TIME AND
NARRATIVE VOLUME 1

TIME AND
NARRATIVE VOLUME I
PAUL RICOEUR

Translated by Kathleen McLaughlin and David Pellauer

The University of Chicago Press · Chicago and London

PAUL RICOEUR has been the dean of the faculty of letters and human sciences at the University of Paris X
(Nanterre) for many years and is currently the John Nu-
veen Professor Emeritus in the Divinity School, the
Department of Philosophy, and the Committee on Social Thought at the University of Chicago.

Originally published as *Temps et Récit*,
© Editions du Seuil, 1983

The University of Chicago Press, Chicago 60637
The University of Chicago Press, Ltd., London

Library of Congress Cataloging in Publication Data
Ricoeur, Paul.
  Time and narrative.

  Translation of: Temps et récit.
  Includes index.
  1. Narration (Rhetoric)   2. Time in literature.
3. Mimesis in literature.   4. Plots (Drama, novel, etc.)
5. History—Philosophy.   I. Title.
PN212.R5213   1984   809'.923   83-17995
ISBN: 0-226-71331-8 (cloth); 0-226-71332-6 (paper) (volume 1)

In Memory of
Henri-Irénée Marrou

Contents

Preface

The Rule of Metaphor and *Time and Narrative* form a pair: published one after the other, these works were conceived together. Although metaphor has traditionally belonged to the theory of "tropes" (or figures of discourse) and narrative to the theory of literary "genres," the meaning-effects produced by each of them belong to the same basic phenomenon of semantic innovation. In both cases this innovation is produced entirely on the level of discourse, that is, the level of acts of language equal to or greater than the sentence.

With metaphor, the innovation lies in the producing of a new semantic pertinence by means of an impertinent attribution: "Nature is a temple where living pillars. . . ." The metaphor is alive as long as we can perceive, through the new semantic pertinence—and so to speak in its denseness—the resistance of the words in their ordinary use and therefore their incompatibility at the level of a literal interpretation of the sentence. The displacement in meaning the words undergo in the metaphorical utterance, a displacement to which ancient rhetoric reduced metaphor, is not the whole of metaphor. It is just one means serving the process that takes place on the level of the entire sentence, whose function it is to save the new pertinence of the "odd" predication threatened by the literal incongruity of the attribution.

With narrative, the semantic innovation lies in the inventing of another work of synthesis—a plot. By means of the plot, goals, causes, and chance are brought together within the temporal unity of a whole and complete action. It is this synthesis of the heterogeneous that brings narrative close to metaphor. In both cases, the new thing—the as yet unsaid, the unwritten—springs up in language. Here a living metaphor, that is, a new pertinence in the predication, there a feigned plot, that is, a new congruence in the organization of the events.

In both cases the semantic innovation can be carried back to the productive imagination and, more precisely, to the schematism that is its signifying matrix. In new metaphors the birth of a new semantic pertinence marvelously demonstrates what an imagination can be that produces things according to rules: "being good at making metaphors," said Aristotle, "is equivalent to being perceptive of resemblances." But what is it to be perceptive of resemblance if not to inaugurate the similarity by bringing together terms that at first seem "distant," then suddenly "close"? It is this change of distance in logical space that is the work of the productive imagination. This consists of schematizing the synthetic operation, of figuring the predicative assimilation from whence results the semantic innovation. The productive imagination at work in the metaphorical process is thus our competence for producing new logical species by predicative assimilation, in spite of the resistance of our current categorizations of language. The plot of a narrative is comparable to this predicative assimilation. It "grasps together" and integrates into one whole and complete story multiple and scattered events, thereby schematizing the intelligible signification attached to the narrative taken as a whole.

Finally, in both cases the intelligibility brought to light by this process of schematization is to be distinguished from the combinatory rationality put into play by structural semantics, in the case of metaphor, and the legislating rationality at work in narratology and scholarly history, in the case of narrative. This rationality aims instead at simulating, at the higher level of a metalanguage, the kind of comprehension rooted in this schematization.

As a result, whether it be a question of metaphor or of plot, to explain more is to understand better. Understanding, in the first case, is grasping the dynamism in virtue of which a metaphorical utterance, a new semantic pertinence, emerges from the ruins of the semantic pertinence as it appears in a literal reading of the sentence. Understanding, in the second case, is grasping the operation that unifies into one whole and complete action the miscellany constituted by the circumstances, ends and means, initiatives and interactions, the reversals of fortune, and all the unintended consequences issuing from human action. In large part, the epistemological problem posed by metaphor or by narrative consists in tying the explanation set to work by the semio-linguistic sciences to the prior understanding resulting from an acquired familiarity with the use of language, be it poetic or narrative use. In both cases it is a question of accounting at the same time for the autonomy of these rational disciplines and their direct or indirect, close or distant filiation, beginning from our poetic understanding.

The parallel between metaphor and narrative goes even further. The study of living metaphor led me to pose, beyond the problem of structure or sense, that of reference or of its truth claim. In the *Rule of Metaphor* I defended the thesis that the poetic function of language is not limited to the celebration of language for its own sake, at the expense of the referential function, which is predominant in descriptive language. I maintained that the suspension of this direct, descriptive referential function is only the reverse side, or the negative condition, of a more covered over referential function of discourse, which is, so to speak, liberated by the suspending of the descriptive value of statements. In this way poetic discourse brings to language aspects, qualities, and values of reality that lack access to language that is directly descriptive and that can be spoken only by means of the complex interplay between the metaphorical utterance and the rule-governed transgression of the usual meanings of our words. I risked speaking not just of a metaphorical sense but also of a metaphorical reference in talking about this power of the metaphorical utterance to redescribe a reality inaccessible to direct description. I even suggested that "seeing-as," which sums up the power of metaphor, could be the revealer of a "being-as" on the deepest ontological level.

The mimetic function of narrative poses a problem exactly parallel to the problem of metaphorical reference. It is, in fact, one particular application of the latter to the sphere of human action. Plot, says Aristotle, is the *mimēsis* of an action. When the time comes, I shall distinguish at least three senses of this term *mimēsis*: a reference back to the familiar pre-understanding we have of the order of action; an entry into the realm of poetic composition; and finally a new configuration by means of this poetic refiguring of the pre-understood order of action. It is through this last sense that the mimetic function of the plot rejoins metaphorical reference. And whereas metaphorical redescription reigns in the field of sensory, emotional, aesthetic, and axiological values, which make the world a habitable world, the mimetic function of plots takes place by preference in the field of action and of its temporal values.

It is this latter feature that I dwell on in this work. I see in the plots we invent the privileged means by which we re-configure our confused, unformed, and at the limit mute temporal experience. "What, then, is time?" asks Augustine. "I know well enough what it is, provided that nobody asks me; but if I am asked what it is and try to explain, I am baffled." In the capacity of poetic composition to re-figure this temporal experience, which is prey to the aporias of philosophical speculation, resides the referential function of the plot.

The frontier between these two functions is unstable. In the first place, the plots that configure and transfigure the practical field encompass not just acting but also suffering, hence characters as agents and as victims. Lyric poetry thereby skirts dramatic poetry. Furthermore, the circumstances that, as the word indicates, encircle action, and the unintended consequences that make up one part of the tragic aspect of action, also consist of a dimension of passivity accessible through poetic discourse, in particular in the modes of elegy and of lamentation. In this way, metaphorical redescription and mimesis are closely bound up with each other, to the point that we can exchange the two vocabularies and speak of the mimetic value of poetic discourse and the re-descriptive power of narrative fiction.

What unfolds, then, is one vast poetic sphere that includes metaphorical utterance and narrative discourse.

The core of this book was first formulated as the Brick Lectures, which I gave at the University of Missouri at Columbia, Missouri, in 1978. (The original French version of these lectures is printed as the first three chapters of *La Narrativité* [Paris: Ed. du C.N.R.S., 1980].) Joined to this is my Zaharɔff Lecture of 1978–79, given at the Taylor Institution, St. Giles College, Oxford: *The Contribution of French Historiography to the Theory of History* (Oxford: Clarendon Press, 1980). Various parts of the work were also developed schematically in two seminars given at the University of Toronto, when I held the Northrop Frye Chair in the Program in Comparative Literature. And several outlines of the whole project were the subject of my own seminars at the Centre d'Etudes Phénoménologiques et Herméneutiques in Paris and at the University of Chicago.

I wish to thank Professors Joseph Bien and Noble Cunningham of the University of Missouri at Columbia, G. P. V. Collyer of the Taylor Institution, and Northrop Frye and Mario Valdès of the University of Toronto for their kind invitations, as well as my colleagues and students at the University of Chicago for their gracious reception of me and this work, their inspiration, and their helpful criticism. My thanks, too, to the National Humanities Center for the opportunity to pursue my work there in 1979–80 and again in 1980–81. I must particularly acknowledge all the participants in my seminar at the Centre d'Etudes Phénoménologiques et Herméneutiques in Paris, who accompanied the whole course of research behind this work and who contributed to our collective volume, *La Narrativité*.

I owe a particular debt of thanks to my two translators, Kathleen McLaughlin and David Pellauer. They have taken the original French text and have truly rethought and rewritten it in English. This arduous labor has strengthened our ties of friendship through the bond of our common work.

Part I
The Circle of
Narrative and Temporality

The first part of this work is concerned with bringing to light the major presuppositions which in the following sections will be submitted to the scrutiny of the various disciplines dealing with either historical or fictional narrative. These presuppositions have a common core. Whether it is a question of affirming the structural identity of historiography, including the philosophy of history, and fictional narrative, as I shall attempt to prove in Part II of this volume and in volume 2, or whether it is a matter of affirming the deep kinship between the truth claims of these two narrative modes, as I shall do in volume 2, one presupposition commands all the others, namely, that what is ultimately at stake in the case of the structural identity of the narrative function as well as in that of the truth claim of every narrative work, is the temporal character of human experience. The world unfolded by every narrative work is always a temporal world. Or, as will often be repeated in the course of this study: time becomes human time to the extent that it is organized after the manner of a narrative; narrative, in turn, is meaningful to the extent that it portrays the features of temporal experience. It is with this major presupposition that Part I of this work is concerned.

This thesis is undeniably circular. But such is the case, after all, in every hermeneutical assertion. Part I will examine this objection. In chapter 3, I shall strive to demonstrate that the circle of narrativity and temporality is not a vicious but a healthy circle, whose two halves mutually reinforce one another. To pave the way for this discussion, I thought it might be well to provide two independent historical introductions to the thesis of the reciprocity between narrativity and temporality. The first (chapter 1) deals with the theory of time in Augustine, the second (chapter 2) with the theory of plot in Aristotle.

There is a twofold justification for the choice of these two authors.

First, they offer us two independent ways of entering into the circle that constitutes our problem: one from the side of the paradoxes of time, the other from the side of the intelligible organization of a narrative. Their indepen-

3

dence does not lie solely in the fact that Augustine's *Confessions* and Aristotle's *Poetics* belong to two profoundly different cultural universes separated by several centuries and involving problematics that are not identical. What is even more important for my purpose is that the first author inquires into the nature of time without any apparent concern for grounding his inquiry on the narrative structure of the spiritual autobiography developed in the first nine books of the *Confessions*. And the second constructs his theory of dramatic plot without paying any attention to the temporal implications of his analysis, leaving to the *Physics* the problem of how to go about analyzing time. It is in this precise sense that the *Confessions* and the *Poetics* offer two points of access, independent of one another, to our circular problem.

However, the independence of these two analyses is not what principally holds our attention. They do not simply converge upon the same interrogation after starting from two radically different philosophical horizons: each engenders the inverted image of the other. The Augustinian analysis gives a representation of time in which discordance never ceases to belie the desire for that concordance that forms the very essence of the *animus*. The Aristotelian analysis, on the other hand, establishes the dominance of concordance over discordance in the configuration of the plot. It is this inverse relationship between concordance and discordance that seemed to me to constitute the major interest of a confrontation between the *Confessions* and the *Poetics*—a confrontation that may seem all the more incongruous in that it goes from Augustine to Aristotle, contrary to the chronological order. But I thought that the meeting of the *Confessions* and the *Poetics* in the mind of one and the same reader would be all the more dramatic if it were to move from the work in which the perplexity created by the paradox of time predominates toward the work in which, on the contrary, confidence reigns in the power of the poet and the poem to make order triumph over disorder.

It is in chapter 3 of Part I that the reader will find the melodic line of which the rest of the work forms the development and sometimes the counterpoint. There I shall consider in and for itself—without any further concern for historical exegesis—the inverted interplay of concordance and discordance, bequeathed to us by the sovereign analyses of time by Augustine and of plot by Aristotle.[1]

The Aporias of the Experience of Time
Book 11 of
Augustine's *Confessions*

The major antithesis around which my reflection will revolve finds its sharpest expression toward the end of Book 11 of Augustine's *Confessions*.[1] Two features of the human soul are set in opposition to one another, features which the author, with his marked taste for sonorous antithesis, coins *intentio* and *distentio animi*. It is this contrast that I shall later compare with that of *muthos* and *peripeteia* in Aristotle.

Two prior remarks have to be made. First, I begin my reading of Book 11 of the *Confessions* at chapter 14:17 with the question: "What, then, is time?" I am not unaware that the analysis of time is set within a meditation on the relations between eternity and time, inspired by the first verse of Genesis, *in principio fecit Deus. . . .*[2] In this sense, to isolate the analysis of time from this meditation is to do violence to the text, in a way that is not wholly justified by my intention to situate within the same sphere of reflection the Augustinian antithesis between *intentio* and *distentio* and the Aristotelian antithesis between *muthos* and *peripeteia*. Nevertheless, a certain justification can be found for this violence in Augustine's own reasoning, which, when it is concerned with time, no longer refers to eternity except to more strongly emphasize the ontological deficiency characteristic of human time and to wrestle directly with the aporias afflicting the conception of time as such. In order to right somewhat this wrong done to Augustine's text, I shall reintroduce the meditation on eternity at a later stage in the analysis with the intention of seeking in it an intensification of the experience of time.

Second, isolated from the meditation on eternity, due to the artifice in method to which I have just admitted, the Augustinian analysis of time offers a highly interrogative and even aporetical character which none of the ancient theories of time, from Plato to Plotinus, had carried to such a degree of acuteness. Not only does Augustine, like Aristotle, always proceed on the basis of aporias handed down by the tradition, but the resolution of each aporia gives rise to new difficulties which never cease to spur on his inquiry. This style, where every advance in thinking gives rise to a new difficulty, places Augustine by turns in the camp of the skeptics, who do not know, and in that of the Platonists and Neoplatonists, who do know. Augustine is seeking (the verb *quaerere*, we shall see, appears repeatedly throughout the text). Perhaps one must go so far as to say that what is called the Augustinian thesis on time, and which I intentionally term a psychological thesis in order to distinguish it from that of Aristotle and even from that of Plotinus, is itself more aporetical than Augustine would admit. This, in any case, is what I shall attempt to show.

These two initial remarks have to be joined together. Inserting an analysis of time within a meditation on eternity gives the Augustinian search the peculiar tone of a "lamentation" full of hope, something which disappears in an analysis that isolates what is properly speaking the argument on time. But it is precisely in separating the analysis of time from its backdrop of eternity that its aporetical features can be brought out. Of course, this aporetical mode differs from that of the skeptics in that it does not disallow some sort of firm certitude. But it also differs from that of the Neoplatonists in that the assertive core can never be apprehended simply in itself outside of the aporias it engenders.[3]

This aporetical character of the pure reflection on time is of the utmost importance for all that follows in the present investigation. And this is so in two respects.

First, it must be admitted that in Augustine there is no pure phenomenology of time. Perhaps there never will be one.[4] Hence, the Augustinian "theory" of time is inseparable from the argumentative operation by which this thinker chops off, one after the other, the continually self-regenerating heads of the hydra of skepticism. As a result, there is no description without a discussion. This is why it is extremely difficult—and perhaps impossible—to isolate a phenomenological core from the mass of argumentation. The "psychological solution" attributed to Augustine is perhaps neither a "psychology" which could be isolated from the rhetoric of argumentation nor even a "solution" which could be removed once and for all from the aporetical domain.

This aporetical style, in addition, takes on a special significance in the overall strategy of the present work. A constant thesis of this book will be that speculation on time is an inconclusive rumination to which narrative activity alone can respond. Not that this activity solves the aporias through substitution. If it does resolve them, it is in a poetical and not a theoretical sense of the word. Emplotment, I shall say below, replies to the speculative aporia with a poetic making of something capable, certainly, of clarifying the aporia (this will be the primary sense of Aristotelian *catharsis*), but not of resolving it theoretically. In one sense Augustine himself moves toward a resolution of this sort. The fusion of argument and hymn in Part I of Book 11—which I am at first going to bracket—already leads us to understand that a poetical trans-figuration alone, not only of the solution but of the question itself, will free the aporia from the meaninglessness it skirts.

THE APORIA OF THE BEING AND THE NONBEING OF TIME

The notion of *distentio animi*, coupled with that of *intentio*, is only slowly and painfully sifted out from the major aporia with which Augustine is strug-gling, that of the measurement of time. This aporia itself, however, is in-scribed within the circle of an aporia that is even more fundamental, that of the being or the nonbeing of time. For what can be measured is only what, in some way, exists. We may deplore the fact if we like, but the phenomenology of time emerges out of an ontological question: *quid est enim tempus?* ("What, then, is time?" [11 14:17].)[5] As soon as this question is posed, all the ancient difficulties regarding the being and the nonbeing of time surge forth. But it is noteworthy that, from the start, Augustine's inquisitive style imposes itself. On the one hand, the skeptical argument leans toward non-being, while on the other hand a guarded confidence in the everyday use of language forces us to say that, in some way, which we do not yet know how to account for, time exists. The skeptical argument is well-known: time has no being since the future is not yet, the past is no longer, and the present does not remain. And yet we do speak of time as having being. We say that things to come *will be*, that things past *were*, and that things present *are passing away*. Even passing away is not nothing. It is remarkable that it is language usage that provisionally provides the resistance to the thesis of nonbeing. We speak of time and we speak meaningfully about it, and this shores up an assertion about the being of time. "We certainly understand what is meant by the word both when we use it ourselves and when we hear it used by others" (14:15).[6]

However, if it is true that we speak of time in a meaningful way and in positive terms (will be, was, is), our powerlessness to explain how this comes about arises precisely from this certitude. Talk about time certainly resists the skeptical argument, but language is itself put into question by the gap between the "that" and the "how." We know by heart the cry uttered by Augustine on the threshold of his meditation: "What, then, is time? I know well enough what it is, provided that nobody asks me; but if I am asked what it is and try to explain, I am baffled" (14:17). In this way the ontological paradox opposes language not only to the skeptical argument but to itself. How can the positive quality of the verbs "to have taken place," "to occur," "to be," be reconciled with the negativity of the adverbs "no longer," "not yet," "not always"? The question is thus narrowed down. How can time exist if the past is no longer, if the future is not yet, and if the present is not always?

Onto this initial paradox is grafted the central paradox from which the theme of distension will emerge. How can we measure that which does not exist? The paradox of measurement is a direct result of the paradox of the being and nonbeing of time. Here again language is a relatively sure guide. We speak of a long time and a short time and in a certain way we observe its length and take its measurement (cf. the aside in 15:19, where the soul addresses itself: "for we are gifted with the ability to feel and measure intervals [moras] of time. What is the answer to be?"). What is more, it is only of the past and of the future that we say that they are long or short. In anticipation of the "solution" of the aporia, it is indeed of the future that we say that it shortens and of the past that it lengthens. But language is limited to attesting to the fact of measuring. The how, once again, eludes him: "But how can anything which does not exist be either long or short [sed quo pacto]?" (15:18).

Augustine will at first appear to turn his back on this certainty that it is the past and the future that we measure. Later, by placing the past and the future within the present, by bringing in memory and expectation, he will be able to rescue this initial certainty from its apparent disaster by transferring onto expectation and onto memory the idea of a long future and a long past. But this certainty of language, of experience, and of action will only be recovered after it has been lost and profoundly transformed. In this regard, it is a feature of the Augustinian quest that the final response is anticipated several times in various ways that must first be submitted to criticism before their true meaning emerges.[7] Indeed Augustine seems first to refuse a certitude based upon too weak an argument: "My Lord, my Light, does not your truth make us look foolish in this case too?" (15:18).[8] He therefore turns first to the present. Was it not when it "was still present" that the past was long? In this question, too, something of the final response is anticipated since memory and expectation will appear as modalities of the present. But at this stage in the argument the present is still opposed to the past and the future. The idea of a threefold present has not yet dawned. This is why the solution based on the present alone has to collapse. The failure of this solution results from a refining of the notion of the present, which is no longer characterized solely by that which does not remain but by that which has no extension.

This refinement, which carries the paradox to its height, is related to a well-known skeptical argument: can a hundred years be present at once (15:19)? (The argument, as we see, is directed solely at attributing length to the present.) Only the current year is present; and in the year, the month; and in the month, the day; and in the day, the hour: "Even that one hour consists of minutes which are continually passing. The minutes which have gone by are past and any part of the hour which remains is future" (15:20).[9]

He must therefore conclude along with the skeptics: "In fact the only time [quid . . . temporis] that can be called present is an instant, if we can conceive [intelligitur] of such, that cannot be divided even into the most minute fractions . . . . when it is present it has no duration [spatium]" (ibid.).[10] At a later stage of this discussion the definition of the present will be further narrowed down to the idea of the pointlike instant. Augustine first gives a dramatic turn to the merciless conclusion of the argumentative machine: "As we have already seen quite clearly, the present cannot possibly have duration" (ibid.).

What is it, then, that holds firm against the onslaughts of skepticism? As always, it is experience, articulated by language and enlightened by the intelligence: "Nevertheless, O Lord, we are aware of [sentimus] periods of time. We compare [comparamus] them with one another and say that some are longer and others shorter. We even calculate [metimur] how much longer or shorter one period is than another" (16:21). The protest conveyed by *sentimus, comparamus*, and *metimur* is that of our sensory, intellectual, and pragmatic activities in relation to the measuring of time. However, this obstinacy of what must indeed be termed experience does not take us any farther as concerns the question of "how." False certainties are still mingled with genuine evidence.

We may believe we take a decisive step forward by substituting for the notion of the present that of passing, of transition, following in the wake of the earlier statement: "If we measure them by our own awareness of time, we must do so while it is passing [praetereuntia]"(ibid.). This speculative formula seems to correspond to our practical certainty. It too, however, will have to be submitted to criticism before returning, precisely, as *distentio*, thanks to the dialectic of the threefold present. So long as we have not formed the idea of the distended relation between expectation, memory, and attention, we do not understand what we are actually saying when we repeat for the second time: "The conclusion is that we can be aware of time and measure it only while it is passing" (ibid.). The formula is at once an anticipation of the solution and a temporary impasse. It is thus not by chance that Augustine stops just when he seems most certain: "These are tentative theories, Father, not downright assertions" (17:22).[11] What is more, it is not due to the impetus of this passing idea that he continues to pursue his search, but by a return to the conclusion of the skeptical argument, "the present cannot possibly have duration." For, in order to pave the way for the idea that what we measure is indeed the future, understood later as expectation, and the past, understood as memory, a case must be made for the being of the past and the future which had been too quickly denied, but it must be made in a way that we are not yet capable of articulating.[12]

In the name of what can the past and the future be accorded the right to exist in some way or other? Once again, in the name of what we say and do with regard to them. What do we say and do in this respect? We recount things which we hold as true and we predict events which occur as we foresaw them.[13] It is therefore still language, along with the experience and the action articulated by language, that holds firm in the face of the skeptics' assault. To predict is to fore-see, and to recount is to "discern [cernere] by the mind." *De Trinitate* (XV 12:21) speaks in this sense of the twofold "testimony" (Meijering, p. 67) of history and of prediction. It is therefore in spite of the skeptical argument that Augustine concludes: "Therefore both the past and the future do exist [sunt ergo]" (17:22).

This declaration is not the mere repetition of the affirmation that was rejected in the first pages, namely, that the future and the past exist. The terms for past and future henceforth appear as adjectives: *futura* and *praeterita*. This nearly imperceptible shift actually opens the way for the denouement of the initial paradox concerning being and nonbeing and, as a result, also for the central paradox of measurement. We are in fact prepared to consider as existing, not the past and the future as such, but the temporal qualities that can exist in the present, without the things of which we speak, when we recount them or predict them, still existing or already existing. We therefore cannot be too attentive to Augustine's shifts in expression.

Just when he is about to reply to the ontological paradox, he pauses once more: "O Lord, my Hope, allow me to explore further [amplius quaerere]" (18:23). This is said not simply for rhetorical effect or as a pious invocation. After this pause, in fact, there follows an audacious step that will lead to the affirmation I have just mentioned, the thesis of the threefold present. This step, however, as is often the case, takes the form of a question: "If the future and the past do exist, I want to know where they are" (ibid.). We began with the question "how?" We continue by way of the question "where?" The question is not naive. It consists in seeking a location for future and past things insofar as they are recounted and predicted. All of the argumentation that follows will be contained within the boundaries of this question, and will end up by situating "within" the soul the temporal qualities implied by narration and prediction. This transition by way of the question "where?" is essential if we are correctly to understand the first response: "So wherever they are and whatever they are [future and past things], it is only by being present that they *are*" (ibid.). We appear to be turning our back on the earlier assertion that what we measure is only the past and the future; even more, we seem to be denying our admission that the present has no duration. But what is in question here is an entirely different present, one that has also become a plural adjective (*praesentia*), in line with *praeterita* and *futura*, and one capable of admitting an internal multiplicity. We also appear to have forgotten the assertion that we "measure [time] only while it is passing" (16:21). But we shall return to it later when we come back to the question of measuring.

It is therefore within the framework of the question "Where?" that we take up once more, in order to carry them further forward, the notions of narration and prediction. Narration, we say, implies memory and prediction implies expectation. Now, what is it to remember? It is to have an image of the past. How is this possible? Because this image is an impression left by events, an impression that remains in the mind.[14]

The reader will have observed that after the calculated delays that preceded, suddenly everything moves very quickly.

Prediction is explained in a way that is scarcely more complex. It is thanks to a present expectation that future things are present to us as things to come. We have a "pre-perception" (*praesensio*) of this which enables us to "foretell" them (*praenuntio*). Expectation is thus the analogue to memory. It consists of an image that already exists, in the sense that it precedes the event that does not yet exist (*nondum*). However, this image is not an impression left by things past but a "sign" and a "cause" of future things which are, in this way, anticipated, foreseen, foretold, predicted, proclaimed beforehand (note the richness of the everyday vocabulary of expectation).

The solution is elegant—but how laborious, how costly, and how fragile!

An elegant solution: by entrusting to memory the fate of things past, and to expectation that of things to come, we can include memory and expectation in an extended and dialectical present which itself is none of the terms rejected previously: neither the past, nor the future, nor the pointlike present, nor even the passing of the present. We know the famous formula whose tie to the aporia it is supposed to resolve we too easily overlook: "It might be correct to say that there are three times, a present of [de] past things, a present of [de] present things, and a present of [de] future things. Some such different times do exist in [in] the mind, but nowhere else [alibi] that I can see" (20:26).

In saying this, Augustine is aware that he is moving away somewhat from ordinary language by which he has, nevertheless, supported his position—prudently, it is true—in his resistance to the argument of the skeptics: "it is not strictly correct [proprie] to say that there are three times, past, present, and future" (ibid.). But he adds as if in a marginal note: "Our use of words is generally inaccurate [non proprie] and seldom completely correct, but our meaning is recognized nonetheless" (ibid.). Nothing, however, prevents us from continuing to speak as we do of the present, past, and future: "I shall not object or argue, nor shall I rebuke anyone who speaks in these terms, provided that he understands what he is saying" (ibid.). Everyday language is thus simply reformulated in a more rigorous manner.

In order to enable us to understand the meaning of this rectification, Augustine relies on a threefold equivalence which, it seems, is self-evident: "The present of past things is the memory; the present of present things is direct perception [contuitus; later the term will be attentio, which better denotes the contrast with distentio]; and the present of future things is expectation" (20:26). How do we know this? Augustine replies laconically: "If we may speak in these terms, I can see [video] three times and I admit [fateorque] that they do exist" (ibid.). This seeing and this admission indeed constitute the phenomenological core of the entire analysis; but the *fateor*, joined to the *video*, bears witness to the sort of debate to which this seeing is the conclusion.

An elegant solution, but a laborious one.

Consider the memory. Certain images must be accorded the power of referring to past things (cf. the Latin preposition *de*)—a strange power indeed! On the one hand, the impression exists now, on the other it stands for past things which, as such, "still" (*adhuc*) exist (18:23) in the memory. This little word "still" (*adhuc*) is at once the solution to the aporia and the source of a new enigma: how is it possible that the impression-images, the *vestigia*, which are present things, engraved in the soul, are at the same time "about" the past? The image of the future presents a similar difficulty: the sign-images are said "to exist already" (*jam sunt*) (18:24). But "already" means two things: "whatever exists already is not future but present" (ibid.), and in this sense, we do not see future things themselves which are "not yet" (*nomdum*). However, "already" denotes, along with the present existence of the sign, its character of anticipation: to say that things "already exist" is to say that by the sign I announce things to come, that I can predict them, and in this way the future is "said in advance" (*ante dicatur*). The anticipatory image is thus no less enigmatic than the vestigial one.[15]

What makes this an enigma lies in the very structure of an image, which sometimes stands as an impression of the past, sometimes as a sign of the future. It seems that for Augustine this structure is seen purely and simply as it presents itself.

What is even more enigmatic is the quasi-spatial language in which the question and the response are couched: "If the future and the past do exist, I want to know where they are" (18:23). To which comes the reply: "Some such different times do exist in [in] the mind, but nowhere else [alibi] that I can see" (20:26). Is it because the question has been posed in terms of "place" (*where* are future and past things?) that we obtain a reply in terms of "place" (*in* the soul, *in* the memory)? Or is it not instead the quasi-spatiality of the impression-image and the sign-image, inscribed in the soul, that calls for the question of the location of the future and past things?[16] This we are unable to state at this stage of our investigation.

The solution of the aporia of the being and nonbeing of time through the notion of a threefold present continues to be fragile so long as the enigma of the measurement of time has not been resolved. The threefold present has not yet received the definitive seal of the *distentio animi* so long as we have not recognized in this very triplicity the slippage [la faille] that permits the soul itself to be accorded an extension of another sort than that which has been denied to the pointlike present. The quasi-spatial language, for its part, remains in suspension so long as this extension of the human soul, the ground of all measurement of time, has not been stripped of any cosmological basis. The inherence of time in the soul takes on its full meaning only when every thesis that would place time within the sphere of physical movement has been eliminated through argumentation. In this sense the "I see it, I admit it" of 20:26 is not firmly established so long as the notion of *distentio animi* has not been formed.

THE MEASUREMENT OF TIME

It is in resolving the enigma of its measurement that Augustine reaches this ultimate characterization of human time (21–31).

The question of measurement is taken up again just where we left it at 16:21: "I said just now that we measure time as it passes [praetereuntia]" (21:27). Now this assertion, which is forcefully repeated ("I know it because we do measure time. We could not measure a thing which did not exist" [ibid.]), is immediately transformed into an aporia. What passes away is, in fact, the present. Yet, we admitted, the present has no extension. The argument, which once again throws us back toward the skeptics, merits a detailed analysis. First of all, it neglects the difference between passing away and being present in the sense in which the present is the indivisible instant (or, as will be stated later, a "point"). Only the dialectic of the threefold present, interpreted as distension, will be able to save an assertion that must first lose its way in the labyrinth of the aporia. But, more important, the adverse argument is constructed precisely with the resources of the quasi-spatial imagery by means of which time is grasped as a threefold present. Passing, in effect, is being in transit. It is therefore legitimate to wonder: "Where is it coming from [unde], what is it passing through [qua], and where is it going [quo]?" (ibid.). As we see, it is the term "passing away" (*transire*) which necessitates dwelling in this way on quasi-spatiality. Now, if we follow the tendency of this figurative expression, we must say that passing is going *from* (*ex*) the future, *through* (*per*) the present, *into* (*in*) the past. This transit thus confirms that the measurement of time is done "in relation to some measurable period" (*in aliquo spatio*) and that all the relations between intervals or time are in relation to "a given period" (*spatia temporum*) (ibid.). This seems to lead to a total impasse: time is not extended in space—and "we cannot measure what has no duration" (ibid.).

At this point, Augustine pauses, as at every previous critical moment. It is also here that the word *puzzle* or enigma is pronounced: "My mind is burning to solve this intricate puzzle [aenigma]" (22:28). Indeed it is our everyday notions that are abstruse, as we have known from the start of this investigation. But, once again, unlike in skepticism, the admission that there is an enigma is accompanied by an ardent desire which, for Augustine, is a figure of love: "Grant me what I love, for it was your gift that I should love it" (ibid.).[17] Here the hymnic aspect of the quest becomes apparent, showing what the investigation of time owes to its inclusion within a meditation on the eternal Word. We shall return to this later. Let us limit ourselves for the moment to underscoring the guarded confidence that Augustine grants to ordinary language: " 'How long [quam diu] did he take to do that?' 'How long is it [quam longo tempore] since . . . !' We use these words and hear others using them. They understand what we mean and we understand them"

(22:28). This is why, I shall say, there is an enigma but not ignorance.

In order to resolve the enigma, the cosmological solution must be rejected so that the investigation will be forced to search in the soul alone, and hence in the multiple structure of the threefold present, for the basis of extension and of measurement. The discussion concerning the relation of time to the movement of the heavenly bodies and to movement in general therefore constitutes neither a digression nor a detour.

Augustine's vision can less than ever be said to be independent of the polemic whose long history stretches from Plato's *Timaeus* and Aristotle's *Physics* to Plotinus's *Enneads* III 7. The *distentio animi* is conquered at great pains during the course of and at the end of a tightly reasoned argument that involves the biting rhetoric of the *reductio ad absurdum*.

First argument: if the movement of the heavenly bodies is time, why should this not also be said of the movement of all other bodies as well? (23:29). This argument anticipates the thesis that the movement of the stars might vary, hence accelerate or slow down, something that is impossible for Aristotle. The stars are thus reduced to the level of other things in motion, whether this be the potter's wheel or the flow of syllables uttered by the human voice.

Second argument: if the lights of the sky ceased to move and if the potter's wheel continued to turn, then time would indeed have to be measured by something other than movement (ibid.). Once again the argument presumes that the thesis of the immutability of celestial movements has been undercut. A variant of this argument: speaking of the movement of the potter's wheel itself takes time, time which is not measured by the astral movement presumed to have been altered or stopped altogether.

Third argument: underlying the earlier presuppositions is the conviction taught by Scripture that the stars are only lights intended to mark out time (ibid.). So disqualified, if we may put it this way, the stars cannot constitute time by their movement.

Fourth argument: if one asks what constitutes the measurement we call a "day" we spontaneously think that the twenty-four hours of the day are measured by the movement of the sun through one complete circuit. But if the sun were to *turn faster* and complete its circuit in an hour, the "day" would no longer be measured by the movement of the sun (23:30). Meijering stresses how, through the hypothesis of a variable speed attributed to the sun, Augustine moves away from all his predecessors. Neither Aristotle nor Plotinus, who do, however, distinguish between time and motion, ever used this argument. For Augustine, since God is the master of creation, he can change the speed of the stars, just as the potter can change that of his wheel, or the speaker the flow of his syllables (Joshua's stopping the sun follows along the same lines as the hypothesis of the acceleration of its motion, which, as such, is independent of the argument from the miraculous). Augustine alone dares to allow that one might speak of a span of time—a day, an hour—without a cosmological reference. The notion of *distentio animi* will serve, precisely, as a substitute for this cosmological basis for the span of time.[18]

It is indeed of essential importance to observe that Augustine introduces the notion of *distentio* for the first time at the end of the argument that totally disassociates the notion of a "day" from that of celestial motion, and this is done without any further elaboration: "I see time, therefore, as an extension [distentio—distension] of some sort. But do I really see this or only seem to see it? You will make it clear to me, my Light and my Truth" (23:30).

Why this reticence just when the breakthrough appears about to be made? In fact, we have not yet finished with cosmology, despite the preceding arguments. We have only dismissed the extreme thesis that "time is constituted by the movement of a material body" (24:31). But Aristotle had also refuted it by affirming that, without itself being movement, time was "something of movement," namely that time is the measurement of movement inasmuch as the latter can be counted. Could not time be the measurement of movement without being movement? For time to exist, is it not enough that movement be potentially measurable? Augustine seems at first sight to make this major concession to Aristotle when he writes: "It is clear then that the movement of a body is not the same as the means by which we measure the duration of its movement. This being so, it must be obvious which of the two ought more properly to be called time" (ibid.).[19] But if Augustine appears to grant that time is the measurement of movement rather than movement itself, this is not because, as was the case with Aristotle, he is thinking of the regular motion of celestial bodies but rather of measuring the movement of the human soul. In fact, if we admit that time is measured by means of a comparison between a longer time and a shorter time, then a fixed term of comparison is required. This cannot be the circular movement of the stars since it has been admitted that that movement could vary. Movement can stop, not time. Do we not in fact measure rest as well as motion? (ibid.).

Were it not for this hesitation, we would not understand why, after the apparently victorious argument against identifying time with movement, Augustine once again falls back into a confession of his utter ignorance: I know that my discourse on time is in time; so I know that time exists and that it is measured. But I know neither what time is nor how it is measured. "I am in a sorry state, for I do not even know what I do not know!" (25:32).

It is, nevertheless, on the following page that the decisive formula is uttered: "It seems to me, then [inde], that time is merely an extension [distentio—distention], though of what it is an extension I do not know. I begin to wonder whether it is an extension of the mind itself" (26:33). Why "then,"—as a result of what? And why this roundabout way ("I begin to wonder whether . . .") of affirming the thesis? Once again, if there is a phenomenological core to this assertion, it is inseparable from the *reductio ad absurdum* that eliminated the other hypotheses: since I measure the movement of a body by time and not the other way around—since a long time can only be measured by a short time—and since no physical movement offers a fixed unit of measurement for comparison, the movement of the stars being assumed to be variable—it *remains that* the extension of time is a distension of the soul. Of course, Plotinus had said this before Augustine; but he was thinking of the soul of the world, not the human soul.[20] This is why everything is resolved and everything is still left up in the air, even once the key phrase *distentio animi* has been pronounced. As long as we have not linked the *distentio animi* to the dialectic of the threefold present, we have not yet understood ourselves.

The whole last part of Book 11 (26:33–28:37) is directed at establishing this connection between the two basic themes of the investigation: between the thesis of the threefold present, which solved the first enigma, that of a being that lacks being, and the thesis of the distension of the mind, summoned in order to resolve the enigma of the extension of a thing that has no extension. What remains, then, is to conceive of the threefold present *as* distension and distension *as* the distension of the threefold present. This is the stroke of genius of Book 11 of Augustine's *Confessions*, in whose wake will follow Husserl, Heidegger, and Merleau-Ponty.

INTENTIO AND DISTENTIO

In order to take this final step, Augustine turns back to an earlier assertion (16:21 and 21:27), which has not only remained in suspension but which seemed to have been bowled over by the the skeptics' assault, namely, that we measure time *when it is passing*; not the future which is not, nor the past which is no longer, nor the present which has no extension, but "time passing." It is in this very passing, in the transit, that both the multiplicity of the present and its tearing apart are to be sought.

The function of the three celebrated examples of a sound that is resonating, a sound that has resonated, and two sounds that resonate one after the other, is to make this tearing apart appear as that of the threefold present.

These examples demand close attention, for the variation from one to the next is quite subtle.

First example (27:34): consider a sound that begins to resonate, that continues to resonate, and that ceases to resonate. How do we speak of it? In order to understand this passage it is important to note that it is written entirely in the past tense. We only speak of a sound's resonance once it has stopped. The not yet (*nondum*) of the future is spoken of in the past tense (*futura erat*). The moment when it resonates, hence its present, is recounted as having disappeared—it could only be measured while it lasted: "but even then [sed et tunc], it was not static [non stabat], because it was transient [ibat], moving continuously [praeteribat]" (ibid.). It is thus in the past tense that we speak of the very passing of the present. Far from securing a comforting reply to the enigma, the first example appears to deepen it. But, as always, the direction in which to search for the solution is in the enigma itself, just as the enigma is in the solution. One feature of the example enables us to steer in this direction: "indeed [enim], while it was transient it was gaining [tendebatur] some extent in time [in aliquod spatium temporis] by which it could be measured, but not in present time, for the present has no extent" (ibid.). The key is indeed to be sought in what passes, as this is distinct from the pointlike present.[21]

The second example exploits this breakthrough, but it does so by varying the hypothesis (27:34ff.). The passage of time will be spoken of not in the past but in the present tense. Here another sound is resonating. Let us assume that it is still (*adhuc*) resonating: "If we are to measure it we must do so while [dum] it lasts." It is now in the future perfect tense that we speak of its stopping, as if of a past future: "once the sound has ceased [cessaverit] it will be [jam] a thing of the past, and if it no longer exists [non erit], it cannot be measured" (ibid.). The question "how long" (*quanta sit*) is then raised in the present tense. Where, then, is the difficulty? It results from the impossibility of measuring the passage while it is "still" (*adhuc*) continuing. For something to stop, it is in fact necessary that there be a beginning and an end, hence a measurable interval.

But if we only measure what has ceased to exist, we slip back into the earlier aporia. It has even deepened a bit more, if we can measure the time that passes neither when it has stopped nor while it continues. The very idea of the time that passes, set aside for this argument, seems to retreat into the same shadows as do the ideas of the future, the past, and the pointlike present: "Therefore we measure neither the future nor the past nor the present nor time that is passing" (ibid.).[22]

From whence then comes our assurance that we *do* measure (the protest: "yet we do measure time" appears twice in this dramatic paragraph), if we do not know *how*? Is there a way to measure time passing both when it has ceased and while it continues? It is indeed in this direction that the third example steers the inquiry.

The third example (27:35), that of reciting a verse by heart—to be exact the *Deus creator omnium*, taken from a hymn by Saint Ambrose—offers a greater complexity than that of the continuous sound, namely, the alternation of four long syllables and of four short syllables within a single expression, a line of verse (*versus*). The complexity of this example necessitates the reintroduction of memory and retrospection that the analysis of the earlier two examples omitted. Thus it is in the third example alone that the connection is made between the question of measurement and that of the threefold present. The alternation of four short and four long syllables in fact introduces an element of comparison that immediately appeals to the senses: "I can tell this because, by pronouncing them, I find it to be the case, insofar as I can rely upon the plain evidence of my own hearing [*quantum sensitur sensu mani-festo*]." [23] But Augustine introduces sensation only in order to sharpen the aporia and to move toward its resolution, not in order to cover it with the cloak of intuition. For if longs and shorts are such only by comparison, we are not able to superimpose them as we would superimpose two beats over one beat. We must be able to retain (*tenere*) the short and to apply it (*applicare*) to the long. But what is it to retain something that has ceased? The aporia fully remains if we speak of the syllables themselves, as we spoke earlier of the sound itself, that is, as past and future things. The aporia is resolved if we speak not of syllables that no longer exist or do not yet exist but of their impressions in the memory and of their signs in expectation: "So it cannot be the syllables themselves [*ipsas*] that I measure, since they no longer exist. I must be measuring something which remains fixed [*in-fixum manet*] in [*in*] my memory" (ibid.).

We again find the present of the past, inherited from the analysis that concluded the first enigma—and with this expression all the difficulties of the impression-image, of the *vestigium*. The advantage gained is, nevertheless, immense. We now know that the measurement of time owes nothing to that of external motion. In addition we have found in the mind itself the fixed element that allows us to compare long periods of time with short periods of time. With the impression-image, the important verb is no longer "to pass" (*tran-sire*) but "to remain" (*manet*). In this sense the two enigmas—that of being/nonbeing and that of measuring what has no extension—are resolved together. On the one hand, we have returned within ourselves: "It is in my own mind, then, that I measure things" (27:36). And how is this? Inasmuch as, after they have passed, the impression (*affectio*) made on the mind by things as they pass remains there: "for everything which happens leaves an impression on it, and this impression remains [*manet*] after the thing itself has ceased to be. It is the impression that I measure, since it is present, not the thing itself, which makes the impression as it passes" (ibid.).

We must not think that this recourse to the impression terminates the inquiry.[24] The notion of *distentio animi* has not been given its due so long as the passivity of the impression has not been contrasted with the activity of a mind stretched in opposite directions, between expectation, memory, and attention. *Only a mind stretched in such different directions can be distended.*

This active side of the process calls for a new look at the earlier example of recitation, but this time in its dynamics. To compose beforehand, to entrust to memory, to begin, to run through—these are all active operations dependent upon the passivity of the sign-images and the impression-images. But it would be to mistake the role of these images if we failed to stress that reciting is an act that moves from an expectation turned first toward the entire poem, then toward what remains of the poem, until (*donec*) the operation is completed. In this new description of the act of reciting, the present changes its meaning. It is no longer a point, not even a point of passage, it is a "present intention" (*praesens intentio*) (27:36). If attention deserves in this way to be called intention, this is so inasmuch as the transit through the present has become an active transition. The present is not simply travelled through, but "man's attentive mind, which is present, is relegating [traicit] the future to the past. The past increases in proportion as the future diminishes, until the future is entirely absorbed and the whole becomes past" (27:36). Of course, the quasi-spatial imagery of a movement from the future toward the past through the present has not been eliminated. No doubt it has its ultimate justification in the passivity that accompanies the entire process. But we are no longer misled by the representation of two places, one of which is filled up as the other is emptied, as soon as we have ascribed a dynamic character to this representation and have discerned the interplay of action and passion that is concealed therein. For, in fact, there would be no future that diminishes, no past that increases, without "the mind, which regulates this process [animus qui illud agit]" (28:37). The shadow of passivity accompanies three actions, now expressed by three verbs. The mind "performs three functions, those of expectation [expectat], attention [adtendit; this verb recalls the intentio praesens], and memory [meminit]" (ibid.). The result is that "the future, which it expects, passes through [transeat] the present, to which it attends, into the past, which it remembers" (ibid.). To relegate is also to pass through. The vocabulary here continues to oscillate between activity and passivity. The mind expects and remembers, and yet expectation and memory are "in" the soul, as impression-images and as sign-images. The contrast appears in the present. On the one hand, inasmuch as it passes, it is reduced to a point (*in puncto praeterit*). This is the most extreme illustration of the present's lack of extension. But, inasmuch as it relegates, inasmuch as through the attention that "which is to be passes towards [pergat] the state in which it is to be no more," it must be said that "the mind's attention persists [perdurat attentio]."

This interplay of action and affection in the complex expression a "long expectation of the future" must be distinguished from what Augustine makes it replace, the absurd notion of a long future, and the same applies to the expression a "long remembrance of the past," which takes the place of the notion of a long past. It is *in* the soul, hence as an impression, that expectation and memory possess extension. But the impression is in the soul only inasmuch as the mind *acts*, that is, expects, attends, and remembers.

In what, then, does distention consist? In the very contrast between the three tensions. If paragraphs 26:33–30:40 constitute the treasure of Book 11, paragraph 28:38, apart from all else, is the crown jewel of this treasure. The example of the song, which includes that of the sound that continues and ceases and that of the long and short syllables, is here more than just a concrete application. It marks the point at which the theory of *distentio* is joined to that of the threefold present. The theory of the threefold present, reformulated in terms of the threefold intention, makes the *distentio* arise out of the *intentio* that has burst asunder. The entire paragraph must be quoted:

> Suppose that I am going to recite a psalm that I know. Before I begin my faculty of expectation is engaged [tenditur] by the whole of it. But once I have begun, as much of the psalm as I have removed from the province of expectation and relegated to the past now engages [tenditur] my memory, and the scope of the action [actionis] which I am performing is divided [distenditur] between the two faculties of memory and expectation, the one looking back to the part which I have already recited, the other looking forward to the part which I have still to recite. But my faculty of attention [attentio] is present all the while, and through it passes [traicitur] what was the future in the process of becoming the past. As the process continues [agitur et agitur], the province of memory is extended in proportion as that of expectation is reduced, until the whole of my expectation is absorbed. This happens when I have finished my recitation and it has all passed into the province of memory. (28:38)

The theme of this entire paragraph is the dialectic of expectation, memory, and attention, each considered no longer in isolation but in interaction with one another. It is thus no longer a question of either impression-images or anticipatory images but of an action that shortens expectation and extends memory. The term *actio* and the verbal expression *agitur*, which is repeated expressly, convey the impulse that governs the whole process. Expectation and memory are themselves both said to be "engaged," the first by the whole of the poem before the start of the song, the second by the part of the song that has already gone by; as for attention, its engagement consists completely in the active "transit" of what was future in the direction of what becomes past. It is this combined action of expectation, memory, and attention that "continues." The *distentio* is then nothing other than the shift in, the noncoincidence of the three modalities of action: "and the scope of the action which I am performing is divided [distenditur] between the two faculties of memory and expectation, the one looking back to the part which I have already recited, the other looking forward to the part which I have still to recite."

Is the *distentio* related in any way to the passivity of the impression? It would seem so, if this beautiful text, from which the *affectio* seems to have disappeared, is compared to the first analytical sketch of the act of reciting (27:36). There the impression appears to be still conceived of as the passive reverse side of the very "tension" of the act, even when silent, of reciting: something remains (*manet*) insofar as we "can go over [peragimus] poems and verses and speech of any sort in our minds." It is "man's attentive mind, which is present, [which] is relegating [traicit] the future to the past" (27:36).

Thus, if we compare, as I believe we can, the passivity of the *affectio* to that of the *distentio animi*, we must say that the three temporal intentions are separate from one another to the extent that intentional activity has as its counterpart the passivity engendered by this very activity and that, for lack of a better name, we designate as impression-image or sign-image. It is not only these three acts that do not coincide, but also the activity and passivity which oppose one another, to say nothing of the discordance between the two passivities, the one related to expectation, the other to memory. Therefore, the more the mind makes itself *intentio*, the more it suffers *distentio*.

Has the aporia of long or short time been resolved? Yes, if we admit: (1) that what is measured is neither future things nor past things, but their expectation and their memory; (2) that these are affections presenting a measurable spatiality of a unique kind; (3) that these affections are like the reverse side of the activity of the mind that continues; and, finally, (4) that this action is itself threefold and thus is distended whenever and wherever it is tensively engaged in.

Yet to tell the truth, each stage in this solution itself constitutes an enigma.

1. How can we measure expectation or memory without taking support from the "points of reference" marking out the space traversed by a moving body, hence without taking into consideration the physical change that produces the trajectory of the moving body in space?

2. What independent mode of access have we to the extension of the impression inasmuch as it is held to be purely "in" the mind?

3. Have we any other means of expressing the connection between *affectio* and *intentio*, outside of a progressive dynamization of the metaphor of the spaces traversed by expectation, attention, and memory? In this respect, the metaphor of the transit of events through the present seems unsurpassable. It is a good metaphor, a living metaphor, in that it holds together the idea of "passing away," in the sense of ceasing, and that of "passing through," in the sense of relegating. There seems to be no concept that "surpasses" (*aufhebt*) this living metaphor.[25]

4. The last thesis, if it can still be termed one, constitutes the most impenetrable enigma, that at the price of which we can say that the aporia of measurement is "resolved" by Augustine: that the soul "distends" itself as it "engages" itself—this is the supreme enigma.

But it is precisely as an enigma that the resolution of the aporia of measurement is valuable. Augustine's inestimable discovery is, by reducing the extension of time to the distention of the soul, to have tied this distention to the slippage that never ceases to find its way into the heart of the threefold present—between the present of the future, the present of the past, and the present of the present. In this way he sees discordance emerge again and again out of the very concordance of the intentions of expectation, attention, and memory.

It is to this enigma of the speculation on time that the poetic act of emplotment replies. But Aristotle's *Poetics* does not resolve the enigma on the speculative level. It does not really resolve it at all. It puts it to work—poetically—by producing an inverted figure of discordance and concordance. For this new solution, Augustine does leave us one word of encouragement. The fragile example of the *canticus* recited by heart suddenly becomes, toward the end of the inquiry, a powerful paradigm for other *actiones* in which, through engaging itself, the soul suffers distension: "What is true of the whole psalm is also true of all its parts and each syllable. It is true of any longer action [in actione longiore] in which I may be engaged and of which the recitation of the psalm may only be a small part. It is true of a man's whole life, of which all his actions [actiones] are parts. It is true of the whole history of mankind, of which each man's life is a part" (28:38). The entire province of narrative is laid out here in its potentiality, from the simple poem, to the story of an entire life, to universal history. It is with these extrapolations, which are simply suggested here, that the present work is concerned.

THE CONTRAST WITH ETERNITY

I have yet to reply to the objection formulated at the beginning of this study. That objection contested a reading of Book 11 of the *Confessions* that artificially isolates sections 14:17–28:37 from the great meditation on eternity that frames them. I provided only a partial response to this objection when I stressed the autonomy that this investigation possesses owing to its repeated confrontations with the skeptical arguments that were essentially concerned with time. In this respect, the thesis that time is "in" the soul and finds "in" the soul the principle of measurement of time, is sufficient in itself inasmuch as it replies to the aporias found within the notion of time. In order to be understood, the notion of *distentio animi* requires no more than to be contrasted with the *intentio* immanent in the "action" of the mind.[26]

And yet something is missing from the full sense of *distentio animi*, which the contrast with eternity alone can provide. But what is missing does not concern what I shall call the sufficient sense of the *distentio animi*. I mean the sense that suffices to reply to the aporias of nonbeing and of measurement. What is missing is of a different order. I discern three major ways in which the meditation on eternity affects the speculation concerning time.

Its first function is to place all speculation about time within the horizon of a limiting idea that forces us to think at once about time and about what is other than time. Its second function is to intensify the experience of *distentio* on the existential level. Its third function is to call upon this experience to surpass itself by moving in the direction of eternity, and hence to display an internal hierarchy in opposition to our fascination with the representation of a rectilinear time.

It is uncontestable that Augustine's meditation is indivisibly concerned with eternity and time. Book 11 of the *Confessions* opens with the first verse of Genesis (in one of the Latin versions known in Africa during the period when the *Confessions* were written): "*in principio fecit Deus. . . .*" Moreover, the meditation that covers the first fourteen chapters of Book 11 joins together, indivisibly, the praise of the psalmist with a type of speculation that is, for the most part, Platonic and Neoplatonic.[27] Such a meditation leaves no place for a derivation, in any conceivable sense of the word, of eternity from time. What is posited, confessed, thought, is in one stroke the contrast of eternity with time. The work of the intelligence bears in no way on the question of whether or not eternity exists. The anteriority of eternity with respect to time—in a sense of anteriority that remains to be determined—is given in the contrast between "something that exists that was not created" and something that has a before and an after that is subject to "change" and to "variation" (4:6). This contrast is given in an exclamation: "Earth and the heavens are before our eyes. The very fact that they are proclaims that they were created, for they are subject to change and variation" (ibid.). And Augustine stresses: "This we know" (ibid.).[28] This said, we can see that the work of the intelligence results from the difficulties raised by this very confession of eternity: "Let me hear and understand the meaning of the words [quomodo]: In the Beginning you made heaven and earth" (3:5). (This question is repeated at the beginning of 5:7.) In this sense, eternity is just like time. That it exists causes no problem; how it exists and acts leaves us puzzled. It is out of this puzzlement that arises the first function of the assertion of eternity in relation to that of time: the function of the limiting idea.

This function results from the linking together of confession and questioning throughout the first fourteen chapters of Book 11 of the *Confessions*. To the first question, "But by what means [quomodo] did you make heaven and earth?" (5:7) comes the answer, in the same spirit of praise, "In your Word alone you created them" (ibid.). But out of this reply a new question arises, "But how did you speak?" (6:8). This is answered, with the same confidence, by the eternity of the *Verbum*: "In your Word all [omnia] is uttered at one and the same time [simul], yet eternally [sempiterne]. If it were not so, your Word would be subject to time and change, and therefore would be neither truly eternal nor truly immortal" (7:9). And he confesses, "This I know, my God, and I thank you for the Knowledge" (7:9).

Let us, then, inquire into this eternity of the Word. A double contrast is examined here, which before becoming a source of new difficulties is a source of negativity with regard to time.

In the first place, to say that things are made in the Word is to deny that God created in the same way as does an artisan, who makes things starting from something else: "Nor was it in the universe that you made the universe, because until [antequam] the universe was made there was no place [quia non erat] where it could be made" (5:7). The creation *ex nihilo* is anticipated here, and this original nothingness henceforth strikes time with an ontological deficiency.

However, the decisive contrast, generating new negations—and new difficulties—is that which opposes the divine *Verbum* to the human *vox*. The creating Word is not like the human voice that "begins" and "ceases," or like syllables that are "heard" and then "die away" (6:8). The Word and the voice are as irreducible to one another and at the same time as inseparable as are the internal ear that hears the Word and receives the teaching of the internal master and the external ear that allows the *verba* to enter and transmits them to the vigilant intelligence. The *Verbum* remains, the *verba* disappear. With this contrast (and the accompanying "comparison"), time is once again struck with a negative characteristic: if the *Verbum* remains, the *verba* "are not at all, because they die away and are lost" (6:8).[29] In this sense, the two functions of nonbeing overlap.

The progression of negation will henceforth never cease to accompany that of the questioning that itself is dependent upon the confession of eternity. Once again, in fact, the question emerges out of the preceding response: "You create them by your Word alone and in no other way. Yet [nec tamen] the things which you create by your Word do not all come into being at one and the same time, nor are they eternal" (7:9). In other words, how can a temporal creature be made in and through the eternal Word? "Why is this so, O Lord my God? In some degree I see why it is, but I do not know how to put it into words" (8:10). Eternity, in this sense, is no less a source of enigmas than is time.

Augustine answers this difficulty by attributing to the Word an "eternal reason" which ascribes a beginning and an end to the being of created things.[30] But this reply contains the seed of a major difficulty that will long occupy Augustine as he ponders what was before creation. Indeed, the way in which eternal reason ascribes a beginning and an end implies that it knows "the moment when" (*quando*) this thing had to begin or end. This *quando* leaves us once more at sea.

To begin, it makes both plausible and respectable the question raised by the Manicheans and by some Platonists, which other Christian thinkers had held to be ridiculous and had treated derisively.

Here, then, Augustine is confronted with his adversary's threefold argument : "What was God doing before [antequam] he made heaven and earth?" "If he was at rest . . . and doing nothing, why did he not continue to do nothing for ever more, just as he had always done in the past?" "But if God's will that there should be a creation was there from all eternity, why is it that what he has created is not also eternal?" (10:12). We shall be concerned, as we consider Augustine's responses, with the progress of the ontological negativity affecting the experience of the *distentio animi*, which is itself negative on the psychological level.

Before proposing his personal response to these difficulties which, once again, result from the confession of eternity, Augustine refines his notion of eternity one last time. Eternity is "for ever still [semper stans]" in contrast to things that are "never still." This stillness lies in the fact that "in eternity nothing moves into the past: all is present [totum esse praesens]. Time, on the other hand, is never all present at once" (11:13). Negativity reaches its highest pitch here. In order to push as far as possible the reflection on the *distentio animi*, that is, on the slippage of the threefold present, it must be "compared" to a present with neither past nor future.[31] This extreme negation underlies his response to the apparently frivolous argument.

If Augustine takes such pains to refute the argument, it is because it constitutes an aporia produced by the very thesis of eternity.[32]

The reply to the first formulation of the argument is forthright: "before he made heaven and earth, God made nothing" (12:14). Certainly, the reply leaves intact the assumption that there was a "before," but the important thing is that this before is struck with nothingness. The "nothing" of "making nothing" is the before that precedes creation. We must therefore think of "nothing" in order to think of time as beginning and ending. In this way, time is, as it were, surrounded by nothingness.

The reply to the second formulation of the argument is even more remarkable. There is no before in relation to creation because in creating the world God created time: "You are the Maker of all time" (13:15). "You must have made that time, for time could not elapse before you made it" (ibid.). With one stroke, the response does away with the question: "If there was not time, there was no 'then' [non erat tunc]" (ibid.). This "no then" is negative to the same extent as is the "nothing" of making nothing. Thought is thus entrusted with the task of forming the idea of the absence of time in order to think time through as far as possible as that which passes. Time must be thought of as *transitory* in order to be fully experienced as *transition*.

However, the thesis that time was created along with the world—a thesis that is already found in Plato, *Timaeus* 38d—leaves open the possibility that there were other times before time. (*Confessions* 11, 30:40–end, mentions this possibility, either as a speculative hypothesis or in order to preserve a temporal dimension peculiar to angelic beings.) Whatever the case, Augustine gives his thesis the extra twist of the *reductio ad absurdum* in order to confront this possibility. Even if there were a time before time, this time would still be a created thing since God is the maker of all time. A time before all creation is thus unthinkable. This argument suffices to dismiss the assumption of God's idleness before creation. To say that God was idle is to say that there was a time in which he never did anything at all before he acted. The temporal categories, therefore, are not suited to characterizing a "before-the-world."

The reply to the third formulation of the adversary's argument provides Augustine with the opportunity to add the final touch to his opposition between time and eternity. In order to dismiss any idea of "newness" in the will of God, the idea of a "before" preceding creation must be given a meaning that excludes all temporality. Antecedence must be thought of as superiority, as excellence, as the supreme height: "It is in eternity, which is supreme [celsitudine] over time because it is a never-ending present, that you are at once before all past time and after all future time" (13:16). The negations are sharpened even more: "Your years are completely present to you all at once, because they are at a permanent standstill [simul stant]" (ibid.). This *simul stant* as well as the "today" of which Exodus speaks assumes the atemporal meaning of that which surpasses without preceding. Passing away is less than surpassing.

If I have so insisted on the ontological negativity that the contrast between eternity and time brings to light in the psychological experience of the *distentio animi*, this is certainly not in order to lock up Augustine's notion of eternity within the Kantian function of a limiting idea. The meeting of the Hebraic tradition and of Platonism in the interpretation of Exodus 3:20—*ego sum qui sum* in its Latin translation—does not allow us to interpret the thought of eternity as a thought lacking an object.[33] Besides, the conjoining of praise and speculation attests to the fact that Augustine does not restrict himself to thinking of eternity. He addresses himself to the Eternal, he invokes the eternal using the form of the second person. The eternal present declares itself in the first person: *sum*, not *esse*.[34] Here again, speculation is inseparable from the recognition of the one who declares himself. It is in this that it is inseparable from the hymn. In this sense, we can speak of an experience of eternity in Augustine, with the reservations that will be stated later. But it is precisely this experience of eternity that has the function of a limiting idea, when the intelligence "compares" time with eternity. It is the recoil effect of this "comparison" on the living experience of the *distentio animi* that makes the thought of eternity the limiting idea against the horizon of which the experience of the *distentio animi* receives, on the ontological level, the negative mark of a lack or a defect in being.[35]

The reverberation—*le retentissement*, as Eugène Minkowski would have said—of this negation that is thought on the living experience of temporality will now convince us that the absence of eternity is not simply a limit that is thought, but a lack that is felt at the heart of temporal experience. The limiting idea then becomes the sorrow proper to the negative.

The contrast between eternity and time is not limited to surrounding our experience of time with negativity, as we do when we link our thought of time to what is other than time. This experience is permeated through and through with negativity. Intensified in this way on the existential level, the experience of distension is raised to the level of a lamentation. The outline of this new contrast is contained in the admirable prayer of 2:3 already mentioned. The hymn includes the lamentation, and the *confessio* brings them both to the level of language.[36]

Against the backdrop of the stillness of eternity, the lamentation unashamedly displays the author's feelings. "What is that light whose gentle beams [interlucet] now and again strike through [percutit] to my heart, causing me to shudder in awe yet firing me with their warmth [et inhorresco et inardesco]? I shudder to feel how different I am from it: yet in so far as I am like it, I am aglow with its fire" (9:11). Already, in the course of the narration of the *Confessions*, as he recounts his vain efforts at Plotinian ecstasy, Augustine laments: "And I discovered that I was far from you in the region of dissimilarity [in regione dissimilitudinis]" (7 10:16). This expression, which comes from Plato (*Statesman* 273d) and which had been transported into the Christian milieu through the intermediary of Plotinus (*Enneads* I, 8:13, 16–17), becomes particularly striking here. It no longer refers, as it did in Plotinus, to the fall into the dark mire but marks instead the radical ontological difference that separates the creature from the creator, the difference that the soul discovers precisely in its movement of returning to its source and by its very effort to know its origin.[37]

If, however, the ability to distinguish the similar from the dissimilar belongs to the intelligence that "compares" (6:8), its reverberation profoundly affects both the scope and the depth of feeling. It is remarkable in this respect that the final pages of Book 11, which complete the setting of the analysis of time into the meditation on the relationship between eternity and time (29:39–31:41), propose a final interpretation of the *distentio animi*, marked by the same tone of praise and lamentation as the first chapters of this book. *Distentio animi* no longer provides just the "solution" to the aporia of the measurement of time. It now expresses the way in which the soul, deprived of the stillness of the eternal present, is torn asunder: "But to win your favor is dearer than life itself. I see now that my life has been wasted in distractions [distentio est vita mea]" (29:39). It is in fact the entire dialectic of *intentio-distentio*, a dialectic within time itself, that is taken up again in terms of the contrast between eternity and time. While the *distentio* becomes synonymous with the dispersal into the many and with the wandering of the old Adam, the *intentio* tends to be identified with the fusion of the inner man ("until . . . I am fused into one with you" [ibid.]). So the *intentio* is no longer the anticipation of the entire poem before its recitation which makes it move from the future toward the past, but the hope of the last things, to the very extent that the past that is to be forgotten is not the storehouse of memory but the emblem of the old Adam according to Paul in Philippians 3:12–14: "forgetting what I have left behind, I look forward [non distentus sed extentus], not to what lies ahead of me in this life and will surely pass away, but to an eternal goal. I am intent [sed secundum intentionem] upon this one purpose, not distracted [secundum distentionem] by other aims" (ibid.). The same words recur: *distentio* and *intentio*, but this is no longer in a purely speculative context of aporia and inquiry but rather in the dialectic of praise and lamentation.[38] With this shift in meaning that affects the *distentio animi*, the borderline separating the condition of created beings from that of fallen beings is tacitly crossed: "I am divided [dissilui] between time gone by and time to come, and its course is a mystery to me" (ibid.). The "lamentations" in which our years pass are inseparably those of the sinner and the created being.

Again it is in relation to eternity that we can fully grasp the sense of all the expressions found in Augustine's other works that lend their metaphorical resources to the central metaphor of the *distentio*.

In an important essay on "Les Catégories de la temporalité chez saint Augustin," in which he pays particular attention to the *Enarrationes in Psalmos* and the *Sermones*, Stanislas Boros arrives at four "synthetic images," each of which joins together what I earlier termed the sorrow of the finite with the celebration of the absolute: to temporality as "dissolution" are linked the images of devastation, of swooning, of gradually sinking, of unfulfilled aim, of dispersal, of alteration, and of extreme indigence; to temporality as "agony" are related images of the deathwatch, of sickness and frailty, of civil warfare, of tearful captivity, of aging, and of sterility; temporality as "banishment" includes the images of tribulation, exile, vulnerability, wandering, nostalgia, and vain desire; and finally, the theme of the "night" governs the images of blindness, darkness, and opacity.[39] There is not one of these four principal images or of their variants that does not receive the strength of its meaning *a contrario* in relation to the opposing symbolism of eternity, in the figures of recollection, living fullness, being at home, and light.

Separated from this branching symbolism, which is engendered by the dialectic of eternity and time, the *distentio animi* would be no more than the sketch of a speculative response brought to the aporias that are continuously produced by skeptical argumentation. Taken up within the dynamics of praise and lamentation, the *distentio animi* becomes a living experience which puts flesh on the skeleton of a counterargument.

The third way in which the dialectic of time and eternity affects the interpretation of the *distentio animi* is no less important. At the very heart of temporal experience, it produces a hierarchy of levels of temporalization, according to how close or how far a given experience approaches or moves away from the pole of eternity.

The accent here is placed less on the dissemblance than on the resemblance between eternity and time in the "comparison" made by the intelligence with regard to each of them (6:8). This resemblance is expressed in time's capacity to approximate eternity, which Plato had included in the very definition of time and which the first Christian thinkers had begun to reinterpret in terms of the ideas of creation, incarnation, and salvation. Augustine gives a unique accent to this reinterpretation by connecting together the themes of the teaching by the inner Word and the return. Between the eternal *Verbum* and the human *vox* there is not only difference and distance but the relation of teaching and communication. The Word is that inner master, sought and heard "within" (*intus*) (8:10): "It is true that I hear [audio] your voice, O Lord, telling me that only a master who really teaches us [docet nos] really speaks to us. . . . But who is our teacher except the Truth which never changes?" (ibid.). In this way, our first relationship to language is not the fact that we talk but that we listen and that, beyond the external *verba*, we hear the inner *Verbum*. The return is nothing other than this listening: for unless the principle "remained when we wandered in error, there would be none to whom we could return and restore ourselves. But when we return from error, we return by knowing the Truth; and in order that we may know the Truth he teaches us, because he is the Beginning and he also speaks to us" (ibid.). Thus are linked together teaching,[40] recognition, and return. The teaching, we could say, bridges the abyss that opens up between the eternal *Verbum* and the temporal *vox*. It elevates time, moving it in the direction of eternity.

This is the very movement that is narrated by the first nine books of the *Confessions*. And in this sense the narration actually accomplishes the itinerary whose conditions of possibility are reflected upon in Book 11. This book, indeed, attests to the fact that the attraction of the eternity of the Word felt by temporal experience is not such as to plunge the narration, which is still temporal, into a contemplation free from the constraints of time. In this respect, the failure of the efforts at Plotinian ecstasy, recounted in Book 7, is definitive. Neither the conversion recounted in Book 8, nor even the ecstasy of Ostia which marks the culmination of the narrative in Book 9, ever eliminate the temporal condition of the soul. These two culminating experiences only put an end to wandering, the fallen form of the *distentio animi*. But this is done in order to inspire a peregrination that sends the soul off again on the roads of time. Peregrination and narration are grounded in time's approximation of eternity, which, far from abolishing their difference, never stops contributing to it. This is indeed why, when Augustine derides the frivolousness of those who attribute a new will to God at the moment of creation, and when he contrasts the way "their thoughts still twist and turn" to the "steady" mind of the one who listens to the Word (11:13), he refers to this steadiness, which is similar to that of the eternal present, only to reiterate the difference between time and eternity: "But if only their minds could be seized and held steady [ut paululum stet], they would be still for awhile and, for that short moment, they would glimpse the splendour of eternity which is forever still [semper stantis]. They would contrast it with time, which is never still, and see that it is not comparable" (ibid.). By opening this distance, proximity also reiterates the

29

limiting function of eternity in relation to time: "If only men's minds could be seized and held still! They would see how eternity, in which there is neither past nor future, determines [dictet] both past and future time" (ibid.)

Of course, when the dialectic of *intentio* and *distentio* is definitively anchored in that of eternity and time, the timid question that has twice been uttered ("Who will hold still . . . ?") is replaced by a more confident affirmation: "Then I shall be cast [stabo] and set firm [solidabor] in the mould of your truth" (30:40). But this firmness remains in the future, the time of hope. It is still in the midst of the experience of distension that the wish for permanence is uttered: "until [donec] I am purified and melted by the fire of your love and fused into one with you" (29:39).

In this way, without losing the autonomy that the discussion of the old aporias concerning time has conferred upon it, the theme of *distension* and *intention* acquires from its setting within the meditation on eternity and time an intensification that will be echoed in all that follows in the present work. This intensification does not just consist of the fact that time is thought of as abolished by the limiting idea of an eternity that strikes time with nothingness. Nor is this intensification reduced to transferring into the sphere of lamentation and wailing what had until then been only a speculative argument. It aims more fundamentally at extracting from the very experience of time the resources of an internal hierarchization, one whose advantage lies not in abolishing time but in deepening it.

The effect of this last remark on my entire undertaking is considerable. If it is true that the major tendency of modern theory of narrative—in historiography and the philosophy of history as well as in narratology—is to "dechronologize" narrative, the struggle against the linear representation of time does not necessarily have as its sole outcome the turning of narrative into "logic," but rather may deepen its temporality. Chronology—or chronography—does not have just one contrary, the a-chronology of laws or models. Its true contrary is temporality itself. Indeed it was necessary to confess what is other than time in order to be in a position to give full justice to human temporality and to propose not to abolish it but to probe deeper into it, to hierarchize it, and to unfold it following levels of temporalization that are less and less "distended" and more and more "held firmly," *non secundum distentionem sed secundum intentionem* (29:39).

2

Emplotment: A Reading of Aristotle's *Poetics*

The second great text that animated my inquiry is Aristotle's *Poetics*. There are two reasons for this choice.

In the first place, I found in his concept of emplotment (*muthos*)[1] the opposite reply to Augustine's *distentio animi*. Augustine groaned under the existential burden of discordance. Aristotle discerns in the poetic act par excellence—the composing of the tragic poem—the triumph of concordance over discordance. It goes without saying that it is I, the reader of Augustine and Aristotle, who establishes this relationship between a lived experience where discordance rends concordance and an eminently verbal experience where concordance mends discordance.

In the second place, the concept of mimetic activity (*mimēsis*) started me on the way to a second problematic, that of the creative imitation, by means of the plot of lived temporal experience. This second theme is difficult to distinguish from the first one in Aristotle, inasmuch as for him mimetic activity tends to be confused with emplotment. It will only be unfolded to its full extent and will only get its full autonomy, therefore, in what follows in this work.[2] Indeed, the *Poetics* is silent about the relationship between poetic activity and temporal experience. As poetic activity, it does not even have any marked temporal character. Aristotle's total silence on this point is not without some advantage, however, insofar as from the beginning it protects our inquiry from the reproach of tautological circularity and thus sets up between the two problematics of time and narrative the most favorable distance for an investigation into the mediating operations between lived experience and discourse.

These few remarks already make clear that I do not intend to use the Aristotelian model as an exclusive norm for the remainder of this work. Rather I am evoking from Aristotle the melodic theme of a twofold reflection whose development is as important as its initial statement. This development will affect both concepts borrowed from Aristotle, emplotment (*muthos*) and mimetic activity (*mimēsis*). On the side of emplotment it will be necessary to remove a certain number of restrictions and prohibitions that are inherent in the privilege the *Poetics* accords to drama (tragedy and comedy) and to the epic. I concede there is something apparently paradoxical in making narrative activity the category encompassing drama, epic, and history, when, on the one hand, what Aristotle calls history (*historia*) in the context of the *Poetics* plays the role of a counterexample and when, on the other hand, narrative—or at least what he calls diegetic poetry—is opposed to drama within the single encompassing category of mimesis. Furthermore, it is not diegetic but tragic poetry that most bears the structural virtues of the art of composition. How can narrative become the encompassing term when at the beginning it is only one species among many? We shall have to say to what point Aristotle's text authorizes us to dissociate this structural model from its statement in terms of tragedy, giving rise by degrees to a reorganization of the whole narrative field. Whatever the case as regards the latitude offered by Aristotle's text, the Aristotelian concept of emplotment can be only the seed for us of a considerable development. To conserve its guiding role, it will have to undergo the test of other, more formidable counterexamples, whether provided by modern fictional narrative, as in the novel, or by contemporary history, which we might call non-narrative history.

On the side of mimetic activity, the full unfolding of the concept of mimesis demands not just that action's referential relation to the "real" be made less allusive, but also that this domain should receive other determinations besides the "ethical" ones—themselves considerable—that Aristotle assigns to it, if it is to rejoin the problematic set up by Augustine concerning our discordant experience of time. Our path beyond Aristotle will be a long one. It will not be possible to say how narrative is related to time until we have posed in its full scope the question of an *interweaving reference* [*référence croisée*]— based upon our lived temporal experience—of fictional and historical narrative. If the concept of mimetic activity comes first in the *Poetics*, this concept of an interweaving reference—as the distant heir of Aristotelian mimesis— has to come last and has to withdraw to the horizon of our whole enterprise. This is why it will not be treated systematically until volume 2.

THE MELODIC LINE: THE PAIR MIMESIS-MUTHOS

I am not proposing to do a commentary on the *Poetics*. My reflection is a second-order one and assumes a certain familiarity with the great commentaries of Lucas, Else, Hardison, and, last but not least, Roselyne Dupont-Roc and Jean Lallot.[3] Readers who have followed the same laborious course will easily recognize what my meditation owes to one or another of these works.

It is not a matter of indifference that the pair mimesis-muthos is approached through the term that both launches and situates the whole analysis: the adjective "poetic" (with its implied noun, "art"). It alone puts the mark of production, construction, dynamism on all the analyses, and first of all on the two terms muthos and mimesis, which have to be taken as operations, not as structures. When Aristotle, substituting the *definiens* for the *definiendum*, says that the muthos is ꞌ"the organization of the events [ē tōn pragmatōn sustasis]" (50a15), we must understand by *sustasis* (or by the equivalent term *sunthesis* [50a5]), not "system" (as Dupont-Roc and Lallot translate it [p. 55]), but the active sense of organizing the events into a system, so as to mark the operative character of all the concepts in the *Poetics*.[4] This is why, from the first lines, muthos is presented as the complement of a verb that means "to compose." Poetics is thereby identified, without further ado, as the art of "composing plots" (47a2). The same mark has to be preserved in the translation of mimesis. Whether we say "imitation" or "representation" (as do the most recent French translators), what has to be understood is the mimetic activity, the active process of imitating or representing something. Imitation or representation, therefore, must be understood in the dynamic sense of making a representation, of a transposition into representative works. Following this same requirement, when Aristotle comes to enumerate and define the six "parts" of tragedy in Chapter 6, we have to understand them not as parts of the poem but of the art of composition.[5]

If I am so insistent about this dynamic aspect which the adjective "poetic" imposes on all of the subsequent analysis, it is by design. When, in the second part of this work and in volume 2, I shall speak in defence of the primacy of our narrative understanding, in relation to explanation (sociological or otherwise) in history and explanation (structural or otherwise) in narrative fiction, I shall be defending the primacy of the activity that produces plots in relation to every sort of static structure, achronological paradigm, or temporal invariant. I will say nothing more about this here. What follows will clarify what I mean.

We shall begin by considering the pair mimesis/muthos.

Aristotle's *Poetics* contains just one all-encompassing concept, that of mimesis. This concept is only defined contextually and through one of its uses, the one that interests us here, imitation or representation of action. Or still more precisely: the imitating or representing of action in the medium of metrical language, hence as accompanied by rhythms (to which are added, in the case of tragedy, the prime example, spectacle and melody).[6] Still it is the imitation or representation of the action proper to tragedy, comedy, and epic that alone is taken into account. This is not yet defined in a form proper to its level of generality. Only the imitation or representation of action proper to tragedy is expressly defined.[7] I shall not directly attack this powerful core of Aristotle's definition of tragedy; instead I shall follow the guideline Aristotle himself offers in the same chapter when he provides the key to the construction of this definition. It is not done generically through some specific difference, but rather by means of an articulation into "parts": "Necessarily, therefore, there are in tragedy as a whole, considered as a special form, six constituent elements, viz. Plot, Character, Language, Thought, Spectacle, and Melody" (50a7–9).

For what follows I shall retain this quasi-identification of the two expressions "imitation or representation of action" and "the organization of the events." The second expression is, as I said, the *definiens* Aristotle substitutes for the *definiendum*, muthos, plot. This quasi-identification is warranted first by placing the six parts into a hierarchy that gives priority to the "what" or object of representation (plot, characters, thought) in relation to the "by which" or means (language and melody) and the "how" or mode (the spectacle); then by a second hierarchization internal to the "what" that sets the action above the characters and the thought. "Tragedy is an imitation of action [mimēsis praxeōs], and it is an imitation of the agents chiefly owing to the action" (50b3). At the conclusion of this double hierarchization, the plot appears as the "first principle," "the end", the "purpose," and, if we may say so, the "soul" of tragedy. This quasi-identification is warranted by the formula: "The imitation of action is the Plot" (50a1).

This text will serve as our guide from here on. It imposes upon us the task of thinking about and defining in terms of each other the imitating or representing of action and the organizing of the events. This equivalence first of all excludes any interpretation of Aristotle's mimesis in terms of a copy or identical replica. Imitating or representing is a mimetic activity inasmuch as it produces something, namely, the organization of events by emplotment. With one stroke we leave behind the Platonic use of mimesis, both in its metaphysical sense and its technical one in Book 3 of the *Republic* which opposes narrative "by mimesis" to "simple" narrative. Let me set aside this latter point for my discussion of the relation between narrative and drama, keeping for the time being the metaphysical sense of mimesis, associated with the concept of participation, by means of which things imitate ideas, and works of art imitate things. Platonic mimesis thereby distances the work of art by twice over from the ideal model which is its ultimate basis.[8] Aristotle's mimesis has just a single space wherein it is unfolded—human making [*faire*], the arts of composition.[9]

If therefore we are to conserve the character of mimesis as being an activity which *poiēsis* confers on it, and if, moreover, we hold tightly to the guideline of defining mimesis by muthos, then we ought not to hesitate in understanding action—action as the object in the expression *mimēsis praxeōs* (50b3)—as the correlate of the mimetic activity governed by the organization of the events (into a system). I shall discuss below other ways of construing the relation of imitation to its "what" (the plot, the characters, and the thought). The strict correlation between mimesis and muthos suggests giving the genitive form *praxeōs* the dominant, although perhaps not the exclusive, sense of being the noematic correlate of a practical noesis.[10] The action is the "construct" of that construction that the mimetic activity consists of. I shall show below that this correlation, which tends to make the poetic text close in on itself, must not be pushed too far. And, as we shall see, this closure is in no way implied by the *Poetics*. This is all the more evident in that the only instruction Aristotle gives us is to construct the muthos, hence the organization of the events, as the "what" of the mimesis. The noematic correlation is therefore between *mimēsis praxeōs*, taken as one syntagmatic expression, and the organization of the events, as another. To extend this relation of correlation within the first expression to include mimesis and praxis is thus plausible, fecund—and risky.

Let us not leave the pair mimesis/muthos without saying a word about the further constraints aimed at accounting for the already constituted genres of tragedy, comedy, and epic, and also at justifying Aristotle's preference for tragedy. We must be very attentive to these additional constraints. For they have somehow to be removed if I am to extract from Aristotle's *Poetics* the model of emplotment I am proposing to extend to every composition we call a narrative.

The first limiting constraint is intended to account for the distinction between comedy, on the one hand, and tragedy and epic, on the other. It is not linked to the action as such but to the characters, whom Aristotle rigorously subordinates to the action, as I shall discuss below. It is, however, introduced as early as the second chapter of the *Poetics*. Indeed the first time that Aristotle has to give a definite correlate to what "the imitators represent," he defines it as the "persons engaged in action" (48a1).[11] If he does not go directly to the only canonical formula in the *Poetics* for mimesis—imitation or representation of action—it is because he needs to introduce early on into the field of representation articulated by rhythmic language an ethical criterion of nobleness or baseness, which applies to the persons represented insofar as they have this or that character. On the basis of this dichotomy, tragedy can be defined as representing a "higher moral type" and comedy a "lower" one.[12]

The second limiting constraint is the one that separates epic, on the one hand, from tragedy and comedy, on the other, which find themselves on the same side of the dividing line this time. This constraint merits the greatest attention since it runs counter to my plan to consider narrative as the common genus and epic as one species of narrative. Here the genus is the imitation or representation of action, of which narrative and drama are two coordinated species. What constraint requires us to oppose them? It is noteworthy, first, that it is not a constraint that divides the objects, the "what" of representation, but its "how" or mode.[13] Yet if the three criteria of means, mode, and object are in principle equal, the whole weight of the subsequent analysis is on the "what." The equivalence between mimesis and muthos is an equivalence by means of the "what." And in terms of its plot, epic closely follows the rules of tragedy except for one variation, the "magnitude" which can be drawn from the composition alone and which in no way affects the basic rules for organizing the events. The essential thing is that the poet—whether narrator or dramatist—be a "maker of plots" (51b27). Next it is notable that the difference in mode, which is already relativized just in being a mode, continues to undergo, even within its field of application, a series of attenuations in the course of the subsequent analyses in the *Poetics*.

In the beginning (Chapter 3), the difference is plainly drawn. It is one thing for whoever does the imitating, therefore for the author of the mimetic activity, no matter what the art form or what the quality of the characters in question, that this author acts as a "narrator" (*apangelia, apangelionta*). It is another thing to make the characters the authors of the representation in that they "are presented as functioning and in action" (48a23).[14] Here there is a distinction taken from the poet's attitude as regards his characters, which is why it constitutes a "mode" of representation. Either the poet speaks directly, and thus narrates what his characters do, or he allows them to speak and speaks indirectly through them, while they "do" the drama (48a29).

Does this distinction prohibit us from reuniting epic and drama under the title "narrative"? Not at all. First, I am not characterizing narrative by its "mode," that is, by the author's attitude, but by its "object," since I am calling narrative exactly what Aristotle calls muthos, the organization of the events. I do not differ from Aristotle, therefore, on the plane he places himself on, that of the "mode." To avoid any confusion, I shall distinguish narrative in the broad sense, defined as the "what" of mimetic activity, and narrative in the narrow sense of the Aristotelian *diēgēsis*, which I shall henceforth call diegetic composition.[15] Next, this transferring of terminology does proportionately less violence to Aristotle's categories in that he continues to minimize the difference, whether he takes up the side of drama or that of epic. On the side of drama, it is said that everything epic has (plot, characters, thought, rhythm), tragedy has too. What tragedy has beyond these (spectacle and music) are not finally essential to it. Spectacle, in particular, is indeed one "part" of tragedy, but "is of all the parts the least technical in the sense of being least germane to the art of poetry. For tragedy fulfills its function even without a public performance and actors" (50b17–19). Further on in the *Poetics*, at the moment when he takes up the classic exercise of handing out prizes, Aristotle can credit tragedy for the fact that it can be seen, but he immediately takes this back again: "And again, tragedy succeeds in producing its proper effect even without any movement at all, just as epic poetry does, since when it is merely read the tragic force is manifested" (62a12).[16] And on the side of epic, the relation of the poet to his characters in the act of narrating is not as direct as the definition would have it. A first attenuation is even incorporated into it right at the start. Aristotle adds a parenthesis to his definition of the poet as narrator: "whether the narrator speaks at times in an assumed role, which is

Homer's way, or always in his own person without change" (48a21–23). More precisely, Homer is praised further on (Chapter 23) for his art of effacing himself behind his characters with their different qualities, letting them act and speak in their own name; in short, for letting them occupy the scene. Aristotle can write, without paradox, at the beginning of his chapter devoted to "the imitative art that . . . employs metrical language" (59a17): "it is evident that, just as in tragedies, its plots should be dramatic in structure, etc." (59a19). Thus in the pair drama/narrative, the first laterally qualifies the second to the point of serving as its model. In various ways, therefore, Aristotle attenuates the "modal" opposition between diegetic imitation (or representation) and dramatic imitation (or representation), an opposition, in any case, that does not affect the object of imitation, the emplotment.

A final constraint merits placement under the pair mimesis/muthos, because it gives an occasion to make more precise the Aristotelian usage of mimesis. It is the one that subordinates consideration of the characters to consideration of the action itself. This constraint seems too restrictive if we consider the modern development of the novel and Henry James's thesis that gives character development an equal, if not higher, place than that of the plot.[17] Yet as Frank Kermode comments, to develop a character means more narration, and to develop a plot means enriching a character.[18] Aristotle is harder to please: "For tragedy is not an imitation of men but of actions and of life. It is in action that happiness and unhappiness are found, and the end we aim at is a kind of activity, not a quality. . . . What is more, without action there could not be a tragedy, but there could be without characterization" (50a16–24). We may of course attenuate the rigor of these hierarchies by observing that it is a question only of ordering the "parts" of tragedy. All the more so as the difference between tragedy and comedy is taken from the ethical differences affecting the characters. Assigning second place to the characters, therefore, does not disqualify the category of character. What is more, we shall encounter in contemporary narrative semiotics—stemming from Propp—attempts comparable to that of Aristotle to reconstruct narrative logic beginning not from characters but from "functions," that is, from abstract segments of action.

But what is essential lies elsewhere. By so giving action priority over character, Aristotle establishes the mimetic status of action. It is in ethics (cf. *Nicomachean Ethics* 1105a30ff.) that the subject precedes the action in the order of ethical qualities. In poetics, the composition of the action by the poet governs the ethical quality of the characters. The subordination of character to action, therefore, is not a constraint of the same nature as the two preceding ones. It seals the equivalence between the two expressions "representation of action" and "organization of the events." If the accent has to be placed on this organization, then the imitation or representation has to be of action rather than of human beings.

THE PLOT: A MODEL OF CONCORDANCE

Let me set the question of the status of mimesis between parentheses for a while, in that it is not uniquely defined by emplotment, and turn directly toward the theory of muthos so as to discern in it the starting point for my own theory of narrative composition.

We should not forget that the theory of muthos is abstracted from the definition of tragedy we find in Chapter 6 of the *Poetics*, which was cited above. Aristotle first provides, therefore, the theory of the tragic muthos.

The question that I shall continue to pursue until the end of this work is whether the paradigm of order, characteristic of tragedy, is capable of extension and transformation to the point where it can be applied to the whole narrative field. This difficulty ought not to stop us here, however. The rigor of the tragic model has the advantage of setting great store on the exigence for order at the very beginning of my investigation of our narrative understanding. Right away, the most extreme contrast is established with the Augustinian *distentio animi*. That is, the tragic muthos is set up as the poetic solution to the speculative paradox of time, inasmuch as the inventing of order is pursued to the exclusion of every temporal characteristic. It will be my task and my responsibility to draw the temporal implications of the model, in connection with the new deployment of the theory of mimesis I propose below. However the enterprise of thinking about Augustine's *distentio animi* and Aristotle's tragic muthos as one will at least appear plausible if we are willing to consider that the Aristotelian theory does not accentuate concordance alone but, in a highly subtle way, the play of discordance internal to concordance. It is this internal dialectic of poetic composition that makes the tragic muthos the inverted figure of the Augustinian paradox.

The definition of muthos as the organization of the events first emphasizes concordance. And this concordance is characterized by three features: completeness, wholeness, and an appropriate magnitude.[19]

The notion of a "whole" (*holos*) is the pivot of the analysis that follows. For, far from being oriented toward an investigation into the temporal character of the organization, this analysis is fixed on its logical character.[20] And it is precisely at the moment when the definition skirts the problem of time that it most distances itself from time: "Now a thing is a whole if it has a beginning, a middle, and an end" (50b26). But it is only in virtue of poetic composition that something counts as a beginning, middle, or end. What defines the beginning is not the absence of some antecedent but the absence of necessity in the succession. As for the end, it is indeed what comes after something else, but "either as its necessary sequel or as its usual [and hence probable] sequel" (50b30). Only the middle seems to be defined just by succession: "A middle is that which both comes after something else and has another thing following it" (50b31). Yet in the tragic model it has its own logic, which is that of a "reversal" (*metabolē, metaballein* [51a14]; *metabasis* [52a16]) of fortune from good to bad. The theory of the "complex" plot will contain a typology of the reversals that have a properly tragic effect. The accent, in the analysis of this idea of a "whole," is therefore put on the absence of chance and on conformity to the requirements of necessity or probability governing succession. If succession can be subordinated in this way to some logical connection, it is because the ideas of beginning, middle, and end are not taken from experience. They are not features of some real action but the effects of the ordering of the poem.

The same applies to the magnitude. It is only in the plot that action has a contour, a limit (*horos*) and, as a consequence, a magnitude. We shall return below, with regard to the aesthetics of reception whose seed is present in Aristotle, to the role of the attention or of memory in the definition of this criterion of perspicacity. Whatever can be said about the spectator's capacity to take in the work in one view, this external criterion comes to terms with an exigency internal to the work which is the only thing important here. "If the length is sufficient to permit a change from bad fortune to good or from good fortune to bad to come about in an inevitable or probable sequence of events, this is a satisfactory limit [horos] of magnitude" (51a12–15). Certainly, this length must be temporal—a reversal takes time. But it is the work's time, not the time of events in the world. The character of necessity applies to the events that the plot makes contiguous with each other (*ephexes*) (ibid.). Vacuous times are excluded. We do not ask what the hero did between two events that would have been separated in his life. In *Oedipus Rex*, notes Else, the messenger returns precisely at the moment the plot requires his presence, "no sooner and no later" (Else, p. 293). It is also for reasons internal to its composition that epic admits of a longer length. More tolerant about its episodic events, it requires greater amplitude, but without ever giving up the requirement for some limit.

Not only is time not considered, it is excluded. For example, in considering epic (Chapter 23), as submitted to the requirements of completeness and wholeness best illustrated by tragedy, Aristotle opposes two sorts of unity to each other: on the one hand, the temporal unity (*henos khronou*) that characterizes "a single period of time with all that happened therein to one or more persons, no matter how little relation one event may have had with another" (59a23–24), and, on the other hand, the dramatic unity that characterizes "a single action" (59a22) (which forms a whole, complete in itself, having a beginning, a middle, and an end). That numerous actions occur during a single period of time does not therefore make a "single action." This is why Homer is praised for having chosen in the story of the Trojan War—even though this too has a beginning and an end—"one part" for which his art alone determined its beginning and its end. These remarks confirm that Aristotle shows no interest in the construction of a time capable of being implicated in the constructing of the plot.

If therefore the internal connection of the plot is logical rather than chronological, what logic is it? The truth is that the word "logic" never appears, although necessity and probability are familiar categories from the *Organon*. If the term "logic" is never used, it is probably because what is at issue is an intelligibility appropriate to the field of *praxis*, not that of *theoria*, and therefore one neighboring on *phronēsis*, which is the intelligent use of action. Poetry is, in fact, a "doing" [*faire*] and a "doing" about "doing"—the "doers" of Aristotle's Chapter 3. But it is not actual, ethical doing, rather fictive and poetic doing. Which is why it is so necessary to discern the specific features of this mimetic and mythic intelligence—in the Aristotelian sense of these two terms.

Aristotle makes clear that it really is a question of a kind of intelligence, beginning in Chapter 4, where he establishes his leading concepts by way of their genesis. Why, he asks, do we take pleasure in regarding the images of things that in themselves are repugnant—the basest animals or corpses? "For this again the reason is that the experience of learning things is highly enjoyable, not only for philosophers but for other people as well . . . when they enjoy seeing images, therefore, it is because as they look at them they have the experience of learning and reasoning out what each thing represents, for example, that 'this figure is so and so'" (48b12–17). Learning, concluding, recognizing the form—here we have the skeleton of meaning for the pleasure found in imitation or representation.[21] But if it is not a question of philosophical universals, what kind of universals are these "poetic" universals? That they are universals is beyond doubt since they can be characterized by the double opposition of the possible to the actual and the general to the particular. The first pair, we know, is illustrated by the famous opposition between poetry and history in the manner of Herodotus.[22] "Thus the difference between the historian and the poet is not that the historian employs prose and the poet verse—the work of Herodotus could be put into verse, and it would be no less history with verses than without them; rather the difference is that the one tells of things that have been and the other of such things as might be. Poetry, therefore, is a more philosophical and a higher thing than history, in that poetry tends rather to express the universal, history rather the particular fact" (51b4–7).

What is at issue is not entirely elucidated, however, for Aristotle is careful to oppose "such things as might happen, things that are possibilities by virtue of being in themselves inevitable or probable" to "things that have happened" (51a37–38). And also a universal is: "The sort of thing that (in the circumstances) a certain kind of person will say or do either probably or necessarily" (51b9). In other words, the possible and the general are not to be sought elsewhere than in the organization of the events, since it is this linkage that has to be necessary or probable. In short, it is the plot that has to be typical. We understand anew why the action takes precedence over the characters. It is the universalizing of the plot that universalizes the characters, even when they have specific names. Whence the precept: first conceive the plot, then add the names.

It might be objected that the argument is circular. The possible and the general characterize the necessary or the probable, but it is the necessary and the probable that qualify the possible and the general. Must we therefore assume that the organization as such, that is, as a connection akin to causality, makes the organized facts typical? For my own part, I lean in the direction of those narrativist theorists of history, such as Louis O. Mink, who put the whole weight of its intelligibility on the connection as such established between the events, or on the judicatory act of "grasping together." To conceive of a causal connection, even among singular events, is already a kind of universalization.

That such is the case is confirmed by the opposition between simple and episodic plots (51b33–35). It is not episodes as such that Aristotle disapproves of; tragedy can forgo them only under the penalty of becoming monotonous, and epic makes the best use of them. What he condemns is disconnected episodes: "I call episodic a plot in which the episodes follow one another [met'allēla] in no probable or inevitable sequence" (ibid.). The key opposition is here: one thing after another and one thing because of another ("in a causal sequence" [di'allēla]) (52a4). One after the other is merely episodic and therefore improbable, one because of the other is a causal sequence and therefore probable. No doubt is allowed. The kind of universality that a plot calls for derives from its ordering, which brings about its completeness and its wholeness. The universals a plot engenders are not Platonic ideas. They are universals related to practical wisdom, hence to ethics and politics. A plot engenders such universals when the structure of its action rests on the connections internal to the action and not on external accidents. These internal connections as such are the beginning of the universalization.

One feature of mimesis, then, is that it is directed more at the coherence of the muthos than at its particular story. Its making [faire] is immediately a universalizing "making." The whole problem of narrative Verstehen is contained here in principle. To make up a plot is already to make the intelligible spring from the accidental, the universal from the singular, the necessary or the probable from the episodic. And is this not finally what Aristotle says in 51b29–32:

> It is clear then from the foregoing remarks that the poet
> should be a maker of plots more than a maker of verse, in
> that he is a poet by virtue of his imitation and he imitates
> actions. So even if on occasion he takes real events as the

subject of a poem, he is none the less a poet, since nothing prevents some of the things that have actually happened from being of the sort that might probably or possibly happen, and it is in accordance with this that he is their poet. (51b27–32)[23]

The two sides of the equation balance each other: maker of plots, imitator of action—this is the poet.

The difficulty is still only partially resolved. We can verify a causal connection in reality, but what about in a poetic composition? This is an embarrassing question. If mimetic activity "composes" action, it is what establishes what is necessary in composing it. It does not see the universal, it makes it spring forth. What then are its criteria? We have a partial answer in the expression referred to above: "it is because as they look at them they have the experience of learning and reasoning out what each thing represents, concluding, for example, that 'this figure is so and so'" (48b16–17). This pleasure of recognition, as Dupont-Roc and Lallot put it, presupposes, I think, a prospective concept of truth, according to which to invent is to rediscover. But this prospective concept of truth has no place in a formal theory of the structure of the plot. It presupposes a more developed theory of mimesis than the one that simply equates mimesis with muthos. I shall return to this point at the end of this study.

INCLUDED DISCORDANCE

The tragic model is not purely a model of concordance, but rather of discordant concordance. This is where it offers a counterpart to the *distentio animi*. Discordance is present at each stage of the Aristotelian analysis, even though it is only dealt with thematically in terms of the complex (versus the simple) plot. It is already manifest in the canonical definition of tragedy as an imitation of action that is serious and "complete" (*teleios*) (49b25).[24] Completeness is not a negligible feature insofar as the end of action is happiness or unhappiness, and insofar as the ethical quality of the characters grounds the plausibility of either outcome. The action is not brought to its conclusion therefore until it produces one or the other. And the space for the "episodes" that bring action to its conclusion is thereby marked out. Aristotle says nothing against episodes as episodes. What he proscribes are not episodes but the episodic texture, the plot where the episodes follow one another by chance. The episodes, controlled by the plot, are what give amplitude to the work and thus a "magnitude."

The definition of tragedy also contains another indication: "and effecting through pity and fear [what we call] the *catharsis* of such emotions" (49b26–27). Let us leave aside the prickly question of catharsis for the moment and concentrate on its means (*dia*). In my opinion Else and Dupont-Roc and

Lallot have well understood Aristotle's intention, as it is reflected in the construction of this sentence. The spectator's emotional response is constructed in the drama, in the quality of the destructive or painful incidents suffered by the characters themselves. The subsequent treatment of the term *pathos*, as the third component of a complex plot, will confirm this. Hence catharsis, whatever the term means, is brought about by the plot. And the first discordance is the fearful and pitiable incidents. They constitute the major threat to the plot's coherence. This is why Aristotle speaks of them again in connection with the necessary and the probable and also in the context of his criticism of episodic examples (Chapter 9). There he no longer uses the nouns pity and fear but the adjectives pitiable and fearful (52a2), which qualify the incidents the poet represents by means of the plot.

Discordant concordance is intended still more directly by the analysis of surprise. Aristotle characterizes it by an extraordinary expression in anacoluthic form, which is lost in the English translation: "when they come unexpectedly and yet occur in a causal sequence in which one thing leads to another [para tēn doxan di'allēla]" (52a4). The "marvelous" things (*to thaumaston*) (ibid.)—the height of the discordant—are those strokes of chance that seem to arrive by design.

We reach the heart of discordant concordance, still common to both simple and episodic plots, with the central phenomenon of the tragic action Aristotle calls "reversal" (*metabolē*) in Chapter 11. In tragedy, reversal turns good fortune into bad, but its direction may be reversed. Tragedy does not exploit this resource, owing no doubt to the role of the fearful or the pitiable incidents. It is this reversal, however, that takes time and governs the magnitude of the work. The art of composition consists in making this discordance appear concordant. The "one because of [dia] the other" thus wins out over "one after [meta] the other" (52a18–22).[25] The discordant overthrows the concordant in life, but not in tragic art.

The reversals characteristic of the complex plot are, as is well known, reversal (*peripeteia*)—*coup de théâtre* in Dupont-Roc and Lallot's apt phrase—and recognition (*anagnōrisis*), to which must be added suffering (*pathos*). The definitions of these modes of reversal are given in Chapter 11 and the commentary that goes with them is well known.[26] What is important for us is that here Aristotle multiplies the constraints on the tragic plot and thereby makes his model both stronger and more limited at the same time. More limited, inasmuch as the theory of the muthos becomes more and more identified with that of the tragic plot. So the question will be whether what we are calling narrative can draw this surprising effect from other procedures than those Aristotle enumerates, and therefore give rise to other constraints than those of tragedy. Yet the model also becomes stronger, inasmuch as reversal, recognition, and suffering—particularly when they are joined together in one work, as in Sophocles' *Oedipus*—bring to their highest degree of tension the fusion of the "paradoxical" and the "causal" sequence, of surprise and necessity.[27] And it is the force of this model that every theory of narrativity tries to preserve by other means than those of the tragic model. In this regard, we might ask whether we do not move away from narrative if we abandon this major constraint constituted by reversal, taken in its broadest sense of "a change from one state of affairs to its exact opposite" (52a22). We shall rediscover this question when we inquire below "what makes a story (or stories) out of action," to use the title of an essay by Hermann Lübbe.[28] The question of unintended effects, as well as that of "perverse" ones, in the theory of history will raise an analogous question. Its implications are numerous: if reversal is essential to every story or history where meaninglessness threatens the meaningful, does not the conjunction of reversal and recognition preserve a universality that goes beyond the case of tragedy? Do not historians, too, seek to replace perplexity with lucidity? And is not our perplexity greatest where reversals of fortune were most unexpected? There is another even more constraining implication: must we not also preserve, along with reversal, the reference to happiness and unhappiness? Does not every narrated story finally have to do with reversals of fortune, whether for better or worse?[29] It is not necessary to take suffering (*pathos*) as the poor cousin in this review of the modes of reversal. Aristotle, it is true, does give it a rather confining definition at the end of Chapter 11. Suffering is linked to the fearful and pitiable incidents inherent in the tragic plot, the leading generators of discordance. Suffering—"the thing suffered," says Else, "*l'effet violent*," according to Dupont-Roc and Lallot—just brings to their peak the fearful and the pitiable in the complex plot.

Such consideration of the emotional quality of the incidents is not foreign to our inquiry, as though concern for the intelligibility proper to the search for completeness and wholeness were to imply an "intellectualism" that should be opposed to some sort of "emotionalism." The pitiable and the fearful are qualities closely tied to the most unexpected changes of fortune oriented toward unhappiness. It is these discordant incidents the plot tends to make necessary and probable. And in so doing, it purifies them, or, better, purges them. We shall return again to this point. By including the discordant in the concordant, the plot includes the affecting within the intelligible. Aristotle thus comes to say that pathos is one ingredient of the imitating or representing of praxis. So poetry conjoins these terms that ethics opposes.[30]

We must go even further. If the pitiable and the fearful can be incorporated into the plot, it is because these emotions have, as Else says (p. 375), their own *rationale*, which, in return, serves as a criterion for the tragic quality of each change in fortune. Two chapters (13 and 14) are devoted to this screening effect which pity and fear exercise with regard to the very structure of the plot. Indeed, to the extent that these emotions are incompatible with the repugnant and the monstrous, or the inhuman (a lack of "philanthropy" that makes us recognize someone like ourselves in the characters), they play the principal role in the typology of plots. This is constructed in terms of two axes: whether the characters are good or evil, and whether their end is happy or unhappy. The two tragic emotions govern its hierarchy of possible combinations "since the first is felt for a person whose misfortune is undeserved and the second for someone like ourselves" (53a3–5).

Finally, it is these tragic emotions that require that the hero be prevented by some "fault" from attaining excellence in the order of virtue and justice, without however vice or wickedness being responsible for his fall into misfortune: "We are left with the man whose place is between these extremes. Such is the man who on the one hand is not pre-eminent in virtue and justice, and yet on the other hand does not fall into misfortune through vice or depravity, but falls because of some mistake [hamartia]" (53a7f.).[31] So even the discernment of the tragic fault is brought about by the emotional quality of pity, fear, and our sense for what is human.[32] The relation therefore is a circular one. It is the composition of the plot that purges the emotions, by bringing to representation the pitiable and fearful incidents, and it is these purged emotions that govern our discernment of the tragic. It seems hardly possible to push any further the inclusion of the fearful and the pitiable in the dramatic texture. Aristotle can, however, conclude this theme in these terms: "And since the pleasure the poet is to provide is that which comes [apo] from pity and fear through [dia] an imitation, clearly this effect must be embodied [empoiēteon] in [en] the events of the plot" (53b12–13).[33]

These are the increasing constraints to which Aristotle submits his tragic model. We may ask then whether, in augmenting the constraints on the tragic plot, he has not made his model both stronger and more limited.[34]

THE TWO SIDES OF THE POETIC CONFIGURATION

To conclude, I would like to return to the question of mimesis, the second focus of my interest in reading the *Poetics*. It does not seem to me to be governed by the equating of the two expressions "the imitation (or representation) of action" and "the organization of the events." It is not that something has to be taken back from this equation. There is no doubt that the prevalent sense of mimesis is the one instituted by its being joined to muthos. If we continue to translate mimesis by "imitation," we have to understand something completely contrary to a copy of some preexisting reality and speak instead of a creative imitation. And if we translate mimesis by "representation" (as do Dupont-Roc and Lallot), we must not understand by this word some redoubling of presence, as we could still do for Platonic mimesis, but rather the break that opens the space for fiction. Artisans who work with words produce not things but quasi-things; they invent the as-if. And in this sense, the Aristotelian mimesis is the emblem of the shift [*décrochage*] that, to use our vocabulary today, produces the "literariness" of the work of literature.

Still the equation of mimesis and muthos does not completely fill up the meaning of the expression *mimēsis praxeōs*. We may of course—as we did above—construe the objective genitive as the noematic correlate of imitation or representation and equate this correlate to the whole expression "the organization of the events," which Aristotle makes the "what"—the object—of mimesis. But that the praxis belongs at the same time to the real domain, covered by ethics, and the imaginary one, covered by poetics, suggests that mimesis functions not just as a break but also as a connection, one which establishes precisely the status of the "metaphorical" transposition of the practical field by the muthos. If such is the case, we have to preserve in the meaning of the term mimesis a reference to the first side of poetic composition. I call this reference mimesis₁ to distinguish it from mimesis₂,—the mimesis of creation—which remains the pivot point. I hope to show that even in Aristotle's text there are scattered references to this prior side of poetic composition. This is not all. Mimesis, we recall, as an activity, the mimetic activity, does not reach its intended term through the dynamism of the poetic text alone. It also requires a spectator or reader. So there is another side of poetic composition as well, which I call mimesis₃, whose indications I shall also look for in the text of the *Poetics*. By so framing the leap of imagination with the two operations that constitute the two sides of the mimesis of invention, I believe we enrich rather than weaken the meaning of the mimetic activity invested in the muthos. I hope to show that this activity draws its intelligibility from its mediating function, which leads us from one side of the text to the other through the power of refiguration.

References are not lacking, in the *Poetics*, to the understanding of action—and also the passions—which the *Ethics* articulates. These are tacit references, although the *Rhetoric* does include a veritable "treatise on the passions." The difference is easy to understand. Rhetoric exploits these passions, while poetics transposes human action and suffering into a poem.

The following chapter will give a more complete idea of the understanding of the order of action implied by narrative activity. The tragic model, as a limited model of narrativity, makes use of borrowings themselves limited by this pre-understanding. The tragic muthos turning on reversals of fortune, and exclusively on those from happiness to unhappiness, is one exploration of the ways in which action throws good people, against all expectation, into unhappiness. It serves as a counterpoint to ethics, which teaches how action, through the exercise of virtue, leads to happiness. At the same time it borrows from the foreknowledge of action only its ethical features.[35]

In the first place, poets have always known that the characters they represent are "persons engaged in action" (48a1). They have always known that "character is that in virtue of which we say that the personages are of such and such quality" (50a4). They have always known that "these persons will necessarily be persons of a higher or lower moral type" (48a2). The parenthesis that follows this last phrase is an ethical one: "for this is the one division that characters submit to almost without exception, goodness or badness being universal criteria of character" (48a2–4). This expression "universal" (*pantes*) is the indication of mimesis₁ in the text of the *Poetics*. In the chapter devoted to the characters (Chapter 15), "the person being imitated" (54a27) is a person according to ethics. And the ethical qualifications come from the real world. What stems from the imitation or representation is the logical requirement of coherence. In the same vein, it is said that tragedy and comedy differ in that "comedy prefers to imitate persons who are worse, tragedy persons who are better, than the present generation [tōn nun]" (48a15–18); this is the second indication of mimesis₁. Therefore, that the characters may be improved or harmed by the action is something the poet knows and takes for granted: "Character is that in virtue of which we say that the personages are of such and such a quality" (50a6).³⁶

In short, if we are to talk of a "mimetic displacement" or a quasi-metaphorical "transposition" from ethics to poetics, we have to conceive of mimetic activity as a connection and not just as a break. It is in fact the movement from mimesis₁ to mimesis₂. If it is beyond doubt that the term muthos indicates discontinuity, the word praxis, by its double allegiance, assures continuity between the two realms of action—ethics and poetics.³⁷

A similar relationship of identity and difference could no doubt be recognized between the *pathē* of which *The Rhetoric*, Book II, gives an ample description and the *pathos*—the suffering—which tragic art makes one "part" of the plot (52b9ff.).

Perhaps we should push this reprise or recovery of ethics in poetics still further. Poets find not only an implicit categorization of the practical field in their cultural stock but also a first narrative organization [*mise en forme*] of this field. If tragic poets, unlike authors of comedy who allow themselves to support their plots with names chosen by chance, retain "historical names" (*genomenōn*) (51b15), that is, ones received from tradition, it is because the probable—an objective feature—must also be persuasive or credible (*pithanon*) (51b16)—a subjective feature. The logical connection of probability cannot therefore be detached from the cultural constraints of acceptability. Certainly art, here again, indicates a break: "So even if on occasion he takes real events [genomena] as the subject of a poem, he is none the less a poet" (51b29–30). Yet without myths that have been passed on there would be nothing to transform poetically. Who can fully put into words the inexhaustible source of violence received from the myths which the poet transforms into a tragic effect? And where is this tragic potential more dense than in the received stories about a few celebrated houses: that of the Atrides, that of Oedipus? It is not by chance therefore that Aristotle, so concerned elsewhere about the autonomy of the poetic act, advises poets to continue to draw upon the most frightful and pitiable matter in this treasury.³⁸

As for the criterion of the probable or the possible by which poets distinguish their plots from the traditional stories—whether they really happened or exist only in the storehouse of tradition—we may doubt that it can be circumscribed by a pure poetic "logic." The reference I made to its tie to the "persuasive" leads me to think it too is somehow received. But this problem relates instead to the problematic of mimesis₃, to which I shall now turn.

At first glance, there seems little to expect from the *Poetics* concerning the second side of poetic composition. Unlike the *Rhetoric*, which subordinates the order of discourse to its effects on its audience, the *Poetics* indicates no explicit interest in the communication of the work to the public. It even reveals in places an impatience regarding the constraints tied to the institution of the public contests (51a7) and even more so regarding the poor taste of the ordinary public (Chapter 25). The reception of the work is not therefore a major category of the *Poetics*. It is a treatise about composition, with almost no concern for anyone who receives the result.

Thus the references that I am now bringing together under the heading of mimesis₃ are all the more valuable in that they are so rare. They testify to the impossibility, for a poetics that puts its principal accent on the internal structures of the text, of locking itself up within the closure of the text.

The line I am going to follow is this. The *Poetics* does not speak of structure but of structuration. Structuration is an oriented activity that is only completed in the spectator or the reader.

From the beginning the term *poiēsis* puts the imprint of its dynamism on all the concepts in the *Poetics* and makes them concepts about operations. Mimesis is a representative *activity*; *sustasis* (or *sunthēsis*) is the operation of organizing the events into a system, not the system itself. Further, the dynamism (*dunamis*) of *poiēsis* is intended from the opening lines of the *Poetics* as an exigency for completeness (47a8–10). It is what, in Chapter 6, requires that the action be brought to its conclusion (*teleios*). Yes, this completeness is the completeness of the work, of its muthos, but it is attested to only by the pleasure "which properly belongs to it" (53b11), which Aristotle calls its *ergon*, "the effect proper to tragedy" (52b30). All the indications of mimesis₃ in Aristotle's text are relative to this pleasure "which properly belongs to" tragedy and its conditions of production. I would like to show in what way this pleasure is both constructed in the work and made actual outside it. It joins inside to outside and requires us to treat in a dialectical fashion this relation of outside to inside, which modern poetics too quickly reduces to a simple disjunction, in the name of an alleged prohibition thrown up by semiotics against everything taken to be extralinguistic.[39] As though language were not always already thrown beyond itself by its ontological vehemence! In the *Ethics* we have a good guide for articulating correctly the inside and the outside of the work. This is its theory of pleasure. If we apply to the work of literature what Aristotle says about pleasure in Books VII and X of the *Nichomachean Eth-*

ics, namely, that it proceeds from unhindered action and is added to accomplished action as a crowning supplement, we ought to articulate in the same fashion the internal finality of the composition and the external finality of its reception.[40]

The pleasure of learning something is the first component of this pleasure of the text. Aristotle takes it as one corollary of the pleasure we take in imitations or representations, which is one of the natural causes of the poetic art, according to the genetic analysis in Chapter 4. And he associates with the act of learning that of "concluding, for example, that 'this figure is so and so'" (59b19). The pleasure of learning is therefore the pleasure of recognition. And this is what the spectators do when they recognize in Oedipus the universal that the plot engenders through its composition. The pleasure of recognition is therefore both constructed in the work and experienced by the reader.

This pleasure of recognition, in turn, is the fruit of the pleasure the spectator takes in the composition as necessary or probable. These "logical" criteria are themselves both constructed in the piece and exercised by the spectator. I have already made an allusion, in discussing extreme cases of dissonant consonance, to the connection Aristotle establishes between the probable and the acceptable—the "persuasive," the major category in the *Rhetoric*. Such is the case as soon as the para-doxical has to be included in the causal sequence of "one by means of the other." It is even more the case when epic accepts the *alogon*, the irrational, that tragedy has to avoid. The probable, under the pressure of the improbable, is thereby stretched to the breaking point. I have not forgotten the astonishing precept: "What is impossible yet probable should be preferred to that which is possible but incredible" (60a26–27). And when, in the following chapter (Chapter 25), Aristotle determines those norms that ought to guide criticism in resolving "problems," he classes representable things under three rubrics: "things as they once were or now are; or things as people say or suppose they were or are; or things as they ought to be" (60b10–11). But what do present (and past) reality, opinion, and things as they ought to be designate if not the realm of the readily believable? We touch here on one of the more concealed sources of the pleasure of recognition, namely, the criterion of what is "persuasive," whose contours are those of the social form of the imagination.[41] It is true that Aristotle does explicitly make the persuasive an attribute of the probable, which is itself the measure of the possible in poetry—"possibility means credibility" (51b16). But whenever the impossible—the extreme figure of the discordant—threatens the structure, is it not the persuasive that becomes the measure of the acceptable impossibility? "Thus in reference to poetic effect, a convincing impossibility is preferable to that which, though possible, is unconvincing" (61b10–11). "Opinion" (ibid.) is the only guide here: "The improbable [or irrational] should be justified by 'what men say'" (61b14).

49

Hence, by its very nature, the intelligibility characteristic of dissonant consonance—what Aristotle puts under the term "probable"—is the common product of the work and the public. The persuasive is born at their intersection.

It is also in the spectator that the properly tragic emotions flower. For the pleasure proper to tragedy is one that engenders fear and pity. Nowhere better than here do we overtake the movement from the work to the spectator. On one side, in effect, the pitiable and the fearful—as adjectives—characterize the "events" themselves that the muthos composes into one. In this sense, the muthos imitates or represents the pitiable and the fearful. How does it bring them to representation? Precisely by making them leave (*ex*) the organization of the events. Here then fear and pity are inscribed *in* the events *by* the composition, insofar as it moves *through* the sieve of the representative activity (53b13). What is experienced by the spectator must first be constructed in the work. In this sense we could say that Aristotle's ideal spectator is an "implied spectator" in the same sense Wolfgang Iser speaks of an "implied reader"—but one of flesh and blood and capable of pleasure.[42]

In this regard I agree with the converging interpretations of catharsis in Else, Golden, Redfield, and Dupont-Roc and Lallot.[43] Catharsis is a purification—or better, as Dupont-Roc and Lallot propose, a purgation—which has its seat in the spectator. It consists precisely in the fact that the pleasure proper to tragedy proceeds from pity and fear. It consists therefore in the transformation of the pain inherent in these emotions into pleasure. Yet this subjective alchemy is also constructed *in* the work *by* the mimetic activity. It results from the fact that the pitiable and fearful incidents are, as we have said, themselves brought to representation. And this poetic representation of these emotions results in turn from the composition itself. In this sense it is not too much to say, with recent commentators, that the purgation first of all is in the poetic construction. I myself have elsewhere suggested treating catharsis as the integrating part of the metaphorical process that conjoins cognition, imagination, and feeling.[44] And in this sense, the dialectic of inside and outside reaches its highest point in catharsis. Experienced by the spectator, it is constructed in the work. This is why Aristotle could include it in his definition of tragedy, without devoting a separate analysis to it: "effecting through [dia] pity and fear [what we call] the *catharsis* of such emotions" (49b28).

I willingly admit that the allusions the *Poetics* makes to pleasure taken as understanding and pleasure taken as experiencing fear and pity—which together, in the *Poetics*, form a single pleasure—constitute just the barest indication of a theory of mimesis₃. This only takes on its full scope when the work deploys a world that the reader appropriates. This world is a cultural world. The principal axis of a theory of reference on the second side of the work passes therefore through the relationship between poetry and culture. As James Redfield so forcefully puts it in his book *Nature and Culture in the Iliad*, the two relations, each the converse of the other, that we can establish between these two terms "must be interpreted . . . in light of a third relation: the poet as a maker of culture" (p. xi).[45] Aristotle's *Poetics* makes no incursion into this domain. It sets up the ideal spectator, and even more so the ideal reader, with his intelligence, his "purged" emotions, and his pleasure, at the junction of the work and the culture it creates. In this, Aristotle's *Poetics*, despite its almost exclusive interest in mimesis as inventive, does offer some indication of an investigation of mimetic activity in all its aspects.

3

Time and Narrative: Threefold *Mimesis*

The moment has come to join together the two preceding independent studies and test my basic hypothesis that between the activity of narrating a story and the temporal character of human experience there exists a correlation that is not merely accidental but that presents a transcultural form of necessity. To put it another way, *time becomes human to the extent that it is articulated through a narrative mode, and narrative attains its full meaning when it becomes a condition of temporal existence.*

The cultural abyss that separates the Augustinian analysis of time in the *Confessions* and the Aristotelian analysis of plot in the *Poetics* compels me to construct at my own risk the intermediary links that articulate their correlation. Indeed, as has been said, Augustine's paradoxes of the experience of time owe nothing to the activity of narrating a story. His key example of reciting a verse or a poem serves to sharpen the paradox rather than to resolve it. And on his side, Aristotle's analysis of plot owes nothing to his theory of time, which is dealt with exclusively in his *Physics*. What is more, in his *Poetics*, the "logic" of emplotment discourages any consideration of time, even when it implies concepts such as beginning, middle, and end, or when it becomes involved in a discourse about the magnitude or the length of the plot.

The mediating construction I am about to propose deliberately bears the same title as does this work as a whole: *Time and Narrative*. At this stage of the investigation, however, it can only be a question of a sketch that will require further expansion, criticism, and revision. In fact, the present study will not take into consideration the fundamental bifurcation between historical and fictional narrative, which will give birth to the more technical studies of the succeeding parts of this work. From the separate investigation of these two fields will proceed the most serious questioning of my whole enterprise, as much on the level of the claim to truth as on that of the internal structure of discourse. What is sketched out here, therefore, is only a sort of reduced model of the thesis that the remainder of this work must attempt to prove.

I am taking as my guideline for exploring the mediation between time and narrative the articulation mentioned earlier, and already partially illustrated by my interpretation of Aristotle's *Poetics*, between the three moments of mimesis that, seriously and playfully, I named mimesis$_1$, mimesis$_2$, and mimesis$_3$. I take it as established that mimesis$_2$ constitutes the pivot of this analysis. By serving as a turning point it opens up the world of the plot and institutes, as I have already suggested, the literariness of the work of literature. But my thesis is that the very meaning of the configurating operation constitutive of emplotment is a result of its intermediary position between the two operations I am calling mimesis$_1$ and mimesis$_3$, which constitute the two sides [*l'amont et l'aval*] of mimesis$_2$. By saying this, I propose to show that mimesis$_2$ draws its intelligibility from its faculty of mediation, which is to conduct us from the one side of the text to the other, transfiguring the one side into the other through its power of configuration. I am reserving for the part of this work devoted to fictional narrative the confrontation between this thesis and what I take to be characteristic of a semiotics of the text, namely, that a science of the text can be established only upon the abstraction of mimesis$_2$, and may consider only the internal laws of a work of literature, without any regard for the two sides of the text. It is the task of hermeneutics, in return, to reconstruct the set of operations by which a work lifts itself above the opaque depths of living, acting, and suffering, to be given by an author to readers who receive it and thereby change their acting. For a semiotic theory, the only operative concept is that of the literary text. Hermeneutics, however, is concerned with reconstructing the entire arc of operations by which practical experience provides itself with works, authors, and readers. It does not confine itself to setting mimesis$_2$ between mimesis$_1$ and mimesis$_3$. It wants to characterize mimesis$_2$ by its mediating function. What is at stake, therefore, is the concrete process by which the textual configuration mediates between the prefiguration of the practical field and its refiguration through the reception of the work. It will appear as a corollary, at the end of this analysis, that the reader is that operator par excellence who takes up through doing something—the act of reading—the unity of the traversal from mimesis$_1$ to mimesis$_3$ by way of mimesis$_2$.

This highlighting of the dynamic of emplotment is to me the key to the problem of the relation between time and narrative. By moving from the initial question of the *mediation* between time and narrative to the new question of connecting the three stages of mimesis, I am basing the whole strategy of my work on the subordination of the second problem to the first one. In constructing the relationship between the three mimetic modes I constitute the mediation between time and narrative. Or to put it another way, to resolve the problem of the relation between time and narrative I must establish the mediating role of emplotment between a stage of practical experience that precedes it and a stage that succeeds it. In this sense my argument in this book consists of constructing the mediation between time and narrative by demonstrating emplotment's mediating role in the mimetic process. Aristotle, we have seen, ignored the temporal aspects of emplotment. I propose to disentangle them from the act of textual configuration and to show the mediating role of the time of emplotment between the temporal aspects prefigured in the practical field and the refiguration of our temporal experience by this constructed time. *We are following therefore the destiny of a prefigured time that becomes a refigured time through the mediation of a configured time.*

On the horizon of this investigation looms the objection of a vicious circle between the act of narrating and temporal existence. Does this circle condemn my whole enterprise to being nothing more than one vast tautology? I seemed to avoid this objection by choosing two starting points as far apart from each other as possible—Augustine on time and Aristotle on emplotment. Still, in seeking a middle term for these two extremes and in assigning a mediating role to emplotment and the time of its structures, have I not given new strength to this objection? I do not intend to deny the circular character of my thesis that temporality is brought to language to the extent that language configures and refigures temporal experience. But I do hope to show, at the end of this chapter, that the circle can be something other than a dead tautology.

MIMESIS₁

Whatever the innovative force of poetic composition within the field of our temporal experience may be, the composition of the plot is grounded in a preunderstanding of the world of action, its meaningful structures, its symbolic resources, and its temporal character. These features are described rather than deduced. But in this sense nothing requires their listing to be a closed one. And in any case their enumeration follows an easily established progression. First, if it is true that plot is an imitation of action, some preliminary competence is required: the capacity for identifying action in general by means of its structural features. A semantics of action makes explicit this competence. Next, if imitating is elaborating an articulated significance of some action, a supplementary competence is required: an aptitude for identifying what I call the symbolic mediations of action, in a sense of the word "symbol" that Cassirer made classic and that cultural anthropology, from which I shall draw several examples, adopted. Finally, these symbolic articulations of action are bearers of more precisely temporal elements, from which proceed more directly the very capacity of action to be narrated and perhaps the need to narrate it. A loan from Heidegger's hermeneutic phenomenology will accompany my description of this third feature.

Let us consider these three features—structural, symbolic, and temporal—in succession.

The intelligibility engendered by emplotment finds a first anchorage in our competence to utilize in a significant manner the conceptual network that structurally distinguishes the domain of action from that of physical move-ment.[1] I say "conceptual network" rather than "concept of action" in order to emphasize the fact that the very term "action," taken in the narrow sense of what someone does, gets its distinct meaning from its capacity for being used in conjunction with other terms of the whole network. Actions imply goals, the anticipation of which is not confused with some foreseen or predicted re-sult, but which commit the one on whom the action depends. Actions, more-over, refer to motives, which explain why someone does or did something, in a way that we clearly distinguish from the way one physical event leads to another. Actions also have agents, who do and can do things which are taken as *their* work, or *their* deed. As a result, these agents can be held responsible for certain consequences of their actions. In this network, the infinite regres-sion opened by the question "Why?" is not incompatible with the finite re-gression opened by the question "Who?" To identify an agent and to recog-nize this agent's motives are complementary operations. We also understand that these agents act and suffer in circumstances they did not make that never-theless do belong to the practical field, precisely inasmuch as they circum-scribe the intervention of historical agents in the course of physical events and offer favorable or unfavorable occasions for their action. This intervention, in turn, implies that acting makes what an agent can do—in terms of "basic ac-tions"—and what, without observation, he knows he is capable of doing, co-incide with the initial state of a closed physical system.[2] Moreover, to act is always to act "with" others. Interaction can take the form of cooperation or competition or struggle. The contingencies of this interaction then rejoin those of our circumstances through their character of helping or hindering us. Finally, the outcome of an action may be a change in fortune toward happiness or misfortune.

In short, these terms or others akin to them occur in our answers to ques-tions that can be classified as questions about "what," "why," "who," "how," "with whom," or "against whom" in regard to any action. But the decisive fact is that to employ any one of these terms in a significant fashion, within a situation of questions and answers, is to be capable of linking that term to every other term of the same set. In this sense, all the members of the set are in a relation of intersignification. To master the conceptual network as a whole, and each term as one member of the set, is to have that competence we can call practical understanding.

What then is the relation of our narrative understanding to this practical understanding? The answer to this question governs the relationship that can be established between the theory of narrative and that of action, in the sense given this term by English-language analytic philosophy. This relationship, in my view, is a twofold one. It is a relation of presupposition and of transformation.

On the one hand, every narrative presupposes a familiarity with terms such as agent, goal, means, circumstance, help, hostility, cooperation, conflict, success, failure, etc., on the part of its narrator and any listener. In this sense, the minimal narrative sentence is an action sentence of the form "X did A in such and such circumstances, taking into account the fact that Y does B in identical or different circumstances." In the final analysis, narratives have acting and suffering as their theme. We saw and said this in discussing Aristotle. We shall see in volume 2 to what point the structural analysis of narrative in terms of functions and actants, from Propp to Greimas, verifies this relation of presupposition which establishes narrative discourse on the basis of the action sentence. In this sense, there is no structural analysis of narrative that does not borrow from an explicit or an implicit phenomenology of "doing something." [3]

On the other hand, narrative is not limited to making use of our familiarity with the conceptual network of action. It adds to it discursive features that distinguish it from a simple sequence of action sentences. These features no longer belong to the conceptual network of the semantics of action. They are syntactic features, whose function is to engender the composing of modes of discourse worthy of being called narratives, whether it be a question of historical narrative or fictional narrative. We can account for the relation between the conceptual network of action and these rules for narrative composition through recourse to the distinction familiar to semiotics between the paradigmatic order and the syntagmatic one. With regard to the paradigmatic order, all terms relative to action are synchronic, in the sense that the relations of intersignification that exist between ends, means, agents, circumstances, and the rest are perfectly reversible. The syntagmatic order of discourse, on the contrary, implies the irreducibly diachronic character of every narrated story. Even if this diachrony does not prevent reading the narrative backwards, which is characteristic, as we shall see, of the act of retelling, this reading backwards from the end to the beginning does not abolish the narrative's fundamental diachrony. In volume 2, I shall draw the consequences of this when I discuss the structuralist attempts to derive the logic of narrative from completely achronological models. For the time being, let us confine ourselves to saying that to understand a narrative is to master the rules that govern its syntagmatic order. Consequently, narrative understanding is not limited to presuppposing a familiarity with the conceptual network constitutive of the semantics of action. It further requires a familiarity with the rules of composition that govern the diachronic order of a story. Plot, understood broadly, as it was in the preceding chapter, that is, as the ordering of the events (and therefore as interconnecting the action sentences) into the total action constitutive of the narrated story, is the literary equivalent of the syntagmatic order that narrative introduces into the practical field.

We may sum up this twofold relation between narrative understanding and practical understanding as follows. In passing from the paradigmatic order of action to the syntagmatic order of narrative, the terms of the semantics of action acquire integration and actuality. Actuality, because the terms, which had only a virtual signification in the paradigmatic order, that is, a pure capacity to be used, receive an actual [*effective*] signification thanks to the sequential interconnections the plot confers on the agents, their deeds, and their sufferings. Integration, because terms as heterogeneous as agents, motives, and circumstances are rendered compatible and work together in actual temporal wholes. It is in this sense that the twofold relation between rules of emplotment and action-terms constitutes both a relation of presuppposition and one of transformation. To understand a story is to understand both the language of "doing something" and the cultural tradition from which proceeds the typology of plots.

The second anchorage that narrative composition finds in our practical understanding lies in the symbolic resources of the practical field. This second feature will govern those aspects of doing something, being able to do something, and knowing how to do something that stem from the poetic transposition.

If, in fact, human action can be narrated, it is because it is always already articulated by signs, rules, and norms. It is always already symbolically mediated. As stated earlier, I am drawing here on the work of anthropologists who in various ways make use of *Verstehen* sociology, including Clifford Geertz, the author of *The Interpretation of Cultures*.[4] The word "symbol" in this work is taken in what we might call a middle sense, halfway between its being identified with a simple notation (I have in mind Leibniz's opposition between intuitive knowledge based on direct insight and symbolic knowledge by way of abbreviated signs, substituted for a long chain of logical operations) and its being identified with double-meaning expressions following the model of metaphor, or even hidden meanings, accessible only to esoteric knowledge. Between too poor and too rich an acceptation I have opted for one close to that of Cassirer, in his *Philosophy of Symbolic Forms*, inasmuch as, for him, symbolic forms are cultural processes that articulate experience. If I speak more precisely of symbolic mediation, it is to distinguish, among symbols of a cultural nature, the ones that underlie action and that constitute its first signification, before autonomous symbolic wholes dependent upon speaking or writing become detached from the practical level. In this sense we might speak of an implicit or immanent symbolism, in opposition to an explicit or autonomous one.[5]

For anthropologists and sociologists, the term "symbol" immediately accentuates the public character of any meaningful articulation. In Geertz's words, "culture is public because meaning is" (p. 12). I readily adopt this initial characterization which clearly indicates that symbolism is not in the mind, not a psychological operation destined to guide action, but a meaning incorporated into action and decipherable from it by other actors in the social interplay

Next, the term "symbol"—or better, symbolic mediation—signals the structured character of a symbolic system. Geertz speaks in this sense of "systems of interacting symbols," of "patterns of interworking meanings" (p. 207). Before being a text, symbolic mediation has a texture. To understand a ritual act is to situate it within a ritual, set within a cultic system, and by degrees within the whole set of conventions, beliefs, and institutions that make up the symbolic framework of a culture.

A symbolic system thus furnishes a descriptive context for particular actions. In other words, it is "as a function of" such a symbolic convention that we can interpret this gesture as meaning this or that. The same gesture of raising one's arm, depending on the context, may be understood as a way of greeting someone, of hailing a taxi, or of voting. Before being submitted to interpretation, symbols are interpretants internally related to some action.[6]

In this way, symbolism confers an initial *readability* on action. In saying this we must not confuse the texture of action with the text the ethnologist writes, the ethno-*graphic* text which is written in categories, with concepts, using nomological principles that are the contribution of the discipline and that must not, consequently, be confused with those categories by which a culture understands itself. If we may nevertheless speak of action as a quasi-text, it is insofar as the symbols, understood as interpretants, provide the rules of meaning as a function of which this or that behavior can be interpreted.[7]

The term "symbol" further introduces the idea of a rule, not only in the sense we have just spoken of about rules for description and interpretation of individual actions, but in the sense of a norm. Some authors such as Peter Winch emphasize this feature in particular, by characterizing meaningful action as "rule-governed behavior."[8] We can clarify this function of social regulation by comparing cultural codes to genetic ones. Like the latter, the former are "programs" for behavior; they give form, order, and direction to life. Yet unlike genetic codes, cultural codes arise in zones not subject to genetic regulation and only prolong their efficacy at the price of a complete rearrangement of the encoding system. Manners and customs, along with everything Hegel put under the title "ethical substance," the *Sittlichkeit* prior to any *Moralität* of a reflective order, thus take over from the genetic codes.

So we pass without difficulty, with the term "symbolic mediation," from the idea of an immanent meaning to that of a rule, taken in the sense of a rule for description, then to that of a norm, which is equivalent to the idea of a rule taken in the prescriptive sense of this term.

As a function of the norms immanent in a culture, actions can be estimated or evaluated, that is, judged according to a scale of moral preferences. They thereby receive a relative value, which says that this action is more valuable than that one. These degrees of value, first attributed to actions, can be extended to the agents themselves, who are held to be good or bad, better or worse.

We thus rejoin, by way of cultural anthropology, some of the "ethical" presuppositions of Aristotle's *Poetics*, which I can therefore attach to the level of mimesis₁. The *Poetics* presupposes not just "doers" but characters endowed with ethical qualities that make them noble or vile. If tragedy can represent them as "better" and comedy as "worse" than actual human beings, it is because the practical understanding authors share with their audiences necessarily involves an evaluation of the characters and their actions in terms of good and bad. There is no action that does not give rise to approbation or reprobation, to however small a degree, as a function of a hierarchy of values for which goodness and wickedness are the poles. When the time comes, I shall discuss the question of whether a mode of reading that would entirely suspend all evaluation of an ethical character is possible. What, in particular, would remain of the pity Aristotle taught us to link to unmerited misfortune, if aesthetic pleasure were to be totally dissociated from any sympathy or antipathy for the characters' ethical quality? We shall see that this possible ethical neutrality has to be conquered by force in an encounter with one originary and inherent feature of action: precisely that it can never be ethically neutral. One reason for thinking that this neutrality is neither possible nor desirable is that the actual order of action does not just offer the artist conventions and convictions to dissolve, but also ambiguities and perplexities to resolve in a hypothetical mode. Many contemporary critics, reflecting on the relation between art and culture, have emphasized the conflicting character of the norms that culture offers for poets' mimetic activity.[9] They were preceded on this score by Hegel in his famous meditation on Sophocles' *Antigone*. But, at the same time, does not such ethical neutrality of the artist suppress one of the oldest functions of art, that it constitutes an ethical laboratory where the artist pursues through the mode of fiction experimentation with values? Whatever our response to these questions, poetics does not stop borrowing from ethics, even when it advocates the suspension of all ethical judgment or its ironic inversion. The very project of ethical neutrality presupposes the original ethical quality of action on the prior side of fiction. This ethical quality is itself only a corollary of the major characteristic of action, that it is always symbolically mediated.

The third feature of a preunderstanding of action which mimetic activity at level two presupposes is just what is at stake in our inquiry. It concerns the temporal elements onto which narrative time grafts its configurations. The understanding of action, in effect, is not limited to a familiarity with the conceptual network of action and with its symbolic mediations. It goes so far as to recognize in action temporal structures that call for narration. At this level, the equation between narrative and time remains implicit. In any case, I shall not push my analysis of the temporal elements of action to the point where we could rightfully speak of a narrative structure, or at least of a prenarrative structure of temporal experience, as suggested by our ordinary way of talking about stories that happen to us or which we are caught up in, or simply about the story of someone's life. I am leaving to the end of this chapter the notion of a prenarrative structure of experience. There it will provide a good opportunity for facing the objection about a vicious circle that haunts my whole analysis. I limit myself here to examining the temporal features that remain implicit in symbolic mediations of action and that we may take as the inductors of narrative.

I shall not linger over the all too evident correlation that can be established, almost term for term, between this or that member of the conceptual network of action and this or that temporal dimension considered in isolation. It is easy to see that the project has to do with the future, in a very specific way that distinguishes the future from prevision or prediction. The close kinship between motivation and the ability to mobilize in the present experience inherited from the past is no less evident. Finally, "I can," "I do," and "I suffer" manifestly contribute to the sense we spontaneously give to the present.

More important than this loose correlation between certain categories of action and temporal dimensions taken one by one, is the exchange that real action makes appear between the temporal dimensions. Augustine's discordant-concordant structure of time develops some paradoxical features on the plane of reflective thought for which a phenomenology of action can sketch a first draft. By saying that there is not a future time, a past time, and a present time, but a threefold present, a present of future things, a present of past things, and a present of present things, Augustine set us on the path of an investigation into the most primitive temporal structure of action. It is easy to rewrite each of the three temporal structures of action in terms of this threefold present. The present of the future? *Henceforth*, that is, from now on, I commit myself to doing that *tomorrow*. The present of the past? *Now* I intend to do that because I *just* realized that. . . . The present of the present? *Now* I am doing it, because *now* I can do it. The actual present of doing something bears witness to the potential present of the capacity to do something and is constituted as the present of the present.

However the phenomenology of action can advance even further than this term-by-term correlation along the way opened by Augustine's meditation on the *distentio animi*. What counts here is the way in which everyday praxis orders the present of the future, the present of the past, and the present of the present in terms of one another. For it is this practical articulation that constitutes the most elementary inductor of narrative.

Here the relay station of Heidegger's existential analysis can play a decisive role, but only under certain conditions that must be clearly laid out. I am well aware that a reading of *Being and Time* in a purely anthropological sense runs the risk of completely missing the meaning of the entire work inasmuch as its ontological aim may be misconceived. *Dasein* is the "place" where the being that we are is constituted through its capacity of posing the question of Being or the meaning of Being. To isolate the philosophical anthropology of *Being and Time*, therefore, is to overlook this major signification of the central existential category of that work. Yet in *Being and Time*, the question of Being is opened up precisely by an analysis that must first have some consistency as a philosophical anthropology, if it is to achieve the ontological breakthrough that is expected of it. What is more, this philosophical anthropology is organized on the basis of a thematic concept, Care (*Sorge*), that, without ever exhausting itself in a praxieology, draws from descriptions borrowed from the practical order the subversive force that allows it to overthrow the primacy of knowledge of objects and to uncover the structure of being-in-the-world that is more fundamental than any relation of a subject to an object. This is how, in *Being and Time*, the recourse to practice has an indirectly ontological import. In this regard, its analyses of tools and the toward-which, which furnish the first framework of meaningful relations, before any explicit cognitive process and any developed propositional expression, are well known.

I find the same powerful breakthrough in the analyses that conclude the study of temporality in the second division of *Being and Time*. These analyses are centered on our relation to time as that "within which" we ordinarily act. This structure of within-time-ness (*Innerzeitigkeit*) seems the best characterization of the temporality of action for my present analysis. It is also the one that accords best with a phenomenology of the voluntary and the involuntary, and with a semantics of action.

Someone may object that it is highly dangerous to enter *Being and Time* by way of its last chapter. What must be understood, however, is why it is the last one in the economy of this work. There are two reasons. First, the meditation on time, which occupies the second division of the book, is itself placed in a position that we may characterize as one of delay. The first division is recapitulated in it under the sign of a question that can be expressed as follows. What makes *Dasein* a unity? The meditation on time is supposed to respond to this problematic for reasons I shall return to in volume 2 of this work. In its turn, the study of within-time-ness, the only one that interests me at this stage of my own analysis, is itself slowed down by the hierarchical organization that Heidegger imposes on his meditation on time. This hierarchical organization follows a downward order of derivation and one of decreasing authenticity at the same time. As is well known, Heidegger reserves the term temporality (*Zeitlichkeit*) for the most originary form and the most authentic experience of time, that is, the dialectic of coming to be, having been, and making present. In this dialectic, time is entirely desubstantialized. The words "future," "past," and "present" disappear, and time itself figures as the exploded unity of the three temporal extases. This dialectic is the temporal constitution of Care. As is also well known, being-towards-death imposes, counter to Augustine, the primacy of the future over the present and the closure of this future by a limit internal to all anticipation and every project. Next

Heidegger reserves the term "historicality" (*Geschichtlichkeit*) for the immediately contiguous level of derivation. Here two features are emphasized: the
extension of time between birth and death, and the displacement of accent
from the future to the past. Heidegger tries to tie the historical disciplines to
this level by means of a third feature—repetition—which indicates the derived character of this historicality with regard to deep temporality.[10]

It is only at the third level, therefore, that the within-time-ness occurs that I
want to consider now.[11] This temporal structure is put in last place because it
is the one most likely to be flattened out by the linear representation of time as
a simple succession of abstract "nows." I am interested in it here precisely
because of the features by which this structure is distinguished from the linear
representation of time and by which it resists that flattening or leveling which
Heidegger calls the "vulgar" conception of time.

Within-time-ness is defined by a basic characteristic of Care, our being
thrown among things, which tends to make our description of temporality dependent on the description of the things about which we care. This feature
reduces Care to the dimensions of preoccupation (*Besorgen*) (p. 157). Yet
however inauthentic this relation may be, it still presents some features that
wrest it from the external domain of the objects of our Care and subter-
raneously reattach it to Care itself in its fundamental constitution. It is noteworthy that, to discern these properly existential characteristics, Heidegger
willingly addresses himself to what we say and do with regard to time. This
procedure is close to the one we meet in ordinary-language philosophy. This is
not surprising. The plane we occupy, at this initial stage of our traversal, is
precisely the one where ordinary language is truly what Austin and others
have said it is, namely, the storehouse of those expressions that are most appropriate to what is properly human in our experience. It is language, therefore, with its store of meanings, that prevents the description of Care, in the
mode of preoccupation, from becoming prey to the description of the things
we care about.

In this way, within-time-ness or being-"within"-time deploys features irreducible to the representation of linear time. Being-"within"-time is already
something other than measuring the intervals between limit-instants.
Being-"within"-time is above all to reckon with time and, as a consequence
of this, to calculate. It is because we do reckon with time and do make calculations that we must have recourse to measuring, not vice versa. It must be
possible, therefore, to give an existential description of this "reckoning with"
before the measuring it calls for. Here expressions such as "have the time to,"
"take the time to," "to lose time," etc. are very revealing. A similar thing can
be said about the grammatical network of the verbal tenses and the highly
ramified network of temporal adverbs: then, after, later, earlier, since, until,
so long as, during, all the while that, now that, etc. All these expressions,

with their extreme subtlety and fine differentiations, are oriented toward the datable and the public character of the time of preoccupation. Yet it is always preoccupation that determines the meaning of this time, not the things we care about. If being-"within"-time is nevertheless so easily interpreted as a function of the ordinary representation of time, it is because the first measurements of this time of our preoccupation are borrowed from the natural environment and first of all from the play of light and of the seasons. In this respect, a day is the most natural of measures.[12] Yet a day is not an abstract measure; it is a length that corresponds to our Care and the world in which it is "time to" do something, where "now" signifies "now that. . . ." It is the time of works and days.

It is important, therefore, to see the difference in signifcation that distinguishes the "now" proper to this time of preoccupation from "now" in the sense of an abstract instant. The existential now is determined by the present of preoccupation, which is a "making-present," inseparable from "awaiting" and "retaining" (p. 473). It is only because, in preoccupation, Care tends to get contracted into this making-present and its difference with respect to awaiting and retaining is obliterated, that the "now" so isolated can become prey to the representation of "now" as an abstract moment.

In order to preserve the meaning of "now" from this reduction to an abstraction, it is important to note those occasions in which we say "now" in our everyday acting and suffering. "Saying 'now,'" says Heidegger, "is the discursive articulation of a *making present* which temporalizes itself in a unity with a retentive awaiting" (p. 469). And again: "The making-present which interprets itself—in other words, that which has been interpreted and is addressed in the 'now'—is what we call 'time'" (p. 460). It is understandable how, in certain practical circumstances, this interpretation can go adrift in the direction of the representation of linear time. Saying "now" becomes synonymous for us with reading the hour on the clock. But to the extent that the hour and the clock are perceived as derivations from the day, which itself links Care to the world's light, saying-now retains its existential meaning, but when the machines that serve to measure time are divested of this primary reference to natural measures, that saying-now returns to the abstract representation of time.

At first glance, the relation between this analysis of within-time-ness and narrative seems quite distant. Heidegger's text, as we shall see in volume 2, even seems to leave no place for it, inasmuch as the tie between history and time occurs, in *Being and Time*, at the level of historicality, not at that of within-time-ness. The advantage of his analysis of within-time-ness lies elsewhere. It lies in the break this analysis makes with the linear representation of time, understood as a simple succession of nows. An initial threshold is thereby crossed with the primacy given to Care. With the recognition of this threshold, a bridge is constructed for the first time between the narrative order and Care. Narrative configurations and the most elaborated forms of temporality corresponding to them share the same foundation of within-time-ness.

We can see the richness in the meaning of mimesis$_1$. To imitate or represent action is first to preunderstand what human acting is, in its semantics, its symbolic system, its temporality. Upon this preunderstanding, common to both poets and their readers, emplotment is constructed and, with it, textual and literary mimetics.

It is true that, within the domain of the literary work, this preunderstanding of the world withdraws to the rank of the "repertoire," to use the language of Wolfgang Iser, in his *The Act of Reading*,[13] or to the rank of "mention," to use a vocabulary more familiar to analytic philosophy. Yet despite the break it institutes, literature would be incomprehensible if it did not give a configuration to what was already a figure in human action.

MIMESIS$_2$

With mimesis$_2$ opens the kingdom of the *as if*. I might have said the kingdom of fiction, in accordance with current usage in literary criticism. I will not, however, allow myself the advantages of this expression so appropriate to the analysis of mimesis$_2$, in order to avoid the equivocation created by the use of this term in two different senses: first as a synonym for narrative configurations, second as an antonym to historical narrative's claim to constitute a "true" narrative. Literary criticism can ignore this difficulty inasmuch as it does not take into account the division of narrative discourse into two large classes. It can thus also ignore the difference that affects the referential dimension of narrative and limit itself to the common structural characteristics of fictional and historical narrative. The word "fiction" is then available for designating the configuration of a narrative for which emplotment is the paradigm, without regard for the differences that concern the truth claims of the two classes of narrative. Whatever the scope of the revisions that the distinction between the fictive or "imaginary" and the "real" must undergo, a difference will remain between fictional and historical narrative that will have to be reformulated in volume 2. While awaiting that clarification, I choose to preserve the term "fiction" for the second of the senses just considered and to oppose fictional to historical narrative. I shall speak of composition or of configuration for the other sense, which does not bring into play the problems of reference or of truth. This is the meaning of the Aristotelian muthos that the *Poetics*, as we saw, defines as the "organization of the events."

I now propose to disengage this configuring activity from the limiting constraints the paradigm of tragedy imposes upon the concept of emplotment for Aristotle. Further I want to complete my model by an analysis of its temporal structures. This analysis, we have seen, had no place in the *Poetics*. I hope to demonstrate here and in volume 2 that, under the condition of a larger degree of abstraction and with the addition of appropriate temporal features, the Aristotelian model will not be radically altered by the amplifications and corrections that the theory of history and the theory of literary narrative will bring to it.

The model of emplotment that will be tested in the remainder of this work responds to one fundamental requirement that was already referred to in the preceding chapter. By placing mimesis$_2$ between an earlier and a later stage of mimesis in general, I am seeking not just to locate and frame it. I want to understand better its mediating function between what precedes fiction and what follows it. Mimesis$_2$ has an intermediary position because it has a mediating function. This mediating function derives from the dynamic character of the configurating operation that has led us to prefer the term emplotment to that of plot and ordering to that of system. In fact all the concepts relative to this level designate operations. The dynamism lies in the fact that a plot already exercises, within its own textual field, an integrating and, in this sense, a mediating function, which allows it to bring about, beyond this field, a mediation of a larger amplitude between the preunderstanding and, if I may dare to put it this way, the postunderstanding of the order of action and its temporal features.

Plot is mediating in at least three ways.

First, it is a mediation between the individual events or incidents and a story taken as a whole. In this respect, we may say equivalently that it draws a meaningful story from a diversity of events or incidents (Aristotle's *pragmata*) or that it transforms the events or incidents into a story. The two reciprocal relations expressed by *from* and *into* characterize the plot as mediating between events and a narrated story. As a consequence, an event must be more than just a singular occurrence. It gets its definition from its contribution to the development of the plot. A story, too, must be more than just an enumeration of events in serial order; it must organize them into an intelligible whole, of a sort such that we can always ask what is the "thought" of this story. In short, emplotment is the operation that draws a configuration out of a simple succession.

Furthermore, emplotment brings together factors as heterogeneous as agents, goals, means, interactions, circumstances, unexpected results. Aristotle anticipates this mediating character in several ways. First, he makes a subset of the three "parts" of tragedy—plot, characters, and thought—with the title the "what" (of the imitation). Nothing therefore forbids extending the concept of plot to the whole triad. This first extension gives the concept of plot the initial scope that allows it to receive subsequent embellishments.

The concept of plot allows an even greater extension. By including pitiable and fearful incidents, sudden reversals, recognitions, and violent effects within the complex plot, Aristotle equates plot with the configuring we have characterized as concordant discordance. This is the feature that, in the final analysis, constitutes the mediating function of the plot. I anticipated this feature in my previous section in saying that a narrative makes appear within a syntagmatic order all the components capable of figuring in the paradigmatic tableau established by the semantics of action. This passage from the paradigmatic to the syntagmatic constitutes the transition from mimesis$_1$ to mimesis$_2$. It is the work of the configurating activity.

Plot is mediating in a third way, that of its temporal characteristics. These allow us to call plot, by means of generalization, a synthesis of the heterogeneous.[14]

Aristotle did not consider these temporal characteristics. They are directly implied, however, in the constitutive dynamism of the narrative configuration. As such, they give the full meaning of the concept of concordant discordance from the preceding chapter. In this respect, we may say of the operation of emplotment both that it reflects the Augustinian paradox of time and that it resolves it, not in a speculative but rather in a poetic mode.

It reflects the paradox inasmuch as the act of emplotment combines in variable proportions two temporal dimensions, one chronological and the other not. The former constitutes the episodic dimension of narrative. It characterizes the story insofar as it is made up of events. The second is the configurational dimension properly speaking, thanks to which the plot transforms the events into a story. This configurational act consists of "grasping together" the detailed actions or what I have called the story's incidents.[15] It draws from this manifold of events the unity of one temporal whole. I cannot overemphasize the kinship between this "grasping together," proper to the configurational act, and what Kant has to say about the operation of judging. It will be recalled that for Kant the transcendental meaning of judging consists not so much in joining a subject and a predicate as in placing an intuitive manifold under the rule of a concept. The kinship is greater still with the reflective judgment which Kant opposes to the determining one, in the sense that it reflects upon the work of thinking at work in the aesthetic judgment of taste and in the teleological judgment applied to organic wholes. The act of emplotment has a similar function inasmuch as it extracts a configuration from a succession.[16]

Yet *poiēsis* does more than reflect the paradox of temporality. By mediating between the two poles of event and story, emplotment brings to the paradox a solution that is the poetic act itself. This act, which I just said extracts a figure from a succession, reveals itself to the listener or the reader in the story's capacity to be followed.[17]

To follow a story is to move forward in the midst of contingencies and peripeteia under the guidance of an expectation that finds its fulfilment in the "conclusion" of the story. This conclusion is not logically implied by some previous premises. It gives the story an "end point," which, in turn, furnishes the point of view from which the story can be perceived as forming a whole. To understand the story is to understand how and why the successive episodes led to this conclusion, which, far from being foreseeable, must finally be acceptable, as congruent with the episodes brought together by the story.

It is this "followability" of a story that constitutes the poetic solution to the paradox of distention and intention. The fact that the story can be followed converts the paradox into a living dialectic.

On the one hand, the episodic dimension of a narrative draws narrative time in the direction of the linear representation of time. It does so in several ways. First, the "then, and then," by which we answer the question "and then what?" suggests that the phases of action are in an external relation. Next, the episodes constitute an open series of events, which allows us to add to the "then, and then" a "and so forth." Finally, the episodes follow upon one another in accord with the irreversible order of time common to physical and human events.

The configurational dimension, in its turn, presents temporal features directly opposed to those of the episodic dimension. Again it does so in several ways.

First, the configurational arrangement transforms the succession of events into one meaningful whole which is the correlate of the act of assembling the events together and which makes the story followable. Thanks to this reflective act, the entire plot can be translated into one "thought," which is nothing other than its "point" or "theme." However, we would be completely mistaken if we took such a point as atemporal. The time of the "fable and theme," to use Northrop Frye's expression, is the narrative time that mediates between the episodic aspect and the configurational aspect.

Second, the configuration of the plot imposes the "sense of an ending" (to use the title of Frank Kermode's well-known book) on the indefinite succession of incidents. I just spoke of the "end point" as the point from where the story can be seen as a whole. I may now add that it is in the act of retelling rather than in that of telling that this structural function of closure can be discerned. As soon as a story is well known—and this is the case for most traditional or popular narratives, as well as for those national chronicles reporting the founding events of a given community—to follow the story is not so much to enclose its surprises or discoveries within our recognition of the meaning attached to the story, as to apprehend the episodes which are themselves well known as leading to this end. A new quality of time emerges from this understanding.

Finally, the repetition of a story, governed as a whole by its way of ending, constitutes an alternative to the representation of time as flowing from the past toward the future, following the well-known metaphor of the "arrow of time." It is as though recollection inverted the so-called "natural" order of time. In reading the ending in the beginning and the beginning in the ending, we also learn to read time itself backwards, as the recapitulation of the initial conditions of a course of action in its terminal consequences.

In short, the act of narrating, reflected in the act of following a story, makes productive the paradoxes that disquieted Augustine to the point of reducing him to silence.

Two complementary features that assure the continuity of the process that joins mimesis$_3$ to mimesis$_2$ remain to be added to our analysis of the configurational act. More visibly than the preceding ones, these two features require the support of reading if they are to be reactivated. It is a question of the schematization and the character of traditionality characteristic of the configurational act, each of which has a specific relation to time.

It will be recalled that I compared the "grasping together" characteristic of the configurational act to judgment as understood by Kant. Remaining in a Kantian vein, we ought not to hesitate in comparing the production of the configurational act to the work of the productive imagination. This latter must be understood not as a psychologizing faculty but as a transcendental one. The productive imagination is not only rule-governed, it constitutes the generative matrix of rules. In Kant's first *Critique*, the categories of the understanding are first schematized by the productive imagination. The schematism has this power because the productive imagination fundamentally has a synthetic function. It connects understanding and intuition by engendering syntheses that are intellectual and intuitive at the same time. Emplotment, too, engenders a mixed intelligibility between what has been called the point, theme, or thought of a story, and the intuitive presentation of circumstances, characters, episodes, and changes of fortune that make up the denouement. In this way, we may speak of a schematism of the narrative function. Like every schematism, this one lends itself to a typology of the sort that Northrop Frye, for example, elaborates in his *Anatomy of Criticism*.[18]

This schematism, in turn, is constituted within a history that has all the characteristics of a tradition. Let us understand by this term not the inert transmission of some already dead deposit of material but the living transmission of an innovation always capable of being reactivated by a return to the most creative moments of poetic activity. So understood, traditionality enriches the relationship between plot and time with a new feature.

In fact, a tradition is constituted by the interplay of innovation and sedimentation. To sedimentation must be referred the paradigms that constitute the typology of emplotment. These paradigms have issued from a sedimented history whose genesis has been covered over.

The sedimentation is produced on multiple levels, and this requires of us a broad discernment in our use of the term paradigmatic. Thus Aristotle seems to us today to have done two, if not three, things at once. On the one hand, he establishes the concept of plot in terms of its most formal features, those which I have identified as the discordant concordance. On the other hand, he describes the genre of Greek tragedy (and accessorily that of epic, but as measured by the criteria of the tragic model). This genre satisfies both the formal conditions which make it a muthos and the restrictive ones which make it a tragic muthos: the reversal of meaning from good to bad fortune, pitiable and frightening incidents, unmerited misfortune, the tragic fault of a character also marked by excellence and free of vice or wickedness. To a large extent, this genre dominated the subsequent development of dramatic literature in the West. It is no less true that our culture is the heir to several narrative traditions: Hebrew and Christian, but also Celtic, Germanic, Icelandic, and Slavic.[19]

This is not all. What makes a paradigm is not just the form of discordant concordance or the model that subsequent tradition identified as a stable literary genre; there are also the individual works—the *Iliad* and *Oedipus Rex* in Aristotle's *Poetics*. To the extent that in the ordering of events the causal connection (one thing as a cause of another) prevails over pure succession (one thing after another), a universal emerges that is, as we have interpreted it, the ordering itself erected as a type. This is why the narrative tradition has been marked not just by the sedimentation of the form of discordant concordance and by that of the tragic genre (and the other models of the same level), but also by the types engendered at the level of individual works. If we encompass form, genre, and type under the heading "paradigm," we shall say that the paradigms are born from the labor of the productive imagination on these various levels.

These paradigms, themselves issuing from a previous innovation, furnish the rules for a subsequent experimentation within the narrative field. These rules change under the pressure of new inventions, but they change slowly and even resist change, in virtue of the very process of sedimentation.

As for the other pole of tradition, innovation, its status is correlative to that of sedimentation. There is always a place for innovation inasmuch as what is produced, in the *poiēsis* of the poem, is always, in the last analysis, a singular work, this work. This is why the paradigms only constitute the grammar that governs the composition of new works—new before becoming typical. In the same way as the grammar of a language governs the production of well-formed sentences, whose number and content are unforeseeable, a work of art—a poem, play, novel—is an original production, a new existence in the linguistic [*langagier*] kingdom.[20] Yet the reverse is no less true. Innovation remains a form of behavior governed by rules. The labor of imagination is not born from nothing. It is bound in one way or another to the tradition's paradigms. But the range of solutions is vast. It is deployed between the two poles of servile application and calculated deviation, passing through every degree of "rule-governed deformation." The folktale, the myth, and in general the traditional narrative stand closest to the first pole. But to the extent we distance ourselves from traditional narrative, deviation becomes the rule. Thus the contemporary novel, in large part, may be defined as an antinovel, to the extent that contestation wins out over the taste for simply varying the application of the paradigms.

What is more, this deviation may come into play on every level, in relation to the types, the genres, even to the formal principle of concordant discordance. The first type of deviation, it would seem, is constitutive of every individual work. Each work stands apart from every other work. Less frequent is a change of genre. Such a change is equivalent to the creation of a new genre, the novel, for example, in relation to drama or the romance, or history in relation to chronicle. Still more radical is the contesting of the formal principle of discordant concordance. I shall inquire later about the room for variation allowed by this formal paradigm. I shall ask whether this contestation, made into a schism, does not signify the death of the narrative form itself. It remains, however, that the possibility of deviation is inscribed in the relation between sedimented paradigms and actual works. Short of the extreme case of schism, it is just the opposite of servile application. Rule-governed deformation constitutes the axis around which the various changes of paradigm through application are arranged. It is this variety of applications that confers a history on the productive imagination and that, in counterpoint to sedimentation, makes a narrative tradition possible. This is the final enrichment by which the relationship of narrative to time is augmented at the level of mimesis$_2$.

MIMESIS$_3$

I want now to show how mimesis$_2$, brought back to its first level of intelligibility, requires a third representative stage as its complement, which also merits being called mimesis.

Allow me to recall once again that the interest brought to bear here on the unfolding of mimesis does not contain its end within itself. My explication of mimesis remains subordinated to my investigation of the mediation between time and narrative. It is only at the end of our traversal of mimesis that the thesis stated at the beginning of this chapter will receive a concrete content: narrative has its full meaning when it is restored to the time of action and of suffering in mimesis$_3$.

This stage corresponds to what H.-G. Gadamer, in his philosophical hermeneutics, calls "application." Aristotle himself suggests this last sense of mimesis-praxeos in various passages of his *Poetics*, although he is less concerned about the audience there than he is in his *Rhetoric*, where the theory of persuasion is entirely governed by the hearer's capacity for receiving the message. Still, when he says that poetry "teaches" the universal, that tragedy "in representing pity and fear . . . effects the purgation of these emotions," or even when he refers to the pleasure we get in seeing the frightening and piti-able events concur with the reversal of fortune that makes a tragedy, he does signify that it is in the hearer or the reader that the traversal of mimesis reaches its fulfilment.

Generalizing beyond Aristotle, I shall say that mimesis₃ marks the intersec-tion of the world of the text and the world of the hearer or reader; the intersec-tion, therefore, of the world configured by the poem and the world wherein real action occurs and unfolds its specific temporality.

I shall proceed in four steps.

1. If it is true that it is by linking together the three stages of mimesis that we institute the mediation between time and narrative, one preliminary ques-tion arises as to whether this linking together really marks a progression. I shall respond here to the objection of *circularity* raised at the beginning of this chapter.

2. If it is true that the act of reading is our connection to the capacity of a plot to model our experience, it has to be shown how this act is articulated by the dynamism belonging to the configuring act, prolonging it and bringing it to its end.

3. Next, approaching head-on the thesis of the refiguration of temporal ex-perience by emplotment, I shall show how the entry of the work, through reading, into the field of communication marks at the same time its entry into the field of reference. Taking up the problem where I left it in *The Rule of Metaphor*, I want to outline the particular difficulties attached to the notion of reference in the narrative order.

4. Insofar, finally, as the world that narrative refigures is a temporal world, the question arises of how much aid a hermeneutics of narrated time can ex-pect from the phenomenology of Time. The answer to this question will make appear a much more radical circularity than the one that engenders the rela-tion from mimesis₃ to mimesis₁ across mimesis₂. The study of the Augustinian theory of time with which I began this work has already provided an occasion for anticipating this. It concerns the relation between a phenomenology that does not stop engendering aporias and what I earlier called the *poetic* "solu-tion" to these aporias. The question of the relationship between time and nar-rative culminates in this dialectic between an aporetics and a poetics.

The Circle of Mimesis

Before taking on the central problematic of mimesis₃, I want to face the suspi-cion of a vicious circle which the traversal from mimesis₁ to mimesis₃ across mimesis₂ must give rise to. Whether we consider the semantic structure of action, its resources for symbolization, or its temporal character, the end point seems to lead back to the starting point or, worse, the end point seems anticipated in the starting point. If such were the case, the hermeneutical circle of mimesis and temporality would resolve into the vicious circle of mimesis alone.

That the analysis is circular is indisputable. But that the circle is a vicious one can be refuted. In this regard, I would rather speak of an endless spiral that would carry the meditation past the same point a number of times, but at different altitudes. The accusation about a vicious circle proceeds from the seduction of one or the other of two versions of circularity. The first emphasizes the violence of interpretation, the second its redundance.

1. In the first case we may be tempted to say that narrative puts consonance where there was only dissonance. In this way, narrative gives form to what is unformed. But then this formation by narrative may be suspected of treachery. At best, it furnishes the "as if" proper to any fiction we know to be just fiction, a literary artifice. This is how it consoles us in the face of death. But as soon as we no longer fool ourselves by having recourse to the consolation offered by the paradigms, we become aware of the violence and the lie. We are then at the point of succumbing to the fascination of the absolutely unformed and to the plea for that radical intellectual honesty Nietzsche called *Redlichkeit*. It is only through a kind of nostalgia for order that we resist this fascination and that we adhere desperately to the idea that order is our homeland *despite everything*. From then on, the narrative consonance imposed on temporal dissonance remains the work of what it is convenient to call a violence of interpretation. The narrative solution to the paradox is just the outgrowth of this violence.

I in no way mean to deny that such a dramatization of the dialectic between narrativity and temporality reveals in a wholly appropriate fashion the characteristic of discordant concordance that is attached to the relationship between narrative and time. But so long as we place the consonance on the side of the narrative and the dissonance on the side of temporality in a unilateral fashion, as the argument suggests, we miss the properly dialectical character of their relationship.

In the first place, our experience of temporality cannot be reduced to simple discordance. As we saw with Augustine, *distentio* and *intentio* mutually confront each other at the heart of our most authentic experience. We must preserve the paradox of time from the leveling out brought about by reducing it to simple discordance. We ought to ask instead whether the plea for a radically unformed temporal experience is not itself the product of a fascination for the unformed that is one of the features of modernity. In short, when thinkers or literary critics seem to yield to a nostalgia for order or, worse, to the horror of chaos, what really moves them, in the final analysis, may be a genuine recognition of the paradoxes of time beyond the loss of meaning characteristic of one particular culture—our own.

In the second place, the consonance characteristic of narrative which we are tempted to oppose in a nondialectical fashion to the dissonance of our temporal experience, must itself also be tempered. Emplotment is never the simple triumph of "order." Even the paradigm of Greek tragedy makes a place for the upsetting role of the *peripeteia*, those contingencies and reversals of fortune that solicit horror and pity. The plots themselves coordinate distention and intention. The same must be said for the other paradigm that, according to Frank Kermode, has governed the "sense of an ending" in our Western tradition. I am thinking of the apocalyptic model that so magnificently underscores the correspondence between beginning—Genesis—and end—the Apocalypse. Kermode himself does not fail to emphasize the innumerable tensions engendered by this model for everything touching those events that come "between times" and above all in the "end times." Reversal is magnified by the apocalyptic model to the extent that the end is the catastrophe that abolishes time and prefigures "the terrors of the last days." Yet the apocalyptic model, in spite of its persistence as attested to by its modern resurgence in the form of utopias or, better, uchronias, is only one paradigm among others, which in no way exhausts the dynamics of narrative.

Other paradigms than those of Greek tragedy or the Apocalypse continue to be engendered by the same process of the formation of traditions that we earlier attached to the power of schematization proper to the productive imagination. In volume 2 I shall show that this rebirth of paradigms does not abolish the fundamental dialectic of discordant concordance. Even the rejection of any paradigm, illustrated today by the antinovel, stems from the paradoxical history of "concordance." By means of the frustrations engendered by their ironic mistrust of any paradigm, and thanks to the more or less perverse pleasure the reader takes in being excited and gulled by them, these works satisfy both the tradition they leave behind and the disorganized experiences they finally end up imitating by dint of not imitating the received paradigms.

The suspicion of interpretative violence is no less legitimate in this extreme case. It is no longer "concordance" that is imposed by force on the "discordance" of our experience of time. Now it is the "discordance" engendered in discourse by the ironic distance in regard to any paradigm that undermines from within the view of "concordance" sustaining our temporal experience and that overthrows the *intentio* without which there would be no *distentio animi*. We can then legitimately suspect the alleged discordance of our temporal experience as being only a literary artifice.

Reflection on the limits of concordance never loses its legitimacy. It applies to every instance of a "figure" of discordant concordance and to concordant discordance at the level of narrative as well as at the level of time. But in every instance the circle is inevitable without being vicious.

2. The objection about a vicious circle can take on another form. Having confronted the violence of interpretation, we have also to face the opposite possibility—a redundancy of interpretation. This would be the case if mime-

sis$_1$ were itself a meaning effect of mimesis$_3$. Mimesis$_2$ would then only restore to mimesis$_3$ what it had taken from mimesis$_1$ since mimesis$_1$ would already be a work of mimesis$_3$.

The objection of redundancy seems to be suggested by the analysis of mimesis$_1$. If there is no human experience that is not already mediated by symbolic systems and, among them, by narratives, it seems vain to say, as I have, that action is in quest of narrative. How, indeed, can we speak of a human life as a story in its nascent state, since we do not have access to the temporal dramas of existence outside of stories told about them by others or by ourselves?

I shall oppose to this objection a series of situations that in my opinion, constrain us to accord already to experience as such an inchoate narrativity that does not proceed from projecting, as some say, literature on life but that constitutes a genuine demand for narrative. To characterize these situations I shall not hesitate to speak of a prenarrative quality of experience.

My analysis of the temporal features of action on the level of mimesis$_1$ led to the threshold of this concept. If I did not cross it at that moment, it was with the thought that the objection of a vicious circle through redundancy would offer a more propitious occasion to indicate the strategic importance of the situations I am about to speak of in the circle of mimesis.

Without leaving everyday experience, are we not inclined to see in a given sequence of the episodes of our lives "(as yet) untold" stories, stories that demand to be told, stories that offer anchorage points for narrative? I am not unaware how incongruous the expression "(as yet) untold story" is. Are not stories told by definition? There is no argument if we are speaking of actual stories. Yet is the notion of a potential story unacceptable?

I would like to point to two less common situations in which the expression "(as yet) untold story" imposes itself upon us with a surprising force. The patient who talks to a psychoanalyst presents bits and pieces of lived stories, of dreams, of "primitive scenes," conflictual episodes. We may rightfully say of such analytic sessions that their goal and effect is for the analysand to draw from these bits and pieces a narrative that will be both more supportable and more intelligible. Roy Schafer has even taught us to consider Freud's metapsychological theories as a system of rules for retelling our life stories and raising them to the rank of case histories.[21] This narrative interpretation implies that a life story proceeds from untold and repressed stories in the direction of actual stories the subject can take up and hold as constitutive of his personal identity. It is the quest for this personal identity that assures the continuity between the potential or inchoate story and the actual story we assume responsibility for.

There is also another situation which the notion of an untold story seems to fit. Wilhelm Schapp describes the case where a judge undertakes to understand a course of actions, a character, by unraveling the tangle of plots the subject is caught up in.[22] The accent here is on "being entangled" (*verstrickt-sein*) (p. 85), a verb whose passive voice emphasizes that the story "happens to" someone before anyone tells it. The entanglement seems more like the "prehistory" of the told story, whose beginning has to be chosen by the narrator. This "prehistory" of the story is what binds it to a larger whole and gives it a "background." This background is made up of the "living imbrication" of every lived story with every other such story. Told stories therefore have to "emerge" (*auftauchen*) from this background. With this emergence also emerges the implied subject. We may thus say, "the story stands for the person" (*die Geschichte steht für den Mann*) (p. 100). The principal consequence of this existential analysis of human beings as "entangled in stories" is that narrating is a secondary process, that of "the story's becoming known" (*das Bekanntwerden der Geschichte*) (p. 101). Telling, following, understanding stories is simply the "continuation" of these untold stories.

Literary criticism shaped by the Aristotelian tradition, for which a story is an artifice created by a writer, will hardly be satisfied with this notion of a told story that would be in "continuity" with the passive entanglement of subjects in stories that disappear into a foggy horizon. Nevertheless, the priority given the as yet untold story can serve as a critical example for every emphasis on the artificial character of the art of narrating. We tell stories because in the last analysis human lives need and merit being narrated. This remark takes on its full force when we refer to the necessity to save the history of the defeated and the lost. The whole history of suffering cries out for vengeance and calls for narrative.

Literary criticism will experience less repugnance in accepting the notion of story as that within which we are entangled, if it pays attention to one recent suggestion stemming from its own domain. In *The Genesis of Secrecy*, Frank Kermode introduces the idea that certain narratives may aim not at illumination but at obscurity and dissimulation.[23] This may be the case, among others, with Jesus' parables which, according to the interpretation of the evangelist Mark, were told with the view of not being understood by "those outside" and which, according to Kermode, also rather severely expel those "inside" from their privileged position. But there are many other narratives that have this enigmatic power of "banishing interpreters from their secret places" (see pp. 33–34). Of course, these secret places are places in the text. They are the internal mark of its inexhaustibility. Yet can we not say that the "hermeneutic potential" (p. 40) of this kind of narrative finds, if not a consonance, at least a resonance in the untold stories of our lives? Is there not a hidden complicity between the "secrecy" engendered by the narrative itself— or at least by narratives like those of Mark or Kafka—and the as yet untold stories of our lives that constitute the prehistory, the background, the living imbrication from which the told story emerges? In other words, is there not a hidden affinity between the secret of *where* the story emerges from and the secret *to which* it returns?

Whatever the constraining force of this last suggestion, we can find reinforcement in it for my principal argument, which says that the manifest circularity of every analysis of narrative, an analysis that does not stop interpreting in terms of each other the temporal form inherent in experience and the narrative structure, is not a lifeless tautology. We should see in it instead a "healthy circle" in which the arguments advanced about each side of the problem aid one another.

Configuration, Refiguration, and Reading

Thus the hermeneutic circle of narrative and time never stops being reborn from the circle that the stages of mimesis form. The moment has come to concentrate our reflection on the transition between mimesis$_2$ and mimesis$_3$ brought about by the act of reading.

If this act may be taken, as stated earlier, as our connection to the plot's capacity to model experience, it is because it takes up again and fulfills the configurational act, for which I emphasized the kinship with judgment that com-prehends, that "grasps together" the details of action into the unity of the plot.

Nothing bears witness to this better than the two features by means of which I characterized plot at the stage of mimesis$_2$, namely, schematization and traditionality. These features contribute particularly to breaking down the prejudice that opposes an "inside" and an "outside" of a text. Indeed, this opposition is closely knit to a static and closed conception of the structure of any text. The notion of a structuring activity, visible in the operation of emplotment, transcends this opposition. Schematization and traditionality are thus from the start categories of the interaction between the operations [*operativité*] of writing and of reading.

On the one hand, the received paradigms structure readers' expectations and aid them in recognizing the formal rule, the genre, or the type exemplified by the narrated story. They furnish guidelines for the encounter between a text and its readers. In short, they govern the story's capacity to be followed. On the other hand, it is the act of reading that accompanies the narrative's configuration and actualizes its capacity to be followed. To follow a story is to actualize it by reading it.

And if emplotment can be described as an act of judgment and of the productive imagination, it is so insofar as this act is the joint work of the text and reader, just as Aristotle said that sensation is the common work of sensing and what is sensed.

Furthermore, it is the act of reading that accompanies the interplay of the innovation and sedimentation of paradigms that schematizes emplotment. In the act of reading, the receiver plays with the narrative constraints, brings about gaps, takes part in the combat between the novel and the antinovel, and enjoys the pleasure that Roland Barthes calls the pleasure of the text.

Finally, it is the reader who completes the work inasmuch as (if we follow Roman Ingarden in *The Literary Work of Art*, and Wolfgang Iser in *The Act of Reading*) the written work is a sketch for reading.[24] Indeed, it consists of holes, lacunae, zones of indetermination, which, as in Joyce's *Ulysses*, challenge the reader's capacity to configure what the author seems to take malign delight in defiguring. In such an extreme case, it is the reader, almost abandoned by the work, who carries the burden of emplotment.

The act of reading is thus the operator that joins mimesis$_3$ to mimesis$_2$. It is the final indicator of the refiguring of the world of action under the sign of the plot. One of the critical problems that will occupy me in volume 2 will be to start from this point and to coordinate the relationships of a theory of reading, such as Wolfgang Iser's, and a theory of reception, such as that of Robert Jauss. For the moment, let us say that what they both have in common is seeing in the effect the text produces on its receiver, whether individual or collective, an intrinsic component of the present or actual meaning of the text. For both, the text is a set of instructions that the individual reader or the reading public executes in a passive or a creative way. Their different approaches in *The Act of Reading* and *Toward an Aesthetic of Reception* start from this common base.

Narrativity and Reference

To complete a theory of writing with a theory of reading constitutes only the first step along the way of mimesis$_3$. An aesthetic of reception cannot take up the problem of communication without also taking up that of reference. What is communicated, in the final analysis, is, beyond the sense of a work, the world it projects and that constitutes its horizon. In this sense, the listeners or readers receive it according to their own receptive capacity, which itself is defined by a situation that is both limited and open to the world's horizon. Thus the term "horizon" and its correlative, "world," appeared twice in the definition of mimesis$_3$ suggested earlier: the intersection of the world of the text and that of the listener or reader. This definition, close to H.-G. Gadamer's notion of a "fusion of horizons," rests upon three presuppositions which underlie, respectively, acts of discourse in general, literary works among these acts of discourse, and narratives among these literary works. The order that ties together these three presuppositions is thus one of increasing specification.

Concerning the first point, I shall limit myself to repeating the thesis argued at length in *The Rule of Metaphor* regarding the relationship between sense and reference in all discourse. According to this thesis, if (following Benveniste rather than de Saussure) we take the sentence as the unit of discourse, then the *intended* of discourse ceases to be confused with the signified correlative to each signifier within the immanence of a system of signs. With the sentence, language is oriented beyond itself. It says something *about* something. This intending of a referent by discourse is completely contemporaneous with its event character and its dialogical functioning. It is the other side of the instance of discourse. The complete event is not only that someone speaks and addresses himself to an interlocuter, it is also the speaker's ambition to bring a new *experience* to language and share it with someone else. It is this experience, in turn, that has the world for its horizon. Reference and horizon are correlative as are figure and ground. All experience both possesses a contour that circumscribes it and distinguishes it, and arises against a horizon of potentialities that constitutes at once an internal and an external horizon for experience: internal in the sense that it is always possible to give more details and be more precise about whatever is considered within some stable contour; external in the sense that the intended thing stands in potential relationships to everything else within the horizon of a total world, which itself never figures as the object of discourse. It is in this twofold sense of the word "horizon" that situation and horizon are correlative notions. This quite general presupposition implies that language does not constitute a world for itself. It is not even a world. Because we are in the world and are affected by situations, we try to orient ourselves in them by means of understanding; we also have something to say, an experience to bring to language and to share.

This is the ontological presupposition of reference, a presupposition reflected inside language itself as a postulate lacking any immanent justification. Language is for itself the order of the Same. The world is its Other. The attestation of this otherness arises from language's reflexivity with regard to itself, whereby it knows itself as being *in* being in order to bear *on* being.

This presupposition does not stem from linguistics or semiotics. On the contrary, these disciplines reject as a postulate of their method the idea of an intention oriented toward the extralinguistic. What I have just called an ontological attestation must appear to them, once their methodological postulates are stated, as an unjustifiable and inadmissable leap. In fact, this ontological attestation would remain an irrational leap if the externalization it required were not the counterpart of a prior and more originary notion, starting from our experience of being in the world and in time, and proceeding from this ontological condition toward its expression in language.

This first presupposition must be coordinated with my preceding reflections on the reception of a text. An ability to communicate and a capacity to refer must be simultaneously posited. All reference is co-reference—dialogical or dialogal reference. There is thus no need to choose between an aesthetic of reception and an ontology of the work of art. What a reader receives is not just the sense of the work, but, through its sense, its reference, that is, the experience it brings to language and, in the last analysis, the world and the temporality it unfolds in the face of this experience.

Consideration of "works of art," among all acts of discourse, calls for a second presupposition which does not abolish the first one but does make it more complex. According to the thesis I presented in *The Rule of Metaphor* and that I shall recall here, literary works, too, bring an experience to language and thus come into the world, just as all discourse does. This second presupposition runs head-on into the dominant theory of contemporary poetics, which rejects any taking into account of reference, something it regards as extralinguistic, in the name of the strict immanence of literary language in relation to itself. When literary texts contain allegations concerning truth or falsity, lies, or secrets, which ineluctably bring back the dialectic of being and appearance,[25] this poetics undertakes to consider as a simple meaning effect what it decides, by a methodological decree, to call a referential illusion. Yet the problem of the relation of literature to the reader's world is not thereby abolished. It is simply set aside. "Referential illusions" are not just any textual meaning effect whatever. They require a detailed theory of the modes of "veridiction." These modes, in turn, stand out against the background of a horizon of the world that constitutes the world of the text. We may certainly include the very notion of a horizon within the immanence of the text and take the concept of the world of the text for an outgrowth of the referential illusion. But reading poses anew the problem of the fusion of two horizons, that of the text and that of the reader, and hence the intersection of the world of the text and the world of the reader.

We might try to deny the problem, and take the question of the impact of literature on everyday experience as not pertinent. But then we paradoxically ratify the positivism we generally fight against, namely, the prejudice that only a datum that is given in such a way that it can be empirically observed and scientifically described is real. We also enclose literature within a world of its own and break off the subversive point it turns against the moral and social orders. We forget that fiction is precisely what makes language that supreme danger which Walter Benjamin, following Hölderlin, speaks of with such awe and admiration.

A whole range of cases is opened by this phenomenon of interaction: from ideological confirmation of the established order, as in official art or state chronicles, to social criticism and even derision for everything "real." Even extreme alienation in relation to reality is still a case of intersection. And this conflictive fusion of horizons is not without some relation to the dynamics of the text, in particular the dialectic of sedimentation and innovation. The shock of the possible, which is no less than that of the real, is amplified by the internal interplay, in the works themselves, between the received paradigms and the proliferation of divergencies, through the deviation of individual works. Thus narrative literature, among all poetic works, is a model of practical actuality by its deviations as much as by its paradigms.

If therefore we do not simply reject the problem of the fusion of the text's and the reader's horizons, or of the intersection between the world of the text and that of the reader, we have to find in the very functioning of poetic language the means to cross the abyss opened between these two worlds by the method of immanence characteristic of antipoetics. I tried to demonstrate in *The Rule of Metaphor* that language's capacity for reference was not exhausted by descriptive discourse and that poetic works referred to the world in their own specific way, that of metaphorical reference.[26] This thesis covers every nondescriptive use of language, and therefore every poetic text, whether it be lyrical or narrative. It implies that poetic texts, too, speak *of* the world, even though they may not do so in a descriptive fashion. Metaphorical reference, it will be recalled, consists in the fact that the effacement of descriptive reference—an effacement that, as a first approximation, makes language refer to itself—is revealed to be, in a second approximation, the negative condition for freeing a more radical power of reference to those aspects of our being-in-the-world that cannot be talked about directly. These aspects are intended, in an indirect but positively assertive way, by means of the new pertinence that the metaphorical utterance establishes at the level of sense, on the ruins of the literal sense abolished by its impertinence. This articulating of a metaphorical reference on the metaphorical sense cannot be clothed with a full ontological meaning unless we go so far as to metaphorize the verb "to be" itself and recognize in "being-as" the correlate of "seeing-as," in which is summed up the work of metaphor. This "being-as" brings my second presupposition to the ontological level of my first presupposition. At the same time, it enriches it. The concept of horizon and world does not just concern descriptive references but also nondescriptive references, those of poetic diction. To take up again one of my earlier statements, I will say that, for me, the world is the whole set of references opened by every sort of descriptive or poetic text I have read, interpreted, and loved.[27] To understand these texts is to interpolate among the predicates of our situation all those meanings that, from a simple environment (*Umwelt*), make a world (*Welt*). Indeed, we owe a large part of the enlarging of our horizon of existence to poetic works. Far from producing only weakened images of reality—shadows, as in the Platonic treatment of the *eikōn* in painting or writing (*Phaedrus* 274e–77e)—literary works depict reality by *augmenting* it with meanings that themselves depend upon the virtues of abbreviation, saturation, and culmination, so strikingly illustrated by emplotment. In *Ecriture et Iconographie*, François Dagognet, replying to Plato's argument directed against writing and against every *eikōn*, characterizes as *iconic augmentation* the painter's strategy of reconstructing reality on the basis of an optical alphabet that is limited and dense at the same time.[28] This concept should be extended to every mode of iconicity, that is, to what we are here calling fiction. In a related sense, Eugen Fink compares *Bild*, which he distinguishes from simple, entirely perceived presentations of reality, to a "window" whose narrow opening looks out onto the immensity of a countryside. And from his side, Gadamer recognizes in *Bild* the power of bringing about an increase in being in our vision of the world which is impoverished by everyday affairs.[29]

The postulate underlying this recognition of the function of refiguration that belongs to the poetic work in general is part of a hermeneutics that aims less at restoring the author's intention behind the text than at making explicit the movement by which the text unfolds, as it were, a world in front of itself. Elsewhere I have discussed this shift in focus of post-Heideggerian hermeneutics in relation to Romantic hermeneutics.[30] For some years now I have maintained that what is interpreted in a text is the proposing of a world that I might inhabit and into which I might project my ownmost powers. In the *Rule of Metaphor*, I held that poetry, through its muthos, redescribes the world. In the same way, in this work I will say that making a narrative [*le faire narratif*] resignifies the world in its temporal dimension, to the extent that narrating, telling, reciting is to remake action following the poem's invitation.[31]

A third presupposition comes into play here, if the referential capacity of narrative works is to be subsumed under those of poetic works in general. The problem posed by narrativity is, in fact, both more simple and more complicated than the one posed by lyric poetry. More simple, because the world, here, is apprehended from the angle of human praxis rather than from that of cosmic pathos. What is resignified by narrative is what was already presignified at the level of human acting. It will be recalled that our preunderstanding of the world of action under the governance of mimesis₁ is characterized by the mastering of a network of intersignifications constitutive of the semantics of action, by familiarity with the symbolic mediations and the prenarrative resources of human acting. Being-in-the-world according to narrativity is a being-in-the-world already marked by the linguistic [*langagière*] practice leading back to this preunderstanding. The iconic augmentation in question here depends upon the prior augmentation of readability that action owes to the interpretants already at work there. Human action can be oversignified, because it is already presignified by all the modes of its symbolic articulation. This is the sense in which the problem of reference is simpler in the case of the narrative mode than in that of the lyrical mode of poetry. Just as, in the *Rule of Metaphor*, it was by extrapolation from the tragic muthos that I elaborated the theory of poetic reference that joins muthos and redescription, it is the metaphorization of action and suffering that is easiest to decipher.

The problem posed by narrativity, with respect to its referential intention and its truth claim, is in another sense more complicated than that posed by lyric poetry. The existence of two large classes of narrative discourse, fictional and historical narrative, poses a series of specific problems that will be treated in volume 2 of this work. I limit myself here to listing a few of them. The most apparent, and perhaps also the most intractable one, proceeds from the undeniable asymmetry between the referential modes of historical and fictional narrative. Only history can claim a reference inscribed in empirical reality, inasmuch as historical intentionality aims at events that have actually occurred. Even if the past no longer exists and if, in Augustine's expression, it can be reached only in the present of the past, that is, through the traces of the past that have become documents for the historian, still it did happen. The past event, however absent it may be from present perception, nonetheless governs the historical intentionality, conferring upon it a realistic note that literature will never equal, even if it makes a claim to be "realistic." This reference through traces to a real past calls for a specific analysis to which one whole chapter of volume 2 will be devoted. I shall have to speak, on the one hand, about what this reference through traces borrows from the metaphorical reference common to every poetic work, inasmuch as the past can only be reconstructed by the imagination, and also what it adds to it, inasmuch as it is polarized by past reality. Conversely, the question will arise whether fictional narrative does not borrow, in turn, a part of its referential dynamics from this reference through traces. Is not every narrative told as though it had taken place, as is evident from the ordinary usage of verbal past tenses to narrate the unreal? In this sense, fiction would borrow as much from history as history borrows from fiction. It is this reciprocal borrowing that authorizes my posing the problem of the *interweaving* reference between history and narrative fiction. This problem can be avoided only by a positivist conception of history that would not recognize the aspect of fiction in its reference through traces, and by an antireferential conception of literature that would not recognize the importance of the metaphorical reference in all poetry. This problem of interweaving reference constitutes one of the major concerns of volume 2 of this work.

But where [*sur quoi*] do the reference by traces and the metaphorical reference interweave if not through the temporality of human action? Is it not human time that history and literary fiction in common refigure, by this interweaving of their referential modes?

Narrated Time

To narrow the framework further in which the question of the interweaving reference between history and fictional narrative will be raised again in the final part of this work, I must sketch the temporal features of the world refigured by the configurational act.

I would like to begin from the notion of iconic augmentation introduced above. We may then take up once more each of the features by which the

preunderstanding of action was characterized: the network of intersignifications between practical categories, the symbolism immanent to this preunderstanding, and above all its properly practical temporality. It can then said that
each of these features is intensified, is iconically augmented.

I shall not say much about the first two features. The intersignifying of project, circumstances, and chance is exactly what plot, which I have described
as a synthesis of the heterogeneous, orders. The narrative work is an invitation to see our praxis as it is ordered by this or that plot articulated in our
literature. As for the symbolism internal to action, we may say that it is exactly what is resymbolized or desymbolized—or resymbolized through de-
symbolization—by means of the schematism turn by turn traditionalized and
subverted by the historicity of our paradigms. Lastly, it is the time of action
that, more than anything, is refigured by the configurational act.

A long detour is required here. A theory of refigured time—or, we might
say, narrated time—cannot be brought to term without the mediation of the
third partner in the conversation already begun between the epistemology of
history and literary criticism applied to narrativity, in the discussion of interweaving reference.

This third partner is the phenomenology of time, only the initial phase of
which was considered in our study of time in Augustine. The rest of this work,
from Part II through volume 2, will be a long and difficult threeway conversation between history, literary criticism, and phenomenological philosophy.
The dialectic of time and narrative is the ultimate stake of this confrontation,
without precedent as far as I know, between three partners who usually ignore
one another.

To give sufficient attention to the third partner's words it will be important
to set forth the phenomenology of time from Augustine to Husserl and
Heidegger, not to write its history, but to give body to a remark tossed out
without any further justification in the course of my study of Book 11 of the
Confessions. There is, I said, no pure phenomenology of time in Augustine.
And I added, perhaps there can never be one. This impossibility of a pure
phenomenology of time is what has to be demonstrated. By a pure phenomenology I mean an intuitive apprehension of the structure of time, which
not only can be isolated from the procedures of argumentation by which phenomenology undertakes to resolve the aporias received from an earlier tradition, but which would not pay for its discovery with new aporias bearing a
higher price. My thesis is that the genuine discoveries of the phenomenology
of time cannot be definitively removed from the aporetic realm that so
strongly characterizes the Augustinian theory of time. We shall have to take
up again therefore our examination of the aporias created by Augustine and
demonstrate their exemplary character. In this regard, Husserl's analysis and
discussion in his lectures on the phenomenology of internal time consciousness will constitute the major counterexample to my thesis about the defini-

tively aporetic character of the phenomenology of time. In an almost unexpected way, at least for me, we shall be brought back by our discussion to the very Kantian thesis that time cannot be directly observed, that it is properly invisible. In this sense, the endless aporias of the phenomenology of time will be the price we have to pay for each and every attempt to make time itself appear, the ambition that defines the phenomenology of time as pure phenomenology. One major step in volume 2 will be to prove this, in principle, aporetic character of the pure phenomenology of time.

This proof is necessary if we are to hold as universally valid my thesis that the poetics of narrativity responds and corresponds to the aporetics of temporality. The rapprochement between Aristotle's *Poetics* and Augustine's *Confessions* provided only a partial and in a way a circumstantial verification of this thesis. If the aporetic character of every pure phenomenology of time may be augmented in at least a plausible way, the hermeneutic circle of narrativity and temporality will be enlarged well beyond the circle of mimesis, to which the discussion in this first part had to be limited, so long as historiography and the philosophy of history along with literary criticism have not had their say about historical time and the games fiction plays with time. It is only at the end of what I have called the three-way conversation, in which the phenomenology of time joins its voice to those of these other disciplines, that the hermeneutic circle can then be compared with the circle of a poetics of narrativity (itself culminating in the problem of interweaving reference referred to above) and an aporetics of temporality.

It might already be objected with respect to my thesis about the universally aporetic character of the pure phenomenology of time that Heidegger's hermeneutics marks a decisive break with Augustine's and Husserl's subjectivist hermeneutics. By founding his phenomenology on an ontology of *Dasein* and of being-in-the-world, is Heidegger not correct in affirming that temporality, as he describes it, is "more subjective" than any subject and "more objective" than any object, inasmuch as his ontology is not bound by the subject/object dichotomy? I do not deny this. The analyses I shall devote to Heidegger will do full justice to the originality that a phenomenology founded upon an ontology and that presents itself as a hermeneutics can boast of.

To say it already, the properly phenomenological originality of the Heideggerian analysis of time—an originality due entirely to its anchorage in an ontology of Care—consists in a hierarchization of the levels of temporality or rather of temporalization. Having shown this, we shall be able to rediscover a presentiment of this theme in Augustine. Indeed, by interpreting the extension of time in terms of distension and by describing human time as raised beyond its inside by the attraction of its polar opposite, eternity, Augustine gave credit in advance to the idea of a plurality of temporal levels. Intervals of time do not simply fit into one another according to their numerical quantities, days into years, years into centuries. In a general way, the problems relative to the extension of time do not exhaust the question of human time. In fact, insofar as extension reflects a dialectic of intention and distention, the extension of time does not have just a quantitative aspect in responding to the questions: for how long a time? during how much time? in how much time? It has a qualitative aspect of graduated tension.

In my study of time in Augustine I indicated the principal epistemological incidence of this notion of a temporal hierarchy: historiography, in its battle against the history of events, and narratology, in its ambition to dechronologize narrative, seem to leave only a single choice: either chronology or achronic systemic relations. Chronology, however, does have another contrary term: temporality itself, brought to its level of greatest tension.

In the Heideggerian analysis of temporality, in *Being and Time*, Augustine's breakthrough is exploited in the most decisive way, even though this occurs, as we shall see, beginning from Heidegger's meditation on being-towards-death and not, as in Augustine, from the structure of the threefold present. I take as one invaluable result of the Heideggerian analysis its having established, with the resources of a hermeneutic phenomenology, that our experience of temporality is capable of unfolding itself on several levels of radicality, and that it belongs to the analytic of *Dasein* to traverse them, whether from above to below, in the order followed in *Being and Time*, from authentic and mortal time toward everyday and public time where everything happens "in" time, or from below to above, as in *The Basic Problems of Phenomenology*.[32] The direction in which the range of temporalization is traversed is less important than the hierarchization of temporal experience.[33]

Along the ascending or regressive path, a stop at the middle level, between within-time-ness and radical temporality, marked by being-towards-death, seems of greatest importance to me. For reasons I shall mention later, Heidegger distinguishes it by the title *Geschichtlichkeit*, historicality. Augustine's and Heidegger's two analyses are closest to each other at this level, before diverging radically—at least in appearance—as the one directs himself toward Pauline hope, the other toward quasi-Stoic resoluteness in the face of death. In volume 2 I shall set forth an intrinsic reason for returning to this analysis of *Geschichtlichkeit*. Indeed, my analysis of repetition—*Wiederholung*—in which I shall seek an ontological answer to the epistemological problems posed by the interweaving reference between the truth claims of historical intentionality and literary fiction, leads back to it. This is why I am already indicating its point of insertion.

There is no question therefore of denying the properly phenomenological originality that the Heideggerian description of temporality owes to its anchorage in the ontology of Care. Nonetheless, on this side of the turn—the *Kehre*—from which proceed the works subsequent to *Being and Time*, it must be admitted that the ontology of *Dasein* remains tied up with a phenomenology that poses problems analogous to those raised by Augustine's and Husserl's phenomenology. Here, too, the breakthrough on the phenomenological plane engenders difficulties of a new sort that again augment the aporetic character of pure phenomenology. This aggravation is in proportion to this phenomenology's ambition, which is not just to owe nothing to an epistemology of the physical and the human sciences, but to serve as their *foundation*.

The paradox is that the aporia has to do precisely with the relations between the phenomenology of time and the human sciences—principally history, but also contemporary narratology. Yes, the paradox is that Heidegger has made more difficult the three-way conversation between history, literary criticism, and phenomenology. We may even doubt whether he might have succeeded in deriving the concept of history familiar to professional historians, as well as the general thematic of the human sciences received from Dilthey, from the historicality of *Dasein*, which, for hermeneutic phenomenology, constitutes the middle level in the hierarchy of degrees of temporality. More serious yet, if the most radical temporality bears the stamp of death, how, we might ask, do we pass from a temporality so privatized by being-towards-death to that common time that requires interaction among multiple characters in every narrative and, all the more, to the public time required by history?

In this sense our passage through Heidegger's phenomenology will require a supplementary effort, which sometimes will distance us from him, to maintain the dialectic of narrative and time. It will be one of the major concerns of volume 2 to show how, in spite of the abyss that seems to lie between the two poles, narrative and time simultaneously and mutually arrange themselves in hierarchies. At times it will be the hermeneutic phenomenology of time that provides the key to the hierarchizing of narrative, other times it will be the disciplines concerned with historical and fictional narrative that allow us to resolve poetically—to use an expression already employed—the most speculatively intractable aporias of the phenomenology of time.

Hence the very difficulty of deriving the historical disciplines from the analysis of *Dasein* and the still more formidable difficulty of bringing together in our thought the *mortal* time of the phenomenology of time and the *public* time of the narrative disciplines, will spur us to think through more thoroughly the relationships of time and narrative. The preliminary reflection that constitutes the first part of this work has already brought us from a conception where the hermeneutic circle is identified with the circle of the stages of mimesis to one that inscribes this dialectic within the larger circle of a poetics of narrative and an aporetics of time.

A final problem appears: that of *the upper limit to the process of the hierarchization of temporality*. For Augustine and the whole Christian tradition, the internalizing of the purely extensive relations of time refers to an eternity where everything is present at the same time. The approximating of eternity by time thus lies in the stability of a soul in respose: "Then I shall be cast and set firm in the mould of your truth" (*Confessions*, Book 11, 30:40). Yet

Heidegger's philosophy of time, at least during the period of *Being and Time*, even while taking up again and developing with great rigor the theme of levels of temporality, orients its meditation not toward divine eternity but toward finitude sealed by being-towards-death. Are these two irreducible ways of guiding the most extensive duration back toward the most tensive duration? Or is this disjunction only apparent? Are we to think that only a mortal can form the plan of "giving the things of life a dignity that makes them eternal"? Can the eternity that works of art oppose to the fugacity of things be constituted only in a history? And does this history in turn remain historical only if, going beyond death, it guards against the forgetfulness of death and the dead, and remains a recollection of death and a remembrance of the dead? The most serious question this work may be able to pose is to what degree a philosophical reflection on narrativity and time may aid us in thinking about eternity and death at the same time.

Part II
History and Narrative

In the first part of this work I attempted to characterize narrative discourse without taking into account the major bifurcation that today divides its field between historiography (including work in philosophy of history) and narrative fiction. By so doing, I tacitly admitted that historiography does genuinely belong to this field. Whether it does belong to this field is what now must be examined.

Two convictions of equal strength lie at the origin of this investigation. The first says that today it is a lost cause to bind the narrative character of history to one particular form of history, narrative history. In this regard, *my thesis concerning the ultimately narrative character of history in no way is to be confused with a defense of narrative history.* My second conviction is that if history were to break every connection to *our basic competence for following a story* and to the cognitive operations constitutive of our narrative understanding, as I described them in the first part of this work, it would lose its distinctive place in the chorus of social sciences. It would cease to be historical. What is the nature of this connection?

To resolve this problem I did not wish to surrender to the easy solution that would consist in saying that history is an ambiguous discipline, half literary, half scientific, and that the epistemology of history can only register this state of affairs with regret, ceasing to work toward a history that would no longer be a kind of narrative. This easy eclecticism is contrary to my ambition. My thesis is that history the most removed from the narrative form continues to be bound to our narrative understanding by a line of derivation that we can reconstruct step by step and degree by degree with an appropriate method. This method does not stem from the methodology of the historical sciences per se but from a second-order reflection upon the ultimate conditions of intelligibility of a discipline that, in virtue of its scientific ambition, tends to forget this line of derivation which continues nevertheless tacitly to preserve its specificity as a historical science.

This thesis has one immediate implication concerning historical time. I do not doubt that historians have the privilege of constructing temporal parameters appropriate to their object and their method. I do maintain, however, that the significance of these constructions is borrowed, that it derives indirectly from the significance of those narrative configurations I described in terms of mimesis₂ and that, by way of these, it is rooted in the temporality characteristic of the world of action. So, construction of historical time will be one of the major stakes of my enterprise. A stake—that is, both a consequence and a touchstone.

My thesis, therefore, is equally distant from two others: the one that would see in the retreat of historical narrative the negation of any connection between history and narrative, making historical time a construction without any support from narrative time or the time of action; and the one that would establish between history and narrative a relation as direct as that, for example, between a species and a genus, along with a directly readable continuity between the time of action and historical time. My thesis rests on the assertion of an indirect connection of derivation, by which historical knowledge proceeds from our narrative understanding without losing anything of its scientific ambition. In this sense, it is not a thesis that seeks to stand in the middle of the road.[1]

To reconstruct the indirect connections of history to narrative is finally to bring to light the intentionality of the historian's thought by which history continues obliquely to intend the field of human action and its basic temporality.

By means of this oblique intention, historiography comes to be inscribed within that great mimetic circle which we traversed in the first part of this study. It too, albeit in a derived way, is rooted in our pragmatic competence, with its handling of events that occur "in" time, as described in my discussion of mimesis₁. It too configures the field of praxis by means of temporal constructions of a higher rank which historiography grafts to the narrative time characteristic of mimesis₂. It too, finally, reaches its meaning in the refiguring of the field of praxis and contributes to recapitulating the existence wherein mimesis₃ culminates.

Such is the farthest horizon of my enterprise. I shall not take it so far in this part. I must reserve for a separate investigation the final segment corresponding to mimesis₃. Indeed, the inserting of history into action and into life, its capacity for reconfigurating time, brings into play the question of truth in history. This question is inseparable from what I call the interweaving reference between history's claim to truth and that of fiction. The investigation to which Part II of this work is devoted, therefore, does not cover the whole field of the problematic of history. To retain the vocabulary I used in *The Rule of Metaphor*, it separates the question of "sense" from that of "reference." Or, remaining faithful to the vocabulary of Part I of this work, the present investigation undertakes to connect together again, in the mode of *oratio obliqua*, explanation and our narrative understanding described in terms of mimesis₂.

The order of questions dealt with in this second part is governed by my argument for the thesis just sketched.

In chapter 4, entitled "The Eclipse of Narrative," I take my distance from modern history as related to an expressly narrative form. I try to establish a convergence, in the attack against narrative history, between two currents of thought largely independent of one another. The first, closer to historical practice, and therefore more methodological than epistemological, seemed to me best illustrated by contemporary French historiography. The second stems from logical positivism's theses about the unity of science. It, therefore, is more epistemological than methodological.

In chapter 5, entitled "Defenses of Narrative," I take account of the various attempts—borrowed for the most part, with one important exception, from English-speaking authors—to extend our narrative competence directly to historical discourse. Despite my great sympathy for these analyses, which I try to integrate into my own project, I must confess that they do not seem to me to have fully reached their goal inasmuch as they only account for those forms of historiography where the relation to narrative is direct, and therefore visible.

Chapter 6, entitled "Historical Intentionality," contains the major thesis of this second part, namely my thesis of the indirect derivation of historical knowledge, beginning from narrative understanding. Within this framework I take up again the analysis I have already begun elsewhere concerning the relations between explanation and understanding.[2] To conclude, I give a partial answer to the question that inaugurates chapter 4, the question regarding the status of an event. This answer cannot be complete because the epistemological status of an event—the only thing at issue in this second part—is inseparable from its ontological status, which is one of the stakes in volume 2.

I must ask for my reader's patience at this point. You need to know that you will find, in the three chapters that follow, only a preparatory analysis as regards my central question about time and narrative. It is necessary first of all to elucidate the relationship between historical *explanation* and narrative *understanding* if we are to be able to pose the question of the contribution of historical narrative to the refiguring of time in a worthwhile manner. And this elucidation itself requires a long analysis. The nomological theory and the narrativist one must, under the pressure of the appropriate arguments, reveal their respective insufficiency if the indirect relationship between historiography and narrative is, in its turn, to be restored step by step and degree by degree. This long epistemological preparation ought not, however, to cause us to lose sight of the final ontological stake. One additional reason may be added to my plea for extending the lines of this battle. The refiguring of time by narrative is, I hold, the joint work of historical and fictional narrative. Only in the second volume of this work, devoted to fictional narrative, therefore, will we be able to take up as a whole the problematic of narrated time.

4

The Eclipse of Narrative

French historiography and neopositivist epistemology belong to two very different universes of discourse. The first is traditionally and unfailingly distrustful of philosophy, which it readily identifies with the philosophy of history in a Hegelian style, itself conveniently confused with the speculations of Spengler or Toynbee. As for the critical philosophy of history, inherited from Dilthey, Rickert, Simmel, and Max Weber, and continued by Raymond Aron and Henri Marrou, it has never truly been integrated into the main current of French historiography.[1] This is why we do not find, in those works most concerned about methodology, a reflection comparable to that of the German school at the beginning of this century, or to that in English of contemporary logical positivism and its adversaries concerning the epistemological structure of explanation in history. Its strength lies elsewhere, in strict adherence to the profession of the historian. The best accomplishment of this French school of history is a methodology for those actually in the field. In this regard, it provides philosophers all the more to think about in that it borrows nothing from them. The superiority of the works arising out of neopositivism, on the contrary, stems from their constant concern to measure explanation in history against models presumed to define scientific knowledge, the profound unity of this project, and its successes. In this sense these works do stem more from epistemology than from methodology. But their strength is often their weakness, in that historians' actual practice is absent from their discussion of the models of explanation. This fault is unfortunately shared by logical positivism's adversaries. As we shall see later, in our examination of "narrativist" arguments, the examples which positivist as well as antipositivist epistemology borrows from historians are rarely at the level of complexity attained today in the historical disciplines.

As heterogeneous as these two currents of thought may be, they have at least in common, besides their denial of the philosophy of history (which does not concern us here), their denial of the narrative character of history as it is written today.

This convergence in outcome is all the more striking in that the arguments are so different. For French historiography, the eclipse of narrative proceeds principally from a displacement of the object of history, which is no longer the active individual but the total social fact. For positivism, the eclipse of narrative proceeds instead from the epistemological break between historical explanation and our narrative understanding.

In this chapter I shall place the accent on the convergence of these two attacks, taking as my guideline the destiny of both what counts as an event and the historical time-span in each perspective.

THE ECLIPSE OF THE EVENT IN FRENCH HISTORIOGRAPHY

My choice of the concept of an event as a touchstone for my discussion is particularly appropriate for an examination of the contribution of French historiography to the theory of history, inasmuch as the criticism of the history of events [*l'histoire événementielle*] has its well-known place there and because this criticism is taken as equivalent to the rejection of the category "narrative." [2]

Prior to reflection, the concept of a historical event shares the misleading assumptions of most common-sense notions. It implies two series of assertions which are not criticized: ontological ones and epistemological ones, the latter being built on the former.

In an ontological sense, we mean by historical event what actually happened in the past. This assertion itself has several aspects. First, we admit that the property of having already occurred differs radically from that of not yet having occurred. In this sense, the pastness of what has happened is taken as an absolute property, independent of our constructions and reconstructions. This first feature is common to physical events and to historical ones. A second feature delimits the field of the historical event. Of all the things that have happened, certain ones are the work of agents similar to ourselves. Historical events therefore are what these active beings make happen or undergo. The ordinary definition of history as knowledge of the actions of past human beings proceeds from this restricting of our interest to the sphere of events assignable to human agents. A third feature results from a delimitation within the practical field of the sphere of possible communication. To the notion of the human past is added, as a constitutive obstacle, the idea of an otherness or an absolute difference affecting our capacity for communication. It seems as though one implication of our competence to seek understanding and agreement, wherein Habermas sees the norm of a universal pragmatics, is that our competence to communicate encounters the strangeness of strangers as a challenge and an obstacle, and that we can hope to understand them only at the price of recognizing their irreducible otherness.

To this threefold ontological presupposition—absolute having been, absolutely past human action, and absolute otherness—corresponds a threefold epistemological one. First, we oppose the unrepeatable singularity of a physical or a human event to the universality of a law. Whether it be a question of statistical frequency, causal connection, or functional relation, an event is what happens only once. Next, we oppose practical contingency to logical or physical necessity. An event is what could have been done differently. Finally, otherness has its epistemological counterpart in the notion of the gap between an event and any constructed model or any invariant.

Broadly speaking, these are the tacit presuppositions of our uncritical use of the notion of a historical event. At the beginning of our investigation we do not know what stems from prejudice, what from philosophical or theological sedimentation, what from universally normative constraints. Sifting it all out can be accomplished only through criticism brought about by actual historical investigations. In the following pages I shall appraise French historiography in light of its contribution to this criticism of our presuppositions concerning events.

I shall refer only briefly to Raymond Aron's key work, *Introduction to the Philosophy of History: An Essay on the Limits of Historical Objectivity* (1938),[3] which appeared shortly before Lucien Febvre and Marc Bloch founded *Annales d'histoire économique et sociale* in 1939, which after 1945 became *Annales. Economiques, Sociétés, Civilisations.* I shall return to Aron's work below in my discussion of the dialectic between explanation and understanding. Still, this book is worth mentioning here for having greatly contributed to dissolving the first presupposition of common sense, that of the absolute character of events, events as what really happened. In setting out the limits of historical objectivity, Aron was led to proclaim what he called the "dissolution of the object" (p. 118). This famous thesis unfortunately gave rise to more than one misunderstanding. It was aimed more at the reigning positivism under the aegis of Langlois and Seignobos than at any ontological thesis.[4] It meant no more than this: to the extent that historians are implicated in the understanding and explanation of past events, an absolute event cannot be attested to by historical discourse. Understanding—even the understanding of another person in everyday life—is never a direct intuition but always a reconstruction. Understanding is always more than simple empathy. In short, no "such thing as a *historical reality* exists ready made, so that science merely has to reproduce it faithfully" (p. 118). "Jean sans Terre was there" is a historical fact only in virtue of a whole bundle of intentions, motives, and values that incorporate this statement into some intelligible whole. Consequently, diverse reconstructions only accentuate the break separating the objectivity claimed by the work of understanding from lived nonrepeatable experience. If this "dissolution of the object" is already accomplished by the most humble forms of understanding, the disappearance of the object is even more complete on the level of causal thinking, to use the vocabulary Aron employed at the time of this work. We shall come back to this point in chapter 6. For Aron, as for Max Weber, historical causality is a relation of one particular to another particular, through the medium of retrospective probability. On the scale of probabilities, the lowest degree defines what is accidental, the highest degree defines what Weber calls adequation. Just as such adequation differs from logical or physical necessity, the accidental is no longer equivalent to absolute singularity. "As for the probability born of the partial character of historical analyses and causal relations, it exists in our minds, not in things" (p. 165). In this respect, historical appraisal of probability differs from the logic of the scientist and is closer to that of the judge. For Aron, the philosophical stake in all this was the destruction of every retrospective illusion of fatality and the opening of the theory of history to the spontaneity of action oriented toward the future.

For our present investigation, the clear result of Aron's book is that the past, conceived of as the sum of what has actually happened, is out of reach of the historian.

We find an argument similar to Aron's in H. I. Marrou's *The Meaning of History* (first published in 1954).[5] There the practice of historians is even more evident. I shall set aside here one problem to which I shall return in volume 2, namely, the connection between understanding another person and knowing the human past.[6]

The continuity between mortal time and public time, referred to at the end of Part I, is directly implied in this. Here I shall only retain the major methodological implications of this recourse to our understanding of others that link up with Aron's axiom concerning the dissolution of the object.

First, historical knowledge, resting on the the testimony of others, is "not a science properly speaking, but only a knowedge by faith" (Marrou, p. 152). Understanding envelops the whole work of the historian inasmuch as history "is a spiritual adventure wherein the historian's personality is brought into play. History is thus endowed, for the historian, with an existential value, and from this existential value it receives its importance, its meaning and its value" (p. 204). And, Marrou adds, "this conception forms the very heart of our critical philosophy, and the focal point around which all else takes on order and clarity" (ibid.). Understanding is thereby incorporated into "The Truth of History"—the title of Marrou's chapter 9; that is, into the truth that history is capable of. Understanding is not the subjective side and explanation the objective one. Subjectivity is not a prison and objectivity is not our liberation from this prison. Far from conflicting, subjectivity and objectivity reinforce each other. "Indeed once history is true, its truth is double, for it is composed of truth both about the past and about the testimony offered by the historian" (p. 238).

If historians are implicated in historical knowing, they cannot propose the impossible task for themselves of re-actualizing the past.[7] It is impossible for two reasons. First, history is a form of knowledge only through the relation it establishes between the lived experience of people of other times and today's historian. The set of procedures used in history is part of the equation for historical knowing. The result of this is that humanity's lived past can only be postulated, like the Kantian noumena at the origin of all empirical phenomena. Further, if this lived past were accessible to us, it would not be so as an object of knowledge. For, when it was present, this past was like our present, confused, multiform, and unintelligible. Instead, history aims at knowledge, an organized vision, established upon chains of causal or teleological relations, on the basis of meanings and values. In essence, Marrou here links up with Aron, at the precise moment when Aron announces the dissolution of the object, in the sense we spoke of above.[8]

The same argument that forbids us to conceive of history as reminiscence also condemns the positivism that the new French historiography takes as its bête noire. If history is the relationship of the historian to the past, we cannot treat the historian as some perturbing factor added to the past that must be eliminated. This methodological argument, we see, exactly repeats the argument drawn from understanding. If hypercriticism attaches more value to suspicion than to empathy, its moral tenor is quite in accord with the methodological illusion that the historical fact exists in some latent state in the documents and that the historian is a parasite on the historical equation. Against this methodological illusion it has to be affirmed that the initiative in history does not belong to the document (see ibid., chapter 3) but to the question posed by the historian. This question takes logical priority in historical inquiry.

In this way Marrou's work reinforces Aron's in its battle against the prejudice about the past in-itself. At the same time, it assures a connection with the antipositivist orientation of the Annales school.

The contribution of the Annales school to our problem differs greatly from that of Aron, the philosopher, and even from that of Marrou, the philosopher-historian, marked as they both are by the German problem of *Verstehen*. With this school, we have to deal with the methodology of professional historians, who for the most part are not concerned about the problem of "understanding."[9] The most theoretical essays by the historians of this school are treatises by artisans reflecting on their craft.

Their tone was set by Marc Bloch in *The Historian's Craft*, a work written far from any library and interrupted two-thirds of the way through by a Nazi firing squad in 1942.[10] This unfinished book means to be "the memorandum of a craftsman who has always liked to reflect over his daily task, the notebook of a journeyman who has long handled the ruler and the level, without imagining himself to be a mathematician" (p. 19). Its hesitations, audacities, and prudences are still valuable today. This is all the more true in that it chooses to accentuate the "unresolvable" aspects of historiography.[11]

Of course, narratives only constitute the class of "voluntary witnesses," whose sway over history needs to be limited with the help of those "witnesses in spite of themselves" which are all the other tracks familiar to the archaeologist and the economic or social historian. But this endless enlarging of documentary sources does not mean that the notion of a witness does not encompass that of a document or does not remain the model for every observation of "tracks" (p. 64). The result is that "criticism" will essentially, if not exclusively, be a criticism of testimony, that is, a test of its veracity, a search for imposture, whether it be misleading information about an author or a date (misinformation in the juridical sense) or more fundamental deception (plagiarism, sheer invention, reshuffling the facts, or the hawking of prejudices and rumors). This considerable place given to criticism of testimony, at the expense of questions about causes or laws, which at this same time occupied English-language epistemology, is due essentially to the specifying of the notion of a track by the psychic character of historical phenomena.[12] Social conditions are, "in their underlying nature, mental" (p. 194). The result is that criticism of testimony, "since it deals with psychic realities, will always remain a subtle art. . . . However, it is also a rational art, which depends on methodical use of certain basic mental processes" (p. 110).The prudences, perhaps the timidities, of this work are the counterpart of this submission of the notion of a document to that of testimony. In fact, even the subsection entitled "Toward a Logic of the Critical Method" (pp. 110–39) remains a prisoner of a psycho-sociological analysis of testimony, albeit a refined one. Even though this rational art compares testimonies, looking for mutual contradictions, and weighs the reasons for lies, it still remains the heir of the erudite methods forged by Richard Simon, the Bollandists, and the Benedictines. Not that Bloch did not glimpse, and in this sense anticipate, the role of statistical criticism, but he did not see that the logic of probability, treated twenty years earlier by Max Weber and then taken up again by Raymond Aron, no longer stemmed from the criticism of testimony but from the problem of causality in history.[13] To use it just to disclose and explain the imperfections of testimony is inevitably to limit its import.[14]

The real breakthrough brought about by *The Historian's Craft* is rather to be found in the remarks devoted to "historical analysis"—the title of chapter 4. Marc Bloch grasped perfectly that historical explanation essentially consists in the constituting of chains of similar phenomena and in establishing their interactions. This primacy of analysis over synthesis allowed him to set in place—under the cover of a quotation from Focillon, the author of the admirable *Vie des Formes*[15]—the phenomenon of the discrepancy between the political, economic, and artistic aspects thereby distinguished within the overall historical phenomenon, to which we shall return below with George Duby.[16] Above all, it gave him the occasion for a remarkable discussion of the problem of nomenclature (see pp. 156–89).

This problem is clearly bound up with that of classifying facts. However, it poses the specific problem of the propriety of our language. Ought we to name past entities with the terms already used by the documents to designate them, at the risk of forgetting that "the vocabulary of documents is, in its way, only another form of evidence. . . . hence subject to criticism" (p. 168)? Or ought we to project modern terms on them, at the risk of missing, through anachronism, the specificity of past phenomena and of arrogantly eternalizing our own categories? As can be seen, the dialectic of the similar and the dissimilar governs historical analysis as it does historical criticism.

These insightful views make all the more regrettable the violent interruption of this work at the moment when it was beginning to discuss the formidable problem of causal relations in history. The final sentence is all the more precious in that it is left unfinished: "In a word, in history, as elsewhere, the causes cannot be assumed. They are to be looked for . . ." (p. 197).

The real manifesto of the Annales school has to be Fernand Braudel's chief work, *The Mediterranean and the Mediterranean World in the Age of Philip II.*[17]

For the sake of didactic clarity, I shall concentrate upon what in Braudel's essays and in those by historians of his school goes directly against the second of our initial presuppositions, namely, that events are what active agents make happen, and, that as a consequence, events share in the contingency proper to action. The model of action implied by the very notion of "making events happen" (along with its corollary of "undergoing them") is what is called into question. Action, according to this implicit model, can always be attributed to some individual agents, authors, or victims of events. Even if we include the concept of interaction in that of action, we never escape the assumption that the author of an action must always be an identifiable agent.

This tacit assumption that events are what individuals make happen or undergo is overthrown by Braudel along with two other assumptions which are closely connected with each other—and which undergo the direct fire of Braudel's and his successors' criticism. They are that the individual is the ultimate bearer of historical change and that the most significant changes are pointlike ones, those in fact that affect individual lives due to their brevity and their suddenness. In fact, Braudel reserves the title "event" just for such changes.

These two explicit corollaries entail a third one which is never discussed by itself, namely that a history of events, a *histoire événementielle*, can only be a narrative history. Political history, a history of events, and narrative history are taken consequently as almost synonymous expressions. Most surprising, for us who are inquiring precisely into the narrative status of history, this notion of narrative is never interrogated for itself, as the notions of primacy of political history and of events are. These historians are content to disown narrative history à la Ranke with a single sentence. (We have seen how narrative for Marc Bloch is one part of voluntary testimony, therefore a document.) Nor does it ever occur to Lucien Febvre, the co-founder of the Annales school with Marc Bloch, that his vehement criticism of the notion of a historical fact, conceived of as an atom of history completely given by the sources, and his plea for a historical reality constructed by the historian, fundamentally bring together historical reality, so created by history, and narrative fiction, created by the narrator.[18] The criticism of narrative history, therefore, is done only by way of the criticism of political history, which emphasizes individuals and events. Only these two primary assumptions are attacked head-on.

To methodological individualism in the social sciences, the new historians oppose the thesis that the object of history is not the individual but the "total social fact" (a term borrowed from Marcel Mauss) in every one of its human dimensions—economic, social, political, cultural, religious, etc. To the notion of an event as a temporal leap, they oppose that of a *social time* whose major categories—conjuncture, structure, trend, cycle, growth, crisis, etc.— are borrowed from economics, demography, and sociology.

The important thing to grasp is the connection between these two types of contestation, one directed against the primacy of the individual as the ultimate atom of historical investigation, and the other against the primacy of events, in the pointlike sense of this word, as the ultimate atom of social change.

These two rejections do not result from any speculation about action and time. Instead they are the direct consequence of the displacment of the principal axis of historical investigation from political history toward social history. Political history, including military, diplomatic, and ecclesiastical history, is where individuals—heads of state, generals, ministers, diplomats, prelates— are supposed to make history. It is also the realm where events go off like explosions. The "history of battles" and the "history of events" (to use an expression of Paul Lacombe's taken up by François Simiand and Henri Berr) go hand in hand.[19] The primacy of the individual and of the pointlike event are the two necessary corollaries of the preeminence of political history.

It is noteworthy that this criticism of the history of events in no way results from philosophical criticism of a conception, itself philosophical, of history in the Hegelian tradition. It results instead from a methodological fight against the positivist tradition that prevailed in historical studies in France during the first third of our century. For this tradition, major events are already deposited in archives, which themselves moreover are already instituted and constituted as a result of the vicissitudes and accidents affecting the distribution of power. This is why the twofold denunciation of the history of battles and that of events constitutes the polemical side of a plea for a history of the total human phenomenon, always with a strong emphasis on its economic and social conditions. In this regard, the most conspicuous and no doubt the most numerous works of this historical school are devoted to social history, in which groups, social categories and classes, cities and the country, the bourgeois, artisans, peasants, and workers become the collective heroes of history. For Braudel, history even becomes a geohistory whose hero is the Mediterranean and the Mediterranean world, until this is succeeded, for Huguette and Pierre Chaunu, by the Atlantic between Seville and the New World.[20]

The concept of a long time-span [*la longue durée*], opposed to the concept of event taken in the sense of a short time-span, was born in this critical context. In his Preface to *The Mediterranean*, then in his inaugural lecture at the Collège de France in 1950, and again in his *Annales* article on "The *Longue Durée*," Braudel never stops driving home the same point. The most superficial history is history concerned with the dimension of individuals. The history of events is the history of short, sharp, and nervous vibrations. It is richest in humanity but also most dangerous. Under this history and its individual time unfolds "a history of gentle rhythms" (*On History*, p. 3) with its "long time span" (pp. 25ff.). This is social history, the history of groups and of deep-lying trends. It is the economist who teaches the historian about this long time-span, but it is also the time of political institutions and of *mentalités*. Finally, even deeper, reigns "a history that is almost changeless, the history of man in relation to his surroundings" (p. 3). With this history, we must speak of a "geographical time" (p. 4).

This series of time-spans is one of the more noteworthy contributions of French historiography to the epistemology of history—given the lack of a more subtle discussion of the ideas of causes and laws.

The idea that the individual and the event are to be simultaneously surpassed is the strong point of this school. For Braudel, the plea for history becomes a plea for "anonymous history, working in the depths, and most often in silence" (p. 10), and thereby for social time that "goes at a thousand different paces, swift or slow" (p. 12). It is a plea and a credo: "Thus I believe in the reality of a particularly slow-paced history of civilizations" (ibid.). Still, it is the historian's profession, not philosophical reflection, affirms Braudel, in "History and the Social Sciences: The *Longue Durée*," that suggests the "living, intimate, infinitely repeated opposition," close to the heart of social reality, "between the instant of time and that time which flows only slowly" (p. 26). Awareness of this plurality of social times must become a component of the common methodology of all the human sciences. Pushing this axiom close to the point of becoming a paradox, Braudel goes so far as to say, "Social science has almost what amounts to a horror of the event. And not without some justification, for the short time span is the most capricious and the most delusive of all" (p. 28).

A reader interested in epistemology may be surprised by the lack of rigor in the expressions that characterize the plurality of temporalities. For example, Braudel not only speaks of short time and long time, that is, of quantitative differences, but also of rapid and slow time. Absolutely speaking, speed does not apply to intervals of time but to movements traversing them.

And, in the final analysis, the question has to do with these movements. Several metaphors, induced by the image of speed or slowness, confirm this. We can begin with those that deprecate events, a synonym for short time-spans. A "surface disturbance, the waves stirred up by the powerful movement of tides. A history of short, sharp, nervous vibrations" (p. 3). "We must beware of that history which still simmers with the passions of the contemporaries who felt it, described it, lived it, to the rhythm of their brief lives, lives as brief as our own" (p. 4). "A world of vivid passions, certainly, but a blind world, as any living world must be, as ours is, oblivious of the deep currents of history, of those living waters on which our frail barks are tossed like Rimbaud's drunken boat" (ibid.). A whole group of metaphors speak of the misleading character of the short time-span: sorcery, smoke, caprice, glimmers without clarity, the short term of our illusions, Ranke's delusive fallacies. Others speak of its prating assumptions: "to react against a history arbitrarily reduced to the role of quintessential heroes," "against Treitschke's proud and unilateral declaration: 'Men make history'" (p. 10). Traditional history, "the narrative history so dear to the heart of Ranke" offers us a "gleam but no illumination; facts but no humanity" (p. 11). Then there are the metaphors that speak of "the exceptional value of the long time span" (p. 27). Anonymous history, "working in the depths and most often in silence," which makes human beings more than they make it (p. 10); "a ponderous history whose time cannot be measured by any of our long-established instruments" (p. 12); "that most silent but imperious history of civilizations" (p. 16).

What do these metaphors conceal? What do they reveal? First, a concern for veracity as much as for modesty, the admission that we do not make history, if by "we" we mean Hegel's great world-historical figures. Hence a willingness to make visible and audible the pressure of a deep time which the clamorous drama of the short time-span has eclipsed and reduced to silence. If we now plumb this modesty, what do we find? Two contrary insights held in equilibrium.

On the one side, by means of the slowness, the weightiness, the silence of long-lasting time, history reaches an intelligibility that belongs only to the long time-span, a coherence that belongs only to durable equilibriums, in short, a kind of stability within change. "As realities of the inexhaustibly *longue durée*, civilizations, endlessly readapting themselves to their destiny, exceed in longevity any other collective reality; they outlive them all" (p. 210). In his discussion of civilizations, Braudel ends up designating them as "a reality that time makes poor use of and carries along very slowly." Yes, "civilizations are realities of the extreme *longue durée*" (p. 209). Toynbee, in spite of everything that can be said against him, saw this perfectly. "He has committed himself to 'societies,' to social realities, or at least to those social realities which persist forever. He has committed himself to events which continue to have violent repercussions whole centuries after they have occurred, or to men well above the general run of mankind, whether Jesus, Buddha, or Mahomet, men who are equally of the *longue durée*" (pp. 196–97). To the smoke of events is opposed the rock of endurance. Especially when time becomes inscribed in geography, when it is gathered up in the perenniality of landscapes. "A civilization is first of all a space, a 'cultural area,' . . . a locus" (p. 202). "The *longue durée* is the endless, inexhaustible history of structures and groups of structures" (p. 75). We might say that here Braudel reaches, by way of the notion of endurance, not so much what changes as what remains the same. The verb "to endure" says this better than does the substantive "endurance." A discrete wisdom, opposed to the frenzy of events, can be discerned behind this respect for the extreme slowness of real changes.

However the opposite perception also appears, as soon as social mathematics proposes to apply its achronological structures and its atemporal models to the long time-span. Against this pretension and this temptation historians stand as the guardians of change. They may oppose to traditional narrative an "account of conjunctures," but far beyond "this second account we find a history capable of traversing even greater distances, a history to be measured in centuries this time: the history of the long, even of the very long time span, of the *longue durée*" (p. 27). But a time-span, even the very long time-span, is still a time-span. And it is there that historians stand guard, at the threshold where history might step over into sociology. We can see this in the section of the essay "History and the Social Sciences: The *Longue Durée*" devoted to social mathematics (see pp. 38–47), as well as in the essay "History and Sociology" (pp. 64–82). "In fact, as far as the language of history is concerned," Braudel protests, "there can be no question of perfect synchrony" (p. 39). Mathematical sociologists may indeed construct almost timeless models—almost timeless, that is, "in actual fact, traveling the dark, untended byways of the extreme *longue durée*" (p. 41). In fact, such models are of varying duration: "they are valid for as long as the reality with which they are dealing. . . . for even more significant than the deep-rooted structures of life are their points of rupture, their swift or slow deterioration under the effect of contradictory pressures" (pp. 44–45). What counts for the historian, in the end, is the range of a model. Here a marine metaphor is again in force: "The significant moment is when it can keep afloat no longer, and sinks" (p. 45). Qualitative mathematical models are ill-suited to voyages in time, "above all because they are committed to traveling along one of time's many possible highways, that of the extreme *longue durée*, sheltered from all accidents, crises, and sudden breaks" (ibid.). Such is the case for the models constructed by Claude Lévi-Strauss. In each instance they are applied to "a phenomenon which develops only very slowly, almost timelessly" (ibid.). The prohibition of incest is one of these realities of the long time-span. Myths, which are slow to develop, also correspond to structures of an extreme longevity. Their mythemes, their atoms of intelligibility, conjoin the infinitely small and the very long time-span. But for the historian this extreme *longue durée* is the "excessive *longue durée*," which makes us forget "the diversity of life—the movement, the different time spans, the rifts and variations" (p. 47).

So we see the theoretician of the long time-span engaged in combat on two fronts, on the side of events and on the side of the excessively long time-span. I shall attempt to say in chapter 6 to what extent this apology for the long time-span with its twofold refusal is compatible with the narrative model of emplotment. If such were the case, the attack against the history of events would not be the historian's last word about the notion of an event, inasmuch as it is more important that an event contribute to the progress of a plot than that it be short and nervous, like an explosion.[21]

Following Braudel, the whole of the Annales school was swallowed up into the breach of the long time-span. I would like next to dwell upon another of the more significant developments of contemporary French historiography, the large-scale introduction into history of quantitative procedures borrowed from economics and extended to demographic, social, cultural, and even spiritual history. With this development another major assumption about the nature of historical events was called into question, namely, that of their uniqueness, the fact that an event never repeats itself.

Quantitative history, in fact, is basically a "serial history"—to use the expresion that Pierre Chaunu made classic.[22] It rests upon the constitution of a homogeneous series of "items," hence of repeatable facts, eventually amenable to processing by a computer. All the major categories of historical time can be ever more closely redefined in terms of a "serial" basis. For example, conjuncture moves from economic history to social history, then to history in general, with the result that it can be conceived of as a method for integrating at some given moment the greatest possible number of correlations between remote series.[23] Similarly, the notion of a structure, understood by historians in the twofold sense of the static architectural relationships of a given set and the dynamics of a durable stability, only conserves its precision if it can be referred to the intersection of numerous variables which all presuppose that they can be put in a series. Hence conjuncture tends to refer to a short span of time and structure to a long one, but as set within the perspective of "serial" history. Taken together, the two notions thus tend to designate a polarity for historical inquiry, depending whether the victory over the accidental and the event-like is carried so far as to absorb conjuncture into structure, or whether the long time-span—which is generally favored by French historiography—refuses to be dissolved into the immobile time of "frozen societies" (p. 527).

In a general way, historians—particularly specialists in economic history—are different from their economist or sociologist colleagues in that they tend to conserve a temporal connotation even for the notion of structure. The notion of the long time-span has helped them, in this battle on two fronts, to resist both the complete dechronologizing of their models and the fascination of the accidental and isolated event. But, since the first temptation comes from the neighboring social sciences and the second from the historical tradition itself, the battle has always been hottest on the front against events. In large measure the development of economic history was a response to the challenge posed by the great depression of 1929, as a means of long-term analysis that would divest that event of its catastrophic singularity. As for the battle on the front against atemporal structures, it has never been completely absent from the scene. In the face of the development of a purely quantitative economics by Simon Kuznets and Jean Marczewski, serial history was forced to distinguish itself from purely quantitative history, which was reproached for becoming locked into a nation-oriented framework by adopting national accounting as its model. What the quantitative history of the economists sacrifices on the altar of the exact sciences is precisely the long time-span, regained at such great price from the dramatic time of events. This is why a foothold in large geographic areas and an alliance with Braudel's geopolitics were necessary if serial history was to remain faithful to the long time-span and, thanks to that mediation, stay grafted to the trunk of traditional history. It is also why conjuncture and structure, even when they are opposed to each other, imprint on diachrony the primacy of an immanent logic over the accidental, isolated event.

With his history of prices, Ernest Labrousse, pursuing the trail opened by François Simiand, turned out to be the first historian to incorporate the notions of conjuncture and structure into his discipline.[24] At the same time, he showed the way to an enlarging of the field opened to quantitative analysis, by guiding his discipline from economic history to social history based on socio-professional inquiries. For Labrousse, structure is a social category. It has to do with human beings in their relationships to production and to other human beings, within those social circles that he calls classes. Since 1950, he has been engaged in calculating "social quantities," thereby indicating the exodus of statistical apparatus toward regions ever more resistant to quantification. Social quantity represents the passage from the first level, that of economics, to the second, social, level, following Marx's line but without any concern for Marxist orthodoxy. As an analytic model, economic history was thereby revealed to be capable of a branching development: on one side, demography, and even, as we shall see later, a sociocultural side, the side of *mentalités*— the third level, according to Labrousse.

The methodology of economic history marked a continuity more than a break with Marc Bloch's and Lucien Febvre's antipositivist battle. In fact, what the founders of the Annales school had wanted to fight against in the first place was fascination with the unique, unrepeatable event, then the identification of history with an improved chronology of the state, and finally—and perhaps above all—the absence of a criterion of choice, and therefore of any problem, in the elaboration of what counts as a "fact" in history. The facts, these historians never stop repeating, are not given in the documents, rather documents are selected as a function of a certain problem. Documents themselves are not just given. Official archives are institutions that reflect an implicit choice in favor of history conceived of as an anthology of events and as the chronicle of a state. Since this choice was not stated, the historical fact could appear to be governed by the document and historians could appear to receive their problems from these things as given.

In this conquest of the whole historical field by quantitative or serial history, special mention must be made of demographic history, particularly because of its temporal implications. For this discipline, what counts is first of all the number of people and then plotting these numbers in relation to the scale of the replacement of generations on this planet. Demographic history, which is to say demography in a temporal perspective, graphs the biological evolution of humanity considered as a whole.[25] At the same time, it reveals the worldwide rhythms of populations that set the long time-span on a scale of half-millennia and call into question the periodization of traditional history. Demography, finally, as taken up by historians, brings to light the link between the size of populations and levels of culture and civilization.[26]

In this sense, historical demography assures the transition between serial history on the economic level and serial history on the social level, then to the cultural and spiritual level, to recall Labrousse's three levels.

By social level we must understand a wide range of phenomena running from what Fernand Braudel in his other major work calls material civilization (or the structures of everyday life) to what others call the history of *mentalités*.[27] Material civilization constitutes a veritable subset of this level due to its own wide-ranging character: gestures, housing, food, etc. This is why its arrangement into stages of temporality, following the model of *The Mediterranean*, is held by Braudel to be so appropriate, as are the pertinence of long time-spans and number series.[28]

Our brief incursion into the field of quantitative history has had but one goal, to indicate the continuity in French historiography's struggle against the history of events and, by implication, against a directly narrative way of writing history. In this regard it is noteworthy that the new history, in order to free itself from the clutch of events, had to join together with another discipline for which time is not a major preoccupation. We have seen the history of long time-spans born from this coupling with geography, and quantitative history, insofar as it too is a history of long time-spans, is born from a coupling with economics. Such coupling of history with another discipline makes all the more pointed the question to what extent history remains historical in this marriage of convenience. In each instance, the relationship to events furnishes an appropriate touchstone.

Such is the case with historical anthropology, which seeks to transfer to historical distance the kind of detachment which geographical distance gives to anthropologists, and thereby to recover beyond the official discourse of the scribes in the era under consideration, hence beyond the learned culture, costume, gesture, and imagination—in short, popular culture. The best example of this type of study is that of Jacques Le Goff in *Time, Work, and Culture in the Middle Ages*.[29] He proposes to constitute "a historical anthropology of the preindustrial West" (p. xiv).

But the philosopher cannot fail to be interested in what is said there precisely about time. Not the time of recounted events, but time as it is represented by people of the Middle Ages. It is amusing that it should be just this representation of time that, for the historian, makes up an event. "The conflict, then, between the Church's time and the merchants' time takes its place as one of the major events of the mental history of these centuries at the heart of the Middle Ages, when the ideology of the modern world was being formed under the pressure from deteriorating economic structures and practices" (p. 30). To reach this time of people, which has become an object for the anthropological historian, and in particular to spot the advance of the merchants' time, we must interrogate the manuals of confession, where we can follow the changes in the definition and categorization of sins. To appraise this mental and spiritual unsettling of the chronological framework, we must take note of the birth and diffusion of clocks, which substitute an exact time for the rural workday and the canonical hours, punctuated by the sound of bells. It is especially when the opposition between learned and popular culture is taken as the axis of their problem that historians become anthropologists. The question then is whether such history remains historical. It does so in that the long time-span remains a time-span. And in this regard, Le Goff's mistrust about a place for the vocabulary of diachrony, a vocabulary imported from semiology and structural anthropology, recalls that of Braudel about the place of Lévi-Strauss's models.[30]

In truth, what interests the historian are not just "value systems" and their resistance to change, but also their mutations. I shall return, at the end of chapter 6, to a suggestion I will risk making now as a stepping-stone for our discussion. We may inquire whether, to remain historical, history must not elaborate as quasi-events the slow changes that it foreshortens in its memory by an effect similar to that of a speeded-up film. Does not Le Goff treat the major conflict concerning the appraisal of time itself as "one of the major events of the mental history of these centuries"? We can do justice to this expression only when we are capable of giving an appropriate epistemological framework to what I am calling here, provisionally, a quasi-event.[31]

Another way of joining history together with disciplines for which time is not a major category is expressed in the history of *mentalités*. The main disciplines referred to here are the sociology of ideologies, with a Marxist origin,

Freudian (and sometimes, though rarely, Jungian) psychoanalysis, structural semantics, and the rhetoric of forms of discourse. The kinship to anthropological history is evident. Attending to ideologies, the collective unconscious, and unrehearsed speech confers on history a sense of strangeness, of distance and difference, comparable to that of the anthropologist's gaze referred to a bit earlier. It is ordinary people, often denied the right to speak by the dominant form of discourse, who regain their voice through this type of history. Its type of rationality is also indicative of the most interesting attempt to carry quantitative analysis to the third level, that of attitudes regarding such things as sex, love, death, spoken or written discourse, ideology, and religion. If it is to remain serial history, this form of history has to find appropriate documents for establishing homogeneous series of statistically manipulatable facts. Here, as was already the case for economic history, historians are the inventors of their documents. In the earlier case these were market prices, then the required tithes. Here the emphasis is on written materials, lists of grievances, parish registers, ecclesiastical dispensations, and above all wills—"those old, sleeping documents" as someone has called them.[32]

The question of historical time will henceforth appear in a new form. According to Chaunu, quantitative analysis is only a mediating device intended to bring to light a structure, at its best a mutation, that is, the end of some structure, the rhythm of whose breakup is closely scrutinized. In this way, quantitative analysis preserves something qualitative, but it is "carefully selected and homogenized."[33] Thus it is through their temporal aspect of stability or mutation or breaking up that structures come into the field of history.

Georges Duby, whose work is an excellent illustration of the history of *mentalités*, poses the problem in similar terms. On the one hand, he accepts Althusser's definition of an ideology as "a system (possessing its own logic and rigor) of representations (images, myths, ideas, or concepts as the case may be) endowed with both existence and a historical role in some particular society."[34] Hence it is as a sociologist that he characterizes ideologies as all-encompassing, distorting, in competition with one another, stabilizing, or a source of action. These features do not refer to either chronology or narration. Yet his sociology leaves a place for history inasmuch as value systems "have their own history, whose allure and phases do not coincide with the history of population or that of production" (p. 148). And in fact it is historians who are interested in the transformation of structures, whether under the pressure of changes in material conditions and social relations, or through protest and conflict.

I should like to end this review of the contributions of French historiography to the exploration of historical time by referring to some works devoted to the relationship of people to death. They provide the most significant and most fascinating example of the conquest by quantitative analysis of the qualitative dimension of history. What is more intimate to life, more a part of it than death, or rather dying? And what is more public than people's attitudes in the face of death as inscribed in last wills and testaments? What more social than the anticipations excited by the thought of their own funerals? What more cultural than how people represent death? Hence it is easy to comprehend that the typology of death proposed by Philippe Aries, in his great book *The Hour of Our Death*, with its four models of death—the accepted death of the patriarch in the Old Testament, of the knight's test in the *Chansons de gestes*, of Tolstoy's peasant; the baroque death of the sixteenth and seventeenth centuries; the intimate death of the eighteenth and nineteenth centuries; and the forbidden and hidden-away death of postindustrial societies—should have both furnished a conceptual formulation for serial inquiries such as those of Vovelle and Chaunu, and received from them the only verification that history is capable of, given its inability to experiment with the past, namely, repeatable numerical frequencies.[35] In this respect, the history of death may not be just the farthest point reached by serial history, but perhaps by all history, for reasons that I shall discuss in volume 2.[36]

THE ECLIPSE OF UNDERSTANDING: THE COVERING LAW MODEL IN ANALYTICAL PHILOSOPHY

In leaving the methodology of French historians for the epistemology of history issuing from logical positivism, we change thought-worlds (and sometimes, although not always, continents). It is not the practice of history that fuels the argument but a more normative than descriptive concern for affirming the unity of science in the tradition of the Vienna Circle. This plea for the unity of science is incompatible with the distinction established by Windelband between an "idiographic" method and a "nomothetic" one.[37] Nor was the relation of history to narrative directly at issue in the first phase of the debate during the forties and fifties. Still, the very possibility of deriving history from narrative was directly undermined by an argument directed essentially against the thesis of the irreducibility of "understanding" to "explanation" which, in the critical philosophy of history in Germany at the beginning of the century, prolonged the distinction between idiographic and nomothetic methods.[38] If I have thought it possible to put under the single title of "eclipse of narrative" two attacks coming from two horizons as different as the French historiography of the Annales school and the epistemology stemming from English-language analytic philosophy (which stands in continuity on this point with the epistemology inherited from the Vienna Circle), it is because both take the notion of event as their touchstone and take it as given that the fate of narrative is sealed at the same time as that of events, understood as the atomic elements of historical change. This is so true that the question of the narrative status of history, which was never at stake in the first phase of the epistemological discussion (the only one considered here), did not move to the forefront, at least in the English-speaking world, until later, due to the battle over the covering law model, where it served as a counterexample opposed to this model. This diagnosis is confirmed by the case of the only French historian—Paul Veyne—who has pleaded for a return to the notion of plot in history. For him too, as we shall see, this return is tied to a vehement criticism of any claim to a scientific status that would be incompatible with the "sublunar" status of history—thereby imitating Aristotle at the same time that he rehabilitates Max Weber!

As the subsequent discussion will confirm, the attack on understanding by the partisans of the covering law model has the same result, if not the same stake, as the attack against events does for the historians of the long timespan: the eclipse of narrative.

I will take as my starting point Karl Hempel's famous article "The Function of General Laws in History." [39]

The central thesis of this article is that "general laws have quite analogous functions in history and in the natural sciences" (p. 345). Hempel is not unaware of history's interest in particular past events. On the contrary, his thesis concerns precisely the status of an event. But it does not take it as important, not to say decisive, that in history events get their properly historical status from having been initially included in an official chronicle, eyewitness testimony, or a narrative based on personal memories. The specificity of this first level of discourse is completely ignored *in favor of a direct relationship between an individual event and the assertion of a universal hypothesis, therefore of some form of regularity*. It is only owing to the subsequent discussion of the covering law model by upholders of the narrativist thesis that we can underscore the fact that, from the beginning of this analysis, the notion of a historical event was divested of its narrative status and placed within the framework of an opposition between particular and universal. The historical event was subsumed under a general concept of event that included all physical events and every noteworthy occurrence, such as the bursting of a dam, a geological cataclysm, a change in some physical state, etc. Once this homogeneous conception of what counts as an event was posited, the argument unfolded as follows.

The occurrence of an event of a specific type can be deduced from two premises. The first describes the initial conditions: prior events, prevailing conditions, and the like. The second states a regularity of a certain type, that is, a hypothesis of a universal form that, if verified, merits being called a law. [40]

If these two premises can be established correctly, we can say that the occurrence of the event under consideration has been logically deduced and therefore it has been explained. This explanation can be vitiated in three ways: the empirical statements establishing the initial conditions may be faulty; the alleged generalities may not be real laws; or the logical link between premises and conclusion may be vitiated by a sophistry or an error in reasoning.

Three comments are called for concerning the structure of explanation in this model, which, since Dray's criticism, is called the covering law model.

First, the three concepts of law, cause, and explanation overlap. An event is explained when it is "covered" by a law and when its antecedents are legitimately called its causes. The key idea is that of regularity. That is, every time an event of type C occurs at a certain place and time, an event of the specific type E will occur at a place and time related to those of the first event. The Humean idea of a cause is therefore unreservedly taken for granted. Hempel speaks indifferently of "causes" or of "determining conditions" (ibid.). This is why he attaches no importance to objections addressed to the terminology of causality, and the attempt, offered among others by Russell, to use only the terms "condition" and "function."[41] This dispute is not, however, a simple one of semantics. I shall ask below if a causal explanation—especially in history—might be possible independently of, or prior to, the idea of a law in the sense of a verified regularity.[42]

Next it must be emphasized that, in a covering law model, explanation and prediction go hand in hand. We can expect any occurrence of type C to be followed by an occurrence of type E. Prediction is just the inverted statement of the explanation in terms of an if/then statement. One result is that the predictive value of a hypothesis becomes one criterion of the validity of an explanation, and the absence of a predictive value is a sign of the incomplete character of the explanation. This remark, too, has to apply to history.

Finally, it will have been noticed that it is a question of events of only one specific type—not singular events, but eminently repeatable ones (the drop in temperature under such and such a conditions, say). Hempel sees no difficulty in this. To express every property of some individual object is an impossible task, which no one, no more in physics than anywhere else, would propose. There could be no explanation of any individual event if the explanation had to account for every characteristic of the event. All we can ask of an explanation is that it be precise and specific, not that it be exhaustive. The unique character of any event, as a consequence, is a myth which must be put beyond the horizon of science. The discussion will again and again return to this traditional chopping block in the theory of history.

If this is the universal structure of explanation applied to all events—whether natural or historical—the question is whether history satisfies this model.

Obviously, it is a highly prescriptive model. It says what an ideal explanation must be. Hempel does not think he is doing any injustice to history in so proceeding. On the contrary, assigning it such an elevated ideal is a way of acknowledging its ambition to be recognized as a science and not an art. Indeed history wants to demonstrate that events are not the result of chance, rather that they happen in conformity with the prediction we can give them, once we know about certain antecedents or certain simultaneous conditions, and once the universal hypotheses which form the major premise of the deduction of the event are stated and verified. Only at this price can prediction be distinguished from prophecy.

But the fact is that history is not yet a fully developed science, principally because the general propositions which ground its ambition to be explanatory do not merit the title of regularities. Either, as a first case, these generalities are not completely stated, as in the case of the incomplete explanations of daily life, where we take for granted tacit generalities drawn from individual or social psychology. Or, as a second case, the alleged regularities lack empirical confirmation. Apart from economics and demography, history contents itself with approximately universal hypotheses. We must place among such laws, whose verification is still too loose, all statements made in terms of probabilities, yet lacking any statistical framework. It is not their probabilistic status that is criticizable but their lack of statistical precision. In this respect, the boundary does not run between causal and probabilistic explanation but between levels of exactitude, whether this be empirical or statistical. Finally, as a third case, the alleged generalities may simply be pseudo-laws, borrowed from popular wisdom or unscientific psychology, when they are not obvious prejudices, the residue of magical or mythical "explanations" of human and cosmic realities. Therefore the line must be clearly drawn between genuine explanations and pseudo ones.

The only nuance Hempel allows to his uncompromising thesis is that, in the best case, history offers "explanation sketchs" (p. 351), resting upon regularities that, while not being explicit and verified laws, do neverthless point in the direction where precise regularities are to be discovered, and that, further, prescribe the steps that must be taken in order to satisfy the model of scientific explanation. In this sense, such explanatory sketchs stand on the side of genuine explanations, not on that of pseudo ones.

Apart from this one concession, Hempel vehemently refuses to accord any actual epistemological value to the procedures warranted by the terms empathy, understanding, or interpretation, which refer to such so-called distinctive features of the historical object as meaning, relevance, determination, or dependence. The alleged method of empathetic understanding is not a method. At most it is a heuristic procedure which is neither necessary nor sufficient, for it is possible to explain things in history without any empathetic understanding.

Nothing in the construction of this model, therefore, refers to the narrative nature of history, or to the narrative status of events, much less to the particular specificity of historical time in relation to cosmological time. As I said earlier, these distinctions are tacitly excluded as soon as no difference in principle is allowed between a historical event and a physical one which simply occurs, and as soon as it is not taken as pertinent to the historical status of an event that it was recounted in chronicles, or legendary narratives, or reports. Even an author such as Charles Frankel, who is, as we shall see, so attentive to the originality of the problematic of interpretation in history, does not incorporate within the notion of an event its contribution to the form of a narrative.[43] The events treated by historians in their works are inscribed, as are physical ones, in "singular statements asserting the occurrence of unique events at specific places and times" (p. 411). Historians simply "give an account of individual events that have occurred once and only once" (p. 410). An explanation, because it is an explanation, abolishes this feature. The logical definition of event requires that of a singular occurrence, without any intrinsic relation to narrative. This identification is so tenacious that at first even the adversaries of the covering law model were themselves in agreement that an explanation would abolish the uniqueness, the unrepeatability of events.

Following Hempel, and in his wake, the partisans of the covering law model in essence gave themselves over to the apologetic task of minimizing the discordances between the requirements of this "strong" model and the specific features of historical knowledge. The price was a "weakening" of the model so as to ensure its viability.[44]

It is not a question of depreciating the work produced by the Hempelian school when I qualify it as being apologetic. This is the case, first, because in weakening the model, these authors brought to light some features of historical knowledge that genuinely depend upon explanation and that any adverse theory must take into account.[45] Weakening a model is a positive work if it augments its applicability. Further, the work of reformulation led to an encounter with the actual work of historians—which we have become familiar with through the example of French historiography—in seeking to resolve the real or alleged difficulties afflicting historical knowledge.

The first major concession, which will be exploited in various ways by the adversaries of the model, is to allow that the explanations offered by historians do not function in history as they do in the natural sciences. History does not establish laws that figure in the major premise of the Hempelian model of deduction. It employs them.[46] This is why they can remain implicit. It is also why they can depend upon heterogeneous levels of universality and regularity. For example, Gardiner, in his *The Nature of Historical Explanation*, admitted to the rank of regularities allowed in history what he calls "law-like explanations." [47] These are a matter principally of regularities of the "dispositional" type to which Gilbert Ryle, in *The Concept of Mind*, assigned a major role in the explanation of behavior. One of the functions of the connective "because"

115

is to set an agent's action within the framework of his "habitual" behavior. This case of explanation in terms of dispositions opens the way to reflection upon the diversity of levels of imprecision that the notion of regularity allows.

This heterogeneity is completely accepted by the reader of historical works. Such a reader does not come to the text with a unique, unchanging, monolithic model of explanation in mind, but with a very broad range of expectations. This flexibility testifies that the question bearing on the structure of explanation must be completed by one bearing on its function. By function, we are to understand the correspondence between a certain type of answer and a certain type of question. For instance, the question "Why?" is one that opens the range of acceptable answers of the form "Because. . . ." In this regard, the strong model only accounts for a limited segment of the range of expectations opened by the question "Why?" and the range of acceptable answers of the form "Because. . . ." The problem, from here on, is to know what extension, and therefore what weakening, the covering law model is capable of, if we exclude any shameful return to an intuitionist or empathetic conception of historical "understanding," or, in a more general fashion, to the pure and simple substitution of understanding for explanation.

For the partisans of the covering law model, the only way to resist the dilution of explanation into more and more varied uses of "Why?" and "Because . . ." is always to refer the weak forms of the model to the strong one, and to assign the former the task of approximating the latter. In this sense, a liberal attitude with regard to the functioning of the model allows us to preserve great rigor concerning the structure of explanation. The strong model thereby remains the "logical marker" for every approximation of the same model by the weaker forms.

A second debate bears witness to the effort referred to earlier about meeting historians in their struggle to elevate their discipline to the rank of a thoroughgoing science. It has to do with the role of selection procedures in history. There is something exemplary about this debate inasmuch as it touches upon one of the difficulties most often referred to in the *Verstehen* tradition, which refuses to history an "objectivity" comparable to that of the natural sciences. In France, Raymond Aron's book remains the unsurpassed witness to this thesis. Neopositivist epistemology responded to this attack by firmly tying the fate of objectivity in history to that of the covering law model. This is why, for this school of thought, defense of this model was equivalent to a plea for objectivity in history.

Ernst Nagel's sharp reply is exemplary in this regard, for it demonstrates in practice what an analytic argument is and how it responds to the massiveness of the objection with a work of decomposition and distinctions.[48]

Do we mean by selectivity the historian's choice of a domain or a problem? No researcher escapes this. The only interesting question is whether, once a field of inquiry has been chosen, researchers are capable of taking their distance with regard to the values or passions which they have for their object. This emancipation of one's mind is not inaccessible to historians. It even defines history as "inquiry."

Do we wish to speak of the limitation of the subject matter resulting from this choice? It need not be a necessary cause of distortion unless we presuppose that to know anything we must know everything. The underlying philosophical thesis, Hegelian in origin, of the "internal" character of every relation is refuted by scientific practice, which verifies the "analytic" character of discourse.

What of selection of hypotheses? All inquiry is selective in this sense. The ending of inquiry at some point? The argument about an infinite regress is a sophism. To a definite problem there is a definite answer. The possibility of pushing the analysis further only bears witness to the progressive character of inquiry.

Finally, what if someone says that history cannot escape collective or personal prejudices? It is a truism to admit that the ideals of any inquiry are causally linked to other cultural, social, and political features. What is significant is that such prejudices can be detected and investigated. The single fact that we can distinguish what is assumed from what is not, proves that the ideal of objectivity is not a hopeless one. If not, the skeptical thesis would fall under its own claim and its validity would be limited to the circle of those who professed it. But if it escapes its own criterion, this attests that it is possible to formulate worthwhile statements about human affairs.[49]

A new obstacle to the realization of a "warranted" explanation results from the limiting of historical inquiry to what it takes as the "principal" cause of a course of events. This imputation of relative importance to causal variables appeals to a "weighing" of them which does not seem capable of being made objective. We may respond that the notion of importance is not inaccessible to analysis. Even if the truth of judgments of importance is subject to debate, it is still the case that we signify something in speaking of importance. Therefore we can set up a table of meanings associated with the assigning of degrees of importance (see Nagel, pp. 382–85).[50] Only perfecting the statistical material involved can reconcile this logic of the "weighing" of degrees of importance and practice. Until this is achieved, limited skepticism is called for, but there is no reason to transform this into wholesale skepticism. There is "substantial agreement among men experienced in relevant matters on the relative probabilities to be assigned to many hypotheses" (p. 385).

We can see that here this argument drawn from the practice of history rejoins that of the upholders of quantitative serial history in French historiography.

Let us follow this apology for the covering law model to the point where weakening the model leads to its abandonment. In this regard, the article I have already referred to by Charles Frankel is exemplary. The model is weakened in the sense that interpretation, taken in a sense close to that of *Verstehen* in the critical philosophy of history, is admitted as one necessary moment of historical knowing. The moment of interpretation is the one when historians appraise something, that is, when they attribute meaning and value to it. This moment must be distinguished from the moment of explanation, which establishes causal connections between events. Yet the effort to articulate these two moments stays within the realm of the covering law model inasmuch as, on the one hand, it is admitted that every good historian wants to distinguish between the two levels of operation and to justify epistemology in its ambition to isolate the explanatory kernel, and, on the other hand, interpretation itself is submitted to the limiting requirements of explanation.

In truth, the weakening of the model starts with a reformulating of the explanatory stage, even though Frankel holds that, ideally, the historian does not proceed any differently than do other scientists. The discordances with the model characterize the current state of affairs in history, not its epistemological ideal. Are its generalizations, as Hempel said, explanation sketchs? This is a contingent feature which does not create a gap between history and other sciences. Instead, it points to "a need for filling in the details" (p. 411). Is the tie between explanation and prediction broken? Does the historian only succeed in giving the necessary but not the sufficient conditions of an event? What is important is not that the explanation is incomplete but that "on many occasions, it seems fully to satisfy our demand for an explanation" (p. 412). For example, we can accept a simple summary of the steps of a process as an explanation. We do so in embryology as well as in all the other sciences dealing with development or evolution. Such genetic explanation suggests that "not all satisfactory explanations supply us with exactly the same type of information, and that not all requests to have something explained are unequivocal requests for a single kind of answer" (ibid.).[51] From here on, the boundary between scientific and commonsense explanations, and the type of prudential judgment we ordinarily make about human affairs, tends to become erased.

Now for the last distinctive feature about historical knowledge that is incompatible with the covering law model. In history, where generalities are highly frequent correlations rather than invariable relations, counterexamples do not invalidate general laws. It is not always true that power corrupts and it is impossible to verify that absolute power corrupts absolutely. What do historians do when they encounter exceptions to their explanations? They add restrictive clauses, thereby narrowing the applicable area of their generalizations. In this way, they disencumber themselves of proposed counterexamples.

Pushing his argument to the limits of the initial model's tolerance, Frankel accepts the fact that explanation is articulated on the basis of interpretation. But, so as not to break with the model, he holds that, to be acceptable, the more encompassing interpretations must rest upon rigorous partial explanations. How can we assign values if they are not set upon well-established causal connections? Someone may say that the opposite is equally true. Certainly in history a cause defines not just any condition but one we may act upon.[52] And in this sense, the values of action do infiltrate every assigning of causes. So we must say that to assign a cause is to admit a fact *and* to stipulate a value. But then, once again, we must apply to the concept of interpretation the same analytic spirit we applied to judgments of importance. In interpreting, we do three things that are unequally compatible with the ideal of explanation. The least compatible undertaking consists in making pronouncements about the meaning of history in terms of ends, of goals, or of ideals. We then set into play an implicit philosophy of "internal" relations that are incompatible, as we said earlier, with the "analytic" spirit, and we impose from without a transcendent, secret project on the course of history. Less contestable is the designation of *the most important cause*, be it economic or something else. Interpretation here is compatible with explanation, to the extent that it is confined to providing inquiry with the guidance of some seminal idea and to indicating degrees of importance. It is no longer, as a consequence, the only worthwhile interpretation, to the exclusion of all others. But the most interesting interpretation is the one that assigns itself the task of evaluating a sequence of events or a set of institutions in terms of their *"terminal consequences"* (p. 421), themselves evaluated in terms of their value or lack thereof.[53] The overall meaning of a process is these very terminal consequences, some of which coincide with variables in the present situation upon which we may act.[54] Thus, for Marx, the emergence of the industrial proletariat is taken as the principal cause, because it is also what bears the "cause" to be defended. This does not prevent a close attention to the facts, if the choice of terminal consequences must itself be a responsible choice. We must therefore admit that two rival interpretations account for different facts, the same events being placed according to the perspective of the different terminal consequences. Either interpetation can be objective and true with regard to the causal sequences upon which it is elaborated. We do not rewrite the same history, we write another history. But we can always discuss the two. History is not condemned to remain a battlefield between irreconcilable points of view. There is a place for a critical pluralism, which, if it admits more than one point of view, does not take them all as equally legitimate.[55]

It is difficult to go any further in the acceptance of the adverse point of view without breaking with the basic hypothesis that explanation in history does not differ fundamentally from explanation in the rest of science. Here at last lies the critical point of the whole discussion. It is to save this essential stake that the upholders of the covering law model endeavor to refer the features of historical methodology that seem discordant with the explanatory model to the present state of affairs of historical science. The declared motivation of their arguments is to defend history against skepticism and to justify its struggle for objectivity. This is why the plea for objectivity and that for the covering law model, having started hand in hand, tend to become indistinguishable.

5

Defenses of Narrative

The question of the narrative status of historical writing was not directly at stake for the epistemology of the historical sciences, neither for French historiography nor in the first phase of the discussion within the analytic school. Throughout this debate it was taken for granted that narrative is too elementary a form of discourse to satisfy, even from afar, the requirements for any science posed by the covering law model of explanation. The subsequent appearance of "narrativist" theses in the field of discussion was born from the conjunction of two currents of thought. On one side, the criticism of the covering law model had ended up in a breaking apart of the very concept of explanation, and this opened a breach for an approach to the problem from the opposite direction. On the other side, narrative became the object of a revaluation bearing essentially on its resources of intelligibility. Our narrative understanding thus found itself brought into prominence, while historical explanation lost some of its importance. This chapter is devoted to this conjunction of these two movements.

THE BREAKING UP OF THE COVERING LAW MODEL

An Explanation Lacking Legality: W. Dray

We saw at the end of the preceding chapter how the partisans of the covering law model tried to account for the gap between the model and the actual state of affairs in historical science by a double tactic, consisting on one side of weakening the model and on the other of taking a stand on historians' efforts to elevate their discipline to the rank of science. The attitude of those who discern the symptom of a basic error in the construction of the model itself, in the gap between the covering law model and the actual methodology of history, is wholly different.

William H. Dray's work, *Laws and Explanations in History*, is the best witness in this regard to the crisis in the covering law model.[1] His book responds to a disjointed problematic with a mutlifaceted structure. Three fronts are opened which are relatively discontinuous with one another. On the first one, a purely negative criticism is carried out that concludes by disconnecting the concept of explanation from that of law. On the second front, he pleads for a type of causal analysis that cannot be reduced to subsumption under laws. The positive thesis underlying the first part, namely, that we can explain things in history without recourse to general laws, thereby receives an initial application, without it being affirmed that every explanation in history must assume causal language. Finally, Dray explores a type of "rational explanation" that covers only a part of the field emancipated by the criticism of explanation in terms of empirical laws. The plea for causal analysis and that for rational explanation are not derived logically from the negative thesis that explanation in history does not need a law to be an explanation, even though they do presuppose it. They must, therefore, be discussed on their own merits.[2] Underlying the criticism of the covering law model is the conviction that it "is unlikely that we shall find any *logical* features according to which all historical explanations can be grasped together as historical. For the explanations found in history books are a logically miscellaneous lot" (p. 85, his emphasis). It is the recognition of this logical dispersion of explanation in history that opened the way to a reevaluation of our narrative understanding.

Beginning with the negative thesis that the idea of explanation in history does not imply the idea of law, Dray finds support for his criticism in the oscillations between the "strong" and the "weak" models of the partisans of the covering law model, which he was the first to call by this name. Already on a formal level, Dray notes, the formulation of the alleged tie between a law and the case it "covers" leaves room for hesitation. The term "because" does not commit us to any particular determinate logical structure, except perhaps in a dictionary written by the logicians of the covering law school. As for the relation of implication affirmed by the "deduced" character of the event, it is far from being univocal. And finally, the concept of explanation does not constrain us to affirm further a "covering" relation between laws and instances.

To these oscillations in the formulation of the bonds of implication are added variations in the formulation of the model itself. We have seen that some authors would rather weaken the model than call it into question. A scale of decreasing rigor can in this sense be traversed, from the most strict requirement for deduction to the idea of a lawlike form, passing through that of an assumed but not yet established law, one that is tacit rather than explicit, sketched out but not complete.

These oscillations are the symptom of a logical deficiency in the model itself. Indeed it can be shown that the covering law model is neither a necessary nor a sufficient condition for the events explained. It is not a sufficient condition because the alleged explanation cannot be converted into a prediction.

Something is still missing. What? Let us consider the example of a mechanical accident, say, when an automobile motor seizes. To attribute the cause to an oil leak, it does not suffice that we know the various physical laws involved. We must also be able to consider a continuous series of incidents between the onset of the leak and the motor's breakdown. In saying "continuous," we are not commiting ourselves to some philosophical aporia concerning the infinite divisibility of space and time. We limit ourselves to identifying the lower order of events and to placing them in a series that does not allow any other events lower than those cited. This "reference to a series of facts constituting the story of what happened between the leakage of the oil and the seizure of the engine does explain the seizure" (p. 70).[3] It is the same in history; the divisibility of time ends where the most detailed analysis does.

If not sufficient, explanation in terms of laws is also not necessary. Indeed, for what condition could it be necessary? Consider the example of an explanation a historian might give or has given: Louis XIV was unpopular when he died because he pursued a political program harmful to the national interests of France. Let us imagine a dialogue between this historian and a logician from the Hempelian school. How would this logician convince the historian that laws are in fact required by the preceding explanation? The logician will say, your explanation is valid due to some implicit law, such as "governments that pursue political programs harmful to the interests of their subjects become unpopular." The historian will object that he had not just any political program in mind but one such that had really been followed in the particular case under consideration. The logician will then try to fill in the gap between the law and the historian's explanation by making the law more precise through a series of additions, such as governments that commit their countries to foreign wars, that persecute religious minorities, that entertain parasites at their courts, become unpopular. Still other precisions can be added: that certain political measures failed, that they involved the king's personal responsibility, and so on without mentioning the measures the king neglected to take. The logician must then allow that, to be complete, an explanation requires an indefinite process of specifications, for at no stage can it be proved that the case covered by the historian is the only one covered by the law.[4] Just one law logically binds the historian: any government taking the same political measures, in exactly the same circumstances as those of Louis XIV, will become unpopular. But this formulation is no longer that of a law. It has to mention, in effect, all the particular circumstances of the case in question. (For example, it must not speak of war in general, but of the attack against the Jansenists, and so on.) It takes on an air of generality only by introducing the expression "exactly." The result of this operation is the production of an empty limit-case, an empty one because the notion of "exactly the same policies and circumstances" (p. 36) cannot be given meaning for any conceivable inquiry.

In return, the historian will accept a general statement such as every people similar to the French people "in the aspects specified" (p. 38) will detest a leader similar to Louis "in the respects specified" (ibid.). This law is not an empty one, since the dialectic between the logician and the historian will have furnished the means to "satisfy" the expressions in quotation marks. But this is no longer the sort of law required by the covering law model. For, far from being vague and general like implicit laws, it is so detailed a law that it is equivalent to a "law" for a single case.

In reality, such a law for a single case is not a law at all, but the reformulation, in the guise of an empirical law, of the historian's process of reasoning. The historian says, "E because $c_1 \ldots c_n$," where E designates the event to be explained and $c_1 \ldots c_n$ are the factors listed by the historian in his explanation. The logician rewrites this as "if $c_1 \ldots c_n$, then E," where "if" is equivalent to "whenever." But this equivalence is misleading, for the hypothetical form can express something other than an empirical law. It can express the principle of inference that, in similar cases, we *can* reasonably predict a result of this sort. Yet this principle is only an "inference license," stated in hypothetical form. The logical phantom of a "law" thus proceeds from the confusion between an empirical law and a principle of inference.

Two provisional conclusions follow, which later I propose to incorporate into my own analysis of the relationships between explanation and understanding in history.

The first one concerns the notion of an event, which is also at stake in the discussion in French historiography. Rejecting the covering law model seems, in effect, to imply a return to the conception of an event as unique. This assertion is false if we attach to the idea of uniqueness the metaphysical thesis that the world is made up of radically dissimilar particulars. Explanation then becomes impossible. The assertion is true, though, if we mean that, in contrast to the practitioners of the nomological sciences, historians want to describe and explain what actually happened in all its concrete details. But then what historians understand by "unique" means that nothing exists exactly like their object of inquiry. Their concept of uniqueness, therefore, is relative to the level of precision chosen for their inquiries. What is more, this assertion does not prevent them from employing general terms such as revolution, conquest of one country by another, and the like. In fact, these general terms do not commit historians to the formulation of general laws, but rather to the search for those respects in which the events considered and their circumstances *differ* from those with which it would be natural to group them under one classificatory term. Historians are not interested in explaining the French Revolution insofar as it is a revolution but insofar as its course differed from those of other members of the class of revolutions. As the definite article indicates in *the* French Revolution, historians do not proceed from the classificatory term toward the general law but from the classificatory term toward the explanation of differences.[5]

The second conclusion concerns this very explanation of differences. To the extent that it gathers together unique factors in the sense just mentioned, we can affirm that it stems from judgment rather than from deduction, where by judgment we are to understand the sort of operation undertaken by judges when they weigh opposing arguments and render a decision. In the same way, for historians to explain is to defend their conclusions against adversaries who would refer to another set of factors to uphold their own thesis. They justify their conclusions by bringing in new details to support their thesis. This way of judging about particular cases does not consist in placing a case under a law but in gathering together scattered factors and weighing their respective importance in producing the final result. Here historians follow the logic of practical choices instead of that of scientific deduction. In this exercise of judgment, another explanation different from that by laws is referred to as a "warrant"—which will be called *causal* explanation.

The plea for *causal analysis* which occupies chapter 4 of Dray's book is relatively independent of his criticism of the covering law model of explanation. Causal analysis is just one of the alternatives to explanation by the covering law model. If Dray discusses it, it is first of all because the contested model has often been presented in terms of the language of causality, for example, by Karl Popper.[6] In this sense, the causal version of the covering law model provides an appropriate transition from negative criticism to positive exploration of causal analysis. Aside from this connection offered by the polemical aspect of Dray's book, however, the examining of causal analysis finds its own justification in the use of causal language in history. Dray takes this language to be inevitable and legitimate, in spite of all the equivocations and difficulties attached to its use. Historians, in fact and legitimately, do use expressions of the form "X is the cause of Y" (which we shall distinguish later from the causal law, "the cause of Y is X"). They use them in fact with numerous variations on "cause": produces, leads to, sets in motion (or their contraries: prevented, omits, stops). They use them legitimately by assuming the explanatory force of a cause. This is what is at stake in this debate. The underlying thesis is that the *polysemy* of the word "cause" is no more an obstacle to the rule-governed usage of this term than is that of the term "to explain," with which we began. The problem is to regulate this polysemy, not to conclude that the term must be rejected.[7]

If we set aside the case in which by a cause we mean a causal law, a discussion about causal analysis in history is interesting only if there are singular causal connections whose explanatory force does not depend on a law.

Dray is fighting here on two fronts: against those who link the fate of the idea of a cause to that of the idea of a law, and against those who want to exclude all explanation from the field of historiography. Yes, historians do attempt to given causal explanations. No, causal analysis of some particular course of events cannot be reduced to the application of some causal law. Yes, historians do use expressions of the form "X causes Y" in a legitimate way; no, these explanations are not the application of a law of the form "if X, then Y."

What then is a causal analysis? It is an essentially selective analysis, aimed at verifying the credentials of this or that candidate for the function of being a cause; that is, its credentials for occupying the place of "Because . . ." in response to the question "Why?" This selection process therefore takes on the character of a contest in which the candidates must pass a certain number of tests. Causal analysis, I would put it, is a causal criteriology. It consists essentially of two tests. The first is an *inductive one*. The factor in question must be a really necessary one. The second is a *pragmatic* test. There must be a reason for selecting the condition in question from among the conditions that as a whole constitute the sufficient condition for the phenomenon.

This pragmatic test corresponds in part to the considerations of manipulability by which Collingwood defines one of the senses of the idea of a cause, namely, that which human action "has a handle on." In another way, it takes into account what *ought* to have been done, thus what can be blamed (as, for example, when we inquire as to the causes of a war). And in yet another way, the pragmatic criterion includes what precipitated the course of events, the spark or catalyst. In essence, such an inquiry is necessarily incomplete. It constitutes an eminently open inquiry.

The inductive test is the most difficult one to define correctly. It consists in justifying the assertion that "if not X, then not Y," in the absence of any rule saying "whenever X, then Y." A historian who is assumed to use similar formulas means that in this particular situation—everthing else otherwise being equal (or better, the situation being what it is)—if *this* X had not occurred, *that* Y which did occur would not have happened or would have been different. Such justification stems from a use of judgment as described earlier, which, we said, does not require a law with the form "only if." The historian "thinks away" the suggested cause "in order to *judge* what difference its nonoccurrence would have made in the light of what else he knows about the situation studied" (p. 104, his emphasis). This inductive test is not equivalent to a sufficient explanation. At most it constitutes a necessary explanation, by eliminating from the list of candidates for the role of cause those factors whose absence would not have changed the course of events. To obtain a complete explanation—or one as complete as possible—the imputed cause must still be justified positively through the process described earlier, that of "filling in" the details.[8]

The important thing for causal analysis is that the imputation of a cause in regard to some particular event does not derive from the application of a causal law. Often it is even the opposite case that is true. Many causal laws are in reality second-order generalizations based on some series of individual diagnoses of causality, established through a use of judgment and validated independently of one another. The alleged causal law, "tyranny causes revolution," is undoubtedly of this order. The same may be said of "the cause of war is greed." Such a law assumes that we have at our command particular explanations of particular wars, then that we observe a trend in the stated law. As useful as these generalizations may be for subsequent research, they are not what justify the individual explanations they rest upon.

If there is therefore no need to give up the idea of cause in history, this is so to the extent that we respect its particular logic, such as I have outlined it.

I will conclude with several strictly conservative comments. First, as concerns explanation, it seems to me that we must apply to the theory of causal analysis—as well as to rational explanations, which I have not yet spoken of—the warning addressed to the partisans of the covering law model, namely, that the explanations encountered in works of history constitute "a logically miscellaneous lot." This assertion holds against every claim to take one model of explanation as the exclusive one. This polysemy can also serve as an argument against Dray's opposite claim to separate explanation in history from the covering law model. If we limit ourselves to saying that no explanation satisfies the covering law model and that there are causal analyses that are not explanations in terms of a law, we are in error. This is why, for my part, I would prefer to emphasize the fact that laws are interpolated into the narrative fabric instead of insisting upon their inappropriateness. This is all the more true in that Dray opens the way to a more subtle dialectic between explanation and understanding when he considers the procedures for justifying a causal attribution and links them to the procedures that occur in juridical cases. The search for warrants, the weighing and evaluating of causes, the testing of candidates for the role of cause, all these activities of judgment stem from an analogy between historical and juridical argumentation which needs to be made more explicit.[9] And in this regard, the kinship among the reconstitution of a continuous series of events, the procedure of the elimination of candidates for singular causality, and the exercise of judgment needs to be shown more clearly. Hence the range must be left open from explanation by laws, to singular causal explanation, to judgment procedures, . . . to rational explanation.

On the other hand, despite the prefatory assertion of always drawing upon historians' actual argumentation, the few examples considered by Dray seem borrowed from the sort of history the French historians struggle against. In the dialectic between the logician and the historian as well as in the description of the causal analysis of singular events, it seems taken for granted that explanation always has to do with singular events. Of course, I am ready to admit that particular causal analysis is valid for any short-term or long-term change, on the condition that historians do take into account the particularity of the changes they consider. In this respect, everything said about the relativity of the notion of a unique event to the scale of an inquiry must be retained. But the broadening of the notion of event to include other changes than the kind that is illustrated by the example of the death of Louis XIV remains to be done.[10]

Most critics have seen his examination of the model of rational explanation as Dray's positive contribution to our problem (see pp. 118–55). This is not wholly wrong inasmuch as this model constitutes one coherent alternative to the covering law model. But neither is it exact, inasmuch as causal analysis already constituted an alternative to explanation in terms of laws. What is more, rational explanation does not cover the whole field opened by Dray's criticism. It is not even addressed to exactly the same examples of explanation. The previous discussion—including that of causal analysis—was applied "to explanations given of fairly large scale historical events or conditions" (p. 118). Rational explanation is applied "to a narrower range of cases," namely, "the kind of explanations historians generally give of the *actions* of those individuals who are important enough to be mentioned in the course of historical narrative" (ibid., his emphasis).

This is why, even though contesting the covering law model remains the negative central thread of Dray's whole book, we must respect the relative autonomy of the three fronts upon which he fights: *against* the covering law model; *for* causal analysis; *for* rational explanation. The relative discontinuity in these analyses bears witness precisely to what I have called the breakdown of the covering law.

The name that Dray gives to this mode of explanation sums up his program. For one thing, it applies to *actions* done by agents similar to ourselves. It thereby marks the intersection of the theory of history with that of action, therefore with what I have called our competence for using a conceptual framework for action in a meaningful way. However, because of this, it runs the risk of confining historical explanation to the domain of the "history of events," from which the new historians take their distance. This point must be kept in mind for our discussion in the next chapter. For another thing, the model still means to be a model of *explanation*. In this, Dray takes his stand equally distant from those for whom explaining something is to "cover" it with an empirical law, and those for whom understanding an action is to re-live, reenact, or rethink the intentions, conceptions, and thoughts of agents. Once again Dray is fighting on two fronts, that of the positivists and that of the idealists, to the extent that these latter theorists lock themselves into a theory of empathy which the former thinkers denounce because of its non-scientific character. In truth, among the "idealists," it is Collingwood whom Dray remains closest to. Relive, reenact, rethink, are Collingwood's terms. What needs to be demonstrated is that these operations do have their own logic which distinguishes them from psychology or heuristics, and which sets them on the terrain of explanations. The stake is therefore really "a *logical* analysis of explanation as it is given in history" (p. 121, his emphasis).[11]

To explain an individual's action in terms of reasons is to provide "a reconstruction of the agent's *calculation* of means to be adopted toward his chosen end in the light of the circumstances in which he found himself" (p. 122, his emphasis). In other words, to explain such actions "we need to know what considerations convinced him that he should act as he did" (ibid.).

Clearly we are involved here with an argument that leads directly back to the Aristotelian theory of deliberation. But let us not misunderstand the term "calculation." It is not necessarily a question of strictly deductive reasoning "recited in propositional form" (p. 123). As soon as we have to do with an intentional action, every level of conscious deliberation is allowed, from the moment these levels permit the construction of such a calculation, "the one the agent would have gone through if he had the time, if he had not seen what to do in a flash, if he had been called upon to account for what he did after the event, etc." (ibid.). To explain the action is to bring to light this calculation. It constitutes the agent's "reasons" for acting as he did. Whence the term "rational explanation."

Dray adds one important touch that goes beyond "logic." To explain is to show that what was done was "the thing to have done for the reasons given" (p. 124). To explain, therefore, is to justify, with the nuance of "appraisal" attached to this term. It means to explain in what way the action was "appropriate." Here again we need to be clear about the meaning of these words. To justify is not to ratify the choice following our moral criteria, so as to say, what the agent in question did is what I would have done too. It means "weighing" the action in terms of the agent's goals, his beliefs (even if they were erroneous ones), the circumstances he was aware of. "Rational explanation may be regarded as an attempt to reach a kind of logical equilibrium at which point an action is *matched* with a calculation" (p. 125, his emphasis). We look for an explanation precisely when we do not see the relationship between what was done and what we think we know about the agents involved. When such logical equilibrium is lacking, we seek to reconstitute it.

"Logical equilibrium" is the best term Dray could have chosen to distance himself from understanding through empathy, projection, or identification, and at the same time remove his explanation from Hempel's criticism. For to reach this point of equilibrium, we must inductively gather the evidence that allows us to evaluate the problem as the agent saw it. Only work with the documents allows this reconstruction. There is nothing instantaneous or dogmatic about this procedure. It requires work and is open to corrections. It requires these features with causal analysis.

Dray did not ask about the relations between his analysis and that of *emplotment*. The kinship between the two approaches is therefore all the more remarkable. It is particularly striking on one point. Dray observes that rational explanation involves a type of generality or universality that is not the same as for an empirical law: "If y is a good reason for A to do x, then y would be a good reason for anyone sufficiently like A to do x under sufficiently similar circumstances" (p. 132). We recognize here the notion of "probability" referred to by Aristotle: "What a man would necessarily or reasonably say or do." Dray is too occupied with polemicizing against the covering law model and distinguishing a "principle of action" from an empirical generalization to take interest in this intersection of the theory of history with that of narrative, as he had done with the theory of action. Yet we cannot forget the Aristotelian distinction between "one because of another" and "one after the other" when Dray pleads for the polysemy of the term "because," against any reduction to univocity in covering law terms.[12]

There remains, to my eyes, the major difficulty, which is not the one Dray is arguing about. To the extent that the model of rational explanation makes the theory of history intersect with the theory of action, the problem is to account for those reasons for actions that cannot be attributed to *individual* agents. Here, we shall see, is the critical point for any "narrativist" theory.

Dray is not unaware of this difficulty and does devote a section to it (pp. 137–42). He proposes three responses which do not exactly correspond with one another. We can begin by saying that there is a presumption that a given action lends itself to rational explanation "if we study it closely enough" (p. 137). This presumption is the wager that it is always possible to "save the appearance" of rationality by discovering, through hard work, the distant—and perhaps strange—beliefs allowing us to construct the presumed calculation and to reach the sought-for point of equilibrium between reasons and actions. This presumption of rationality has no limits. It includes recourse to unconscious motives, and even an "irrational" explanation is still a case of explanation by reasons.

However, this first response only holds to the degree that we can identify the individual agents of an action. What happens when rational explanation is applied to groups? Dray suggests that by an elliptical process historians do find it legitimate to personify entities such as Germany and Russia and to apply a quasi-rational explanation to these super-agents. For example, Germany's attack on Russia in 1941 can be explained by referring to Germany's fear of being attacked from the rear by Russia—as though a calculation of this sort did hold for the actions of a super-agent named Germany (see p. 140).

This ellipsis itself is justified in two ways. We can, through very detailed studies, demonstrate that the calculation in question is in the final analysis one that applies to those individuals authorized to act "for Germany." And in other cases, we extend by analogy a "typical" explanation for an individual to a group. (For example, the Puritans in the eighteenth century fought against the system of taxation in England.)

The third response is that with large-scale historical phenomena we run into what Whitehead called the "senseless side" of history, that is, that rationally explainable actions produce unintended and unwanted effects, even adverse ones. For example, Christopher Columbus's voyage can be said to be the cause of the spread of European culture, in a sense of the word "cause" that has nothing to do with Columbus's intentions. The same may be said for most large-scale social phenomena. At this point, an objection might be made that links up with French historiography's considerations about the long time-span and social history. Dray grants that the result of such large-scale changes cannot be explained by the purposes of some individual "who stage-managed the whole thing." In other words, there is no place here for referring to some equivalent or substitute for the Hegelian cunning of reason, which would still allow us to speak of unintended results of action in intentional terms. Yet this admission does not prevent more detailed inquiry into individuals' or groups' contribution to the final result and therefore into the calculations that presided over their activities. There is no one super-calculation but rather a batch of calculations to be treated in a "piecemeal" fashion.

As we see, the argument is valid only if we take the social process as equivalent to the sum of individual processes analyzed in intentional terms and if we take the gap that separates them as simply "meaningless." This equivalence, however, is a problem. There is the question, in fact, whether what distinguishes historical explanation from rational explanations of action is not first of all the scale of phenomena it refers to, namely, entities with a societal character that are not reducible to the sum of their individual members. Next there is the appearance of effects not reducible to the sum of individual intentions, and hence to their calculations. Finally, there are those changes not reducible to variations in the time experienced by individuals taken one at a time.[13] In short, how are we to tie social processes to the acts of individuals and their calculations without professing a "methodological individualism" that has yet to produce its credentials?

William Dray confines himself to the resources of a theory of action close to the one I developed in Part I under the title of mimesis$_1$. It remains to be seen whether a "narrativist" treatment of our historical understanding, which would draw upon the resources of the intelligibility of narrative stemming from mimesis$_2$, might span the gulf that remains between explanation in terms of an individual or quasi-individual agent's reasons and explanation of large-scale historical processes in terms of nonindividual social forces.

Historical Explanation According to G. H. Von Wright

Criticism of the covering law model takes a decisive step with the work of Georg von Wright.[14] It does not, as with Dray, consist in opposing causal explanation to explanation in terms of laws and constructing, as a partial alternative model, rational explanations. It aims instead at conjoining causal explanation and teleological inference within a "mixed" model, that of quasi-causal explanation, intended to account for the most typical mode of explanation in the human sciences and in history.

It is not insignificant that von Wright, a specialist in deontological logic,[15] should recognize, at the threshold of his enterprise, the duality of traditions that have presided over theory-building in the "humanistic and social" disciplines. The first tradition, which goes back to Galileo, and even Plato, gives priority to causal and mechanistic explanation. The second, which goes back to Aristotle, pleads for the specificity of teleological or finalistic explanation. The former requires a unified scientific method. The latter defends a methodological pluralism. Von Wright rediscovers this ancient polarity in the opposition, familiar to the German tradition, between *Verstehen* (understanding) and *Erklären* (explanation).[16] But even though the covering law model was forced to deny that understanding possessed any explanatory value, without for all that succeeding in accounting for the intellectual operations actually at work in the human sciences, von Wright proposes a sufficiently powerful model to get close to, through a series of successive extensions of the initial language of classical propositional logic, the domain of historical understanding, with regard to which he always recognizes an originary capacity of apprehension as regards the meaning of human action. What is interesting, for our investigation, lies exactly in this approximation without annexation of the domain of understanding through a model stemming from the enrichment of propositional logic by modal logic and the theory of dynamic systems.[17]

Whoever speaks of approximation speaks at the same time of the construction through successive extensions of some initial language of a richer model, yet one that is coherent with the theoretical requirements of this language, and also of the polarization of the theoretical model due to the attraction exercised upon it of some originary apprehension of meaning, which in the end remains external to the purely internal process of enriching the model. The question will be whether this approximation goes as far as becoming a logical reformulation of the underlying concepts of historical understanding.

Unlike the covering law model, which limits itself to superimposing a covering law upon what is given without any internal logical connection, von Wright's model extends its empire to the conditional relations between earlier and later states implied in dynamic physical systems. This extension constitutes the underlying structure for his logical reformulation of the whole problem of understanding.

There is no question here of reproducing the argumentation that governs this passage from propositional logic to the logic of dynamic physical systems. I shall limit myself to a rapid presentation of the formal-logical apparatus that governs von Wright's work.[18] He makes the following assumptions: a set of logically independent generic states of affairs (that the sun is shining, that someone is opening a door, etc.);[19] the occurrence of these states of affairs on given (spatial or temporal) occasions; the assumption that logically independent states of affairs combine with one another in a finite number of ways constituting a total state or world; the possibility of constructing a language that, through a conjunction of its sentences, describes those states that are the atoms or elements of this possible world; and, finally, the possibility of considering, among the set of states of affairs, "state-spaces" and, among these, finite state-spaces. This set of presuppositions can be summed up as follows. "Assume that the total state of the world on a given occasion can be completely described by stating for any given member of some state-space, whether or not this member obtains on that occasion. A world which satisfies this conditon might be called a *Tractatus*-world. It is the kind of world which Wittgenstein envisaged in the *Tractatus*. It is a species of a more general conception of how the world is constituted. We can call this general conception *logical atomism*" (p. 44, his emphasis).

As to saying whether the world in which we actually live satisfies this model, that remains "a deep and difficult metaphysical question, and I do not know how to answer it" (ibid.). The model indicates only that states of affairs are the sole "ontological building-bricks" of those worlds we are studying and that we do not attend to the internal structure of these bricks.

At this stage of the analysis, it is difficult to see what step has been taken in the direction of practical and historical understanding. A first significant extension concerns the addition to this system of a principle of development. Von Wright does this in the simplest possible way, by adding a rudimentary "tense-logic" to his two-valued propositional logic. Using the vocabulary of this logic, we add a new symbol T which is reducible to a binary connector. "The expression 'pTq' can be read: '(now) the state p obtains *and next*, viz., on the next occasion, the state q obtains'. . . . Of particular interest is the case when they are state-descriptions. The whole expression then says that the world is now in a certain state and on the next occasion in a certain total state, the same or a different one as the case may be" (p. 45). If we consider further that the p and q that frame the T can also themselves contain the symbol T, we can construct chains of states marked by succession which allow us to state fragments of the world's history, where the term "history" indicates both the succession of total states of the world and the expressions depicting that succession. We must further enrich the calculus of the connective T, first with a temporal quantifier ("always" "never," "sometimes"), then by a modal operator M. These successive additions govern the formalizing of the logic of conditions as well as what von Wright will later call causal analysis.

Instead of developing this calculus further, he limits himself to a "quasi-formal method of exposition and illustration" bringing into play simple to-pological figures (or "trees") (p. 48). These figures consist only of total states of the world (made up of n elementary states of affairs), represented by small circles, a progression from left to right from one total state to another, hence a "history," represented by the line connecting the circles, and finally alternate possible progressions, represented by branches of the tree.

As formal as this model may be, it already bears the imprint of every subsequent development. The most fundamental condition of history is constituted by the "freedom of movement"—the theoretically unlimited indetermination—the world has, or would have had, at each stage of the progression. We must never lose sight of the fact that, when we speak of a system, we have only to do with "a fragment of the history of the world." "A system, in this sense, is defined through a state-space, an initial state, a number of stages of development, and a set of alternative moves for each stage" (p. 49). Far then from the idea of a system excluding the intervention of free and responsible subjects—whether it be a question of making a plan or a physical experiment—it fundamentally conserves this possibility and calls for it as its complement. How?

A second addition is necessary here, if the logic of dynamic physical systems is to rejoin our originary understanding of action and history. It concerns the status of causal explanation in relation to causal analysis, it being understood that it is the former that is of interest to understanding.

Causal analysis is an activity that runs through systems in the form of topological trees. Considering some final state, it inquires into the "causes" of its coming into being and its composition in terms of necessary and sufficient conditions. Let us briefly recall the distinction between these two types of condition. To say that p is a sufficient condition of q is to say that whenever p, then q (p suffices to assure the presence of q). To say that p is the necessary condition of q is to say that whenever q, then p (q suffices to assure the presence of p). The difference between these two types of conditions is illustrated by the asymmetry in how the system is considered, that is, whether it is approached retrogressively or progressively, due to the alternatives opened by the branches. Causal *explanation* differs from causal *analysis* in that in the latter a system is given and we explore the conditional relations internal to the system, whereas in causal explanation an individual occurrence of a generic phenomenon (an event, process, or state) is given and we look for a system wherein this generic phenomenon—the *explanandum*—can be linked to another one following some relation of conditionality.

The reader will recognize the step being taken in the direction of the human sciences by this passing from causal analysis to causal explanation, and by the application to the latter of the distinction between a necessary and a sufficient condition. The sufficient condition relation governs manipulation (in producing p we bring about q). The necessary condition relation governs prevention (in setting aside p we prevent everything from happening for which p is a necessary condition). We respond to the question "Why did such a state necessarily happen?" in terms of a sufficient condition. On the other hand, we respond to the question "How was it possible for such a state to occur?" in terms of a necessary, but not sufficient, condition. In the explanation of the first kind, prediction is possible. Explanations of the second kind do not authorize prediction, but rather retrodiction, in the sense that, beginning from the fact that something has happened, we infer, backward through time, that the antecedent necessary condition must have occurred and we look for its traces in the present, as is the case in cosmology, geology, and biology, as well as, I shall say later, in certain historical explanations.

We are now ready for the decisive step, the articulation of causal explanation on the basis of what we originally understand *action* as being. (Note that at this stage the theories of action and of history overlap.) The phenomenon of "interference," which we anticipated in speaking of producing and bringing about, or of setting aside and preventing, requires such articulation, in the sense that it conjoins that ability to do something of which an agent has an immediate understanding, with the internal conditional relations of a system. The originality of *Explanation and Understanding* is that it seeks the condition of such interference in terms of the very structure of systems.

The key concept is that of the closure of a system, which comes from causal analysis. In fact a system can be called closed only on some occasion, for a given exemplification. An occasion—or a sequence of occasions—is given, where its initial state occurs and the system unfolds following one of its possible courses of development over *n* given steps. Among the possible types of closure we can include isolating a system from external causal influences. No state, at any step of the system, has an antecedent causal condition outside the system. Action realizes another noteworthy type of closure, in that it is in doing something that an agent learns to "isolate" a closed system from its environment and to discover the possibilities of development inherent to this system. The agent learns this by setting the system in motion, beginning from some initial state the agent has "isolated." It is this setting things in motion that constitutes interference, at the intersection between one of the agent's abilities and the resources of the system.

How does this intersection occur? Von Wright's argument runs as follows. Given *a*, the initial state of a system for a given occasion, assume "now there is a state α such that we feel confident, on the basis of past experience, that α *will not change* to a state *a*, unless *we change it* to *a*. And assume this is something (we know) *we can do*" (p. 60, his emphases). These sentences contain the whole theory of interference. Here we touch something irreducible. I am certain that I can. . . . No action would happen and, in particular, no scientific experiments would occur, without this confidence and this assurance that through our interference we can produce changes in the world. And this assurance does not depend upon a relation of conditionality. Instead α marks an interruption of the chain: "α, we assumed, will not change to a unless *we* change it" (p. 61, his emphasis). Conversely, we can simply let the world change without our interference. Thus we have "to isolate a fragment of the world's history to a closed system and get to know the possibilities (and necessities) which govern the developments inside a system. . . . partly by repeatedly putting the system in motion through acts of producing its initial stage and then watching ('passively') the successive stages of its development, and partly by comparing these successive stages with developments in systems originating from different initial states" (pp. 63–64).

Von Wright is correct when he states that "in the idea of putting systems in motion the ideas of action and causation meet" (p. 64). Here he renews a relationship with one of the oldest meanings of the idea of a cause, of which language has conserved a trace. Science may well struggle against analogical and abusive uses of the idea of a cause as some responsible agent, but this idea has its roots in the idea of *doing something* and of intentionally interfering with the course of nature.[20]

As for the logical structure of "doing something," von Wright adopts the distinctions introduced by Arthur Danto.[21] With Danto, he distinguishes between *doing something* (without having to do something else in the meantime) and *bringing something about* (by doing something else). We have to decide whether to say: "The thing done is the result of an action; the thing brought about is the consequence of an action" (p. 67). This distinction is important because interference in a system rests finally on the first type of actions, which Danto calls "basic actions." The tie between a basic action and its result is intrinsic and logical, not causal (if we retain from the Humean model the idea that cause and effect are logically extrinsic to each other). Action is therefore not the cause of its result—the result is a part of the action. So in this sense, the action of putting a system in motion, reduced to a basic action, identifies the initial state of a system with the result of an action, in a non-causal sense of the word "result."

The metaphysical consequences of this concept of interference are important and indirectly concern history, inasmuch as it relates actions. Being able to do something, we say, is to be free: "In the 'race' between causation and agency, the latter will always win. It is a contradiction in terms to think that agency could be completely caught in the nets of causality" (p. 81). If we doubt this, it is first because we take as our models the phenomena of disabilities and incapacitations, rather than successful interferences, which rest upon the intimate certainty we have of being able to do something. This certitude is not derived from acquired knowledge bearing on our inabilities. If we doubt our freedom to do something, it is because we extrapolate to the whole world the regular sequences we have observed. We forget that causal relations are relative to the fragments of the history of a world that has the characteristics of a closed system. But the capacity to put systems in motion by producing their initial states is a condition for their closure. Action is therefore implied in the discovery of causal relations.

Let us stop at this stage of the demonstration. Are we justified in saying that the theory of dynamic systems furnishes a logical reformulation of what we have already understood as being an action, in the strong sense of the term, that is, as implying an agent's conviction of being able to do something? It does not seem so. Action's lead over causality, suggested in the text just cited, is definitive. Causal explanation runs after our conviction of being able to do something but can never catch up. Approximation, in this sense, is not a logical reformulation without any remainder, but rather the progressive reduction of the interval that allows logical theory to explore the frontier it has in common with understanding.

The reader will have noted that, in my analysis of the phenomenon of interference, I have not distinguished the theory of action and that of history. Or rather, the theory of history has been considered as only one mode of the theory of action.

The extension of the initial logical model is guided, in its approximation of the historical field, by another phenomenon of which we have an understanding just as originary as that of our ability to do something, namely, the understanding we have of the intentional character of action. This intentional character was in one sense implicitly contained in the earlier analysis of "doing something." With Danto, we in effect distinguished basic actions, by which we do something without an intervening intermediary action, and those other actions, by means of which we do something *so that* something else happens—that is, those things we bring about, and, among them, those which we bring about through other people. We are going to see what extending of the model this originary apprehension of meaning gives rise to, and we shall ask ourselves whether the new approximation this extension gives rise to can take advantage of a full logical reformulation of our understanding of the intentional character of action.

The adding of teleological explanation to causal explanation is called for by the logic of "in order that." Let us set aside the case of quasi-teleological explanation which is only disguised causal explanation, as when we say a wild animal is attracted by its prey, or that a rocket is drawn to its target. The teleological language cannot conceal the fact that the validity of these explanations rests entirely on the truth of their nomic connections. Adaptive phenomena, and in general functional explanations in biology and history, arise from this type of explanation. (Conversely, we shall see later, history presents quasi-causal explanations which, in this instance, conceal in a causal vocabulary, in the nomic sense of this word, genuine segments of teleological explanation.) Teleological explanation bears on actionlike forms of behavior. The phases of an action, in its outer aspect, are not tied together here by a causal bond. Their unity is constituted by their being subsumed under the same *intention*, defined by what the agent intends to do (or to abstain from doing, or to neglect to do).

Von Wright's thesis is that intention cannot be treated as a Humean cause of behavior, if we define such causes by the distinctive feature that the cause and effect are logically independent of each other. Von Wright is here adopting the "logical connection argument," which says that the tie between a reason for acting and the action itself is an intrinsic, not an extrinsic, one. "It is a motivational mechanism and, as such, not causal but teleological" (p. 69).

The question posed here is knowing to what point the logic of teleological explanation accounts for what has already been understood as an intention. As previously in the analysis of interference, we discover a new relation between understanding and explaining. It is no longer a matter of incorporating an "I can" into a causal chain but an intention into a teleological explanation. To succeed at this, it suffices to take teleological explanation as an inverted practical inference, written as follows.

> A intends to bring about *p*.
> A considers that he cannot bring about *p* unless he does *a*.
> Therefore A sets himself to do *a*.

In a teleological explanation, the conclusion of the practical inference is both a premise and the major term of the conclusion: A sets himself to do *a* "because" A intends to bring about *p*. The practical inference, therefore, is what has to be considered. But in order "to become *teleologically explicable*. . . . behavior must first be *intentionalistically understood*" (p. 121, his emphasis). "Intentional" and "teleological" are thus terms that overlap without being identical with each other. The *description* in which the action to be explained is stated, von Wright calls intentional; the *explanation* itself which brings into play a practical inference, he calls teleological. The two terms overlap inasmuch as the intentional description is required in order to constitute the premise of a practical inference. They are distinct inasmuch as the teleological explanation is applied to objects distant from an intention, which are reached precisely at the end of the practical inference. On one side, therefore, the intentional description only constitutes the rudimentary form of a teleological explanation. Only the practical inference brings about the passage from the intentional description to the teleological explanation properly speaking. On the other side, there would be no need for a logic of the practical syllogism if an immediate apprehension of the meaning bearing on the intentional character of the action did not give rise to it. Just as in the movement between our lived experience of acting and causal explanation, action always won, must we not say that in the movement between intentional interpretation of action and teleological explanation, the former always wins? Von Wright comes close to admitting this in the passage already cited: "In order to become *teleologically explicable*. . . . behavior [mentioned in the conclusion of the practical syllogism] must first be *intentionalistically understood*." And he also says: "a teleological explanation of action is normally preceded by an act of intentionalist *understanding* of some behavioral data" (p. 132, his emphasis).[22]

Let me make my point another way: in completing causal explanation with teleological explanation, have we reached that understanding of history that I tie to narrative understanding?[23] In truth, we have not yet accounted for what distinguishes the theory of history from that of action. The practical syllogism as just described allowed me to lengthen, if I may put it this way, the range of the intentional aim of action. This is why teleological explanation by itself does not allow us to distinguish history from action. In fact, we have only spoken until now of history in an extremely formal sense. A system, we said, is "a fragment of the history of a world." But this assertion is valid for every possible world satisfying the criteria for a "*Tractatus*-world." The term "history," in the concrete sense of a "story," appears just once in the analysis of teleological explanation. It is introduced in the following way. We can observe with Wittgenstein that intentional behavior resembles the use of language. "It is a gesture whereby I mean something" (p. 114). The use and the understanding of language presuppose the context of a linguistic community, which is a life-community. "An intention," we are told in Wittgenstein's *Philosophical Investigations* (section 337), "is embedded in its situation, in human customs and institutions." One result is that we cannot understand or teleologically explain a form of behavior completely foreign to us. It is this reference to the context of an action that calls for the comment that "the behavior's intentionality is its *place* in a story about the agent" (von Wright, p. 115, his emphasis). It is not sufficient therefore to establish the equivalence between intentionality and teleological explanation to account for explanation in history. It is also necessary to give a logical equivalent for the relationship of an intention to its context, which, in history, is made up of all the circumstances and all the unintended effects of the action.

It is to approach a degree closer to this particular status of explanation in history that von Wright introduces the concept of quasi-causal explanation.

In a general way, quasi-causal explanation takes the form: "this happened because. . . ." For example, a people rose up in rebellion because the government was corrupt. This explanation is said to be causal because the *explanans* refers to a factor that preceded the *explanandum*. But it is only quasi-causal, for two reasons. The negative reason is that the validity of the two statements does not require—as is the case for causal explanation and for quasi-teleological explanation—the truth of a lawlike connection. The positive reason is that the second statement contains an implicitly teleological structure. The goal of the uprising was to throw off the evil the people were suffering.

What therefore is the relation between quasi-causal explanation and teleological explanation?

Let us say first of all that it is not the only mode of explanation in history. History seems rather, from an explanatory point of view, to constitute a mixed genre. Hence, if there is a place for explanations of a causal type, that place "is peculiar and in a characteristic sense subordinate to other types of explanation" (p. 135).[24]

Causal explanation occurs in two major forms: explanation in terms of sufficient conditions (why did this type of state of affairs necessarily occur?) and explanations in terms of necessary conditions (how was it possible that . . . ?). The subordination of these two forms of causal explanation to other types of explanation can be shown in the following way. Consider the ruins of a city. What was the cause of its destruction? A flood or an invasion? We have a Humean cause (a physical event) and a Humean effect (another physical event, the conquest being considered as a physical agent). But this fragment of causal explanation is not, as such, the province of history. It arises only indirectly from history, inasmuch as, behind the material cause, a background of political rivalries takes shape between cities and inasmuch as, beyond the material effect, political, economic, and cultural consequences of the disaster develop. It is this non-Humean cause and non-Humean effect that historical explanation wants to tie together. In this first type, therefore, the "role of the causal explanation proper is often to link the nonhumean causes of its *explanans* with the nonhumean effects of its *explanandum*" (p. 137).[25]

Here is an explanation in terms of necessary conditions. How could the inhabitants of this place have been able to construct such a colossal city wall! The *explanandum* is a Humean effect: the walls are still standing. The *explanans* is also a Humean cause: the material means used for their construction. But the explanation is only a historical one if it takes a detour through action (city planning, architecture, etc.). The *explanandum* is then the result of this action, in the sense that we said that a result of action is not a Humean effect. Once again the causal explanation is one segment of the historical explanation, which also includes a non-lawlike (causal) segment.[26]

As for quasi-causal explanation, it is significantly more complex than are the preceding forms. The answer to the question "Why?" is extraordinarily ramified in it. The example introduced earlier (that the people rose up because their government was corrupt) masks the real complexity of the historian's work. Consider the thesis that the First World War broke out "because" the Austrian archduke was assassinated at Sarajevo in July 1914. What kind of explanation is this supposed to be? Concede for the sake of argument that the cause and effect are logically independent; in other words, that the two events are considered as different from each other.[27] In this sense, the explanation clearly has a causal form. Yet true *mediation* is assured by the whole range of motivations affecting the parties involved. This range of motivations must be schematized by an equal number of practical inferences, which engender new facts (in virtue of the link we have spoken of between intention and action in a practical syllogism). These facts constitute new situations for all the agents, who evaluate their situation by incorporating the new fact into the premises of their new practical inferences, which in turn engender new facts which affect the premises of the practical inferences utilized by the various parties involved.[28]

Quasi-causal explanation thus turns out to be more complex than rational explanation in Dray's sense of this term. This latter form only overlaps the properly teleological segments of the "mixed" model—the causal-teleological aspects. These segments do derive from "a set of singular statements which constitute the premises of practical inferences" (p. 142). But, if it is true that these segments of a practical inference are not reducible to nomic connections, quasi-causal explanation, in turn, is not reducible to the reconstruction of a calculation, as in rational explanation.

In sum, quasi-causal explanation correctly restores several specific characteristics of explanation in history. First, the conjunction between causal explanation and the theory of action due to the phenomenon of interference allows us to include within the mixed model the reference of history to human actions, whose signification as action is attested to by the conviction the agent has that he is able to do what he does. Further, the teleological segments of the explanatory schema testify to the fact that it is reasonable for the historian to inquire about the intentions of actors in history in terms of a practical inference arising out of a specific logic, that which was inaugurated by the Aristotelian theory of the practical syllogism. Finally, the model expresses the necessity of coordinating these modes of an ability to do something and these segments of practical inference with nonpractical and nontelelogical segments of a properly causal type.

In return, we can ask whether, despite the extraordinary effort at attaching the various modes of explanation to a very powerful logical model, the types of explanation are not more scattered than ever.

We have, in fact, a proposal for three schemas of historical explanation, without having been shown how the first two are incorporated into the third one. Moreover, an important scattering factor appears on the causal level. In a properly analytic approach, we are led to distinguish between "external" factors (climate, technology, etc.) and "internal" ones (motives, reasons, etc.), without being able to say which are "causes" and which are "effects." An integrating factor appears to be lacking here, whose importance and perhaps unavoidability are indicated by ideologies. From its side, the motivational field contains factors as disparate as commands, hindrances, normative pressures, badges of authority, sanctions, and the like which add to the scattering of explanation. It is difficult to see how all these heterogeneous causes are to be incorporated into the premises of a practical syllogism. Here we touch upon the claim of overall explanations such as those of historical materialism. Since it is equally impossible to prove them with a priori reasons or to refute them on the basis of experience alone, we have to admit that the "prime measure of their truth is their fertility for furthering our understanding of history or the social process" (p. 145). The boundary between scientific explanation and ideology is revealed as a fragile one, owing to the lack of an effort, which we shall only encounter in Hayden White, to integrate into historical explanation more numerous variables than those considered by von Wright and to confer on all these explanatory modes the unity of a style.

To stick with the model of quasi-causal explanation, in its most elementary presentation, however, we might ask what assures the unity of the nomic and the teleological segments inside the overall schema. This discontinuity inside the model, joined to the other scattering factors of explanation just referred to, leads us to ask whether a guideline from the order of understanding is not lacking for holding together the nomic and the teleological segments of a quasi-causal explanation. For me, this guideline is plot, insofar as it is a synthesis of the heterogeneous. Plot, in effect, "comprehends" in one intelligible whole, circumstances, goals, interactions, and unintended results. May we not say, therefore, that plot is to quasi-causal explanation what the assurance of our ability to do something was earlier to an agent's interfering in a nomic system, and what intentionality was to teleological explanation? Must we not, in the same way, say that causal explanation must be preceded by our narrative understanding, in the sense that we could say with von Wright that a "teleological explanation of action is normally preceded by an act of intentionalist *understanding* of some behavioral data"? Is this not so because in understanding a plot, we take as a whole nomic and teleological segments, because we look for a model of explanation appropriate to that eminently heterogeneous concatenation that the diagram for quasi-causal explanation so well throws into relief?

I find some justification for my interpretation in von Wright's own analysis. Each result of a practical syllogism is said to create a new fact which changes the "motivation background" assignable to the action of different historical agents. Is not this change what we have constantly called the circumstances of an action, and what narrative incorporates into the unity of the plot? Is not the virtue of the explanatory schema, consequently, that it generalizes the notion of circumstances, to the point of making it designate not just an initial situation, but all the interpolated situations which, by their novelty, constitute a motivation background within the field of interactions? That a fact affects the premises of a practical inference, that a new fact emerges from the conclusion drawn from the premises, is what must be understood as a synthesis of the heterogeneous, before the logic of explanation proposes a more adequate reformulation of it. But this reformulation, far from substituting itself for our narrative understanding, remains an approximation of a more original operation on the same level as our certitude of being able to do something and an intentional description of behavior.

NARRATIVIST ARGUMENTS

The bringing together of history and narrative, I said at the beginning of this chapter, is born from the conjunction of two movements of thought. To the weakening and breaking up of the covering law model corresponded a reevaluation of narrative and its resources of intelligibility. The fact is that for the advocates of the covering law model, narrative was too elementary and too poor a mode of articulation to claim as explanatory. I shall say, using the vocabulary proposed in Part I of this work, that for these authors narrative has only an episodic character, not a configurational one.[29] This is why they saw an epistemological break between history and narrative.

The question now is whether the reconquest of the configurational features of narrative justifies hope that our narrative understanding can take on an explanatory value, at the same time that historical explanation ceases to be measured by the standard of the covering law model. My own contribution to this problem will be born, in the next chapter, from the admission that a "narrativist" conception of history only partially answers this expectation. This conception does tell us what prior mode of understanding explanation is grafted to, but it does not give us a narrative equivalent or substitute for explanation. This is why I am looking for a more indirect tie between historical explanation and our narrative understanding. The present investigation will not have been in vain, however, inasmuch as it will have allowed us to isolate one necessary but not sufficient component of historical knowledge. A half failure remains a half success.

"Narrative Sentences" According to Arthur Danto

It is noteworthy that the first plea in favor of a narrativist interpretation of history should have been formulated within the framework of analytic philosophy itself. It is found in Arthur C. Danto's book, *Analytic Philosophy of History*.[30]

The guiding thread of his argument is not so much the epistemology of historiography, as it is practiced by historians, as it is the conceptual framework governing our use of a certain type of sentences called narrative sentences. This inquiry stems from analytic philosophy, if we mean by this term the description of our ways of thinking and talking about the world, and correlatively the description of the world such as these ways of thinking and speaking oblige us to conceive it. Analytic philosophy, so understood, is in essence a theory of descriptions.

Applied to history, this analytic conception of philosophy comes down to asking to what extent our ways of thinking and speaking about the world involve sentences using verbs in the past tense and irreducibly narrative statements. This type of question, according to Danto, is carefully avoided by empiricism, which only deals with present-tense verbs corresponding to statements about perception. Linguistic analysis in this way implies a metaphysical description of historical existence.[31] By this quasi-Kantian turn, analytic philosophy of history excludes in principle and as a hypothesis what Danto calls "substantive philosophy of history." Generally speaking, this is any Hegelian type of philosophy of history. Analytic philosophy of history rightly attributes to such philosophy the claim to grasp the whole of history, but it interprets this claim as follows. To talk about the whole of history is to compose a complete picture of the past and the future. But to pronounce on the future is to extrapolate from the configurations and concatenations of the past in the direction of what is still to come. This extrapolation, constitutive of prophecy, consists, in turn, of speaking about the future in terms appropriate to the past. But there is no history of the future (nor, as we shall see later, a history of the present) due to the nature of narrative sentences, which redescribe past events in light of subsequent ones unknown to the actors themselves. Such a meaning can be conferred on events "only in the context of a *story*" (p. 11, his emphasis). The vice of substantive philosophies of history, as a consequence, is that they write narrative sentences with regard to the future when they can only be written with regard to the past.

The argument is an impecable one so long as it is formulated in negative terms. If the philosophy of history is thought concerning the whole of history, it cannot be the expression of a narrative discourse appropriate to the past. But the argument cannot eliminate the hypothesis that discourse about the whole of history does not have a narrative nature and constitutes its meaning in another way. Hegelian philosophy of history is assuredly not narrative. Nor can we say that the anticipation of the future in a philosophy or theology of hope is narrative. On the contrary, narration is there reinterpreted beginning from hope, certain founding events—for example, the Exodus or the Resurrection—being interpreted as marking out the path of hope.

As long as we keep the argument in its negative form it has the twofold virtue of delimiting in an almost Kantian way the space where narrative sentences are valid and imposing a limit on them. Not only, as Danto rightly says, is narrative discourse intrinsically incomplete, since every narrative sentence is subject to revision by a later historian, but also every intelligible thing we can say about history does not inevitably have a narrative character. This second implication is directed against what remains dogmatic in the analytic philosophy of history, in spite of its deliberately critical turn when it sets out the internal limits of historical knowledge. It is not certain that "what the substantive philosophy of history attempts is to make the same kind of statement about the future that historians try to make about the past" (p. 26).

The presuppositions for an analytic philosophy of history having been stated, the study of narrative sentences presents itself as the study of a *class* of sentences. It establishes the differentiating feature of historical knowledge and, in this sense, provides a minimal characterization of history. I am not saying, however, that it attains the core of historical understanding, inasmuch as the "context of history" is not defined by the structure of the narrative sentence. The properly discursive feature of history is missing, as we shall see later.

This study rests on the theory of descriptions as applied to one particular sector of reality, namely, the changes produced by human action. The same change stemming from human action can be variously described and a narrative sentence is one of the possible descriptions of such action. I shall speak later about what distinguishes these accounts that we give of action, within the framework of what is usually called the theory of action.

Danto's ingenious idea is to approach the theory of narrative sentences by way of a detour: criticism of the prejudice that the past is determined, fixed, eternally standing still in its being, while the future is open and undecided (in the sense of Aristotle's and the Stoics' "future contigencies"). This presupposition rests upon the hypothesis that events fall into a receptacle where they accumulate without being able to be altered; neither their order of appearance can be changed, nor can anything be added to their content, except by adding to what follows them. A complete description of an event should therefore register everything that happened, in the order in which it happened. But who could do such a thing? Only an Ideal Chronicler could be such an absolutely faithful witness and absolutely sure about this entirely determined past. This Ideal Chronicler would be gifted with the faculty of being able to give an instantaneous transcription of whatever happens, augmenting his testimony in a purely additive and cumulative way as events are added to events. In relation to this ideal of a complete and definitive description, the historian's task would be merely to eliminate false sentences, to reestablish any upset in the order of true sentences, and to add whatever is lacking in this testimony.

The refutation of this hypothesis is simple. One class of descriptions is missing from this absolute chronicle, the one precisely in terms of which an event cannot be witnessed; that is, the whole truth concerning this event cannot be known until *after the fact* and long after it has taken place. This is just the sort of story only a historian can tell. In short, we have neglected to equip the Ideal Chronicler with a knowledge of the future.

We can now define narrative sentences: "they refer to at least two time-separated events though they only *describe* (are only *about*) the earliest event

145

to which they refer" (p. 143, his emphasis). Or more exactly, they "refer to two distinct and time-separated events, E_1 and E_2." And they "*describe* the earliest of the events referred to" (p. 152, his emphasis). It is also necessary to add that the two events must both be in the past as related to the time of the utterance. Three temporal positions are therefore implied in a narrative sentence: that of the event described, that of the event in terms of which the first event is described, and that of the narrator. The first two concern the statement, the third its being stated.

The paradigmatic example which this analysis rests upon is illustrated by the following sentence. In 1717, the author of *Rameau's Nephew* was born. No one, at that time, could utter such a sentence, which redescribes the birth of a child in light of another event, the publication of Diderot's famous book. In other words, writing *Rameau's Nephew* is the event in terms of which the first event—Diderot's birth—is redescribed. In a while I shall pose the question whether this type of sentence, by itself, is typical of historical narrative.

This analysis of narrative sentences has several implications. The first one takes the form of a paradox concerning causality. If an event is significant in light of future events, the characterization of one event as the cause of another one may occur subsequent to the event itself. It might seem, then, that a subsequent event transforms a prior one into a cause, therefore that a sufficient condition for the earlier event is produced later than the event. But this is a sophism, for what is determined after the fact is not some part of the event but the predicate "is the cause of. . . ." We must say therefore that E_2 is a necessary condition for E_1 to be a cause, given an appropriate description. We are simply repeating in another way that "is the cause of . . ." is not a predicate available to the Ideal Chronicler and only characterizes narrative sentences. Examples of such a retrospective use of the category "cause" are numerous. A historian will readily say, "Aristarchus, in 270 B.C., anticipated Copernicus's theory published in A.D 1453." Similar expressions—"anticipated," "began," "preceded," "provoked," "gave rise to"—appear only in narrative sentences. A large part of the concept of significance stems from this peculiarity of narrative sentences. For whoever visits the birthplace of a famous person, this site is meaningful or important only in light of subsequent events. In this sense, the category of significance lacks meaning for the Ideal Chronicler, even though he is a perfect witness.

A second epistemological implication is even more interesting, for it allows us to distinguish the properly narrative description of action from ordinary descriptions of it. Here Danto says something that Dray could not anticipate with his model of rational explanations, which takes into account only historical actors' calculations at the moment when they occurred. Both descriptions, it is true, have in common their use of verbs that we may call "project verbs." These verbs do more than simply describe a particular action. Expressions such as "make war" or "raise cattle," or "write a book" contain verbs

that cover many detailed actions, which may be totally discontinuous and im-
plicate numerous individuals in a temporal structure for which the narrator
carries the responsibility. In history we encounter innumerable uses of such
project verbs, which organize numerous microactions into one unique overall
action. But in ordinary discourse about action, the meaning of a project verb is
not affected by the outcome of the action—whether it takes place or not,
whether it succeeds or fails. So if history is characterized by statements that
account for the truth of a particular occurrence in terms of its unintended consequences, the truth of the statements bearing on the subsequent events is important for the meaning of the narrative description.

The theory of narrative sentences thus is valuable in a discriminating way as
regards discourse about action in ordinary language. The discriminating factor
lies in the "retroactive re-alignment of the Past" (p. 168) brought about by the
properly narrative description of action. This realignment is far-reaching. To
the extent that the past is considered temporally in terms of unintended consequences, history tends to weaken the intentional accent in action: "frequently
and almost typically, the actions of men are not intentional under those descriptions given of them by means of narrative sentences" (p. 182). This last
feature accentuates the gap between the theory of action and that of history:
"For the whole point of history is *not* to know about actions as witnesses
might, but as historians do, in connection with later events and as parts of
temporal wholes" (p. 183).[32] This gap between the theory of action and narrative theory helps us better to understand in what sense narrative description is
one kind of description among other kinds.

The final consequence is that *there is no history of the present*, in the
strictly narrative sense of that term. Such a thing could be only an anticipation
of what future historians might write about us. The symmetry between explanation and prediction, characteristic of the nomological sciences, is broken at
the very level of historical statements. If such narration of the present could
be written and known to us, we could in turn falsify it by doing the opposite of
what it predicts. We do not know at all what future historians might write
about us. Not only do we not know what events will occur, we do not know
which ones will be taken as important. We would have to foresee the interests
of future historians to foresee under what descriptions they will place our actions. Peirce's assertion "the future is open" means "no one has written the
history of the present." This latter remark brings us back to our starting point,
the internal limit of narrative statements.

In what measure does the analysis of narrative sentences clarify the problem
of the relationships between our narrative understanding and historical
explanation?

Danto nowhere declares that the theory of history is exhausted by his analysis of narrative sentences. Nowhere does he say that a historical text is reduci-

ble to a succession of narrative sentences. The constraints imposed on the true description of an event by the temporal structure of a narrative sentence only constitute a "minimal characterization of historical activity" (p. 25).

Still it is true that the very choice of narrative sentences as the minimal constraint might leave the impression that the statements describing pointlike events, or at least dated ones, in light of other pointlike or dated events constitute the logical atoms of historical discourse. In fact it is only a question, at least until Danto's chapter 10, of "true descriptions of events in *their* past" (ibid.) (in opposition to the claim of philosophers of history also to describe events in *their* future). It almost seems presumed that historical events, taken one by one, are all of the form, What happened to X during such and such an interval of time? Nothing indicates that historical discourse requires connectives, themselves complex, distinct from the structure of the narrative sentence. This is why "explaining" and "describing"—in the narrative sense— are for so long taken as indistinguishable. Danto wants nothing to do with Croce's distinction between chronicle and history,[33] nor with Walsh's distinction between a pure, plain narrative, limited to reporting what happened, and a significant one which seeks to establish connections between facts. For a simple narrative already does more than report events in their order of appearance. A list of facts without any ties between them is not a narrative. This is why describing and explaining are not distinguished from each other; or, in Danto's forceful expression, why "history is of a piece." What we can distinguish is the narrative and the material evidence warranting it. A narrative does not reduce to a summary of its critical apparatus, whether we understand by this its conceptual or its documentary apparatus. Yet the distinction between a narrative and its conceptual or documentary support does not come down to distinguishing two levels of composition. To explain why something happened and to describe what happened coincide. A narrative that fails to explain is less than a narrative. A narrative that does explain is a pure, plain narrative.

Nothing therefore indicates that the something more that a narrative has in relation to a simple enumeration of events is different from the twofold structure of reference in the narrative sentence, thanks to which the meaning or truth of one event is relative to the meaning and truth of another event. This is why the notion of plot or narrative structure does not seem to be missing in the logic of the narrative sentence. It is as though the description of an earlier event in terms of a later one were already a plot in miniature.

In any case, we can ask whether the two notions are superimposed one on the other. For example, when Danto considers the unavoidably selective activity of historical narrative, he seems to invoke a more complex structural factor: "any narrative is a structure imposed on events, grouping some of them together with others, and ruling some out as lacking relevance" (p. 132). A narrative "mentions only the significant events" (ibid.). However, is the narrative organization which confers on events a meaning or an importance (the two connotations of the term "significance") simply an expansion of the narrative sentence?[34]

In my opinion, if the question of the relationship between text and sentence is not posed as such, it is due to the excessive emphasis placed upon the quarrel Danto has with the phantom of a complete description, and the fact that this phantom is exorcised through the analysis of narrative sentences.

The problem arises again with the question whether explanation in terms of laws still has a place in history, that is, when "a narrative already is, in the nature of the case, a *form of explanation*" (p. 201, his emphasis). Danto, in effect, does not oppose Hempel head-on. He confines himself to observing that the partisans of the covering law model, concerned as they are for the strong structure of the *explanans*, do not see that this *explanans* functions in an *explanandum* that is already a narrative, hence that is already "covered" by a description that counts as an explanation. We can cover an event with a general law only if it figures in language as a phenomenon under a certain description, therefore as inscribed in a narrative sentence. Consequently, Danto can be much more liberal and ambivalent about the covering law model than Dray can.[35]

Following a Story

W. B. Gallie's work, *Philosophy and the Historical Understanding*, centered on the concept of the "followability" of a story, leads us a step further in the direction of a structural principle of narrative.[36] This concept, in my opinion, fills a hole left by Danto's analysis of narrative sentences. If the narrative sentence's twofold reference to the event it describes and a later event in light of which the description is made constitutes a good discriminating factor in relation to other descriptions of action, for example, in terms of the agent's own intentions and reasons, nevertheless the mentioning of a difference between two dates, or two temporal localizations, does not suffice to characterize a narrative as a *connection* between events. A gap remains between the narrative *sentence* and the narrative *text*. This is the gap the notion of the followability of a story tries to fill.

But it is really in terms of one fundamental hypothesis that Gallie sets forth his analysis, namely, "whatever understanding and whatever explanations a work of history contains must be assessed in relation to the narrative form from which they arise and whose development they subserve" (p. xi). This thesis is as prudent as it is resolute. It does not deny that explanation does something more than simply narrate. It just limits itself to affirming, first, that explanation is not born from nothing but "proceeds" in some way or another from some discourse that already has a narrative form. Second, it says that in some way or another, explanation remains "in the service of" the narrative form. This form therefore is both the matrix of explanation and its setting. In this sense, the narrativist thesis says nothing about the structure of explanation. The notion of followability therefore has the ambition of satisfying this twofold requirement.

What, then, is a story? And what does it mean "to follow" a story?

A story describes a sequence of actions and experiences done or undergone by a certain number of people, whether real or imaginary. These people are presented either in situations that change or as reacting to such change. In turn, these changes reveal hidden aspects of the situation and the people involved, and engender a new predicament which calls for thought, action, or both. This response to the new situation leads the story toward its conclusion (p. 22).

As the reader will see, this sketch of the notion of a story is not far from what I have called emplotment. If Gallie did not find it useful to relate his concept of a story to that of plot, it was no doubt because he was less interested in the immanent structural constraints on narrative than in the subjective conditions under which a story is acceptable. These conditions of acceptability are what constitute a story's aptitude for being followed.

To follow a story, in effect, is to understand the successive actions, thoughts, and feelings in the story inasmuch as they present a particular "directedness." Let us understand by this that we are "pulled foward" by the development, as soon as we respond to this force with expectations concerning the completion and outcome of the whole process. The reader will immediately perceive how understanding and explanation are inextricably mixed together in this process. "Ideally, a story should be self-explanatory" (p. 23). It is only when the process is interrupted or blocked that we demand an explanation as a supplement.

To say that we are oriented in a certain direction is to recognize a teleological function in the "conclusion," the same one I emphasized in my analysis of the "ending." [37] However, in response to the covering law model we need to add that a narrative "conclusion" is not something that can be deduced or predicted. A story that included no surprises or coincidences or encounters or recognition scenes would not hold our attention. This is why we have to follow a story to its conclusion, which is something completely different than following an argument whose conclusion is compelled to be what it is. Rather than being predictable, a narrative's conclusion has to be *acceptable*. Looking back from the conclusion toward the intermediary episodes, we must be able to say that this end demanded those events and that chain of actions. Yet this backward look is itself made possible by the teleologically oriented movement of our expectations when we were following the story. An incompatibility, posited abstractly, between the contingency of the incidents and the acceptability of the conclusion is precisely what the followability of a story belies. Contingency is unacceptable only to a mind that attaches the idea of mastery to that of understanding. To follow a story is "to find [the events] intellectually acceptable *after all*" (p. 31, his emphasis). The intelligence exercised here is not the same as that connected with the lawfulness of a process but one that responds to the internal coherence of a story which conjoins contingency and acceptability.

The reader will not have failed to note the surprising kinship of this proposal with the notion of discordant concordance I extracted from the Aristotelian treatment of peripeteia within the framework of Aristotle's theory of muthos. The major difference with regard to criticism stemming from Aristotle is certainly to be found on the side of the subjective factor introduced by the notion of expectation or attraction due to the end; in short, by the subjective teleology that takes the place of structural analysis. In this sense, the concept of "followability" is drawn more from a psychology of reception than from a logic of configuration.[38]

If we now pass from the concept of "story" to that of "history," the continuity between them must be underlined first of all. Gallie's strategy is precisely to inscribe the epistemological discontinuity between them—which he in no way denies—in the framework of the continuity of narrative interest. This strategy, quite clearly, attacks head-on the problematic set forth in the previous chapter. The question will be whether the analysis that follows has any application outside of narrative history, which Gallie takes as exemplary. The object of such history is past actions that were recorded or that we can infer on the basis of records and reports. The history we write is the history of those actions whose projects or results can be seen as akin to our own action. And in this sense, all history is one fragment or segment of a unique world of communication. This is why we expect works of history, even if they are isolated works, to indicate in their margins the unique history which, however, no one can write.

If this narrative continuity between story and history was little noticed in the past, it was because the problems posed by the epistemological break between fiction and history, or between myth and history, turned attention to the question of evidence, at the expense of the more fundamental question of what accounts for the interest of a work of history. It is this interest that assures the continuity between history based on historiography and ordinary narration.

As a narrative, all history has to do with "some major achievement or failure of men living and working together, in societies or nations or any other lastingly organized groups" (p. 65). This is why, in spite of their critical relation to traditional narrative, histories that deal with the unification or the disintegration of an empire, with the rise or fall of a class, a social movement, a religious sect, or a literary style are narratives. In this regard, the difference between an individual and a group is not decisive. Sagas and ancient epics were already centered on groups, not just on isolated figures. "All history is, like saga, basically a narrative of events in which human thought and action play a predominant part" (p. 69). Even when history deals with currents, tendencies, or trends, it is the act of following the narrative that confers an organic unity on them. A trend only manifests itself in the succession of events we follow. It is "a pattern-quality of those particular events" (p. 70). This is why: (1) the reading of these historians' stories derives from our competence to follow stories. We follow them from one end to the other, and we follow them in light of the issue promised or glimpsed through the succession of contingent events. (2) Correlatively, the theme of these stories is worth being recounted and their narratives are worth following, because this theme is superimposed on interests that are our own as human beings, however distant this theme might be from our present feelings. Through these two features, "history is a species of the genus story" (p. 66).

As we see, Gallie delays the moment when he has to take up the problem from the other side. Why do historians seek to explain things in a different way that that given by the contours of traditional stories, which they break away from? And how are we to articulate the discontinuity introduced by critical reason into history on the one hand, and fiction or traditional narratives on the other?

Here the notion of followability offers another face. Every story, we have said, in principle explains itself. In other words, narrative answers the question "Why?" at the same time that it answers the question "What?" To tell what has happened is to tell why it happened. At the same time, following a story is a difficult, laborious process, which can be interrupted or blocked. A story, we also said, has to be acceptable after all (we could have said, in spite of everything). This, we have known since my interpretation of Aristotle, is true of every narrative. The "one because of the other" is not always easy to extract from the "one after the other." Consequently, our most elementary narrative understanding already confronts our expectations governed by our interests and our sympathies with reasons that, to fulfill their meaning, have to correct our prejudices. In this way, critical discontinuity is even incorporated into narrative continuity. We thus see in what way the phenomenology applied to every story's followability is capable of extension, to the point of inserting a critical moment into the very heart of the basic act of following a story.

This interplay between expectations governed by interests and reasons governed by critical rationality provides an appropriate framework for attacking the two specifically epistemological problems set forth in chapter 4 above, namely, the change in scale of the entities treated by contemporary history, and the recourse to laws at the level of scientific history.

The first problem seems to constrain the narrativist to take part in a quarrel between two schools of thought. For the first one, which we can call the "nominalist" school, general propositions that refer to collective entities and attribute predicates of action to them (we speak of a government's politics, the progress of a reform, a change of constitution) have no autonomous meaning. Although these propositions, taken in a strict sense, do not refer to the identifiable actions of singular individuals, in the final analysis an institutional change is only an abbreviation for a multitude of ultimately individual facts. For the second school, which we can call the "realist" one, institutions and every comparable collective phenomenon are real entities, which have their own history, irreducible to goals, efforts, and enterprises attributable to individuals either acting alone or in concert, in their own name or in the name of groups which they represent. Conversely, to understand actions assignable to individuals, we have to refer to those institutional facts within which they act. And finally, we are not really interested in what individuals do as individuals.

Against all expectations, Gallie is very careful not to take sides with the nominalist thesis. Nominalists, in fact, do not explain why it is in the historian's interest to proceed to an abbreviation of individual facts which subordinates them to the abstraction of an institutional one, nor why historians are indifferent about enumerating every individual action and reaction in order to understand the evolution of an institution. Nominalists do not see the close tie between the use of abstractions and the eminently selective character of historical interest. Nor do they see, for the most part, that the actions attributable to individuals are done by them as individuals, but only insofar as they are filling some institutional role. Finally, nominalists do not see that to understand global phenomena such as "social discontent" or "economic institutions" requires use of "dummy variables," some x that marks the place where all the as yet unexplored interactions capable of standing in the place of this x cross.[39] In all these respects, the Weberian method of "ideal-types" turns out to be the best way to explain this sort of abstraction.

Yet if the historian's practice belies the extreme thesis that only individual things exist, including persons, it does not justify the realist thesis that all human action implies a tacit reference to some social institutional fact of a general character, and is sufficiently explained when we have made explicit this reference. The nominalist thesis, despite its epistemological inadequacy, indicates the goal of historical thought, which is to account for the social changes that interest us (because they depend upon the ideas, choices, places, efforts, successes and failures of individual men and women). However the realist does give a better account of the way in which history realizes this goal, namely, by appealing to all knowledge available having something to do with social life, "from traditional truisms to the theorems and abstract models of the social sciences" (p. 84).

Far from aligning his narrativist theory with the nominalist one, therefore, Gallie tries to seek a combination of the epistemology implied by the realist thesis and the fundamentally individualistic ontology implied by the nominalist one. This eclecticism would be a weak solution if it did not represent fairly well what professional historians do in practice when they come to the crucial moments of their work. Their whole effort then consists in determining as exactly as possible how this or that individual or group of individuals adopted, maintained, abandoned, or failed to hold on to certain institutional roles. In return, in between these crucial moments, they content themselves with general summaries, formulated in institutional terms, because during these intervals anonymity prevails until some rupture worth recounting happens to alter the course of the institutional or social phenomenon. Such is the case generally in economic and social history, where the massive anonymity of forces, currents, and structures reigns. Yet even this type of history which, at the limit, is written without dates or proper names, does not fail to account for initiatives, qualities of mind, courage, desperation, the flair of individual human beings, "even if their names have usually been forgotten" (p. 87).

As for our second problem, that of the function of laws in historical explanation, it is important to be on guard in this regard against a false interpretation of what historians expect from these laws. They do not expect them to eliminate contingencies, but rather to provide a better understanding of their contribution to the march of history. This is why their problem is not to deduce or to predict but to understand better the complexity of the intertwinings that have converged into the occurrence of this or that event. In this historians are different than physicists. They do not seek to increase the field of generalities at the price of a reduction in contingencies. Instead they want better to understand what has happened. The same point applies even to those areas where it is contingencies that hold their interest, whether it be a question of conflicts between nation-states, social struggles, scientific discoveries, or artistic innovations.[40] Interest in these events, which I would compare with the Aristotelian peripeteia, does not signify that historians give in to the sensational. Their problem is precisely to incorporate these events into an acceptable narrative, therefore to inscribe contingency within an overall schema. This feature is essential to the followability of any fact capable of being narrated.

One result of this primacy of the concept of followability is that the explanations, for which historians borrow laws from the sciences to which they link their discipline, have no other effect than to allow us better to follow the story, when our vision of its interconnections is obscured or when our capacity to accept the author's vision is carried to the breaking point.

It would be completely erroneous therefore to see here the weakened forms of a strong covering law model. Explanations simply bring their help to our capacity for following a story. In this sense, their function in history is "an ancillary one" (p. 107).

Such a thesis would be unacceptable if we did not know that every narrative explains itself, in the sense that to narrate what has happened is already to explain why it happened. In this sense, the smallest story incorporates generalizations, whether of a classificatory, a causal, or a theoretical order. Consequently, nothing prevents ever more complex generalizations and explanations from being grafted onto and in a way interpolated into historical narrative. However if every narrative so explains itself, in another sense no historical narrative does so. Every historical narrative is looking for an explanation to incorporate into itself, because it has failed to explain itself. It needs to be put back on the trail again. Hence the criterion of a good explanation is a pragmatic one. Its function is an eminently corrective one. Dray's rational explanations satisfied this criterion. We reconstruct an agent's calculations when a course of action surprises us, intrigues us, or leaves us perplexed.

In this regard, history does nothing different from what philology or textual criticism does. When the reading of some received text or interpretation appears to be discordant in relation to other accepted facts, the philologist or textual critic rearranges the details to make everything intelligible again. Writing is rewriting. For historians, everything enigmatic becomes a challenge to those criteria of what, in their eyes, makes a history followable and acceptable.

In this work of recasting earlier ways of writing history, historians come closest to the Hempelian type of explanation. Confronted with a strange course of events, they will construct a model of a normal course of action, then ask how the behavior of the actors in question deviates from it. Every explanation of possible courses of action has recourse to such generalizations. The most frequent and most noteworthy case of such recasting is the one where a historian puts forth an explanation that not only was not accessible to the actors in question but that differs from the explanations offered by previous histories, which have become opaque and enigmatic to the new historian. In this case, to explain is to justify the reorientation of historical attention, which leads to a general re-vision of a whole course of history. The great historian is the one who succeeds in rendering acceptable a new way of following history.

But in no case does explanation exceed its ancillary and corrective function as regards understanding applied to the followability of historical narrative.

In the next chapter, we shall ask whether this "ancillary" function of explanation suffices to account for the "unleveling" brought about by historical inquiry in relation to the entities and procedures of narrative.

The Configurational Act

With the work of Louis O. Mink, we come even closer to the main argument of the "narrativist" conception, that narratives are highly organized wholes, requiring a specific act of understanding that takes the nature of a judgment. This argument is all the more interesting in that it makes no use of the concept of plot from literary criticism. In turn, this lack of reference to the structural resources of fictional narrative may explain a certain shortcoming in Mink's analysis, which I shall discuss at the end of this section. Still nobody has gone as far as Mink has in recognizing the synthetic character of narrative activity.

Already in an article published in 1965, his arguments against the covering law model pave the way for characterizing historical understanding as an act of judgment, in the twofold sense that Kant's first and third *Critiques* assign to this term, namely, the synthetic function of "grasping together" along with the reflective function attached to every synoptic operation.[41] In this article he reviews the main discrepancies, already emphasized by other critics, between the highly prescriptive requirements of the covering law model and the actual understanding displayed by current work in history. He shows that these discrepancies can be accounted for only if the autonomy of historical understanding is correctly established.

Why can historians aspire to explain things when they cannot predict them? Because explaining is not always equivalent to subsuming facts under laws. In history, to explain is often to make use of "colligations"—to use Whewell's and Walsh's term—which comes down to "explaining an event by tracing its intrinsic relations to other events and locating it in its historical context" (p. 171). This procedure is at least characteristic of sequential explanations. Why are hypotheses not falsifiable in history in the same way they are in science? Because hypotheses are not the goal of history, only landmarks for delineating a field of investigation, guides serving a mode of understanding which is fundamentally that of interpretative narrative, which is neither chronology nor "science." Why do historians so willingly make recourse to imaginative reconstruction? Because the task of an overall view is "comprehending [the constitutive events] in an act of judgment which manages to hold them together rather than reviewing them *seriatim*" (p. 178). Consequently, this overall viewpoint is not a "method," nor "a technique of proof nor an organon of discovery but a type of reflective judgment" (p. 179). Why are there no "detachable" conclusions in a historian's argument or work? Because the narrative as a whole is what supports these conclusions. And they are exhibited by the narrative order rather than demonstrated. "The actual meanings are provided by the total context" (p. 181). The notion of a comprehensive synthesis, a synoptic judgment, similar to the operation that allows us to interpret a synthesis as a whole, clearly comes to the forefront with this argument. "The logic of confirmation is appropriate to the testing of detachable conclusions, but ingredient meanings require a theory of judgment" (p. 186). Why can historical events be both unique and similar to other events? Because similarity and uniqueness are alternately accentuated as a function of the contexts at hand. Once again historical understanding comes down to "comprehending a complex event by 'seeing things together' in a total and synoptic judgment which cannot be replaced by any analytic technique" (p. 184). Why do historians aspire to address a potentially universal audience and not simply a scientific forum? Because what they attempt to communicate is a kind of judgment closer to Aristotle's *phronēsis* than to "science." The historian's problem "becomes intelligible . . . if it is seen as an attempt to communicate his experience of seeing-things-together in the necessarily narrative style of one-thing-after-another" (p. 188).

The conclusion of this article is especially worth quoting: the historian "cultivates the specialized habit of understanding which converts congeries of events into concatenations, and emphasizes and increases the scope of synoptic judgment in our reflection on experience" (p. 191). Mink readily admits that this identification of historical thought with "synoptic judgment" leaves open epistemological problems, such as "the questions whether 'interpretative syntheses' can be logically compared, whether there are general grounds for preferring one to another, and whether there are criteria of historical objectivity and truth" (ibid.). But these epistemological questions presuppose that we have identified "what distinguishes sophisticated historical thinking from both the everyday explanations of common sense and the theoretical explanations of natural science" (pp. 191–92).

He makes his own approach to these questions more specific in an article published in 1968, on the basis of a criticism of Gallie's book.[42] The phenomenology applied to our capacity for following a story is not debatable as long as we have to do with stories whose outcomes are unknown to the listener or reader, as is the case when we are following a game. Here our knowing the rules of the game is of no help in predicting the outcome. We have to follow the series of incidents to its conclusion. The contingencies, for a phenomenological understanding, amount to surprising and unexpected incidents in the given circumstances. We expect some conclusion but we do not know which one, out of the several that are possible, will occur. This is why we have to follow the series from one end to the other. It is also why our feelings of sympathy or hostility should help support the dynamism of the whole process. But, argues Mink, this condition of ignorance and with it the unreflective activity that constitute the following of the story are not characteristic of the historian's procedure. History "is not the writing, but the rewriting of stories" (p. 687). Its readers, in turn, apply themselves to a "reflective" following, corresponding to the situation of the historian as re-recounting and rewriting the story. History appears once the game is over.[43] Its task is not to accentuate the accidents but to reduce them. The historian is always tracing the lines backwards, for "there are no contingencies going backwards" (ibid.). It is only when we tell the story that "we retrace forward what we have already traced backward" (ibid.). This does not mean that, knowing the outcome, readers could have predicted it. They follow in order "to see" the series of events as an intelligible "pattern of relationships" (p. 688). This retrospective intelligibility rests upon a construction that no witness could have put together when the events were occurring, since this backward way of proceeding would be unavailable to any contemporary witness.[44]

Mink adds two further comments. In a phenomenology limited to the situation where a story is followed for the first time, the function of explanation runs the risk of being underemphasized and reduced to the act of filling in lacunae or of setting aside anything obscure that obstructs the narrative flow. Explanation appears less ancillary and as a result less theoretical, if the historian's task is to proceed backwards and if, as Mink says, "there are no contingencies going backwards." "The logic of explanation should have something to do with the phenomenology of understanding; the former, one hopes, should serve to correct the latter and the latter to enrich the former." [45]

His second argument is more debatable. Gallie, he says, "wishes to transfer the openness and contingency of our present future to the narrative of past events, since it seems to him that we can think of them in no other way than as once having been future" (p. 688). By doing so, Gallie follows an erroneous ontology of time, the leading feature of which is "the principle that the past and the future are not categorically different from each other: the past consists of past futures and the future of future pasts" (ibid.). This argument does not strike me as convincing. First, I do not think that past futures and future pasts are categorically similar to each other. On the contrary, the lack of symmetry between them nourishes what Mink quite rightly calls "the poignancy of the historical consciousness" (ibid.). Next, the determinate character of the past is not such as to exclude the sort of retroactive changes in meaning to which Danto has so successfully called attention. Third, the process of tracing forward anew the pathway we have already covered going backward may well reopen, if I can put it this way, the space of contingency that once belonged to the past when it was present. It may reinstate a sort of learned wonder, thanks to which "contingencies" recover a part of their initial surprising force. This power may well belong to the fictional character of historical understanding which I shall discuss later. More precisely, it may be tied to that aspect of fiction that Aristotle characterized as the mimesis of action. It is at the level of initial contingencies that some events enjoy the status of having been future with regard to the course of action that is retrospectively reconstructed. In this sense, there must be a place for past futures even in an ontology of time, to the extent that our existential time is shaped by the temporal configurations that history and fiction together establish. I shall return to this discussion in the second volume of this investigation.

Here I would rather emphasize the kind of unilateralness that results from substituting a phenomenology of retrospective grasping for the direct grasping of a story followed for the first time. Does not Mink run the risk of abolishing, at the level of retelling, those features of the narrative operation that telling and retelling really have in common, because they stem from the same structure of narrative, namely, the dialectic between contingency and order, episode and configuration, discordance and concordance? Across this dialectic, is it not the specific temporality of narrative that runs the risk of being misunderstood? The fact is that we can observe in Mink's analyses a tendency to divest the very act of "grasping together," characteristic of the configurational operation, of every temporal attribute. His refusal to attribute having once been future to narrated events already is indicative of this orientation. And it appears to be reinforced by his insistence on the act of retelling at the expense of the act of following a story for the first time. A third article by Mink clearly demonstrates this thesis.[46]

The strong point of this article is its construing of the configurational mode as one of three modes of "comprehension" in the broader sense, which also includes the theoretical and the categoreal modes. According to the theoretical mode, objects are comprehended in terms of a case or as examples of a general theory. The ideal type of this mode is represented by Laplace's system. According to the categoreal mode, often confused with the preceding one, to comprehend an object is to determine what type of object we are dealing with, what system of a priori concepts organizes an experience that otherwise would remain chaotic. Plato aims at this categoreal comprehension, as do most systematic philosophers. The configurational mode puts its elements into a single, concrete complex of relations. It is the type of comprehension that characterizes the narrative operation. All three modes do have a common aim, which is no less implicit in the configurational mode than in the other two. Comprehension in the broad sense is defined as the act "of grasping together in a single mental act things which are not experienced together, or even capable of being so experienced, because they are separated by time, space, or logical kind. And the ability to do this is a necessary (although not a sufficient) condition of *understanding*" (p. 547, his emphasis). Comprehension, in this sense, is not limited to either historical knowledge or temporal acts. To understand a logical conclusion as resulting from its premises is a kind of comprehension without any narrative features, even though it does imply several temporal presuppositions, inasmuch as what we try to think of as a whole consists of "the complicated relationships of parts which can only be experienced *seriatim*" (p. 548). But this is just a way of saying with Kant that all experience occurs in time, even if it also occurs in space, since we have to trace, retain, and recognize all the components and steps of the related experience. In short, "comprehension is an individual act of seeing-things-together, and only that" (p. 553).

Furthermore, comprehension in the broad sense presents one fundamental feature that has important implications for the narrative mode of comprehension. All comprehension, Mink declares, has an ideal aim, even if it is unattainable, of comprehending the world as a *totality*. To put it another way, this goal is unattainable because it would amount to divine comprehension; yet it is significant because "the human project is to take God's place" (p. 549). This sudden intrusion of a theological theme is in no way marginal. The alleged ultimate goal of the three modes of comprehension proceeds from a transposition into epistemology of Boethius's definition of "God's knowledge of the world as a *totum simul*, in which the successive moments of all time are copresent in a single perception, as of a landscape of events" (ibid.).[47]

Mink does not hesitate to apply this goal of comprehension in the broad sense to the configurational mode. "The *totum simul* which Boethius regarded as God's knowledge of the world would of course be the highest degree of configurational comprehension" (p. 551). In light of this declaration, the earlier criticism of a phenomenology confined to the act of following a story takes on a new aspect. What ultimately appears to be refused to narrative comprehension, in the name of the *totum simul*, is the sequential form of stories which this phenomenology had succeeded in preserving. I wonder if the argument, valuable in itself, that history consists more of having followed than of following is not pushed too far, and even weakened, by the subsequent thesis in which he holds that in the act of configurational understanding "actions and events, although represented as occurring in the order of time, can be surveyed as it were in a single glance as bound together in an order of significance, a representation of the *totum simul* which we can never more than partially achieve" (p. 554).

I also wonder whether what is held to be a superior degree of configurational comprehension is not rather the mark of its abolition. To avoid this troublesome consequence for narrative theory, must we not assign an opposite function to the idea of a *totum simul*, namely, precisely to limit comprehension's ambition to abolish the sequential character of time underlying the episodic side of emplotment? The *totum simul* would then have to be recognized as an Idea in the Kantian sense of a limit-idea rather than as a goal or a guide. For the moment, it will suffice to ask ourselves whether this ideal goal is really the appropriate extrapolation of what is implied in the actual comprehension of narratives.

What is debatable, on simply the phenomenological level—the level where "having followed" is rightly opposed to "following"—is the assertion that "in the understanding of a narrative the thought of temporal succession as such vanishes—or perhaps, one might say, remains like the smile of the Cheshire Cat" (ibid.). I refuse to believe that "in the configurational comprehension of a story which one *has followed* . . . the necessity of the backward references cancels out, so to speak, the contingency of the forward references" (ibid., his emphasis). None of the arguments advanced for this conclusion are convincing.

The argument that in current historiography chronology recedes—and along with it the concern for dates—is a perfectly reasonable one. But the question remains open to what point the surpassing of simple chronology implies the abolition of every mode of temporality. From Augustine to Heidegger, every ontology of time tries to disentangle from purely chronological time those temporal properties founded upon succession but not reducible to either simple succession or chronology. The argument that understanding is complete when we grasp a certain action as the response to an event (where "sending a telegram" responds to "receiving an offer") is equally correct. But the link between sending a telegram and the reception of an offer is assured by a mediating term: acceptance of the offer, which engenders a change from the initial state of affairs to the terminal one. We do not have the right, consequently, to generalize on the basis of the "response," and to say that "the actions and events of a story comprehended as a whole are *connected by a network of overlapping descriptions*" (p. 556, his emphasis). The abolition of sentences marked by verbal tenses in this network of overlapping descriptions is the sign that the narrative quality of history has disappeared along with the temporal ties. We may well say that, in retrospect, all the incidents that occur in the *story* of Oedipus can be grasped together in the *portrait* of Oedipus. But this portrait is equivalent to the "thought" of the tragedy *Oedipus Rex*. And the "thought," or what Aristotle named the *dianoia*, is an aspect derived from the plot in the same way the characters are.

It remains to be seen in what way a transferral of the concept of plot from literary criticism to the epistemology of history may illumine the concrete dialectic between discordance and concordance in narrative, a dialectic of narrative which has not been taken into account enough in the analysis of the configurational mode of understanding that tends to dissolve its temporal quality in the name of the goal given it of becoming equal to the *totum simul* of divine knowledge.

Explanation by Emplotment

The procedures of emplotment which I earlier set forth in terms of mimesis$_2$ are for the first time assigned to the narrative structure of history writing in the work of Hayden White.[48] However, they do not cover the whole field.

The force of White's analyses is due to the lucidity with which he makes explicit the presuppositions of his analyses of major historical texts and defines the universe of discourse in which these presuppositions in turn find their place.

His first presupposition runs as follows. Following in the wake of Mink's work, White reorganizes the relationship between history and fiction along other lines than those of an epistemology for which the problematic of objectivity and proof determines the basic criterion of every classification of the modes of discourse. Whatever may be said about this problematic, the first presupposition of a "poetics" of historical discourse is that fiction and history belong to the same class as regards their narrative structure. The second presupposition is that this bringing together of history and fiction entails another one, this time bringing together history and literature. This overturning of the usual classifications requires that the characterization of history as writing be taken seriously. "The writing of history," to use the title of a work by Michel de Certeau, is not external to the conceiving and composing of history.[49] It does not constitute some second-order operation, stemming only from the rhetoric of communication, that we could neglect as belonging simply to the redactional order. It is constitutive of the historical mode of understanding. History is intrinsically historio-graphy—or to put it in a deliberately provocative way, a literary artifact.[50] Hence the third presupposition is that the boundary drawn by epistemologists between historians' history and the philosophy of history must also be called into question, inasmuch as, for one thing, every great historical work unfolds an overall vision of the historical world and, for another, philosophies of history have recourse to the same resources of articulation as do the great works of history. This is why in his own major work, *Metahistory*, White does not hesitate in placing Michelet, Ranke, Tocqueville, Burckhardt, Hegel, Marx, Nietzsche, and Croce all within the same framework.

He calls this "poetics" of historiography "metahistory" to distinguish it from an epistemology oriented to the characteristics of inquiry in history, and therefore riveted on the conditions of objectivity and truth that ground the epistemological break between history as a science and traditional or mythical narrative.

His three presuppositions entail, in effect, a displacement and a reclassification of this problematic, the exclusive attention given to the conditions for the scientific status of history being taken as responsible for the misapprehension of those structures that set history within the space of narrative fiction. Only a metahistory can dare to consider historical narratives as verbal fictions close to their literary counterparts because of their content and their form. Later, the question must arise whether it is possible to reclassify history as a literary artifact without declassifying it as knowledge which claims to be scientific.

It is undeniable that this displacement and reclassification of the problematic of history does imply a transferring to historiography of categories borrowed from literary criticism.

The irony of this situation is that these loans are made from the very authors who are opposed to them. We have not forgotten the firmness with which Aristotle excludes *historia* from his problematic concerning muthos. To grasp the significance of White's gesture that transgresses the Aristotelian interdiction, we need to understand the reasons for this prohibition. Aristotle does not confine himself just to asserting that history is too "episodic" to satisfy the requirements of his *Poetics*—after all, this judgment is easily revocable ever since the work of Thucydides. He also tells why history is episodic: because it reports what really happened. And the real, unlike the possible which the poet conceives, and which the peripeteia illustrate, implies a contingency that escapes the poet's control. It is because poets are the authors of their plots that they can uproot themselves from the contingently real and raise themselves to the level of probable possibility. Transferring history into the circle of poetics is not therefore an innocent act and cannot lack consequences as concerns the treatment of real contingencies.

Transgressing the Aristotelian interdiction meets no less resistance from the side of literary criticism, to which White's work is even closer. For Auerbach, Booth, and Scholes and Kellogg, the imaginary is defined in opposition to the "real" and history continues to be the model for realism of representation. The height of the irony is that Northrop Frye, whom White especially borrows from, is one of the most vigilant guardians of this boundary. Fiction, for Frye, concerns the possible, history has to do with the real. Following Aristotle, Frye will say that the poet works from a form of unification, the historian works toward it.[51] For Frye, only philosophies of history, such as those of Spengler, Toynbee, or H. G. Wells, can seem to belong to the same "poetic" category as do drama and epic.

White's metahistory must therefore break through two resistances: that of the historians who hold that the epistemological break between history and traditional and mythic narrative uproots the former from the circle of fiction, and that of the literary critics for whom the distinction between the imaginary and the real is beyond question.

I shall reserve for my second volume those aspects of verbal fiction that force us to return to the notion of the representation of the real in history, a problem I have chosen to consider in terms of what I have called mimesis$_3$. Here I shall remain within the limits of fiction understood as configuration, in the sense of mimesis$_2$. I am aware of the injustice I am doing to White's work by separating his more formal analyses from those concerning historical reality—the dividing line passes between his considerations concerning emplotment and those that concern the prefiguring of the historical field which he assigns to a theory of tropes (metaphor, metonymy, etc.). The compensation for this loss, in my view, is the advantage gained in not tying the outcome of the formal analyses, which seem more solid to me, to that of the theory of tropes, which I think is more fragile.[52]

It is important to note that emplotment does not receive from White the large-scale treatment I am giving it except on the condition of not entirely identifying the notion of "historical narrative" with it. He is very careful, in his articles as well as in *Metahistory*, to situate emplotment among a number of other operations, whose enumeration varies from one work to another. This is why, for didactic purposes, I shall first consider all that is not "plot" in order then to concentrate the essential part of my remarks on it.

In an article published in 1972, plot is placed between the story and the argument.[53] Story is taken here in a limiting sense, that of "telling stories," in the sense of an essentially sequential narrative, having a beginning, a middle, and an end. In truth, it is the concept of "story-line" rather than that of "story" that serves as a benchmark. White visibly wants to rid himself of the argument that history, as it is written today, is no longer narrative. This objection only holds, he says, if we reduce story to story-line.

This delineation of story from plot, which is disconcerting to many critics, seems to White to be more urgent in history than in literary criticism, because in history the events constituting the narrated story-line are not produced by the historian's imagination but rather are submitted to proof procedures. For my part, I see in this argument one way of responding to Aristotle's interdiction. The price for this exemption is the distinction between story and plot.

This distinction is not always easy to maintain, inasmuch as a story is already a mode of organization in that it is distinguished from a simple chronicle of events and organized in terms of "motifs" and "themes" which unify and delineate subsets within it.[54] In this way, a story is already capable of an "explanatory effect." It is precisely to do justice to this explanatory effect belonging to a story that *Metahistory* distinguishes story from chronicle, which then becomes the very first articulation of the historical field. As for this notion of the "historical field" (see *Metahistory*, p. 30), which we shall rediscover in the work of Paul Veyne, it poses the problem of a still earlier articulation. We can, in fact, speak from inside an already organized narrative only of an "unprocessed historical record" (p. 5), that is, of a preconceptual background open to processes of selection and arrangement.[55]

Emplotment conserves an explanatory effect distinct from that of the story, in the sense that it does not explain the events of the story but rather the story itself, by identifying the class to which it belongs. The story-line allows us to identify a unique configuration, while emplotment invites us to recognize a traditional class of configurations. These plot categories, as a function of which the story itself, not its events, is encoded, are akin to those "relational cryptograms" that, according to E. H. Gombrich, in *Art and Illusion*, govern our way of "reading a painting." [56]

In this way, White thinks he can escape the antinarrativist arguments of the partisans of Hempel's theory by abandoning to them the organization of history in terms of causes and laws, while taking away from them the categorial explanation proper to emplotment. But he does so only at the price of disjoining the explanation of a story and the explanation of an event.

The boundary between plot and argument is no easier to trace. The argument designates "the point of it all" or "what it all adds up to" (*Metahistory*, p. 11), in short, the thesis of a narrative. Aristotle included the argument in the plot under the cloak of the plot's probability and necessity. We might say, in any case, that it is history as different from epic, tragedy, and comedy that requires this distinction at the level of "explanatory effects." It is precisely because explanation by argument can be distinguished from explanation by emplotment that logicians invented the covering law model. Historians do argue in a formal, explicit, discursive way. What the partisans of the covering law model failed to see, however, was that their field of argumentation is considerably vaster than that of general laws, borrowed from the sciences connected to history which are already constituted outside the historical field. Historians have their own modes of arguing, but these belong to the narrative domain. And these modes of arguing are so numerous as to call for a typology. If this is the case, it is because each such mode of arguing expresses at the same time a presupposition of a metahistorical character about the very nature of the historical field and about what we may expect from explanation in history. As for his typology, White borrows it from Stephen Pepper's *World Hypotheses*. In this way he distinguishes four major paradigms: the formist, organist, mechanistic, and contextualist forms.[57] He takes pleasure in emphasizing that if the first two are taken as more orthodox and the latter two as more heterodox and metaphysical (in spite of such masters of these genres as Ranke and Tocqueville), it is due to misapprehending the epistemological status of these global hypotheses. One forgets that "history is *not* a science, or is at best a protoscience with specifically determinable nonscientific elements in its constitution" (p. 21, his emphasis).

In truth, explanation through these major paradigms is little short of the explanation by ideological implication that *Metahistory* puts in the fifth rank of narrative structures. White distinguishes this latter mode of explanation from the preceding one by the ethical stance inherent in a particular manner of writing history. The presuppositions of the preceding mode had to do rather with the nature of the historical field. The presuppositions of the ideological mode bear on the nature of historical consciousness, and therefore on the tie between explaining past facts and present practice.[58] This is why the ideological mode of explanation, too, has a conflictual structure, which calls for an appropriate typology. White borrows it, although he reworks and simplifies it, from Karl Mannheim's *Ideology and Utopia*. In this way, he postulates four basic ideological positions: anarchism, conservatism, radicalism, and liberalism. Whatever the case may be as regards the propriety of this typology for the great historical works of the nineteenth century, whose examination is precisely the major objective of *Metahistory*, it is important to underline the fact that, by adding the ideological mode, White satisfies two distinct, if not opposed, demands. On the one hand, he serves the cause of truth by reintroducing, by way of the post-Marxist concept of ideology, components of historical knowledge that the *Verstehen* tradition, represented in France by Aron and Marrou, has always emphasized, namely, the historian's implication in historical work, the consideration of values, and history's tie to action in the world of the present. Ideological preferences bearing in the final analysis on social change, on its desirable scope and its desirable rhythm, concern metahistory insofar as they are incorporated into the explanation of the historical field and the construction of the verbal model by which history orders events and processes in narratives. On the other hand, in distinguishing argument and ideology, White indicates the place for the critique of ideology, and submits ideology to the same rule of discussion that applies to the mode of explanation by formal arguments.

So enframed by the story-line (a level itself split into chronicle and the chain of motifs) and the argument (split into formal arguments and ideological implications), explanation by emplotment for White takes on a strict and limited sense, which allows him to say both that it is not the whole narrative structure and yet is its pivot.[59]

By emplotment, he means much more than the simple combination of the linear aspect of the story and the argumentative aspect of the proposed thesis. He means the *kind* of story, therefore one of the configurative categories we have learned to distinguish in our culture. Let us say, to clarify this problem, that White appeals to the theme I developed at length in Part I, of the role of paradigms in emplotment, along with the constitution of a narrative tradition by the interplay of innovation and sedimentation. While I characterize the entire scale of exchanges between paradigms and individual stories by emplotment, White retains just their function of categorization for his notion of emplotment. This explains why he carries over to his notion of story the purely linear aspect. Emplotment so conceived constitutes a mode of explanation, "explanation by emplotment" (see *Metahistory*, pp. 7–11). Here, to explain is to provide a guide for progressively identifying the class of emplotment ("The Structure of Historical Narrative," p. 9). "Providing the 'meaning' of a story by identifying the *kind of story* that has been told is called explanation by emplotment" (*Metahistory*, p. 7, his emphasis). A given historian "is forced to emplot the whole set of stories making up his narrative in one comprehensive or *archetypal* story form" (p. 8, his emphasis).

White borrows his typology of emplotment from Frye's *Anatomy of Criticism*: romance, tragedy, comedy, satire. (Epic is left out, because it appears as the implicit form of the chronicle.) The genre of satire has an peculiar position in that, for Frye, stories constructed in the ironic mode draw their effect from the fact that they defraud their readers of the sort of resolution they expect of stories constructed in the romantic, comic, or tragic modes. Satire, in this sense, is diametrically opposed to the romantic genre, which demonstrates the final triumph of the hero, but it is also opposed, at least in part, to tragedy where, in lieu of celebrating humanity's ultimate transcendence over the fallen world, a reconciliation is contrived for the spectators, who are led to perceive the law governing the outcome. Finally, satire also takes its distance from the mutual reconciliation of human beings, society, and the world brought about in comedy by its happy ending. In each case, this opposition is only partial. There can be a satirical tragedy or a satirical comedy. Satire starts from the ultimate inadequacy of the visions of the world dramatized in romance, comedy, and tragedy.

What benefit can the epistemology of historical knowledge draw from this distinction between these "modes of explanation" (and their corresponding "explanatory effects") and the three typologies proposed respectively at the levels of plot, argument, and ideology? Essentially, what is gained is a theory of historiographical style, if we understand by style a remarkable intersecting of the possibilities opened by the diverse narrative categories involved (see pp. 29–31).

We can build up this theory of style degree by degree, by following the combinatory system's order of complexity.

At a first level, the theory of style plays upon the basic trilogy: story, emplotment, argument. Thus, in his 1972 article, this tripartite division is illustrated by three works: explanation as a function of the story-line is illlustrated by Ranke's *History of Germany During the Age of the Reformation*, explanation in terms of plot by Tocqueville's *Democracy in America*, and explanation in terms of argument by Burckhardt's *Culture of the Renaissance in Italy*. Each of these works includes, of course, a story-line, plot, and argument, but in varying proportions. Linear order prevails in Ranke. His history has a beginning, a middle, and an end, and has taken place before the present of the reader. His argument can be reduced to the changes that befall the entity Germany, which conserves its identity. And his plot is confined to showing "how one thing led to another" (p. 6). In this sense, everything for Ranke is a story that illustrates the "narrativist" type of historiography. Tocqueville also has a story, but one open on the end turned toward us, who bear the burden of giving it an end through our own action. Everything he narrates, if you will, is only the extended middle of his story. However the accent is placed on the type of structure binding together social classes, political democracy, culture, religion. With Burckhardt, on the contrary, we can say that everything is argument. His story only serves to illustrate his thesis about individualism in the Renaissance.

Yet imperceptibly, White's theory of historical style passes to a second level, by combining the tripartite division into story, plot, and argument with the typology of emplotment. If Burckhardt illustrates the primacy of argument over plot and story, he also illustrates the ironic mode of emplotment, for a story that does not go anywhere destroys our expectation of a moral or intellectual conclusion, such as it would have been forged by the other paradigms of emplotment: romance, comedy, and tragedy. Michelet, on the other hand, does construct his story in the romantic mode, Ranke in the comic one, and Tocqueville in the tragic one.

Finally, the theory of style passes to a third level by combining the three typologies corresponding to emplotment, argumentation, and ideological implication. We thus obtain a combinatory system that takes account of, if not all the combinations possible, at least those "elective affinities" that outline the network of compatibility from which emerge the identifiable historiographical styles: "In my view, a historiographical style represents a particular *combination* of modes of emplotment, argument, and ideological implication." [60] But we misapprehend things if we see in a style a necessary combination of modes of explanation: "the dialectical tension which characterizes the work of every master historian usually arises from an effort to wed a mode of emplotment with a mode of argument or of ideological implication which is inconsonant with it" (p. 29).[61] We are thus led by way of a long detour to my theme of dissonant consonance.[62] One primary source for it proceeds from the opposition between the three modes, taken together, that confer an explanatory function on the narrative structures.[63] Another source of consonance stems from the confrontation between several manners of emplotment, not only in the work of different historians, but at the heart of a major work.

In sum, the notion of narrative structure, with which we began, covers a larger terrain than what "narrativist" authors usually allow to it, while the notion of plot receives from its opposition to story and argument an uncommon precision.

Most of all, we must not lose sight of the fact that the threefold typology upon which this theory of historical style rests does not claim any "logical" authority. The modes of emplotment, in particular, are the products of a tradition of writing which has given them the configuration that the historian uses. This aspect of traditionality is in the end the most important thing. A historian, as a writer, addresses a public likely to recognize the traditional forms of the art of narration. These structures are not therefore inert rules. They are the forms of a cultural heritage. If we say that no event is in itself tragic and that the historian only makes it appear as such by encoding it in a certain way, it is because the arbitrariness of the encoding is limited, not by the narrated events, but by the reader's expectation of encountering known forms of encoding: "the encodation of events in terms of such plot structures is one of the ways that a culture has of making sense of both personal and public pasts" ("The Historical Text as Literary Artifact," p. 85). The encoding is thus governed more by the expected meaning effects than by the material to be encoded.

Such meaning effects consist essentially of making the unfamiliar familiar. The encoding contributes to this to the extent that the historian shares with his public an understanding of the forms "that significant human situations *must* take by virtue of his participation in the specific processes of sense-making which identify him as a member of one cultural endowment rather than another" (ibid., his emphasis).[64]

In this way, the dynamic character of emplotment is restored through its character of traditionality, even if its generic character is the only one considered. What is more, this trait is counterbalanced by the continuity that the notion of historiographical style reestablishes between chronicle, the chain of motifs, plot, argument, and ideological implication. This is why we may— somewhat counter to White, but thanks to his work—take emplotment as the operation that *dynamizes* every level of narrative articulation. Emplotment is much more than one level among many. It is what brings about the transition between narrating and explaining.

How One Writes History

It struck me that it might be interesting to return at the end of this chapter to French historiography. The work of Paul Veyne, *Comment on écrit l'histoire*—which stands alone on the French landscape—has the noteworthy advantage of uniting a scientific abasement of history with an apology for the notion of plot.[65] Veyne thus finds himself curiously situated at the confluence of the two currents of thought I have just described, even though he starts from Max Weber and not the English-language "narrativist" current, and even though he preserves a tie to logical positivism which that current has broken. Nevertheless, by placing him at this strategic crossroads I hope to add to the sting of a work that is already quite provocative.

His book can, in effect, be read as an expert performance intertwining two motifs: history is "nothing but a truthful narrative" (p. 13), and history is too "sublunar" a science to be explained in terms of laws. To abase the explanatory claim while elevating the narrative capacity—these two movements balance each other in an incessant seesawing.

The goal of elevating the narrative capacity is attained if we join together narrative and plot, something neither Marc Bloch, nor Lucien Febvre, nor Fernand Braudel, nor even Henri-Irénée Marrou ever tried to do, because for them the narrative is what the actors themselves bring about, being given over to the confusion and opacity of their own present. But, precisely because the narrative is a construct, it revives nothing. "History," says Veyne, "is a bookish, not an existential, notion. It is the organization by the intelligence of givens that refer to a temporality other than that of my *Dasein*" (p. 90). "History is an intellectual activity that, through consecrated literary forms, serves the ends of simple curiosity" (p. 103). Nothing links this curiosity to some existential ground.[66]

In one sense, Veyne is calling narrative what Aron and Marrou called reconstruction. But this change in terminology has its own importance. By linking historical understanding to narrative activity, he allows us to push even further the description of "the object of history" (the title of his first section). If, in fact, we cling to the intrinsic character of the notion of an event—that is, every individual and unrepeatable occurrence—nothing qualifies it as historical or as physical. "The true difference does not lie between historical facts and physical ones, but between history and the physical sciences" (p. 21). The latter subsume facts under laws, the former integrates them into plots. Emplotment is what qualifies an event as historical: "the facts only exist in and through plots wherein they take on the relative importance that the human logic of the drama imposes on them" (p. 70). And "since every event is as historical as any other, we can cut up the field of events as we like" (p. 83). Here Veyne rejoins those narrativist authors we have studied. A historical event is not what happens but what can be narrated, or what has already been narrated in chronicles or legends. Furthermore, historians do not despair of having to work only with mutilated fragments. One makes a plot with what one knows, and a plot is by nature "mutilated knowledge."

By so reconnecting event and plot, Paul Veyne can undramatize the argument over events and nonevents [*l'événementiel et du non-événementiel*], started by the Annales School. The long time-span is just as much about an event as is the short time-span, if plot is the only measure of an event. The nonevent marks the gap between the determined field of events and the already plowed region of plots. "What is not an event are those events not yet hailed as such: The history of terrors, of *mentalités*, of madness, or of the search for security across the ages. We shall therefore call the nonevent that historicity which as such we are not yet aware of" (p. 31).

What is more, if we define what counts as a plot broadly enough, even quantitative history reenters its orbit. There is a plot whenever history brings together a set of goals, material causes, and chance. A plot is "a very human and very unscientific mixture of material causes, ends, and chance events" (p. 46). Chronological order is not essential to it. In my opinion, this definition is completely compatible with the notion of the synthesis of the heterogeneous proposed above in Part I.

So long as we can recognize this disparate combination, there is a plot. And in this sense, nonchronological series, series of items for the quantitative historians, remain within the domain of history in virtue of their tie, however tenuous, to a plot. This tie between a plot and a series of items, which is not clearly explained by Veyne, seems to me assured by the notion he borrows from Cournot (to which Aron also referred at the beginning of his 1937 book), of the interweaving of causal series. "The field of events is an interweaving of series" (p. 35). But is every interweaving of series a plot?

Veyne thinks he can extend the notion of plot to the point where the notion of time is no longer indispensable to it. "What would become of a history that succeeded in ridding itself of all remaining singularities, of all units of time and place, so as to present itself completely as just the unity of the plot? This is what has appeared over the course of this book" (p. 84). Veyne thus wants to carry to the extreme one of the possibilities opened by the the Aristotelian notion of plot which, we have seen, also ignores time, even though it implies a beginning, a middle, and an end. This possible achronicity has also been worked out by various English-speaking authors (such as Louis O. Mink, whom I discussed above). This possibility is tied to the fundamental feature of a plot upon which Aristotle constructed his *Poetics*, namely, its capacity to teach the universal. We have also seen above how Hayden White exploits this generic or categorial resource of emplotment.

I find the same accent in Veyne when he develops the apparent paradox that the object of history is not the individual but the specific. Once again it is the notion of plot that turns us away from any plea for history as the science of the concrete. To put an event in a plot is to state something intelligible and therefore something specific. "Everything we can state about an individual possesses a sort of generality" (p. 73). "History is the description of what is specific, that is, understandable, in human events" (p. 75). This thesis blends with the one about description in terms of items and the one about the interweaving of series. The individual is an intersection for a series of items, on the condition that a set of items is still a plot.

With this intelligible component of a plot we pass over to the other side of Veyne's work, that of reducing the explanatory claim.

Here Veyne acts as a *provocateur*. *History*, he says, *has a critique and a topic, but not a method*. No method? Let us take him as meaning no rule for bringing about a synthesis of the facts. If the historical field, as we said, is completely undetermined, everything found there really happened, yet numerous itineraries can be traced through it. As for the art of tracing them out, it stems from the historical genre, with all the different ways that has been conceived across the centuries.

The only "logic" compatible with the notion of a plot is a logic of the probable, whose vocabulary Veyne borrows from Aristotle. Science and its laws do not rule in the sublunar order, for "the sublunar is the kingdom of the probable" (p. 44). To say that history stems from the sublunar order or that it proceeds by plots is the same thing. History "will always be a plot because it is human; sublunar, because it will not be a part of determinism" (p. 46). Probability is a corollary of the historian's capacity freely to slice up the field of events.

But since the probable is a characteristic of the plot itself, there are no grounds for distinguishing between narrative, understanding, and explanation. "What people call explanation is barely anything more than the way the narrative organizes itself into an understandable plot" (p. 111). From this we can expect that, in the sublunar order, explanation in the scientific sense of this word does not exist. "To explain, for a historian, means 'to show the unfolding of the plot, to make it understood'" (p. 112). The explanation of the French Revolution "is the *summary* of it and nothing more" (p. 114, his emphasis). Thus sublunar explanation is not to be distinguished from understanding. With this stroke, the problem of the relationship between understanding and explanation, which had so bothered Raymond Aron, vanishes. As for the word "cause," disconnected from the term "law," Veyne uses it as does Maurice Mandelbaum.[67] "The causes are the various episodes of the plot" (p. 115). And the narrative "is from the outset causal, understandable" (p. 118). In this sense, "to explain more is to narrate better" (p. 119). This is the only depth we can assign to history. If explanation seems to push beyond our immediate understanding, it is because it can explain the factors of a narrative according to all three lines of chance, material cause, and freedom. "The least historical 'fact' includes these three elements, if it is human" (p. 121). This is to say that history is not to be entirely explained by accidental encounters, or by economic causes, or by *mentalités*, projects, or ideas. And there is no rule for ordering these three aspects. This is another way of saying that history has no method.

One apparent exception to the thesis that, in history, to explain is to make understood is represented by retrodiction (see Veyne, pp. 176–209), that inductive operation by which historians fill in a lacuna in their narrative through an analogy with a similar concatentation in another series but one without a fault. Here explanation seems quite clearly to be distinguished from understanding, inasmuch as retrodiction brings into play a causal explanation. And it seems to intervene precisely when the documents do not furnish a plot. We then return through retrodiction to some presumed cause (we might say, for example, too many fiscal laws made Louis XIV unpopular). We reason here from something similar to something else similar, with no guarantee that in this particular circumstance our analogy may not betray us. This is a case for recalling that sublunar causality is irregular, confused, and only valid "most of the time" and "except for . . ."! Within these narrow limits of what is reasonable, retrodiction compensates for the lacunae in our documents. The kind of reasoning retrodiction most resembles is putting things into a series, as practiced by epigraphists, philologists, and iconographers. What provides the historian with the equivalent of a series is the resemblance that assures the relative stability of the customs, conventions, and types from one civilization or era to another. It is what allows us to know, broadly speaking, what to expect from the people of a given era.

Retrodiction, therefore, does not escape the conditions of sublunar knowledge. It has nothing in common with a law of subsumption. It is much closer to causal explanation in Dray's and Mandelbaum's sense. "Historical explanation is not nomological, it is causal" (p. 201). After all, this is what Aristotle said about plot. It makes "one because of another" prevail over "one after another."

We might ask, however, whether causal explanation and understanding through the plot always coincide. This point is not seriously discussed. When action displays nonintentional effects, which is the normal situation a historian encounters, as Danto and Lübbe emphasize, using different arguments, explanation does seem to indicate a defeat for the plot. Veyne even seems to concede this. "The interval between the intention and the effect is the place that we reserve for science, when we are writing history and when we are doing it" (p. 208). Perhaps we should reply that the plot, as not coinciding with the perspective of an agent but as expressing the narrator's "point of view"—the "narrative voice," so to speak—knows nothing of unintended effects.

We must now do justice to the two complementary theses that history does not have a method but that it does have a critique and a topic.

What is its critique? It does not constitute the equivalent of a method, nor does it substitute for one. As the term—which is Kantian—indicates, it refers rather to the vigilance historians exercise with regard to the concepts they use. In this respect, Veyne professes a nominalism without any concessions. "Abstractions cannot be efficient causes, for they do not exist. . . . No more do forces of production exist; only human beings who produce things exist" (p. 138). This abrupt declaration ought not to be separated, I think, from the thesis mentioned earlier that history does not know the individual but rather the specific. Put simply, the generic is not the specific. Here Veyne has in mind something like Weber's ideal-types whose heuristic and nonexplanatory character he underscores. Because they are heuristic, the historian is never finished with readjusting them in order to escape the countermeanings they give rise to. Concepts in history are instead composite representations, extracted from earlier designations, and extended in an exploratory fashion to analogous cases. However, the continuities they suggest are misleading and their genealogies are abusive. But such is the realm of sublunar concepts which are perpetually false and constantly somewhat out of focus. So the historian's vigilance must be particularly severe whenever history enters, as it must, the way of a comparative approach. Marc Bloch was correct, in his *Feudal Society*, to compare serfdom in Europe and Japan. Yet comparison does not uncover a more general reality, nor does it provide for a more explanatory history. It is only a heuristic approach that leads to particular plots. "What do we do other than understand plots? And there are not two ways of understanding" (p. 157).

The topic of history remains to be considered. History does not have a method but it does have a critique and a topic (p. 267). The term "topic" is borrowed, following Vico's example, from the Aristotelian theory of *topoi* or "commonplaces," which itself is related to rhetoric. As is well known, these commonplaces constitute the stock of appropriate questions that an orator must possess to speak effectively before an assembly or a tribunal. What is the purpose of history's topic? It has just one purpose: "to expand the questionnaire" (pp. 253ff.). This expanding of the questionnaire is the only progress history is capable of. How does it come about, if not through a parallel enrichment of the concepts involved? Veyne's nominalism, so strongly associated with his theory of understanding, must therefore be counterbalanced by an apology for the conceptual progress thanks to which the modern historian's vision is richer than that of a Thucydides. Veyne, of course, does not formally contradict himself, inasmuch as he assigns the topic of history to its heuristic aspect, hence to its art of asking questions, and not to explanation, if we take this to apply to the art of answering questions. But does this topic stay within the bounds of heuristics and not encroach upon explanation? In the most frequent case today, of nonevent-oriented history, what we can call "structural history" (p. 263), it is this topic that allows historians to uproot themselves from the perspective of their sources and to conceptualize events differently than the historical agents or their contemporaries would have done so, and therefore to rationalize their reading of the past. Veyne, in fact, puts this quite nicely: "This rationalization translates into a conceptualizing of the experienced world, through an expanding of the topic" (p. 268).

He is here asking us to accept together two theses that at first glance look quite disparate: that there is nothing to understand in history except plots, and that expanding our questionnaire is equivalent to a progressive conceptualization. It is true that the contrast between these two theses is not so strong if we correctly interpret the two assertions. On the one hand, we must admit that his notion of plot is not tied to the history of events. There is also a plot in structural history. So broadened, the understanding of a plot not only does not contradict but even calls for progress in conceptualization. On the other hand, we have to admit that conceptualization does not authorize any confusion between sublunar knowledge and a science in the strong sense of this term. This is the sense in which the topic remains something heuristic and does not change the fundamental character of understanding, which remains the understanding of plots.

To be totally convincing, however, Veyne should explain how history can still be a narrative when it stops being about events, whether it becomes structural, or comparative, or if it regroups into series items drawn from an atemporal continuum. In other words, the question Paul Veyne's book raises is how far we can extend the notion of plot without its losing its discriminating ability. This question today must be addressed to all the upholders of a "narrativist" theory of history. English-speaking authors have been able to avoid it because their examples usually are naive and do not surpass the level of the history of events. Yet it is when history ceases to be the history of events that the narrativist theory is really called into question. The force of Paul Veyne's book is to have brought to this critical point the idea that history is only the construction and understanding of plots.

6

Historical Intentionality

The aim of the present chapter is to examine the *indirect* connection that must be maintained, in my opinion, between history and our narrative competence, as this has been analyzed in the third chapter of Part I. The fact that this connection must be maintained but that it cannot be a direct connection is the result of the confrontation presented in the two preceding chapters.

The analyses in the first chapter establish the idea of an epistemological break between historical knowledge and our ability to follow a story. This break affects this ability on three levels: the level of procedures, the level of entities, and the level of temporality. On the level of procedures, history is born as inquiry—*historia, Forschung, recherche*—out of the specific use it makes of explanation. Even if admit, with W. B. Gallie, that a narrative is "self-explanatory," history as a science removes the explanatory process from the fabric of the narrative and sets it up as a separate problematic. It is not that the narrative is oblivious to the forms "why" and "because," but its connections remain immanent to the emplotment. For historians, the explanatory form is made autonomous; it becomes the distinct object of a process of authentification and justification. In this respect, historians are in the situation of a judge: placed in the real or potential situation of a dispute, they attempt to prove that one given explanation is better than another. They therefore seek "warrants," the most important of which is documentary proof. Now it is one thing to explain by recounting. It is quite another to set up the explanation itself as a problem in order to submit it to discussion and to the judgment of an audience, which, if not universal, is at least reputed to be competent, and is composed first of all of the historian's peers.

Making historical explanation autonomous in this way in relation to the explanatory sketches immanent in the narrative has several corollaries, all of which accentuate the break between history and narrative. The first corollary is that tied to the work of explanation is a work of conceptualization, which some people even hold to be the principal criterion of history.[1] This critical problem can belong only to a discipline which, if it has no method, according to Paul Veyne, does indeed possess a critique and a topic. There is no epistemology of history that does not at one time or another take a stand on the great quarrel over (historical) universals and that does not painfully retrace, following the medieval scholars, the back-and-forth movement between realism and nominalism (Gallie). This is of no concern to narrators. Certainly they use universals, but they are unaware of the question posed by "extending the questionnaire" (Veyne).

Another corollary of the critical status of history as inquiry is that whatever the limits of historical objectivity may be, there is a problem of objectivity in history. According to Maurice Mandelbaum, a judgment is termed "objective" "because we regard its truth as excluding the possibility that its denial can also be true."[2] This is a claim that is never made good but that is included in the very project of historical inquiry. The objectivity in question has two sides to it: first, we can expect that the facts dealt with in historical works, when they are taken one at a time, interlock with one another in the manner of geographical maps, if the same rules of projection and scale are respected, or, yet again, like the different facets of the same precious stone. Whereas there is no sense in placing stories, novels, and plays side by side, it is a legitimate and unavoidable question how the history of a given period interlocks with that of some other period, the history of France with that of England, for example, or how the political or military history of a given country at a given time dovetails with its economic history, with its social history, and its cultural history. A secret dream of emulating the cartographer or the diamond cutter animates the historical enterprise. Even if the idea of universal history must forever remain an Idea in Kant's sense of this term, since it is incapable of constituting a Leibnizian geometral, the work of approximation that brings the concrete results attained by individual or collective inquiry ever closer to this idea is neither useless nor meaningless. To this desire to tie things together on the side of historical facts corresponds the hope that the results reached by different investigators can be combined, due to their complementarity, and that they can mutually correct one another. The credo of objectivity is nothing other than this twofold conviction that the facts related by different histories can be linked together and that the results of these histories can complete one another.

The final corollary is that, precisely because history has objectivity as a project, it can pose the limits of objectivity as a specific problem. This question is foreign to the innocence and naiveté of the narrator, who instead expects from the public, in Coleridge's familiar expression, a "willing suspension of disbelief." Historians address themselves to distrustful readers who expect from them not only that they narrate but that they authenticate their narrative. In this sense, to recognize an "ideological implication" (White) among explanatory modes of history is to be capable of recognizing an ideology as such, hence to pick it out from the properly argumentative modes, hence also to place it within the scope of a critique of ideology. This final corollary might be called the critical reflection of historical inquiry.

Conceptualization, the search for objectivity, and critical reexamination thus mark the three steps in making explanation in history autonomous in relation to the "self-explanatory" character of narrative.

Corresponding to this process of making explanation autonomous is a similar process as regards the entities historians take as their sufficient object. Whereas in the traditional or mythical narrative, and also in the chronicle that precedes history, action is imputed to agents who can be identified, designated by a proper name, and held responsible for the actions imputed to them, history as a science refers to objects of a new type appropriate to its form of explanation. Whether these are nations, societies, civilizations, social classes, or *mentalités*, history replaces the subject of action with entities that are anonymous, in the strict sense of the term. This epistemological break on the level of entities reaches its culmination in the French Annales school, with its expunging of political history in favor of economic, social, and cultural history. The place formerly held by those heroes of historical action whom Hegel called the great figures of world history is henceforth held by social forces, whose action can no longer be ascribed in a distributive manner to individual agents. This new history thus seems to lack characters. And without characters, it could not continue to be narrative.

The third break results from the preceding ones. It concerns the epistemological status of historical time. This appears to have no direct connection to the time of the memory, expectation, and circumspection of individual agents. It no longer seems to refer to the living present of a subjective consciousness. Its structure is exactly proportional to the procedures and the entities that history as a science deals with. On the one hand, historical time appears to resolve itself into a succession of homogeneous intervals, the bearers of causal or nomological explanation. On the other hand, it is scattered into a multiplicity of times, depending on the scale of entities considered: the short time-span of the event, the moderately long time-span of conjunctures, the long time-span of civilizations, the very long time-span of the symbol systems that found the social as such. These "times of history," to use Braudel's expression, seem to be without any apparent relation to the time of action, to that "intratemporality" of which we said, following Heidegger, that it is always a favorable or an unfavorable time, a time "for" something.

And yet, despite this triple epistemological break, history cannot, in my opinion, sever every connection with narrative without losing its historical character. Conversely, this connection cannot be so direct that history can simply be considered a species of the genus story (Gallie). By converging on one another without ever meeting, the two halves of chapter 5 have heightened the necessity for a new type of dialectic between historical inquiry and narrative competence.

On the one hand, the criticism of the covering law model with which we began led to a diversification of explanation that makes it less foreign to narrative understanding, without thereby denying the explanatory vocation that keeps history within the circle of the human sciences. First we saw the covering law model weaken under the pressure of criticism. In this way it became less monolithic, allowing a greater diversity of scientific precision for alleged explanatory generalities, extending from laws worthy of the name to the common-sense generalities that history shares with ordinary language (Berlin), by way of the generalities of a dispositional nature mentioned by Ryle and Gardiner. Then we saw "rational" explanation demand its proper place, with the same requirements of conceptualization, authentification, and critical vigilance as any other mode of explanation. Finally, as we saw with G. H. von Wright, causal explanation was distinguished from causal analysis, and the form of quasi-causal explanation was separated from causal-nomological explanation and was seen to integrate within itself segments of teleological explanation. Following these three lines, the explanation peculiar to historical inquiry does indeed appear to move part of the way along the path separating it from the explanation immanent in a narrative.

To this weakening and diversification of the models of explanation proposed by epistemology corresponds a symmetrical attempt in the analysis of narrative structures to hold up the explanatory resources of the narrative and to bring them, so to speak, to meet the return movement of explanation in the direction of narration.

I stated above that the partial success of the narrativist theories was at the same time a partial failure. This admission must not lessen the acknowledgment of the partial success. The narrativist theses, in my opinion, are basically correct on two points.

First, the narrativists have successfully demonstrated that to narrate is already to explain. The *di' allēla*—the "one because of the other" that, according to Aristotle, forms the logical connection of the plot—is henceforth the necessary starting point for any discussion of historical narration. This basic thesis has a number of corollaries. If every narrative brings about a causal connection merely by reason of the operation of emplotment, this construction is already a victory over simple chronology and makes possible the distinction between history and chronicle. What is more, if plot construction is the work of judgment, it links narration to a narrator, and therefore allows the "point of view" of the latter to be disassociated from the understanding that the agents or the characters of the story may have of their contribution to the progress of the plot. Contrary to the classical objection, a narrative is in no way bound to the confused and limited perspective of the agents and the eyewitnesses of the events. On the contrary, the putting at a distance that constitutes a "point of view" makes possible the passage from the narrator to the historian (Scholes and Kellogg). Finally, if emplotment integrates into a meaningful unity components as heterogeneous as circumstances, calculations, actions, aids and obstacles, and, lastly, results, then it is equally possible for history to take into account the unintended results of action and to produce descriptions of action distinct from its description in purely intentional terms (Danto).

Second, the narrativist theses reply to a diversifying and hierarchizing of the explanatory models with a comparable diversifying and hierarchizing of the explanatory resources of narrative. The structure of the narrative sentence was, for example, seen to lend itself to a certain type of historical narrative based on documented dating (Danto). We then witnessed a certain diversification in the act of configuration (Mink), and we even saw, for the same author, how the configurational explanation itself becomes one explanatory mode among others, along with categoreal explanation and theoretical explanation. Finally with Hayden White, the "explanatory effect" characteristic of emplotment is situated halfway between that of the argumentation and that of the story-line, to the point that what occurs here is no longer a diversification but a breaking apart of the narrative function. Following this, explanation by emplotment, which had already been distinguished from the explanation inherent in the story-line, becomes part of a new explanatory configuration by linking up with explanation by argument and explanation by ideological implication. This redeploying of narrative structures is equivalent to a disavowal of the strictly "narrativist" theses, which are reassigned to the lower level of the story-line.

The simple narrativist thesis has thus suffered a fate comparable to that of the covering law model: to attain the level of properly historical explanation, the narrativist model has been diversified to the point of disintegrating altogether.

This adventure brings us to the brink of the major difficulty: does a narrativist thesis, which has been reworked to the point of becoming antinarrativist, have any chance of replacing the explanatory model? This question must unreservedly be answered in the negative. A gap remains between narrative explanation and historical explanation, a gap that is inquiry as such. This gap prevents us from taking history, as Gallie does, as a species of the genus "story."

And yet the intersections hinted at in the converging movement by the explanatory model toward narration and by the narrative structure toward historical explanation attest to the reality of the problem to which the narrativist thesis gives too brief a reply.

The solution to this problem depends on what could be called a method of "questioning back." This method, practiced by Husserl in his *Krisis*, stems from what Husserl calls a genetic phenomenology—not in the sense of a psychological genesis but of a genesis of meaning.[3] The questions that Husserl raised concerning Galilean and Newtonian science, I am raising concerning the historical sciences. I am asking in turn about what I shall henceforth call the intentionality of historical knowledge or, by abbreviation, *historical intentionality*. By this I refer to *the meaning of the noetic intention* that forms the historical character of history and keeps it from dissolving into the other types of knowledge with which history is joined through its marriage of convenience with economics, geography, demography, ethnology, and the sociology of *mentalités* and of ideologies.

The advantage we may have over Husserl in his investigation of the "lifeworld" to which, according to him, Galilean science refers, is that this questioning back, applied to historiographical knowledge, refers to a cultural world that is already structured and not at all to immediate experience. It refers to a world of action that has already received a configuration through narrative activity, which with regard to its meaning is prior to scientific history.

Indeed, this narrative activity already has its own dialectic that makes it pass through the successive stages of mimesis, starting from the prefigurations inherent in the order of action, by way of the constitutive configurations of emplotment—in the broad sense of the Aristotelian muthos—to the refigurations that arise due to the collision of the world of the text with the life-world.

From this, my working hypothesis becomes more specific. I propose to explore by which indirect paths the paradox of historical knowledge (in which the two preceding chapters culminate) transposes onto a higher level of complexity the paradox constitutive of the operation of narrative configuration. This paradox, we recall, arises from the median position of narrative configuration between that which comes before and that which comes after the poetic text. This narrative operation already presents the opposing features that are sharpened in historical knowledge. On the one hand, it emerges out of the break that sets up the kingdom of the plot and splits it off from the order of real action. On the other hand, it refers back to the understanding immanent in the order of action and to the prenarrative structures stemming from real action.[4]

The question, therefore, is as follows. Through what mediations does historical knowledge succeed in transposing into its own order the twofold constitution of the configuring operation of narrative? Or: by what indirect derivations does the triple epistemological break that makes history a form of inquiry proceed from the break established by the configurating operation on the level of $mimesis_2$? Does history nevertheless continue obliquely to intend the order of action on the level of $mimesis_1$ in accordance with its own resources of intelligibility, of symbolization, and of prenarrative organization?

The task is all the more arduous in that the conquest of the scientific autonomy of history does seem to have as its corollary, if not as its precondition, a concerted forgetfulness of its indirect derivation, starting from the activity of narrative configuration, and of its referring back, through forms that are further and further removed from the narrative base, to the field of praxis and its prenarrative resources. This feature, once again, relates my enterprise to that of Husserl in the *Krisis*. Galilean science, too, broke its ties with the prescientific world, to the point of making it almost impossible to reactivate the active and passive syntheses constituting the "life-world." However, our inquiry may have a second advantage in relation to the Husserlian efforts at genetic phenomenology, directed primarily at "the constitution of the object" by way of perceptual phenomena, the advantage of finding at the very heart of historical knowledge a series of relay stations for our questioning back. In this sense, the derivation is never so completely forgotten that it cannot be reconstructed with some sureness and rigor.

This reconstruction will follow the order in which I presented above the different aspects of the epistemological break: the autonomy of explanatory procedures, the autonomy of the entities referred to, and the autonomy of the time—or rather of the times—of history.

Beginning with the explanatory procedures, I would like, in light of the encouragement provided by von Wright's analyses, to return to the disputed question about causality in history or, more precisely, about singular causal attribution or imputation. I do so not in order to oppose it, in a polemical spirit, to explanation by laws but, on the contrary, in order to discern within it the transitional structure between explanation by laws, often identified with explanation as such, and explanation by emplotment, often identified with understanding. In this sense, singular causal imputation does not constitute one explanation among others, but is rather the nexus of all explanation in history. As such, it constitutes the requisite mediation between the opposing poles of explanation and understanding, to preserve a now obsolete vocabulary, or, better, between nomological explanation and explanation by emplotment. The affinity preserved between singular causal imputation and emplotment authorizes us to speak of the first form, by analogy, in terms of a quasi-plot.

As for the entities set in place by historical discourse, I would like to show that they are not all of the same order but that they can be arranged along the lines of a strict hierarchy. History, in my opinion, remains historical to the extent that all of its objects refer back to first-order entities—peoples, nations, civilizations—that bear the indelible mark of concrete agents' participatory belonging to the sphere of praxis and narrative. These first-order entities serve as the transitional object between all the artifacts produced by history and the characters of a possible narrative. They constitute quasi-characters, capable of guiding the intentional reference back from the level of the science of history to the level of narrative and, through this, to the agents of real action.

Between the relaying by singular causal imputation and that by first-order entities—between the nexus of explanation and the transitional object of the description—there are tight interconnections. The distinction between these two lines of derivation—derivation of procedures, derivation of entities—presents in this respect a purely didactic character, so closely knit are these two lines. It is important, nonetheless, to keep them distinct in order better to understand their complementarity and, if I may put it this way, their reciprocal genesis. The reference back to primary entities, which I am calling "participatory belonging," occurs principally by way of singular causal imputation. Reciprocally, the intention that runs through a causal imputation is guided by the interest the historian continues to have in the contribution made by historical agents to their fate, even though this fate slips out of their hands due to the perverse effects that, precisely, distinguish historical knowledge from the simple understanding of the meaning immanent to their action. In this sense, quasi-plot and quasi-characters belong to the same intermediary level and have a similar function, serving as a relay station for the movement of history's questioning back toward narrative and, beyond the narrative, in the direction of actual practice.

A final test of my working hypothesis concerning historical knowledge is obviously necessary. It concerns the epistemological status of historical time in relation to the temporality of a narrative. Our inquiry about history must venture to this point if it is to remain faithful to the principal subject of this work: narrative and temporality. It is important to show two things: On the one hand, that the time constructed by the historian is constructed to the second, the third, the nth level upon an already constructed temporality, the theory of which was expounded in Part I under the title of $mimesis_2$; and on the other hand, that this is constructed time, however artificial it may be, never ceases to refer back to the temporality of praxis described by $mimesis_1$. Constructed on . . . , referring back to . . . , these two intertwining relations also characterize the procedures and the entities built by history. The parallel with the other two mediations goes even further. Just as I am searching in historical causality and in first-order entities for the relay stations capable of guiding the reference of the structures of historical knowledge back to the work of narrative configuration, which itself refers back to the narrative prefigurations found in the field of praxis, in a similar way I should like to show, in the fate of the historical event, both the indication of the ever-increasing gap separating historical time from the time of narrative and from lived time and the indication of the ineffaceable reference of historical time back to the time of action by way of the time of narrative.

In these three successive spheres I will call upon the testimony of history alone as it pursues to the very end its critical self-reflection.

Singular Causal Imputation

Singular causal imputation is the explanatory procedure that accomplishes the transition between narrative causality—the structure of "one because of the other" which Aristotle distinguished from "one after the other"—and explanatory causality that, in the covering law model, is not distinguished from explanation by laws.

The search for this transition finds support in the analyses of William Dray and G. H. von Wright presented at the beginning of the preceding chapter. Dray familiarized us with the thesis that the causal analysis of a particular course of events cannot be reduced to the application of a causal law. The double test, inductive and pragmatic, by which we verify the credentials of this or that candidate for the function of cause is not far from the logic of causal imputation offered by Max Weber and Raymond Aron. But a connection is lacking between the theory of causal analysis and that of analysis by reasons. This connection is forged by G. H. von Wright in his analysis of quasi-causal explanation. Rational explanation is identified with the segments of teleological inference linked together in this specific type of explanation. Teleological inference, in turn, rests on the prior understanding we have of the intentional character of action. And the latter, too, refers to the familiarity we have with the logical structure of doing something (making something happen, doing something so that something happens). Making something happen is interfering with the course of events by setting a system in motion and, by this, also ensuring that it is a closed system. By this series of connections—teleological inference, intentional understanding, practical interference—quasi-causal explanation, which as causal explanation applies only to individual occurrences of generic phenomena (events, processes, states), ultimately refers back to what I shall now designate by the term "singular causal imputation."

The most precise presentation of the logic of singular causal imputation is found in the critical study Max Weber devoted to Edward Meyer's work *Zur Theorie und Method der Geschichte*,[5] to which must be added the contributions made by Raymond Aron, in the third section of his *Introduction to the Philosophy of History*, which are decisive for our investigation.[6] This kind of logic consists essentially of the constructing by our imagination of a different course of events, then of weighing the probable consequences of this unreal course of events, and, finally, in comparing these consequences with the real course of events. "In order to penetrate the real causal interrelationships, *we construct unreal ones*" (Weber, pp. 185–86, his emphasis). And Aron: "Every historian, to explain what did happen, asks himself what might have happened" (p. 160).

This probabilist, imaginary construction presents a twofold similarity, on the one hand, with emplotment, which is itself a probable imaginary construction, and, on the other hand, with explanation in terms of laws.

Let us examine Max Weber's reasoning more closely.[7]

Consider, as an example, Bismarck's decision to declare war on Austria-Hungary in 1866. As Weber observes, "And yet, despite all this, the problem: what might have happened if, for example, Bismarck had not decided to make war is by no means an 'idle' one" (p. 164). We need to understand this question. It consists in asking what "causal *significance* is properly to be attributed to this individual decision in the context of the totality of infinitely numerous 'factors,' all of which had to be in such and such an arrangement and in no other if *this* result were to emerge, and what role it is therefore to be assigned in an historical explanation" (ibid., his emphases). It is the phrase "all of which had to be in such and such an arrangement and in no other" that marks the entrance on stage of the imagination. Reasoning, from this point on, moves in the arena of unreal past conditionals. But history shifts into the sphere of the unreal only in order better to discern there what is necessary. The question becomes "what consequences were to be anticipated had another decision been taken?" (p. 165). This then involves an exploration of the probable or necessary interconnections. If the historian in his thinking can affirm that, by the modification or omission of an individual event in a complex of historical conditions, there would have followed a different series of events "in certain *historically important* respects" (p. 166, his emphasis), then the historian can make a judgment of causal imputation that decides the historical significance of the event.

This reasoning, in my opinion, runs in two different directions: on the one hand in the direction of emplotment, and on the other in the direction of scientific explanation.

Nothing in Weber's text, in fact, indicates that he perceived the first connection. We shall have to establish it, using the present-day resources of narratology. However, two of Weber's remarks do tend in this direction. He says, first of all, that the historian is and is not in the position of the agent who, before acting, weighs the possible ways of acting, given this or that aim, this or that available means. It is indeed a question that Bismarck could have asked himself that we formulate, except that we know the outcome. This is why we raise it "with better chances of success" (p. 165) than he did. The expression "better chances of success" announces, of course, the logic of probability that will be referred to later. But does it not in the first place refer to that extraordinary laboratory of the probable constituted by the paradigms of emplotment? Max Weber also notes that historians both resemble criminologists and differ from them. By investigating guilt they also investigate causality, although to causal imputation they add ethical imputation. But what is this causal imputation divested of any ethical imputation if not the testing of different plot schemata?

Causal imputation is also related at every stage to scientific explanation. First of all, explanation supposes a detailed analysis of factors, aiming at "the selection of the causal links to be incorporated into an historical exposition" (p. 168, n. 35). Certainly, this "thought process" is guided by our historical curiosity, that is, by our interest in a certain class of results. This is one of the senses of the term "importance." In the murder of Caesar, historians are interested only in the notable consequences of the event for the development of world history, which they consider to be most significant. (In this respect, a discussion that would get bogged down again in the quarrel opposing objectivity and subjectivity in history would miss the highly intellectual character of the operation of abstraction that precedes that of sorting out possibilities.) Next, to modify mentally in a specific way this or that factor, which first has been isolated, is to construct alternate courses of events among which the event whose importance is being weighed acts as the deciding factor. Weighing the consequences of eliminating the supposed event thus gives the causal argument its logical structure. Now, how do we construct the consequences that should have been expected if we assume a particular factor to be eliminated, if not by including in our reasoning what Weber calls "an empirical rule" (p. 173), that is, in the final analysis, a knowledge that must indeed be called "nomological" (p. 174)? Of course, these rules based on experience quite often do not go beyond the level of a dispositional knowledge, as Ryle and Gardiner would put it. Max Weber has specifically in mind those rules "relating to the ways in which human beings are prone to react under given situations" (ibid.). Nevertheless, they are sufficient to show, as we stated earlier, how laws can be used in history even though they are not established by history.

These first two features—analysis into factors and recourse to rules based on experience—are not absolutely foreign to narrative "logic," especially if this is shifted from the surface of the text to its deep grammar. The true mark of the scientific character of a construction, considered as both unreal and necessary, results from applying to the compared weight of different causes the theory of "objective possibility" that Weber borrows from the physiologist von Kries.[8] It is this third feature that marks the true distance separating explanation by narration from explanation by causal imputation.

The theory in question aims mainly at raising such unreal constructions to the level of judgments of objective possibility, which ascribe a degree of relative probability to the various causal factors and in this way allow them to be placed along a single scale, although the gradations resulting from this type of judgment cannot be quantified as is the case in what we call the "calculation of probabilities" in the strict sense. This idea of a graduated causality gives causal imputation an exactness that is lacking in the probability invoked by Aristotle in his theory of the plot. The various degrees of probability thus range in order from a low point, which defines accidental causality (as, for example, between the movement of a hand throwing dice and a particular number turning up), and a high point, which defines, in von Kries' terms, adequate causality (as in the case of Bismarck's decision). Between these two extremes we can speak of the more or less favorable influence of a certain factor. The danger is, obviously, that, by reason of an insidious anthropomorphism, we may materialize the degrees of relative probability ascribed to the various causes that our reasoning sets in competition with one another, in the form of antagonistic tendencies struggling to transform a possibility into a reality. Ordinary language is conducive to this when it has us say that this or that event helped or thwarted the appearance of some other event. In order to rid ourselves of this misunderstanding, it is enough to remember that these possibilities are unreal causal relations that we have constructed mentally, and that the objectivity of the various "chances" belongs to the judgment of possibility.

It is only at the end of this testing process that a factor is attributed the status of a sufficient cause. This is an objective status, in the sense that the argument does not stem from a mere psychology of discovering hypotheses; rather, irrespective of genius, which is no more lacking in a great historian than in a great mathematician, it constitutes the logical structure of historical knowledge or, in Max Weber's own words, a "firm skeletal structure of established causes" (p. 176).

We see where the continuity between emplotment and a singular causal imputation resides and where the discontinuity is to be found. The continuity resides at the level of the role played by the imagination. In this regard we might say of emplotment what Max Weber says of the mental construction of a different course of events: "In order to penetrate the real causal relationships, we construct unreal ones." The discontinuity has to do with the analysis into factors, the insertion of rules from experience, and, especially, the assignment of degrees of probability that determine adequate causality.

It is for this reason that historians are not simply narrators: they give reasons why they consider a particular factor *rather than some other* to be the sufficient cause of a given course of events. Poets also create plots that are held together by causal skeletons. But these latter are not the subject of a process of argumentation. Poets restrict themselves to producing the story and explaining by narrating. In this sense, Northrop Frye is right: poets begin with the form, historians move toward it.[9] The former produce, the latter argue. And they argue because they know that we can explain *in other ways*. They know this because, like a judge, they are in a situation of contestation and of trial, and because their plea is never finished—for the test is more conclusive for eliminating candidates for causality, as William Dray would say, than for crowning any particular one once and for all.

And yet, let me repeat, the filiation of historical explanation, starting from narrative explanation, is unbroken, inasmuch as adequate causality remains irreducible to logical necessity alone. The same relation of continuity and of discontinuity is found between singular causal explanation and explanation by laws as between the former and emplotment.

Let us first consider the discontinuity. It is more clearly stressed in Aron's analysis than in Weber's. In the section he devotes to the relation between causality and chance, Aron does not restrict himself to situating accidents at one end of the scale of retrospective probability, with adequate probability at the opposite end. The definition of an accident as possessing an objective possibility of almost zero is valid only for isolated series. His consideration, borrowed from Cournot, of the notion of coincidences between series or between systems and series throws into relief more clearly the notion of accident and emphasizes the relative character of Weber's probabilist theory: "An event may be said to be accidental with reference to one system of antecedents, adequate with reference to another. Chance, since many series have come together; rational, since at a higher level an ordered whole is found" (Aron, p. 175). We must reckon, in addition, with "the uncertainty which lies in the fixing of the limits of systems and series, with the plurality of fortuitous constructs which the scholar is free to set up or imagine" (p. 176). For all these reasons, a reflection on chance cannot restrict this notion to a simple opposition to adequate causality, within a process of reasoning based on retrospective probability.

The continuity between singular causal explanation and explanation by laws is no less evident than their discontinuity. The relation between history and sociology is exemplary in this respect. Raymond Aron describes it in these words: "sociology is characterized by the attempt to set up laws (or at least regularities or generalities), whereas history is limited to narrating events in their peculiar sequence" (p. 187). In the same sense: "Historical research sticks to the antecedents of a singular fact, sociological research to the causes of a fact which may be repeated" (p. 226). But then the word "cause" changes its meaning: "cause, as seen by sociologists, is the *constant antecedent*" (p. 188, his emphasis). Nevertheless, the points of intersection between the two kinds of causality—historical causality and sociological causality—are more noteworthy than their divergences. For example, when a historian establishes the relative probability of some historical constellation or other, this includes within it, as a nomological segment, empirical generalizations that provoke an inquiry into regularities by the person whom Aron calls the "scholar" in opposition to the "judge." The entire study devoted to sociological causality in his book tends to show both the originality of this enterprise and its dependence with respect to historical causality, hence with respect to singular causal imputation. In this way historical causality has the strange status of being an investigation found lacking in relation to the search for regularities and laws, and yet deemed excessive in relation to the abstractions of sociology. It constitutes an internal limit on sociology's claim to be a science, just when it borrows from the latter the regularities upon which its probabilism is founded.

It is due to this epistemological ambivalence that historical determinism, which claims to be located at an even higher level than that of sociological explanation, is, in its turn, chipped away from inside by the contingency preserved in historical causality: "Causal relations are dispersed, they do not fall into a pattern, so that they do not explain each other as do the classified laws of a theory in physics" (p. 205). In this sense, sociological causality refers back to historical causality rather than absorbing it into itself: "the partial determinism develops regularly only in a single constellation which is never exactly reproduced" (p. 224). And again: "abstract relations never exhaust the unique constellation" (p. 230).

It must therefore be concluded that the same dialectic of continuity and discontinuity is observed on the second side of the mediation performed by singular causal imputation between the narrative level and the epistemological one as is found on the first side: "Both complementary and divergent at the same time, sociological and historical causality complement each other" (p. 187).

Here again, Aron's originality in relation to Weber is confirmed. It results from the philosophical intention that animates his whole book. Thus the insistence with which the dependence of partial determinism on singular historical causality is stressed is in profound harmony with the "historical philosophy" (to use Gaston Fessard's title) that directs the epistemology of *Introduction to the Philosophy of History*, namely, his struggle against the illusion of fatality created by historical retrospection and his plea for the contingency of the present required by political action. Set against the backdrop of this great philosophical design, the logic of retrospective probability bears a precise meaning, which is of direct interest to our investigation into historical temporality. "The investigation of cause by the historian," says Aron, "is directed not so much at tracing the broad outlines of the relief of history as at preserving for or restoring to the past the uncertainty of the future" (p. 179). And again: "Unreal constructions must still remain an integral part of science, even if they do not go beyond an uncertain probability, for they offer the only means of escaping the *retrospective illusion of fatality*" (p. 183, his emphasis). How is this possible? We must understand that the imaginative operation by which the historian assumes in thought that one of the antecedents has disappeared or been modified, and then tries to construct what would have happened in accordance with this hypothesis, has a significance that goes beyond epistemology. The historian acts here as a narrator who redefines the three dimensions of time in relation to a fictive present. Dreaming of a different event, he opposes "uchronia" (a timeless time) to the fascination with what once was. The retrospective estimation of probabilities thus contains a moral and a political significance that exceeds its purely epistemological one. It recalls to the readers of history that the "historian's past has been the future of the characters in history" (p. 184). Due to its probabilist character, causal explanation incorporates into the past the unpredictability that is the mark of the future and introduces into retrospection the uncertainty of the event. The final lines of the section entitled "Limits and Meaning of Historical Causality" (pp. 179–85), which concludes the analysis of historical causality, thus occupy a strategic position in the economy of this book: "Anticipatory calculation is a condition of reasonable conduct, as retrospective probabilities are of the true account. If decisions and moments are neglected, one substitutes for the living world a natural world or fatality. In this sense, historical science, the resurrection of politics, becomes contemporary with its heroes" (p. 184, trans. altered).

I do not want to end this plea on behalf of the mediating role played by historical causality between emplotment and explanation by laws without replying to an objection that will link the current discussion to my discussion in the next section concerning the entities characteristic of historical knowledge.

It may, in fact, be objected that if we are still able to perceive a connection between emplotment and singular causal imputation, this is due to the limitations of the example chosen by Max Weber: Bismarck's decision to attack Austria-Hungary in 1866. Does not this choice confine the argument, from the very start, to the political sphere, hence to the plane of the history of events? Does this not condemn it to being only another version of "rational" explanation? No, not if the argument can be extended by analogy to large-scale historical events in which the cause, while remaining singular, is no longer the individual.

This analogical extension is made possible by the very nature of the question raised concerning the original example.[10] Even when historians inquire into the responsibility an individual has in a course of events, they explicitly distinguish causal imputation from ethical responsibility, on the one hand, and from nomological explanation, on the other. With regard to the first point, we must say that "causal analysis provides absolutely no value judgment and a value judgment is absolutely not causal explanation" (Weber, p. 123). In the example chosen by Weber, following Meyer, causal imputation consists in asking "why the decision to go to war was at that moment the appropriate means to achieve the goal of the unification of Germany" (p. 121). We must not be misled by the use of such categories as means and ends. The argument does, of course, include a teleological segment, but overall it is causal. It concerns the causal value to be attributed to a certain decision in a course of events that includes factors other than the rational core of the decision considered, and among these the nonrational motivations of all the protagonists in this course of action and, in addition, "meaningless factors" stemming from physical nature. It is causal imputation alone that can say up to what point the outcome of an action failed to live up to or betrayed the intentions of the actors. The gap between the intention and the consequences is precisely one of the aspects of the causal value related to decision.

These remarks go along with the thesis I have stated several times, namely, that causal explanation, even when it concerns the historical role of an individual decision, is distinguished from a phenomenology of action inasmuch as it evaluates intentions not only in terms of aims but also in terms of results. In this sense, causal imputation, as presented by Weber, coincides with von Wright's quasi-causal explanation, which contains teleological segments and epistemic segments.[11]

If, then, the argument of singular causal imputation is rightfully extended to series of events in which the cause is not of an individual but a collective nature, it is because already in the original example (the historical meaning of an individual decision) historical imputation is irreducible to moral imputation.

The objection, it is true, could return in another form. Why, someone might ask, continue to speak of imputation when moral responsibility is no longer in question? The notion of imputation, it would seem, preserves a diacritical function in that it provides a criterion for the distinction between causal explanation and nomothetic explanation. Even when the course of events offered for causal explanation involves nonindividual factors, as we shall see later on for other examples, this course of events is considered by the historian in its singularity. In this sense, I should say that the individual (the individual decision) is only the first analogue of singular causality. This is why the argument drawn from the study of the historical significance of an individual decision possesses exemplary value. Consider, for instance, Goethe's letters to Madame de Stein (another example borrowed from Weber's essay on Meyer's theory of history). It is one thing to interpret them causally, that is, to show in what way the facts attested to in these letters are "real links in a causal chain" (p. 139), namely the development of the personality of Goethe's work; it is something quite different to think of them as an example of one way of conceiving of life, or as a case for a psychology of eroticism. Causal explanation is not restricted to an individual point of view, although it remains singular, since this type of behavior can in its turn be integrated into a causal ensemble of the history of German culture. In this case, it is not the individual fact itself that enters into the historical causal series, instead it serves to "disclose the facts which are to be integrated into such causal sequences" (p. 142). These causal series, in their turn, are singular even though they do include typical facts. It is this singularity belonging to causal series that separates causal imputation from nomothetic explanation.[12] It is because causal explanation is singular, and in this sense *real*, that the question of the importance of a given historical factor arises. The notion of importance enters in only on the level of causal explanation, not on that of nomothetic explanation.[13]

The thesis that the notion of singular causal imputation can, in principle, be extended beyond causal imputation to individuals receives confirmation from another example Weber borrows from Meyer. The historian can pose the question of the historical significance of the battle of Salamis without breaking this event up into a dust cloud of individual actions. The battle of Salamis is for the historian, in a particular discourse situation, a single event to the extent that it can as such constitute the object of a singular causal imputation. This is the case insofar as it can be shown that this event is the deciding factor between two possibilities, whose probability can be estimated without being quantified. On the one hand, there is the possibility of a religious-theocratic culture that would have been imposed on Greece if the battle had been lost, and that can be reconstructed on the basis of other known factors and in comparison with similar situations, in particular, that of the Persian protectorate as it concerned the Jews returning from Exile. On the other hand, there is the free Hellenic spirit as this actually developed. The victory of Salamis can be held to be the adequate cause of this development. Indeed, when the event is eliminated in thought, a whole series of factors is eliminated with it: the construction of the Attic fleet, the development of the struggles for freedom, curiosity about history—factors that are summed up under the heading of the "possibility" following upon this event. It is, no doubt, the price we attach to the irreplaceable cultural values of the free Hellenic spirit that creates our interest in the Greco-Persian wars. But it is the construction of the "imaginary tableau" produced by abstraction and the weighing of the consequences of the event assumed to be eliminated that constitutes the logical structure of the argument. In this way, the argument remains that of a singular causal imputation, even when it is no longer applied to an individual decision.

Max Weber's own work offers us an even more remarkable example of singular causal imputation outside of the sphere of individual decision and of politico-military history. The reasoning used in *The Protestant Ethic and the Spirit of Capitalism* exactly satisfies the method of causal inference that has just been described.[14] The alleged connection between certain features of the Protestant ethic and certain features of capitalism constitutes a singular causal chain, even though it does not concern individuals taken one at a time, but rather roles, attitudes, and institutions. What is more, the causal connection provides the structure for a single process that renders irrelevant the distinction between a pointlike event and a long time-span. The thesis upheld in Weber's essay is, in this sense, a remarkable case of singular causal imputation.

How is this argument constructed? Faithful to the method of abstraction, Weber isolates the specific component of the work ethic on the side of the religious phenomenon and, on the side of the economic phenomenon, the spirit of acquisition characterized by rational calculation, the precise adaptation of available means to desired ends, and the value attached to labor as such. The problem is then precisely set out. It is not a question of explaining the birth of capitalism as an overall phenomenon but rather the particular vision of the world it implies. The religious conception of ascetic Protestantism is itself considered only in terms of the relation of adequate causality that it maintains in regard to the spirit of capitalism. When the problem is set out in this way, the question is that of the adequacy of the causal imputation in the absence of any regularity of a nomological type. Empirical generalizations are involved, of course—for example, the assertion that a doctrine such as predestination, which divests the individual of ultimate responsibility, was bearable only when it was compensated by other factors that increased self-assurance such as the belief in personal salvation, attested to by active involvement in work. However, empirical generalizations of this sort are only argumentative segments incorporated into the inductive inference that draws as its conclusion the imputation of the spirit of capitalism to the Protestant ethic, therefore a singular causal imputation, inasmuch as that these two configurations and their conjunction remain unique in history. In order to uphold this causal imputation, Weber does exactly what he recommends in his article on Edward Meyer. He imagines a historical course from which the spiritual factor considered would be absent and in which other factors would have played the hypothetical role assumed by the Protestant work ethic—among these other factors are the rationalization of law, the organization of commerce, the centralization of political power, technological inventions, the development of the scientific method. A probability calculation applied to these various factors suggests that in the absence of the spiritual factor under consideration these other factors would not have been sufficient to produce the effect in question. For example, the advent of the scientific method would have been capable of focusing energy on a specific goal, the precise organization of ends and means. But it would have lacked the emotional force and the power of dissemination that the Protestant ethic alone could contribute. In this sense, the probability that the scientific method might have transformed the traditional ethic into the bourgeois work ethic is slight. The same reasoning has to be repeated with respect to the other candidates for the role of cause before the Protestant ethic can be held to be the adequate cause of the development of the spirit of capitalism. This is why the adequacy of the causal imputation is not equivalent to an argument based on necessity but only to one based on probability.

With this extension of singular causal imputation to historical developments in which neither individual decisions nor pointlike events can any longer be discerned, we have reached the point where historical explanation appears to break its moorings to narrative. And yet the reconstruction of the various stages of filiation I have just made, in my free reading of Weber's text, with the help of Aron's *Introduction to the Philosophy of History*, authorizes us to apply the notion of plot *by analogy* to all singular causal imputation. This is, in my opinion, what justifies the use of the term "plot" by Paul Veyne, who designates by this all the singular configurations that satisfy the criterion that I have proposed for the notion of emplotment, namely, the synthesis of such heterogeneous factors as circumstances, intentions, interactions, adversity, good or bad fortune. This, moreover, as we have seen, approximates Veyne's definition of plot: the conjoining of aims, causes, and chance occurrences. In keeping with my argument for the indirect relation of historical explanation to the structure of the narrative, I shall speak of a quasi-plot in order to indicate the analogous nature of the extension of singular causal imputation on the basis of its prime example, the causal explanation of the results of an individual decision.

I shall take this analogy as my theme as I move from the question of explanatory procedures to that of the basic entities of historical knowledge.

THE FIRST-ORDER ENTITIES OF HISTORY

For didactic reasons, I have distinguished three paths along which we may question back: the one that leads from the explanatory procedures of scientific history back to the explanatory power contained in the emplotment of narrative; the one that leads from the entities constructed by the historian back to the characters in narrative; and, finally, the one that leads from the multiple times of history back to the temporal dialectic of narrative.

These three paths are inseparable, as were the three types of epistemological break described in the introduction to this chapter. They are characterized not only (1) by the same style of indirect filiation linking history to narrative understanding, but also (2) by the same recourse to certain relay stations that history itself provides for the task of reconstructing the historical intentionality.

My emphasis will be placed first on the indirect character of the narrative filiation, a character that can be verified on the level of entities as well as on that of procedures. The epistemological break between historiographical entities and the characters in narratives is, as I see it, the presupposition with which we must start here. Characters can be identified, designated by proper names, and held to be responsible for the actions ascribed to them. They are their authors or their victims. And these actions make them happy or unhappy. Now, the entities to which history refers the changes it attempts to explain are not characters, if we limit ourselves to its explicit epistemology. The social forces that operate in the background of individual actions are, strictly speaking, anonymous. The force of this presupposition seems to me to be overlooked by every form of "epistemological individualism," for which any social change can, in principle, be divided up into simple actions, ascribable to the individuals who are the authors of these actions and who bear the final responsibility for them. The error of methodological individualism lies in requiring in principle a reductive operation that can never actually be accomplished. In this I see the expression of a demand for a direct derivation that fails to grasp the specific nature of the questioning back, which alone is practicable in this domain. Only an indirect derivation can respect the epistemological break without shattering the intentional aim of historical knowledge.

The question is, then, whether this intentional aim actually possesses, on the level of historiographical entities, a relay station similar to that of singular causal imputation on the level of explanatory procedures.

This relay station does exist in the form of the first-order entities of historical knowledge, that is, those societal entities that, while they are indecomposable into a dust cloud of individuals, nevertheless do refer, in their constitution and in their definition, to individuals capable of being considered as the characters in a narrative. In the introduction to this chapter I called these first-order entities "entities of participatory belonging." The following discussion should justify naming them in this way.

The explanatory procedures that I classed under the heading of singular causal imputation apply, in a privileged manner, to these first-order entities. In other words, to the mediation procedures operating between scientific explanation and explanation by emplotment correspond transitional objects that mediate between historiographical entities and the narrative entities I term the characters of a narrative. Participatory belonging is to entities what singular causal imputation is to the procedures of history.

All historians—and the example of Braudel, to whom I shall return in the third section of this chapter, provides ample confirmation of this—are led at one time or another, even if they are wary of the epistemology conceived by philosophers, to order the entities put on stage in their discourse. This work of ordering is precisely what genetic phenomenology wants to follow through and make explicit. Whereas for professional historians the ordering of entities is thoroughly justified by its heuristic fecundity, genetic phenomenology seeks to carry this hierarchization of levels of discourse back to the intentionality of historical knowledge, to its constitutive noetic intention. To do this, it attempts to show that the ordering performed by historians is not reducible to a methodological expedient but contains its own intelligibility, which it is possible to account for reflectively. This intelligibility amounts to the possibility of traversing in both directions the hierarchy established by historical discourse among the entities it refers to. The first traversal—ascending, if one likes—must be able to indicate the ever-widening gap between the level of narrative and the level of history as science. The second—descending—must be able to indicate the series of references leading back from the anonymous entities of historical discourse to the characters in a possible narrative. The intelligibility of the ordering results from the reversibility of these two traversals.

It is within this search for intelligibility that the basic entities of historical discourse are determined. These entities of participatory belonging are located at the intersection of the ascending itinerary and the descending one. It is this strategic position that makes their determination the pivot point of our questioning back.

1. Some help for this attempt at indirect derivation can be found in Maurice Mandelbaum's work, *The Anatomy of Historical Knowledge*, despite the author's hostility to the narrativist theses. From him I have learned a double lesson that I shall incorporate into my method of questioning back. The first concerns the ordering of the entities assumed by the historian's discourse. The second concerns the correlation between what Mandelbaum takes as the first-order entities of historical knowledge and the procedure of causal imputation, the theory of which was worked out above. This second lesson will enable us to tie together the two paths of questioning back, the path of entities and the path of procedures. But let us begin by reflecting on the basic entities.

Maurice Mandelbaum's epistemology places him at an equal distance from the proponents of a subsumption model and from those of the narrativist version. In opposition to the former, he holds that, despite the typical character of the situations and events that history treats and despite its recourse to generalizations, history deals fundamentally with "what was characteristically true of some particular place over some particular span of time. . . . Thus, the familiar thesis that historians are concerned with the particular, rather than with establishing explanatory generalizations, appears to me sound" (p. 5). In other words, Mandelbaum takes into account Windelband's distinction between idiographical and nomothetic sciences. In opposition to the latter, he holds that history is an investigation, that is, a discipline concerned with authenticating its statements, with accounting for the relations it establishes between events. This is why the interest it displays in singular constellations cannot at the same time exclude the interpolation of regularities into its chains of relations. I shall not discuss these presuppositions, which accord quite well with the conclusions of the preceding two chapters.

Against this backdrop, the thesis I shall be attending to stands out clearly; the irreducible object of history is of a *societal* order. History sees the thoughts, feelings, and actions of individuals in the specific context of their social environment: "It is only insofar as individuals are viewed with reference to the nature and changes of a society existing at a particular time and place that they are of interest to historians" (Mandelbaum, p. 10). At first sight, this thesis, taken in isolation, confirms the discontinuity between the level of history and that of a narrative in which characters have to be identifiable as individuals responsible for their actions. A more precise determination of the term "society" sets us on the path of the problematic specific to these basic entities. It results from a distinction between two kinds of history: "general history" and "special histories" (p. 11). General history takes as its theme particular societies, such as peoples and nations, whose existence is continuous. Special histories takes as their theme abstract aspects of culture such as technology, art, science, religion, which lack continuous existence and which are linked together only through the initiative of the historian who is responsible for defining what counts as art, as science, as religion.

The notion of society, as the ultimate reference of history, receives from its opposition to the notion of culture a determination that will later allow me to characterize it as a transitional object between the plane of narrative and the plane of explanatory history.

Let us specify further Mandelbaum's notion of society in its opposition to that of culture: "A *society*, I shall hold, consists of individuals living in an organized community that controls a particular territory; the organization of such a community is provided by institutions that serve to define the status occupied by different individuals and ascribe to them the roles they are expected to play in perpetuating the continuing existence of the community" (ibid., his emphasis).

All three components of this definition are important: the first ties the community, and hence its duration, to places; the second connects it to individuals by assigning to them an institutionalized role; the third characterizes the community in terms of its uninterrupted existence. This third component will later enable us to bridge the gap between the basic entities and the procedures of causal connection that correspond to them at this level.

The notion of culture covers all of the achievements stemming from social creations and implicated in individual use that are transmitted by a tradition: language, techniques, arts, philosophical or religious attitudes and beliefs, insofar as these diverse functions are included in the social heritage of the various individuals living within a particular society.

The difference between society and culture is, of course, difficult to maintain in all cases. Why, it will be asked, are institutions, which define the role of individuals and include kinship systems, the distribution of goods, and the organization of labor, placed on the side of society rather than on that of culture? The answer is provided by the third feature of society, namely, that it is particular and exists continuously. From this it follows that an institution belongs to society and not to culture inasmuch as it constitutes an integrating factor in a particular and continuously existing society. In return, the activities that define culture are abstracted from particular societies and their modes are gathered together under a single classificatory concept by the definition that historians give to them, a definition that can vary widely from one author to another.

This distinction between the history of particular societies and that of classes of activities indicates the two poles at either end of a range of intermediary cases. For example, the societal phenomenon can be analyzed into various aspects—political, economic, social,—and the ways in which these aspects are cut up, defined, and put into relation stem from methodological choices that make them into artifacts in the same way as the activities classed under the heading of culture are made into artifacts. But as long as these aspects are thought of as the "facets" of a particular society, they provide its ultimate characterization. These facets can be referred back to the global societal phenomenon due to a noteworthy feature of the latter, namely, that it constitutes a network of institutions and powers, whose indefinite density lends itself to investigations on varying scales, after the manner of geographical maps. This capacity of the societal phenomenon of being analyzed into aspects, dimensions, or facets ensures the transition from general (I would prefer to say global) history to the special (or better, specialized) histories. But it is one thing to abstract these aspects and to group them together under the classes that then become the dominant subject matter of a specialized history; it is another thing altogether to relate these aspects to a particular society, to characterize it in an ever denser, ever more subtle manner, and in this way to restore its singular identity. The inverse argument can be made concerning specialized histories. In each case they take as their guiding theme a "class" of separate activities—techniques, sciences, arts, literature, philosophy, religion, or ideology. Now a class is not a concrete totality; it is an artifact of method. For example, art historians arrange discontinuous works into a collection following criteria that depend on the conception they may have of art. However, this manner of separating out a class by stipulating conditions is not left to the sole discretion of the art historians. The works themselves are set within traditions and within a framework of influences that mark their rootedness in the historical continuity of particular societies, from which the works receive a borrowed continuity. In this way, specialized histories refer back to general or global history.

Consequently, depending upon whether the accent is placed on the artificial character of the connections between cultural products or upon the traditions that allow them to participate in the temporal continuity of particular societies, the investigation leans to the side of specialized history or to the side of global history. It is the semi-autonomy of institutions and activities that allows us to relate them either to the singular constellations that define a societal phenomenon or to the classes of products and of works that define the cultural phenomenon.[15]

In what sense does the notion of society, in Mandelbaum's sense, offer a relay station in the derivation of historical entities starting from the characters in a narrative? Just as singular causal imputation presents an affinity with emplotment that justifies our speaking with regard to it of a quasi-plot, and even of plot in the broad sense of the word, so too society, once it is considered a singular entity, appears in historical discourse as a quasi-character. And this analogical transfer is not reducible to a rhetorical effect. It is founded twice over, in the theory of narrative and in the structure of the societal phenomenon.

On the one side, nothing in the notion of character, understood in the sense of someone who performs an action, requires that this character be an individual human being. As our literary analysis in volume 2 will amply confirm, the role of character can be held by *whomever* or *whatever* is designated in the narrative as the grammatical subject of an action predicate in the basic narrative sentence "X does R." In this sense history only extends and amplifies the dissociation made between character and real actor in emplotment. It could even be said that history helps to give to the character his, her, or its full narrative dimension. In this sense, individual responsibility is just the first in a series of analogies, among which we find peoples, nations, classes, and all the communities that exemplify the notion of a singular society.

On the other side, the societal phenomenon itself contains a decisive feature that governs the analogical extension of the role of characters. The definition given by Mandelbaum of a singular society is incomplete without an oblique reference to the individuals who make it up. This oblique reference, in turn, allows us to deal with the society itself as one great individual, analogous to the individuals who make it up. It is in this sense that Plato spoke of the City as a soul writ large and that Husserl in his fifth *Cartesian Meditation* calls historical communities "personalities of a higher order."

Two things are to be pointed out in this argument.

The first concerns the oblique reference in every definition of the societal phenomenon to the individuals who compose it. The second concerns the support this oblique reference provides for the analogical extension of the role of characters to the first-order entities of historical discourse.

This oblique reference to individuals is contained in the features by which Mandelbaum defines society: territorial organization, institutional structure, temporal continuity. All three refer back to individuals who inhabit the territory, who fill the roles assigned by the institutions, and who provide, as generation replaces generation, the historical continuity of the society in question. I call this an *oblique* reference because it is not part of the historian's direct discourse, which can, without too many qualms, restrict itself to collective entities and make no explicit reference to their individual components. But if it is not up to history as a scientifically oriented discipline to thematize this oblique reference, it is, on the contrary, the task of a genetic phenomenology to discover in the phenomenon of the we-relation the origin of the connection between individuals and particular societies. It finds this connection in the phenomenon of participatory belonging that relates first-order historical entities to the sphere of action. This connection defines the bearers of action as *members of.* . . . It can be called a real, ontological connection insofar as it has precedence with respect to the consciousness the members have of it. Of course, it is characteristic of this connection that it be capable of being recognized as such, that it be capable of being experienced and stated; but this recognition is grounded in the connection itself, which it brings to the level of language. The same emphasis must be given to both the ontological anteriority of the connection of belonging and the role of symbolic mediations—norms, customs, rites—by which the recognition of this connection is confirmed. As a result, neither varying degrees of consciousness nor the modes of its becoming conscious are actually constitutive of this connection. With this qualification in mind, let us consider for a moment the perspective of the varying degrees of consciousness. The connection of belonging can be experienced with great intensity of feeling, as in patriotism, class-consciousness, or prejudice, but it can also be forgotten, neglected, dissimulated, even vehemently denied by those whom the rest of society considers as outcasts or traitors or by those who consider themselves dissidents, exiles, or outlaws. It can then be the task of a critique of ideology to unmask their hidden allegiance. But this critique, in its turn, presupposes the anteriority of the connection in relation to consciousness (and to the possibility of bringing it into the sphere of explicit consciousness). As for the modes of explicit consciousness, the experience of participatory belonging can be tinged with the widest range of evaluations—

even opposition. It spans the range between the poles of approbation and rejection, commemoration and abhorrence (to use François Furet's expression in *Interpreting the French Revolution*, to which I shall return in the third section of this chapter).

The threefold reference of the societal phenomenon to the individual, which I have extracted from Mandelbaum's definition, clearly derives from this connection of participatory belonging brought to light by genetic phenomenology. To territorial organization corresponds the act of inhabiting, that is, of defining human space by means of a set of founding acts: constructing a shelter, marking out and passing over a threshold, living together, showing hospitality. Corresponding to the way in which individuals are assigned a status by institutions are the various manners in which the members of a group take on a given role, that is, the various ways of working, of performing a craft, of relating labor and leisure, of situating oneself within the relations of class, rank, and power. Corresponding to the perpetuation of societal existence is the connection between generations that intertwines life and death, and provides the living not only with contemporaries but also with predecessors and successors.[16]

Then comes the second part of the argument: namely, that the oblique reference of the societal phenomenon to individuals justifies the analogical extension of the role of character to the first-order entities of history. By virtue of this analogy, first-order historical entities can be designated as the logical subjects of active and passive verbs. In return, the analogy requires nothing more than the oblique reference of the societal phenomenon to individuals. To say that France *does* this or *suffers* that by no means implies that the collective entity in question has to be reduced to the individuals who make it up and that its actions can be distributively ascribed to its members taken one by one. The transfer of the vocabulary of the individual to the first-order entities of history must be said at one and the same time to be only analogical (and therefore implying no reductionism) and to be well-founded in the phenomenon of participatory belonging.

The recognition of this connection between the oblique character of the reference to the individual and the analogous character of the transfer of vocabulary is not without epistemological consequences. It enables history and the other social sciences to avoid the difficulties of methodological individualism. By giving equal weight to the ontological dimension and to the reflective dimension, the connection of participatory belonging accords equal weight to the group and the individual. It shows the individual to be situated from the outset in what Hannah Arendt liked to call "the public sphere of appearance." In this sense, none of the three features that constitute the societal phenomenon can be derived from the isolated individual: not the organizing of a territory, not the instituting of roles, not the continuity of existence. On the other hand, none of these three features can be defined without referring to individual action and to the interaction among individuals. It results from this that the transitional object of historical consciousness presents an unavoidable polarity, which is summed up in the expression "participatory belonging." [17]

The notion of a quasi-character, which I am adopting here in symmetry with that of a quasi-plot, owes an equal debt to each of the two arguments stated above. It is because each society is made up of individuals that it behaves like one great individual on the stage of history and that historians can attribute to these singular entities the initiative for certain courses of action and the historical responsibility—in Aron's sense—for certain results, even when these were not intentionally aimed at. But it is because the technique of narrative has taught us to dissociate characters from individuals that historical discourse can perform this transfer on the syntactical level. In other words, first-order historiographical entities constitute a relay station between second- and even third-order entities only because the narrative idea of a character itself constitutes a relay station on the configurational level between those first-order entities which history deals with and the active individuals implied by real practice. The first-order entities of the historian refer to the entities belonging to the sphere of action—those which I spoke of in Part I under the heading of mimesis$_1$—only by means of the narrative category of character, which comes from mimesis$_2$.

2. The symmetry between the theory of quasi-character and that of quasi-plot is reinforced by the fact that singular causal imputation, in which we saw the transitional procedure between historical explanation and narrative explanation, finds its privileged field of application precisely on the level of the first-order entities of historical discourse. One essential function of causal attribution is, in effect, to reestablish the continuity of a process in which the unity of development appears, for one reason or another, to be interrupted, or even nonexistent. We recall that continuous existence is, in Mandelbaum's vocabulary, a major feature in distinguishing society from culture.

This function of causal explanation is one of the primary theses of Mandelbaum's work. This thesis deliberately breaks with the empiricist tradition stemming from Hume, for which causality expresses a regular connection between two types of logically distinct events. According to this tradition, the nomothetic character of the causal relation is rigorously tied to the atomist character of the notions of cause and effect. Mandelbaum attacks just this atomist character of causal connection when he defines the basic social phenomenon in terms of continuous existence. [18]

Starting from the perceptual level, causality expresses the continuity of a singular process. The cause is the whole process, the effect is its end point. For the observer, the fact that a ball is hit is the cause of its movement, and the cause is included within the complete event. It is only for the sake of convenience that we isolate from the whole process the most variable of its factors and make it a cause distinct from its effect—for example, bad weather for a bad harvest. Against Hume it must be said that an "analysis of the cause of a particular occurrence involves tracing the various factors that are jointly responsible for the occurrence being what it was, and not being different" (p. 74).[19]

Causal explanation always involves linking a cause and its effect together "in such a way that they may be said to constitute aspects of a single ongoing process" (p. 76). Conversely, explanation in terms of *one* discrete antecedent is always the sign of an abbreviated and truncated explanation. The pragmatic advantage of these truncated explanations must not make us forget that the "cause is the whole set of actual ongoing occurrences or events that resulted in this, and no other, particular effect" (p. 93). In this sense there is a logical gap between causal explanation, which always concerns the factors responsible for a particular occurrence, and the statement of a law, which concerns the invariable connection between types of events or properties. Laws have an unlimited range of application, precisely "because they do not attempt to state connections between actual occurrences, but between properties characteristic of occurrences of given types" (p. 98), or, if one prefers, "between types of factors rather than between types of actual events" (p. 100).

This has two consequences, whose importance for the theory of history must not be underestimated. The first concerns the insertion of regularities into a singular causal attribution. If, in the course of the explanation of a singular process, we make recourse to generalities, to laws, this generality characteristic of laws cannot be substituted for the singularity of causal explanation. If we say, X was killed by a bullet that passed through his heart, the physiological laws concerning blood circulation are linked to abstract factors, not to the concrete phases of the actual process. They provide the mortar, not the materials. Laws apply to the sequence of conditions only seriatim. Therefore the series of occurrences leading to the final result must be accounted for causally in order for the laws to be applied to this series.[20]

Second consequence: the explanation makes the effect of a continuous process appear to be determined necessarily, once the initial state of the system is given; nothing other than this particular result could have occurred. But this does not mean that the event, as a whole, has been determined. For it is always in a closed system that a process can be said to be determined. The entire universe would have to be considered as a single system in order to identify the idea of causal determination with that of determinism. The initial conditions cannot be said to lead logically to their effect, since this effect results from the contingent fact that each of the occurrences taken at the start took place at a given moment and at a given place. Causal necessity is therefore a conditional necessity: *given* the complete set of causal conditions that took place (and not others) it was *necessary* that the effect that was actually produced occur. These two consequences confirm the irreducible but nonexclusive position of causal explanation.[21]

The decisive feature—and to my knowledge without equivalent anywhere else—of Maurice Mandelbaum's theory of causal explanation is, as has been stated, its close affinity with the analysis of first-order entities in history. Indeed, it is general history—in the sense defined above—that most fully illustrates his three-point thesis concerning causal explanation: namely, that causality is the internal linkage of a continuous process, that generalizations in the form of laws are to be inserted into singular causal explanation, and that causal necessity is conditional and does not imply a belief in determinism. Let us consider each of these three points further.

The affinity between causal reasoning and the continuous nature of social phenomena is easily explained. As was stated earlier, history passes from description to explanation as soon as the question "Why?" is freed from the question "What?" and becomes a separate theme of inquiry. And the question "Why?" becomes autonomous when the analysis into factors, phases, and structures is itself freed from the overall grasping of the total social phenomenon. Causal explanation must then reconstruct the continuity broken by the analysis. This reconstruction can take two forms, depending on whether it emphasizes temporal continuity or structural unity. In the first case, that of longitudinal analysis, if we may so call it, the social phenomenon calls for analysis and the work of reconstruction due to the fact that the web of events has the noteworthy property of constituting "an infinitely dense series" (p. 123). This property allows every possible change in scale. Any event can thus be analyzed into subevents or integrated into a larger-scale event. In this sense, the difference between short term, middle term, and long term is simply the temporal aspect of the relation of part to whole that predominates in historical explanation.[22]

To these changes of scale in the longitudinal analysis correspond equally variable degrees in the structural analysis. A society is an institutional fabric of tighter or looser stitches that permits variable degrees of abstraction in the institutional *topos*. Thus, the end point of our analysis may lie in the distinction between economics and ideology on the whole, as in Marx, or between political, economic, social, and cultural phenomena, but we may also take each of these terms as a starting point for a functional analysis.

These two lines of analysis are largely autonomous, due to the fact that it "is unlikely that all aspects of societal life and all phases of culture will change in a synchronous fashion" (p. 142). These discordances encourage the splitting apart of general history into special histories. And in turn, this splitting apart renders the task of general history all the more urgent and specific: "the degree of unity to be found in any age becomes not an explanatory principle but something that is itself to be explained" (ibid.). This degree of unity is not to be sought anywhere but in the way in which the parts are related to one another: "the explanation of the whole will depend upon understanding the connections that exist in the patterning of its parts" (ibid.)

The second thesis, the necessary insertion of generalities in singular causal explanation, results from the analytical character of explanation: the historical field is a relational field in which no connection, whether longitudinal or transversal, is taken as given once and for all. This is why generalizations of every order, of every epistemological level, and of every scientific origin are required to "cement" causality together. They concern institutional structures no less than the dispositions that give human conduct a certain stability and make it relatively accessible to prediction. But these generalizations function *historically* only under the condition of accounting for temporal structures and sequences whose cohesiveness is due to the fact that they are parts of a continuous whole.

Finally, the distinction between conditional causal necessity and universal determinism is perfectly homogeneous with the distinction between general history and special histories. Since the individual societies that constitute the ultimate term of reference for general history are ineluctably multiple, the necessity that historians may claim in reconstructing the continuity of their sequential or structural constitution remains fragmentary and somewhat regional. Mandelbaum's reasoning here hooks up with that of G. H. von Wright concerning the closure of systems, the intervening role played by agents in this very operation of closure, and the impossibility for any subject to be at one and the same time the observer of systemic connections and the active operator who puts the system into motion. Mandelbaum also here links up with the distinction made by Max Weber between adequate causality and logical necessity. And lastly, he reinforces Raymond Aron's argument against the retrospective illusion of fatality and Aron's defense of a fragmentary determinism open to free political action.

Yet the root of the distinction between conditional causal necessity and universal determinism is to be sought in the very nature of the first-order entities, which are always individual societies. Whatever lies behind this word, be it nation, class, people, community, or civilization, the participatory belonging that founds the societal bond engenders the quasi-characters who are as numerous as are the quasi-plots of which they are the heroes. Just as, for historians, there is no single plot that could encompass every possible plot, neither is there, for them, a single historical character who would be the superhero of history. The pluralism of peoples and civilizations is an unavoidable fact of every historian's experience because it is an unavoidable fact of the experience of those who make or who suffer history. This is why singular causal attribution, which operates within the limits of this pluralism, can claim only a causal necessity conditioned by the hypothesis that a particular singular society is given in which there exist human beings who are acting in common.

3. I shall only briefly discuss the second- and third-order entities constructed by historians and the correlation between their explanatory procedures and these derived entities.

The passage from general history to special histories in Maurice Mandelbaum is once again a good guide. Let us recall the characteristics he attributes to the cultural phenomena which special histories are concerned with, technology, the sciences, the arts, religion. They are (1) discontinuous phenomena (2) delimited by the historian, who establishes by stipulation what counts as a cultural phenomenon of this or that class, and, consequently, (3) are less inclined toward objectivity than is general history. Since my topic here is not the debate between objectivity and subjectivity in history but the epistemological status of the entities constructed by the historian, I am going to bracket everything that concerns the degree of arbitrariness allowed by special histories and will concentrate instead on the relation of derivation that connects special histories to general history.

This derivation is made possible by the analysis into phases and structures that already prevails on the level of general history, as well as by the recourse made to general terms in the course of causal explanation.

Starting from this twofold work of abstraction the interest of the historian has no difficulty in shifting from the societal phenomenon, taken in its continuity and its singularity, to cultural and generic phenomena. New entities then occupy the stage of history that are simply correlates of the work of conceptualization characteristic of scholarly history. These entities are, we must admit, classes, generic beings, not singular entities. For the most part, they are borrowed from the social sciences with which history combines to form a pair: economics, demography, the sociology of organizations, the sociology of attitudes and of ideologies, political science. Historians will be all the more tempted to take these entities for historical realities if they are successful in dealing with them as invariants, for which singular societies are no more than variants or, better, variables.

This is what Paul Veyne does in *L'Inventaire des Différences*.[23] He constructs an invariant, imperialism, and among its variants the imperialism that consists in occupying all the available space in order to acquire a monopoly of power. Roman singularity is thus localized, without any consideration of space and time, on the specific axis defined by the invariant taken as the starting point. This conceptual mechanism is perfectly legitimate and of great heuristic and explanatory force. It becomes faulty only when it is forgotten that second-order entities, such as imperialism, are derived—with respect to their existence—from first-order entities, to which acting individuals have belonged and in which they have participated through their actions and interactions. Perhaps historians can only "believe" in these conceptual beings by forgetting and reversing the true order of derivation. The merit of Maurice Mandelbaum's argument is that it combats this forgetfulness by reminding us that no history of art, of science, or of any other function of a given society preserves a historical significance unless, at least implicitly, historians keep in mind the concrete entities from which their histories were abstracted. In other words, these histories have no historical significance in themselves but only in reference to the continuously existing entities which are the bearers of these functions.

The derivation of second-order entities from first-order ones has as its corollary the derivation we have continuously observed of nomological explanation from singular causal explanation. I shall not return to this argument itself but rather to one of its aspects that more directly expresses the kinship between the two lines of derivation, that of procedures and that of entities. I have in mind the sort of quarrel over universals occasioned in the area of historical studies by the work of conceptualization, which, as I stated in the introduction to this chapter, is one of the corollaries of the epistemological break that gives rise to history as a scientific investigation. Mandelbaum's thesis, that the objects proper to special histories are classes and not singular entities, helps to strengthen the moderate nominalism professed by many epistemologists concerning the status of the conceptual apparatus employed by the new historians.

Henri-Irénée Marrou, in a chapter of his book, entitled "The Use of the Concept" (pp. 155–76), distinguishes five large categories of concepts. (1) History, he says, uses "concepts having a universal ambition" (p. 157), which are not so rare as the relativist critique would have them be, concerning that which is least variable in human beings. For my part, I would connect them to the conceptual network constituting the semantics of action (mimesis$_1$). (2) History, in addition, makes an "analogical or metaphorical use . . . of some special image" (p. 162); for example, the adjective "baroque" taken out of context and transposed on the basis of a reasoned comparison to periods other than the Baroque, strictly speaking. (3) Next comes the nomenclature of "special terms designating institutions, instruments or tools, manner of acting, thinking or feeling, in short, the facts of civilization" (p. 166). The limits of their validity are not always perceived, for example, when these terms are extrapolated from one specific sector of the past and applied to another—consul, Roman virtue, etc. (4) Of greater importance is Max Weber's class of ideal-types, if by ideal-type we mean "a plan of relatively general value built up by the historian from rudiments observed in the study of special cases, an organic scheme of mutually dependent parts. . . . expressed with precision and severity by the historian in a definition which exhausts the contents" (p. 168). For example, the notion of the ancient City as it was set out by Fustel de Coulanges. However, Marrou observes, "(as Max Weber emphasizes with some insistence), it is only legitimate to use the *Idealtypus* as long as the historian remains fully conscious of its strictly nominalistic character" (p. 171). We cannot, then, be too much on guard against the temptation to reify ideal types. (5) Finally, there are names such as Classical Antiquity, Athens, the Renaissance, the Baroque, the French Revolution. "This time it is a matter of particular terms that are incapable of exhaustive definition. They denote an ensemble, for example a more or less vast period of the history of a certain human milieu, or of the history of art or of thought: the totality of all that we are able to know of the object thus defined" (p. 174).

In my opinion, this last class is heterogeneous in relation to the preceding ones, because it designates third-order entities that combine the themes, procedures, and results of special histories into new holistic entities. These totalities are in no way comparable to the concrete totalities characteristic of first-order entities. They differ from them due to the complex procedures of special histories. Their synthetic character is the counterpart of the deliberately analytical spirit that governs the construction of second-order entities. In this sense, despite their appearance of being concrete, these entities are the most abstract of all. This is why the procedures that govern this level are as far removed as possible from the procedures of emplotment that can be analogously extended to the collective "heroes" of general history.[24]

This nominalism of historical concepts is, in my opinion, the epistemological corollary of the derived nature of the second- and third-order entities. When we consider these entities, we are dealing with "constructs" whose basis in narrative and, all the more so, in experience, is less and less apparent. We can no longer discern in these constructs the equivalent of what we call project, goal, means, strategy, or even occasion and circumstance. In short, at this derived level we may no longer speak of a quasi-character. The language appropriate to second- and third-order entities is too far removed from that of narrative, and even more so from that of real action, to retain any trace of its indirect derivation. It is only by way of the relation of derivation of second-order entities starting from first-order ones that this filiation can be reactivated.

Only the highly refined method of questioning back can, therefore, reconstruct the channels by which not only the procedures but also the entities of historical investigation indirectly refer back to the plane of narrative understanding. Only this questioning back accounts for the intelligibility of history as a *historical* discipline.[25]

HISTORICAL TIME AND THE FATE OF THE EVENT

The reader will not be surprised if I conclude my inquiry into the epistemology of history with the question of historical time. This is, indeed, what is at stake throughout the whole of Part II of this work. The question of the epistemological status of historical time in relation to the temporality of narrative has been constantly anticipated in the two preceding sections. Singular causal imputation has been shown to be closely akin to the historian's positing of first-order entities, one of whose distinctive features is, in its turn, continuous existence. Even if this feature cannot be reduced to temporal continuity, since it concerns all the structural aspects of the relations between the parts and the whole, nevertheless the notion of change applied to structural relations un-ceasingly leads back to the question of historical time.

Does my thesis, that both the procedures and the entities stemming from the epistemological break characteristic of history as science refer back by an indirect path to the procedures and entities of the narrative level, have an equivalent on this third level as well? Can it be demonstrated that the time constructed by the historian stems, through a succession of ever-widening gaps, from the temporality proper to the narrative? Here again I have sought an appropriate relay station. I thought this could be found in the extremely ambiguous use that historians make of the notion of event.

For this demonstration I will once again rely on French historiography. Of course, I am taking as given what has been amply demonstrated above, namely, that the history of long time-spans has now carried the day and tends to occupy the entire field of historical studies.[26] In taking up once more the plea for the long time-span from the viewpoint of the fate of the event, I will attempt to find in it an expansion—one characteristic of history—of the dia-lectic between the configuration of time by narrative composition and the tem-poral prefigurations of practical lived experience.

Let us first recall what the "mythic" configuration—in the Aristotelian sense of the term—makes of the event. We remember the epistemological and ontological postulates related to the notion of event. Let us leave aside for the moment the ontological postulates, which we shall return to in volume 2 when I discuss the reference of history to the past. Let us restrict ourselves to the epistemological postulates implicit in the current use of the term "event" —singularity, contingency, deviation—and let us attempt to reformulate them in terms of my theory of plot, as presented under the heading of mimesis$_2$. This reformulation proceeds from the major connection between event and narrative through the plot. As was shown above, the events themselves re-ceive an intelligibility derived from their contribution to the development of the plot. As a result, the notions of singularity, contingency, and deviation have to be seriously modified.

Plots, in fact, are in themselves both singular and nonsingular. They speak of events that occur only in this particular plot, but there are types of plot that universalize the event.

In addition, plots combine contingency and probability, even necessity. Like the peripeteia in Arisotle's *Poetics*, events occur by surprise, changing, for example, good fortune into bad. But the plot makes contingency itself a component of what Gallie rightly calls the followability of the story. And, as Louis O. Mink has noted, it is really in the case of re-telling a story—reading the story backward from its conclusion to its beginning—that we understand things had to "turn out" as they did.

Plots, finally, combine submission to paradigms with deviation from the established models. The emplotment process oscillates between servile conformity with respect to the narrative tradition and rebellion with respect to any paradigm received from that tradition. Between these two extremes lies the entire range of combinations involving sedimentation and invention. Events, in this regard, follow the fate of the plot. They too follow the rule and break it, their genesis oscillating from side to side of the median point of "rule-governed deformation."

Thus, due to the fact that they are narrated, events are singular *and* typical, contingent *and* expected, deviant *and* dependent on paradigms, even if this is in the ironic mode.

My thesis is that historical events do not differ radically from the events framed by a plot. The indirect derivation of the structures of history starting from the basic structures of narrative, a derivation established in the preceding sections, allows us to think that it is possible, through the appropriate procedures of derivation, to extend to the notion of historical event the reformulation of the concepts of singularity, contingency, and absolute deviation imposed by the notion of emplotted event.

I would like to return to Fernand Braudel's work, despite—or even because of—the case made there against the history of events, in order to show in what sense the very notion of the history of a long time-span derives from the dramatic event in the sense just stated, that is, in the sense of the emplotted event.

I will start from the indisputable achievement of the Braudelian methodology, namely, the idea of the plurality of social times. The "dissecting of history into various planes," to employ the terms of the Preface to the *The Mediterranean* (p. 21), remains a major contribution to the theory of narrative time. The method of questioning back must therefore start from here. We must ask ourselves what enables us to make the very distinction between a "history whose passage is imperceptible," a history "of slow but perceptible rhythms" (p. 20), and a history "on the scale . . . of individual men" (p. 21), namely, that history of events which the history of the long time-span is to dethrone.

It seems to me that the answer is to be sought in the principle of unity which, despite the separation into different spans of time, holds the three parts of Braudel's work together. The reader cannot be content with merely recognizing the right of each of these parts to exist by itself—each part, the Preface states, "is itself an essay in general explanation" (p. 20). This is all the more incumbent in that the title of the work, by its twofold reference—on the one hand to the Mediterranean, on the other to Philip II—invites its readers to ask themselves in what way the long span of time brings about the transition between structure and event. To understand this mediation performed by the long time-span is, in my opinion, to recognize the plot-like character of the whole that is constituted by the three parts of the work.

I would like to base my interpretation not on the declarations concerning method collected in the work *On History*, but on a patient reading of *The Mediterranean and the Mediterranean World in the Age of Philip II* (in the 1976 French third edition).[27] This reading reveals the important role of the transitional structures that ensure the overall coherence of the work. These structures, in turn, allow us to consider the arrangement of the entire work in terms of its quasi-plot.

By transitional structure, I mean all the procedures of analysis and exposition that result in a work's having to be read both forward and backward. In this regard, I would be prepared to say that if the first part itself retains a historical character despite the predominance of geography, this is by virtue of all the elements that point to the second and third parts and set the stage upon which the characters and drama of the rest of the work will be played out. The second part is devoted to the long time-span, properly speaking, and serves to hold the two poles together: the Mediterranean, the referent of the first part, and Philip II, the referent of the third. In this sense it constitutes both a distinct object and a transitional structure. It is this last function that makes it interdependent with the two parts that frame it.

Let me demonstrate this in some detail.

Consider the first level, whose theme seems to be space rather than time. What is immobile is the Inland Sea. And everything he writes about is already part of a history of the Mediterranean.[28] For example, the first three chapters are devoted to this landlocked sea. They refer to inhabited or uninhabitable spaces, including watery plains. Humans are everywhere present and with them a swarm of symptomatic events. The mountains appear as a refuge and a shelter for free people. As for the coastal plains, they are not mentioned without a reference to colonization, to the work of draining them, of improving the soil, the dissemination of populations, displacements of all sorts: migrations, nomadism, invasions.[29] Here, now, are the waters, their coastlines, and their islands. They, too, enter into this geohistory on the scale of human beings and their navigation. The waters are there to be discovered, explored, traveled. Even on this first level, it is not possible to speak of them without mentioning relations of economic and political dominance (Venice, Genoa). The great conflicts between the Spanish and Turkish empires already cast their shadows over the seascape. And with these power struggles, events are already taking shape.[30]

Thus, the second level is not only implied but actually anticipated in the first: geohistory is rapidly transformed into geopolitics. In fact, the first part is essentially concerned with establishing the polarity between the Turkish and Spanish empires.[31] Maritime zones are from the very beginning political zones.[32] Our view may try to concentrate on the silent life of the islands, their slow rhythm of ancient and new. But global history never ceases to come ashore on these islands and to link the peninsulas,[33] so "political supremacy passed from one peninsula to another and along with it supremacy in other fields, economic and cultural" (p. 166). Geography has so little autonomy that the boundaries of the space considered are continually redrawn by history.[34] The Mediterranean is measured by its sphere of influence. The phenomenon of trade is, in the same stroke, already implied. The Mediterranean space must be extended as far as the Sahara and to the European isthmuses. Braudel does not shy from stating right in the middle of his first part: "It is worth repeating that history is not made by geographical features, but by the men who control or discover them" (p. 225). Thus the final chapter of the first level openly leads from a physical unity to that human unity "with which this book is concerned" (p. 276). Consider human labor ("The different regions of the Mediterranean are connected not by the water, but by the peoples of the sea" [ibid.]), it produces a space-in-motion made of roads, markets, and trade. This is why it is necessary to speak of banks and of industrialism and trading families, and especially of cities, whose appearance changes the face of the land.[35]

The second level is, of course, the one where the historian of the long time-span finds himself most at home. But the extent to which this level, considered in itself, lacks coherence must be noted. Oscillating between the sphere of structure and the sphere of conjuncture, it places three competing systems of organization on stage: that of economic conjuncture, in overall expansion; that of the political implications of the physical and geographical relations, as observed in the mobile polarity of Spain and Turkey; and that of civilizations. These three systems do not correspond exactly, and this perhaps explains the increasing temptation, from one edition to the next, to give in to the unifying materialism of the economic conjuncture.

Already under the title of "economies"—the first system of organization—relatively disparate problems are considered: the constraints of space and of the number of people with respect to the governing of the empires, the role of the influx of precious metals, monetary phenomena and the evolution of prices, and finally, trade and transportation. As he is setting up this first system, Braudel raises, with ever increasing emphasis, the question of the specific level at which the totalizing factor, if there is one, is to be located: "Can the model of the Mediterranean economy be constructed?" Yes, if a content can be given to the notion of a "world-economy," considered as an "internally coherent zone" (p. 419) despite its uncertain and variable limits. But this is a risky endeavor, because of a lack of monetary standards by which to draw up an account of all the exchanges. In addition, a flurry of dated events concerning the four corners of the quadrilateral Genoa-Milan-Venice-Florence, as well as the history of the other marketplaces, confirms the fact that level three continually merges with level two. And the growth of states, joined to that of capitalism, makes the long history of economies repeatedly fall back upon the history of events.[36] Discussing trade and transportation, Braudel reiterates his purpose: "My intention is . . . to discover a general pattern" (p. 542). But the pepper trade, the wheat crisis, the invasion of the Mediterranean by ships from the Atlantic, oblige him to cover a great number of events (the history of Portuguese pepper, the Welser and Fugger agreements, the struggle between competing routes) and at the same time to go beyond the appearances of the narrative.[37] The balances and the crises touching Mediterranean wheat—"the vicissitudes of the grain trade" (p. 584)—the arrival of Atlantic sailing ships, which becomes an invasion—these are so many dates ("How the Dutch took Seville after 1570 without firing a shot" [p. 636]). The historian never manages to put events behind him as he moves in the direction of general economics, of the dynamic of world-economies, which are assigned the task of explaining events on the scale of the one I have just mentioned.

And the second level must also make room for other principles of organization: empires, societies, civilizations. It sometimes seems that empires provide the fabric of history: "The story of the Mediterranean in the sixteenth century is in the first place a story of dramatic political growth, with the leviathans taking their positions" (p. 660), the Ottomans to the east, the Hapsburgs to the west. The characters—Charles V, Sulaiman—are accidents, of course, but not their empires. Without denying individuals and circumstances, attention must instead be directed to the conjuncture persistently favorable to vast empires, with the economic ascendancy of the fifteenth and sixteenth centuries, and, more generally, to the factors favorable or unfavorable to the vast political formations which are seen to rise and to begin to decline in the sixteenth century.[38] It can well be said that Iberian unity is in the air, implied by the very meaning of the conjuncture, and along with it the creation of an imperial mystique, one of conquest and expansion in the direction, first, of Africa and, then, of America. But, in the face of events on the scale of the conquest of Constantinople, then of Syria, and finally of Egypt by the Turks, how hard it is not to exclaim: "surely the major event!" (p. 667). How can one fail to give life to characters as imposing as Charles V and Philip II, even if it can be written that "Philip II's withdrawal to Spain was a tactical withdrawal towards American silver" (p. 676). This does not keep the historian from expressing regret Philip II did not move his capital to Lisbon rather than shutting himself up in Madrid. If, despite everything, the long time-span wins out, this is inasmuch as the fates of states and of economies are mutually related. In opposition to Schumpeter, who overemphasizes the economy, one must place an equal weight on politics and on its institutions.[39] But politics cannot be discussed without discussing the agents of its greatness, legislators and their venality, the financial difficulties of the state, fiscal wars. The political enterprise has its actors.

Once again, neither economies nor empires occupy the entire stage of the second level. Civilizations are also to be considered: "Of all the complex and contradictory faces of the Mediterranean world, its civilizations are the most perplexing" (p. 757), so fraternal and so exclusive are they, mobile and permanent, ready to spread their influence and determined not to borrow from the outside. Spain has its Baroque. The Counter-Reformation is its Reformation: "The refusal then was deliberate and categorical" (p. 768). In order to express these "areas of astonishing permanence," Braudel has a magnificent description: "a civilization exists fundamentally in a geographical area which has been structured by men and history. That is why there are cultural frontiers and cultural zones of amazing permanence: all the cross-fertilization in the world will not alter them" (p. 770). Mortal? Of course, civilizations are mortal, but "their foundations remain. They are not indestructible, but they are many times more solid than one might imagine. They have withstood a thousand supposed deaths, their massive bulk unmoved by the monotonous pounding of the centuries" (pp. 775–76). However yet another factor intervenes. Civilizations are many, and it is out of their points of contact, of friction, and of conflict that once again events are born. Even if the Hispanic world's refusal of any mixing is the cause, "the slow shipwreck of Islam on the Iberian Peninsula" (p. 781) has to be recounted, along with the "drama of Grenada," and even the survivals and infiltrations that allow us to speak of "the aftermath of Grenada" (p. 792), until its destruction.[40] Next, the fate of the Jews has to be dealt with by means of the same schema, with a parallel being drawn between the stubbornness of the Marranos and that of the Moriscos. But, here again, we must follow the train of events back until we grasp the hidden connection between Jewish martyrdom and the movement of the conjuncture: "The chief culprit was the general recession of the western world" (p. 820). The date 1492 thus loses a bit of its dark splendor when it is placed at the end of a period of slow regression. Even the moral condemnation is found to be, if not weakened, at least nuanced.[41] The long conjunctures of civilizations are intertwined with those of economies. It remains that the rejection of Islam and of Judaism attests to the specificity of civilizations in relation to economies. Finally, and especially, without returning to the history of battles, forms of warfare have to be placed on the level of long time-span phenomena. And yet events must also be included if we are to appreciate the forms of war, to weigh the cost—the ruin of empires—and, in particular, to discern in war itself the very test of the longevity of civilizations. Opposing ideological conjunctures that present themselves and then are replaced allow us to give their relative weight to events such as the battle of Lepanto, which was grossly overestimated by its protagonists and eyewitnesses. These superimposed conjunctures, the bearers of events, mark on land and on sea the collision of economies, empires, societies, and civilizations. This competition between several principles of organization operating on the second level has not escaped Braudel. At the end of the second part—and in later editions—he weighs the pros and cons of a history governed by economic conjuncture alone or instead by a series of numerous conjunctures: for there is not one conjuncture but several. There is not even one economic conjuncture but a secular "trend" (the limit of its ebb and flow has a different date from one edition to the next) and an entire hierarchy of long, semi-long, and short conjunctures. But, most of all, it must be admitted that cultural conjunctures can only with the greatest difficulty be superimposed on economic conjunctures, even on the secular "trend." Did not the Spanish golden age continue to flower after the greatest secular upheaval? How can these late-season flowerings be explained? The historian hesitates. Despite the sirens of the economic conjuncture, he admits that history once again becomes multiple, uncertain; perhaps it is the whole that will slip through our fingers.

Everything, then, in the first two parts conspires to crown the edifice with a history of events that puts on stage "politics and people." This third part of the work is by no means a concession to traditional history. In a total history stable structures and slow evolutions perhaps constitute the essential part, but "they cannot provide the total picture" (p. 901). Why? First, because events provide testimony of the deep-seated, underlying movements of history. As we saw, the first two parts make frequent use of these "ephemera of history" (ibid.), which are at one and the same time symptoms and testimonies. The great historian is not afraid of stating here: "I am by no means the sworn enemy of the event" (ibid.). But there is another reason, namely, that events raise the problem of their coherence at their own level. Braudel himself gives a twofold justification for the inevitable selection that this level of explanation requires. On the one hand, the historian retains only important events, those that have been made important by their consequences. Without naming it, Braudel encounters here the problem of singular causal explanation as it was posed by Weber and Aron, with its logic of retrodiction and its search for "adequation."[42] On the other hand, the historian cannot ignore the judgment made by contemporaries concerning the importance of events, under pain of failing to take into account the way in which people of the past interpreted their history. (Braudel mentions in this regard the turning point that the Saint Bartholomew's Eve massacre represents for the French.) These interpretations, too, are part of the historical object.

It thus becomes impossible to make these two series coincide, the series of economic conjunctures and that of political events in the broad sense, the series of events that contemporaries chose to consider most significant, especially in a century in which, despite everything, politics led the way. These two series still leave great gaps between them that were, we saw, filled by the history of empires, of societies, of civilizations, and of war itself.[43]

Braudel's art, here, is to structure his history of events—and his history is not lacking in dates, battles, and treaties—not by dividing them into periods, as all historians do, but by reanchoring them in structures and conjunctures, just as he had previously called upon events in order to attest to the structures and conjunctures. Here the event gathers up and draws together the conjunctures and structures: "In Philip II the strengths and weaknesses of the empire were incarnate" (p. 1023). What structures this political history is the sort of "physics of international relations which in the sixteenth century was busy establishing the necessary compensations between the major war fronts along which Turkish power impinged upon the outside world" (p. 1166). A vast shift of power occurs when Philip's empire turns toward the Atlantic and America. Then "Spain leaves the Mediterranean" (p. 1184). At the same time, the Mediterranean steps outside the spotlight of global history.[44]

If this is indeed the history that is being recounted, why was it necessary to conclude with such sumptuous pages on the death of Philip II on September 13, 1598? From the viewpoint of the total history of the Mediterranean, this death is not a great event.[45] But it was an event of the greatest magnitude for all the protagonists "at the end of a long reign that to his adversaries had seemed interminable" (p. 1235). Have we not said that the perspective of contemporaries is also an object for history? Perhaps we ought to go even further—and this remark may well throw into question the beautiful balance of the three parts—and say that death reveals an individual destiny which does not fit exactly within the framework of an explanation that itself is not scaled to of the measurements of mortal time.[46] And without death as it seals a destiny such as this, could we still know that history is human history?

I now come to my second thesis, namely, that it is *together* that the work's three levels constitute a quasi-plot, a plot in the broad sense used by Paul Veyne.

It would be a mistake to limit the kinship between this text and the narrative model of emplotment to just the third level. To do so would be to miss the major contribution of this work, which is to open up a new career for the very notion of plot, and, in this, for that of *event*.

Nor am I prepared to look for this new form of plot in the middle level alone, although certain statements by Braudel himself suggest doing this. Does he not speak of the *récitatif de la conjuncture*, the conjuncture narrative? What might serve as a plot in the economic history is its cyclical character and the role that is played by the notion of crisis.[47] The double movement of growth and decline thus represents a complete intercycle, measured by the time of Europe and more or less by that of the entire world. The third, as yet untranslated, volume of *Civilization and Capitalism: 15th–18th Century*, entitled *Le Temps du Monde*, is built entirely upon this vision of the rise and decline of world economies, in accordance with the slow rhythms of conjuncture. The notion of a "trend" tends, then, to take the place of that of a plot.[48]

Nevertheless, I am not inclined to restrict myself to this equation, not only because it does just as much violence to the notion of cycle as to that of plot but also because it does not account for what occurs in the work at these three levels. Economic history lends itself to a plot when an initial term and a final term are chosen, and these are provided by categories other than conjunctural history itself, which, in principle, is endless, unlimited in the strict sense. A plot has to include not only an intelligible order but a magnitude that cannot be too vast, or it will be unable to be embraced by our eye, as Aristotle stresses in the *Poetics* (51a1). What frames the plot of the Mediterranean? We may say without hesitation: the decline of the Mediterranean as a collective hero on the stage of world history. The end of the plot, in this regard, is not the death of Philip II. It is the end of the conflict between the two political leviathans and the shift of history toward the Atlantic and Northern Europe.

All three levels contribute to this overall plot. But whereas a novelist— Tolstoy in *War and Peace*—would have combined all three together in a single narrative, Braudel proceeds analytically, by separating planes, leaving to the interferences that occur between them the task of producing an implicit image of the whole. In this way a virtual quasi-plot is obtained, which itself is split into several subplots, and these, although explicit, remain partial and in this sense abstract.

The work is placed as a whole under the heading of the mimesis of action by the continual reminder that "history is not made by geographical features but by the men who control or discover them" (*The Mediterranean*, p. 225). In this respect, the history of conjunctures cannot by itself constitute a plot. Even on the plane of economics, several different economies—or, more precisely, the antagonisms of two economic worlds—have to be placed together. I have already quoted this passage from Part I: "Politics merely followed the outline of an underlying reality. These two Mediterraneans, commanded by warring rulers, were physically, economically, and culturally different from each other. Each was a separate historical zone" (p. 137). With one stroke, the fabric of the plot is already suggested: the great opposition between the two Mediterraneans and the decline of their conflict.[49] If this is indeed the history Braudel is narrating, then it is understandable that its second level—which is supposed to be entirely devoted to the long time-span—requires beyond its overview of economies the addition of the physics of international relations that alone governs the subplot of the conflict between empires and the fate of this conflict. In its ascending phases, "The story of the Mediterranean in the sixteenth century is in the first place a story of dramatic political growth, with the leviathans taking up their positions" (p. 660). In addition, high stakes are involved: will the Atlantic belong to the Reformation or to the Spanish? When Turks and Spaniards turn their backs on one another at the same time, the narrative voice inquires: in the Mediterranean, earlier than elsewhere, does not the hour toll for the decline of empires? The question is necessary, for, as in drama, reversal brings with it contingency, that is to say, events that could have turned out differently: "The decline of the Mediterranean, some will say: with reason. But it was more than that. For Spain had every opportunity to turn wholeheartedly towards the Atlantic. Why did she choose not to?" (p. 703). In turn, the subplot of the conflict between empires, and the retreat of this conflict from the Mediterranean area, demands to be linked up with the subplot of the collision of monolithic civilizations. We recall the statement, "Of all the complex and contradictory faces [*personnages*] of the Mediterranean world, its civilizations are the most perplexing" (p. 757).[50] The reversals of these conflicts have been mentioned above: the fate of the Moriscos, the fate of the Jews, foreign wars. We must now speak of the contribution these subplots make to the overall plot. Referring to the alternation of foreign wars and internal wars as "plain to see" (p. 842), the dramatist writes: "it offers a new perspective on a confused period of history, illuminating it in a way which is neither artificial nor illusory. It is impossible to avoid the conviction that contrasting ideological patterns were first established and then replaced" (ibid.). Thus, just as Homer picked from the stories of the Trojan War the set he chose to tell in the *Iliad*, Braudel picks from the great conflict between civilizations in which the Occident and the Orient alternate the conflict whose protagonists are Spain and Turkey at the time of Philip II and whose framework is the decline of the Mediterranean as a historical zone.

Having said this, we must admit that the overall plot that constitutes the unity of the work remains a virtual plot. Didactic reasons require that the "three different conceptions of time" (p. 1238) remain disconnected, the aim being "to bring together in all their multiplicity the different measures of time past, to acquaint the reader with their coexistence, their conflicts and contradictions, and the richness of experience they hold" (ibid.).[51] However, even if it is virtual, the plot is nonetheless effective. It could become real only if a total history were possible without doing violence to any of its parts.[52]

Finally, by his analytical and disjunctive method, Braudel has invented a new type of plot. If it is true that the plot is always to some extent a synthesis of the heterogeneous, the virtual plot of Braudel's book teaches us to unite structures, cycles, and events by joining together heterogeneous temporalities and contradictory chronicles.[53] This virtual structure permits us nevertheless to judge between two opposite ways of reading *The Mediterranean*. The first subordinates the history of events to the history of the long time-span and the long time-span to geographical time—the main emphasis is then placed on the Mediterranean. But then geographical time is in danger of losing its historical character. For the second reading, history remains historical insofar as the first level itself is qualified as historical by its reference to the second level and, in turn, the second level derives its historical quality from its capacity to support the third level. The emphasis is then placed on Philip II. But the history of events lacks the principles of necessity and of probability that Aristotle attributed to a well-constructed plot. The plot that includes the three levels equally authorizes both readings and makes them intersect at the median position of the history of the long time-span, which then becomes the unstable point of equilibrium between them.

In my opinion, it is this long detour by way of the quasi-plot that finally allows us to question once more the notion of event that Braudel holds to be canonical.[54] For me, the event is not necessarily brief and nervous, like some sort of explosion. It is a variable of the plot. As such, it does not belong only to the third level but to all the levels and their various functions. When it emerges on the third level, it appears with the sign of necessity or probability that it owes to having having crossed through the other levels. It is in this way that Lepanto loses its brilliance and falls lower on the scale of importance. The death of Philip II remains a major event only because of the subplot of "Politics and People." This death tends to become a nonevent when it is placed within the overall plot of the struggle between political giants and on the trajectory of the decline of the Mediterranean, which comes to its relative conclusion only several decades later. After all, we have seen events proliferate also on the second and even on the first level; except that the event loses its explosive character there and acts rather as a symptom or a testimony.

The truth is that the event is what distinguishes the historian's concept of structure from that of the sociologist or the economist. For the historian, the event continually appears in the very midst of structures. And this occurs in two ways: on the one hand, all structures do not change at the same pace. It is when "these different time-spans" (*On History*, p. 48) no longer coincide that their dissonance becomes event-like. In the same way, the exchanges between numerous zones of civilization, the borrowings and rejections constitute quasi-pointlike phenomena which do not mark a civilization on all of its levels at the same time: "it is not so much time which is the creation of our own minds, as the way in which we break it up" (ibid.). On the other hand, in contrast to the sociologist, the historian in dealing with structures is attentive to their breaking points, their sudden or slow deterioration, in short, to the consideration that they die out. In this respect Braudel is no less preoccupied with the decay of empires than the traditional historian. In one sense, *The Mediterranean* is the gradual progress, the slowed-down march of the major event: the retreat of the Mediterranean from general history. Once again, the fragility of human works comes to the foreground and with it the dramatic dimension, from which the long time-span was supposed to free history.

I have found in other French historians who come within the sphere of influence of the *Annales* indications—often furtive ones—that betray this return to the event by means of the long time-span itself.

For example, in the marriage between history and anthropology as it is advocated by Le Goff, and which has produced *Time, Work, and Culture in the*

Middle Ages, it is, of course, the long—the very long—time-span that occupies the foreground ("the long stretch of the Middle Ages," "the long period relevant to our history," "the history of preindustrial society" [p. x]). Yet, on the other hand, Le Goff, no less strongly than Braudel, resists the seductiveness of the atemporal models characteristic of a certain type of sociology. First of all, because this very span of time is not without events, but indeed is punctuated by repeated or expected events (festivals, ceremonies, rituals) which recall all that is liturgical in historical societies. Next, because this particular long time-span no longer exists: the name medieval civilization is well chosen, for it is a "transition" society. Of course, the attitudes emphasized by historical ethnology are those that "change least" in historical evolution (p. 229), but "mental systems are historically datable, even if they do carry a heavy freight of debris from archeo-civilizations, dear to André Varagnac" (ibid.). In particular, history, if it is to remain history in its union with anthropology, cannot convert itself into "an ethnology that stands outside time" (p. 236). This is why the historian cannot conform to the vocabulary of diachrony, as it is borrowed from linguistics. The latter, in fact, functions in accordance with "abstract systems of transformation very different from the evolutionary schemes used by the historian in attempting to apprehend the process of becoming in the concrete societies he studies" (p. 235).[55] Instead, the historian has to try to go beyond "the false dilemma of structure versus conjuncture and, even more important, structure versus event" (ibid.).

In fact, in Le Goff I find an intimation of the thesis that the past owes its historical quality to its capacity for being integrated in that memory that Augustine called "the present of the past." Le Goff defines his "total," "long" "Middle Ages of the depths" in the following terms. "It is the time of our grandparents" (p. xi); "the primordial past in which our collective identity, the quarry of that anguished search in which contemporary societies are engaged, acquired certain of its essential characteristics" (ibid.). Given this, it is not surprising if, in this constituting of our memory, the long time-span is shortened into the form of quasi-events. Does not Le Goff describe the conflict between the time of the church and the time of the tradesmen, symbolized by the confrontation between bells and clocks, "as one of the major events in the mental history of these centuries at the heart of the Middle Ages, when the ideology of the modern world was being formed under pressure from deteriorating economic structures and practices"? (p. 30). What, in fact, constitutes the event is "the essential separateness and the contingent encounter" (p. 38, trans. altered) of these two times.

The historian of *mentalités* encounters the same problem. For example, Georges Duby begins with an entirely nonnarrative sociological analysis of ideologies—he calls them total, deforming, competitive, stabilizing, action-generating—yet he sees the event infiltrate these structures due not only to external borrowings, rejections, and internal conflicts but also to dissonances, "deviations of temporality" that appear at the point of intersection of objective situations, mental representations, and individual or collective behavior. The historian is thus brought to stress "critical periods in which the movement of material and political structures ends by reverberating on the level of ideological systems, thereby sharpening the conflict that opposes them."[56] Just as above, I am tempted to speak of a quasi-event to describe what Duby calls here "the burst of acceleration," set off by polemics, "within the tendencies covering long spans of time which guide the evolution of the dominant ideology" (p. 157).

And the vehicle of the quasi-event, as I tried to show in Braudel, is again the quasi-plot. I would like to demonstrate the same thing with regard to Georges Duby's work by placing side by side the article on method just referred to, "Histoire sociale et idéologies des sociétés," and the application of his working hypothesis in one of the works most representative of what he means by the history of ideologies. I have chosen *The Three Orders: Feudal Society Imagined.*[57] I propose to show once again here how the author dramatizes an ideological structure by constructing a quasi-plot containing a beginning, a middle, and an end. The structure in question is the imaginary representation of the entire society in the form of a hierarchy of three orders: those who pray, those who fight, and those who by their labor feed the rest. The formulation of this imaginary representation is taken from a seventeenth-century author, Charles Loyseau, in his *Traité des Ordres et Simples Dignités*, published in 1610. However, Duby does not simply consider a period of six centuries, as it is staked out by descriptions akin to Loyseau's. Instead, renewing the art of the author of the *Iliad*, he picks from among all the vicissitudes of the trifunctional image a history that has a beginning—the initial formulations by Adalbero of Laon and Gerard of Cambrai—and an end—the battle of Bouvines in 1214. The middle is formed by the reversals that dramatize the historical role of this ideological representation. So Duby attacks a problem different from that posed by Georges Dumézil, the untiring advocate of the trifunctional image. Whereas the latter attempts to establish—by comparison and through its recurrence in different historical constellations—that this schema belongs to the latent structures of human thought, in order to lead up to the question of *why* and *how* "the human mind is constantly making choices among its latent riches,"[58] Duby replies to Dumézil's two questions with two other questions, the historian's questions of *where* and *when*. He chooses to show how this trifunctional image "functions as a major cog in an ideological system" (p. 8). The ideological system in question is feudalism as it emerges and then triumphs. And to describe how it functions, he constructs what I am calling a quasi-plot in which the trifunctional image plays the role of, in his own terms, the "book's central character" (ibid.).

The outline Duby follows is very instructive in this respect. Since what is in question is indeed a structure, that is, a mental representation that "has withstood all the pressures of history" (p. 5), he entitles his first part "Revelation," in order to indicate clearly the transcendence of the system in relation to its fragmentary representations. The system is already historicized to a great extent by the variations in the first formulations and by the reconstitution of their political framework, the decline of the Carolingian monarchy and of the power that went along with it, that of the bishops. It is only at the end of this first inquiry that the organization of the "system" can be described (pp. 56–69). This includes the postulate of a perfect coherence between heaven and earth; a concept of order which has become an attribute of the perfect city; the division into the order of bishops and the order of kings; the division into dominant groups—priests and nobles; the addition to this binary arrangement of a third order characterizing the dominant functions—the class of subjects; and, finally, the concept of mutuality, of reciprocity within hierarchy, which in structural terms calls for a ternary division.

The mere description of this system demonstrates how equivocal the notion of trifunctionality actually is and how very little it resembles a true system. First of all, the third function appears in the form of an addition to two binary oppositions (bishop/king, priest/noble). Next, the relation dominant/dominated is added, as another specific binary system, to the internal binarism of domination just mentioned, whence the extreme instability of the system. Finally, the system does not imply that the three parts be filled by roles as well specified as those in Dumézil. *Order* alone is the key word. We can thus understand why the system is so easily a prey to history.[59]

Before entering into the plot properly speaking, Duby attempts, under the title "Genesis," to take a retrospective look at the formation of the system beginning with Gregory the Great, Augustine, and Dionysius the Areopagite. He then shows how the shift could occur from theological speculation on celestial hierarchies to political reflection on order and on orders, linking up in this way the celestial example and the ternary distribution of terrestrial functions.[60]

The quasi-plot really commences when the system is put to the test of "circumstances" (pp. 121–66), undergoes a long "eclipse" (pp. 167–268), and then finally reemerges, this "resurgence" (pp. 269–353) culminating in the system's "adoption," an adoption that is not merely symbolized but realized and finalized by the victory of the king—and hence the victory of the bishops as well—for whom the system had been intended, at Bouvines.

These are the three major reversals between which Duby divides his plot. It is noteworthy that the narrated story is set in motion by a crisis in which royalty appears to founder.[61] This is, first of all, a political crisis. But, above all, on the symbolic level, there is a competition with rival systems, which are themselves tripartite: the heretical model, the model of God's peace, the monastic model created at Cluny. The polemic engaged in by these competing systems is precisely what dramatizes the model. The triumph of Cluny announces the "eclipse."[62] Contributing to this is the feudal revolution which forces a reclassing of all the orders to make room for the third party, the peasants. And this places in competition, at the beginning of the eleventh century, not three but four ideological models (pp. 161–62): the model bound for victory and the three rival models just referred to.

The ideological model of Adalbero and Gerard is placed in the strange position of being not a reflection but an anticipation: an anticipation of the decline of monasticism, an anticipation of the restoration of the episcopate, an anticipation of the renaissance of the monarchic state.[63]

This curious split between an apparent survival and a real anticipation governs the system's "eclipse," as it is told in Part IV. This is "the age of the monks," who benefit from the waning of the Capetian royalty and, with it, of the episcopal institution. But an "eclipse" is by no means a disappearance. The time of eclipse is also the emergence of "new times": the times of the Cistercians, of the merchants, of the clerks, of the schoolmasters and their students.

As for the "resurgence," it is marked by the clerks' reconquest of the first rank at the expense of the monks; the knights' takeover of the second rank, the stronghold of the princes; and the takeover of the third rank by the laborers. But if the time of the eclipse was, for the trifunctional model, a time of anticipation, the time of resurgence is that of delay: "The obstacle," Duby says, "was Royal France . . . , the obstacle was Paris, treasure and symbol of a kingdom allied with the pope, with the bishops, with the reformed Church, with the schools, with the communes, with the people" (p. 307). This is what makes the resurgence the final reversal. "The adoption" alone constitutes a conclusion, inasmuch as it ensures the reconciliation between the model dreamed of and the real institution. Bouvines is the instrument of this encounter. Capetian has taken the place of Carolingian. However, it is curious that, with regard to the systematizing spirit that seems to govern the work, the king is not part of the tripartite schema: "He himself sat enthroned above order, i.e., above the three orders that made up court society" (p. 346).

Regardless of the doubts we may have concerning the coherence of the trifunctional model,[64] the plot ends when the symbol shifts from the dreamed imaginary to the constituting imaginary.[65] So it is indeed the "adoption" that at one and the same time provides an end to the story and confers a sense upon the "middle" represented by the triad: "circumstance," "eclipse," "resurgence."

This is all I wanted to show: the quasi-events that indicate the critical periods of the ideological system are set within quasi-plots, which assure their narrative status.

It is in the field of political history that the return to the event is most urgently felt. "How does one interpret such an event?" asks François Furet at the start of a work that is called, precisely, *Interpreting the French Revolution*.[66]

Interpreting—this the historian can do if he frees himself from the alternative of commemoration or execration in which he is caught up as long as he continues to participate in "the obsession with origins, the underlying thread of all national history" (p. 2) since 1789. Then the historian is inspired by intellectual curiosity alone, in the same way as any other scholar. Thanks to this assumed distance, he can claim to conceptualize the event, without himself assuming the actors' belief in the meaning of the event as a break with the past and as the origin of new times, in short, without sharing the French Revolution's illusion about itself. But at what price does the historian arrive at interpreting the French Revolution as an *event*? It is noteworthy that he only partially succeeds by combining two explanations which, separately and perhaps even together, leave a remainder, and this remainder is the event itself.

To interpret the French Revolution with Tocqueville is to see it not as a break and an origin, but as the completion of the work of the monarchy, as the dissolution of the social body to the benefit of the state administration. There is an enormous gap here between historiography and the tyranny of the actors' lived historical experience, with its myth of origin. What Furet is inquiring into is precisely the gap between the actors' intentions and the role they play. In the same stroke, the event disappears, at least as a break, when the analysis proceeds by means of explicit concepts. This analysis actually breaks off the historical narrative: Tocqueville, Furet notes, "treats a problem rather than a period" (p. 17).

The event, however, has not been eliminated in every respect. If Tocqueville accounts well for the result of the Revolution (Furet says of "the revolution-as-content"), the very process of the Revolution (what Furet calls "the revolution-as-mode") remains to be explained, that is to say, the particular dynamics of collective action which were responsible for the fact that this result of the Revolution, according to Tocqueville, was not achieved by an English-style evolution but by a revolution. This is where the event resides: "the fact remains that the revolutionary event, *from the very outset*, transformed the existing situation and created a new mode of historical action that was not intrinsically a part of that situation" (p. 22, his emphasis).

A second model must therefore be introduced in order to account for the appearance on the stage of history of a practical and ideological mode of social action that is nowhere inscribed in what preceded it. This second model must take into account what it is that makes the Revolution "one of the basic forms of historical consciousness of action" (p. 24), namely, the way "it was ever ready to place ideas above actual history, as if it were called upon to restructure a fragmented society by means of its own concepts" (p. 25). The Jacobin phenomenon is described in this way.

Augustin Cochin's explanatory model then takes over from Tocqueville's model in order to show how a new political sensibility was produced alongside the old, one which gives rise to a new world based on the individual and not on institutional groups, built upon the tie of opinion alone. Cochin indeed finds in the "philosophical societies [*sociétés de pensée*]" the matrix of a conception of power that rests on the principle of equality, on the transformation of isolated individuals into a people—the sole imaginary actor of the Revolution—and on the suppression of every sort of screen between the people and its self-designated spokesmen.

Jacobinism, however, is not just an ideology, it is an ideology that took power. Consequently, the revolution-as-event is totally accounted for neither by the historian's dismantling of what he holds to be an "illusion of politics," nor by identifying the channels through which this new power is exercised over society. The series of splits and conspiracies that ensue are indeed plots, in the most common sense of the word. Of course, it can be shown how the conspiracy mentality proceeds from the new political sociability that casts as an enemy anyone who has been unable to occupy the symbolic seat of power as the system defines it. In this respect, the pages on conspiracy as the consequence of the new political symbolism are quite brilliant and convincing. Nevertheless, it seems to me that taking power continues to be an event that is not deduced from the ideological system that defines power. Events, chronology, and great individuals come back in full force under the cloak of conspiracy. Even when it is deduced from the ideological system, I would say that conspiracy *brings back the event with the plot.* For even if conspiracy is a theater of madness, this madness is at work, generating events.

This is why Thermidor is an event, for interpretation of course, but only up to a certain point. It "marked the end of the Revolution because it is the victory of representative over revolutionary legitimacy . . . , and as Marx said, the reassertion of real society on *the illusion of politics*" (p. 58). But this "ideological coding" (p. 59) of the Robespierre phenomenon, in turn, does not exhaust, it seems to me, its historical meaning. To say that it incarnates an ideology—the struggle for one imaginary system against another—is only, as in Greek tragedy, to name the theme that corresponds to a plot. For it is as a result of the plot that "he was the mouthpiece of [the Revolution's] purest and most tragic discourse" (p. 61). From the Jacobin ideology has been deduced "what is purest" but not "what is most tragic" in the event.

This is why I would not venture to say, with François Furet, that Thermidor, in that it represents "society's revenge on ideology" (p. 74), leads from Cochin back to Tocqueville, for the continuation of the *ancien régime* passes not only by way of the ideological acceleration of Jacobinism but by the actions that this political illusion engendered. In this sense, the second schema of the French Revolution, that provided by Augustin Cochin, is no more capable of getting to the bottom of the event than is the first, provided by Tocqueville. No conceptual reconstruction will ever be able to make the continuity with the *ancien régime* pass by way of the rise to power of an imaginary order experienced as a break and as an origin. This rise to power is itself on the order of an event. And it results in the fact that the fantasy of an origin is itself an origin, to reverse François Furet's formula.[67]

Has Furet then been successful in "interpreting" the event that is the French

Revolution? I would say, in line with my reflection on Braudel's long time-span, that the event is restored at the end of each attempted explanation as a remainder left by every such attempt (in the way that the third part of Braudel's *The Mediterranean* constitutes both a supplement and a complement), as a dissonance between explanatory structures, and finally, as the life and death of the structures themselves.

If the discovery of the long time-span did not lead us back to the event in accordance with one of these three modes, the long time-span would be in danger of severing historical time from the living dialectic of past, present, and future. A long time can be a time without any present and, so, without past or future as well. But then it is no longer a historical time, and the long time-span only leads back from human time to the time of nature. Evidence of this temptation can be seen in Braudel himself and results from the absence of a philosophical reflection on the relation between what he somewhat too hastily calls the subjective time of the philosophers and the long time of civilizations. For the discovery of the long time-span may simply express the fact that human time, which always requires the reference point of a present, is itself *forgotten*. If the brief event can act as a screen hiding our consciousness of the time that is not of our making, the long time-span can, likewise, act as a screen hiding the time that we are.

This disastrous consequence can be avoided only if an analogy is preserved between the time of individuals and the time of civilizations: the analogy of growth and decline, of creation and death, the analogy of fate.

This analogy on the level of temporality is of the same nature as the analogy I tried to maintain on the level of procedures between causal attribution and emplotment, and then on the level of entities between societies (or civilizations) and the characters in a drama. In this sense, *all change enters the field of history as a quasi-event*.

This declaration is by no means equivalent to a cunning return to the brief event, which has been criticized by the history of the long time-span. When it was not the reflection of the actors' confused consciousness and of their illusions, this brief event was just as much a methodological artifact, even the expression of a world view. In this respect, Braudel is perfectly justified in exclaiming: "I argue against Ranke or Karl Brande, that the narrative is not a method, or even the objective method *par excellence*, but quite simply a philosophy of history" (*The Mediterranean*, p. 21).

By *quasi-event* we signify that the extension of the notion of event, beyond short and brief time, remains correlative to a similar extending of the notions of plot and character. There is a quasi-event wherever we can discern, even if only very indirectly, very obliquely, a quasi-plot and quasi-characters. The event in history corresponds to what Arisotle called a change in fortune—*metabolē*—in his formal theory of emplotment. An event, once again, is not only what contributes to the unfolding of a plot but what gives it the dramatic form of a change in fortune.

It follows from this kinship between quasi-events and quasi-plots that the plurality of historical times extolled by Braudel is an expansion of the cardinal feature of narrative time, namely, its ability to combine in variable proportions the chronological component of the episode and the achronological component of the configuration. Every one of the temporal levels required by historical explanation may be seen as a duplication of this dialectic. It might perhaps even be said that with the brief event the episodic continues to dominate in plots that are nevertheless extremely complex, and that the long time-span gives precedence to the configuration. However, the emergence of a new event-like quality at the end of our effort to work out the historical structures echoes as a reminder. It reminds us that something happens to even the most stable structures. Something happens to them—in particular, they die out. This is why, despite his reticence, Braudel was unable to avoid ending his magnificent work with the description of a death, not, of course, the death of the Mediterranean but of Philip II.

Conclusions

I would now like to sum up the results attained at the end of this second part of my study. With respect to the aims advanced in chapter 3 of the first part, these results stand within precise limits.

To begin with, only one of the two great narrative modes has been submitted to examination—history. I have excluded from the field of investigation all that will be placed, in volume 2, under the title of "Fictional Narrative"— let us say, from the ancient epic to the modern novel. Therefore, only half of the ground to be covered by the inquiry has actually been traveled.

The restriction of my analysis to historical narrative has not only resulted in leaving other narrative modes *outside*, it has resulted in an amputating of the internal problematic of history itself. In fact, the *ambition of truth* by which history, in Paul Veyne's apt expression, claims the title "true" [*véridique*], displays its full meaning only when it can be opposed to the deliberate suspension of the true/false alternative, characteristic of the fictional narrative.[1] I do not deny that this opposition between a "true" narrative and a "half true, half false" one rests on a naive notion of truth that will have to be thoroughly reexamined in volume 2.

This first limitation, in turn, leads to a second, more serious one that directly concerns the relation of narrative to time. As I have just said, by bracketing history's ambition to attain the truth, I have set aside any attempt to thematize, in and of itself, the relation of history to the past. In fact, I have deliberately abstained from taking a stand on the ontological status of the historical past as having-been. In this way, when I have discussed the concept of event, I have carefully dissociated the epistemological criteria currently associated with this notion (unity, singularity, divergence) from the ontological criteria by which we distinguish what is only feigned from what actually took place (occur, make happen, differ in novelty from every reality that has already taken place). With this stroke, the relation between history, as the guardian of humanity's past, and the whole set of attitudes by which we relate to the present and to the future, is left in abeyance.

Consequently the question of historical time has not been unfolded to its full extent. Only the aspects of time directly implied in the configurational operations that connect history to narrative have been taken into consideration. Even my discussion concerning the long time-span remained within the limits of an epistemology applied to the constructions characteristic of explanation in history. The relations between the long time-span and the event were discussed, but there was no attempt to find out what is actually involved in the relation between the multiple temporalities distinguished by historians and what they, casting a mistrustful eye, regard as the subjective time of the philosophers—whether by this is meant Bergsonian duration, the absolute flow of consciousness in Husserl, or Heidegger's historicality. Once again, the contribution of history to this debate could not be clarified without that of fictional narrative. I implied this when, in chapter 3 of Part I, I subordinated the question of time as refigured by narrative to the resolution of the problem of the intertwining reference of true narrative and fictional narrative. It must even be suspected that, thanks to the greater freedom it has with respect to events that actually occurred in the past, fiction displays, concerning temporality, resources not allowed to the historian. As I shall say in volume 2, literary fiction can produce "fables about time" that are not merely "fables of time." Hence it is not inconceivable that we must wait until after our long detour by way of the time of fiction before making any definite statement about the relation of history to time.

Admitting the limits of the analyses in my second part by no means forces me to minimize the importance of the results I think I have attained. It is just that these limits remind us that the investigation was placed on the level of mimesis$_2$ and did not take into account the mediating function performed by this mimetic stage between prenarrative experience and an experience that is refigured by the work of narrative in all its forms.

The whole of my second part has been an investigation of the relations between the writing of history and the operation of emplotment, which Aristotle elevates to the rank of the dominant category in the art of composing works that imitate an action. If, indeed, the subsequent confrontation between historical narrative and fictional narrative is to make sense, I had first of all to be sure that history belongs to the narrative field defined by this configurating operation. And this relation, as it was progressively verified, revealed itself to be extraordinarily complex.

In order to circumscribe it, I first of all had to employ, in chapters 4 and 5, an antithetical strategy in which theses that were on the whole nomological were contrasted with wholly narrativist theses. In the course of this polemic, there was no thesis submitted to criticism that did not in some way contribute, at the cost of a series of rectifications, to an initial approximation of the relation between history and narrative. Some of these rectifications appeared only later. Thus, in part one of chapter 4, the plea for a nonevent history, which is held by French historians to be incompatible with a narrativist interpretation of history, was left without any immediate critical response, until a more sophisticated concept of historical plot, in the last part of chapter 6, permitted the reintegration of nonevent history into the narrative field. But, first, it was necessary, in setting aside a naive narrative reading of history, to pose the problem within the epistemological situation most unfavorable to a direct and immediate relation between history and narrative.

If, in return, the covering law model was promptly submitted to rather strong criticism, first internally at the end of chapter 4 and then externally in chapter 5, this double criticism was not purely negative. From examining the covering law model, I retained the idea of an epistemological break which distances historical explanation armed with generalizations in the form of laws, from simple narrative understanding.

Once this epistemological break was recognized, it was no longer possible to adopt the overly simple thesis that history must be held to be a species of the genus story. Even if, on the whole, a narrativist interpretation of history seemed to me more correct than a nomological one, the narrativist theses examined in chapter 5—even if they were reworked and refined—did not appear really to do justice to the specificity of history in the narrative field. Their main drawback is that they do not sufficiently take into account the transformations that have driven contemporary historiography further and further away from a naive narrative style of writing, and that they have not been successful in integrating explanation in terms of laws into the narrative fabric of history. And yet the narrativist interpretation is correct in its clear perception that the specifically historical property of history is preserved only by the ties, however tenuous and well-hidden they may be, which continue to connect historical explanation to our narrative understanding, despite the epistemological break separating the first from the second.

This twofold requirement, doing justice to the specificity of historical explanation *and* maintaining history's belonging within the narrative field, led me in the sixth chapter to join the antithetical strategy of chapters 4 and 5 to the method of questioning back, related to the genetic phenomenology of the later Husserl. This method aims at accounting for the indirect character of the filiation that connects history to our narrative understanding by reactivating the phases of the derivation by which this filiation is realized. To be precise, this questioning back is no longer epistemological, strictly speaking, nor does it correspond to a simple methodology adapted to the historian's day-to-day work. It corresponds to a genesis of meaning, which is the responsibility of the philosopher. This genesis of meaning would not be possible if it were not supported by the epistemology and the methodology of the historical sciences. The latter provide the relay stations capable of guiding, in each of the three spheres under consideration, the reactivation of the narrative sources of scholarly history. For example, singular causal explanation provides the transitional structure between explanation in terms of laws and understanding by means of the plot. In their turn, the first-level entities to which the historian's discourse ultimately refers make us look in the direction of the modes of participatory belonging that maintain the kinship between the object of history and the characters in a narrative. Finally, the discordant rhythms of the multiple temporalities, interwoven in the overall becoming of societies, reveal a profound kinship between the least pointlike historical changes and the sudden changes in fortune that, in narrative, are considered to be events.

Thus the historians' profession, the epistemology of the historical sciences, and genetic phenomenology combine their resources to reactivate that fundamental noetic vision of history which, for the sake of brevity, I have called *historical intentionality*.

The most significant result of this critical examination of history has not yet been stressed. It results from the subsequent impact of the examination on the initial model proposed in chapter 3 of Part I.

Certainly, the essential features of the basic model have been preserved in the analyses of the second part. These include: the dynamic character of the configurational operation, the primacy of order over succession, the competition between concordance and discordance, the narration's schematization of generalities in the form of laws, the conflict between sedimentation and innovation in the formation of traditions throughout the course of the development of the historical sciences. But, as I noted at the time, a study based on a simple confrontation between the Augustinian *distentio animi* and the Aristotelian *muthos* could only be expected to provide "a sketch, that will require further expansion, criticism, and revision."

In fact, my examination of history was not limited to verifying the relevance of this model by applying it to a rather vast area of narrative composition. A good example of expanding the model was provided by the complexity of the discordant concordance offered by historical narration, which has no parallel in Aristotle's *Poetics*. The idea of the synthesis of the heterogeneous, which was merely suggested in Part I, is completely freed from the limits imposed upon it by the literary "genres" and "types" with which it is still confused in the *Poetics*.

For this very reason, the expansion of the initial example tends toward a critique, if not of the model as such, at least of the interpretations of historical explanation that have remained too closely tied to this model. This is so whenever the theory of history is not clearly distinguished from a theory of action and does not give to the circumstances, the anonymous forces, and, especially, the unintended consequences the place that is due them. "What transforms actions into histories?" asks a philosopher. Precisely those factors that escape a simple reconstruction of the calculations made by the agents of the action. These factors give the emplotment a complexity unequaled in the small-scale model that, in Aristotle, is still patterned on Greek tragedy (without forgetting, as well, epic and, to a lesser extent, comedy). The model of explanation proposed by von Wright, which combines teleological segments and law-like segments within a composite model, gives a good idea of the critique to which a model of historical explanation based purely on the concept of action must be submitted.

Would I go so far as to speak of a revision of the initial model by the theory of history? Yes, up to a certain point. This is attested to by the concepts of quasi-plot, quasi-character, and quasi-event that I had to construct in order to respect the very indirect form of filiation by which the history that is the least narrative in its style of writing nevertheless continues to rely on narrative understanding.

In speaking of quasi-plot, quasi-character, and quasi-event I wanted to bring the initial concepts worked out within the sphere of mimesis$_2$ close to their breaking point. The reader will recall to what extent the plot that threads through Braudel's great work, *The Mediterranean and the Mediterranean World in the Age of Philip II*, is deeply buried and difficult to reconstruct. Nor have I forgotten the care with which proper names have to be used when they are applied to the first-level entities of history. Finally, the notion of event had to lose its usual qualities of brevity and suddenness in order to measure up to the discordances and ruptures that punctuate the life of economic, social, and ideological structures of an individual society. The term "quasi" in the expressions "quasi-plot," "quasi-character," and "quasi-event" bears witness to the highly analogical nature of the use of narrative categories in scholarly history. In any event, this analogy expresses the tenuous and deeply hidden tie that holds history within the sphere of narrative and thereby preserves the historical dimension itself.

Notes

1. My choice of vocabulary owes a great deal to Frank Kermode's work, *The Sense of an Ending: Studies in the Theory of Fiction* (New York: Oxford University Press, 1966), which will be the object of a separate analysis in volume 2 of the present work.

CHAPTER ONE

1. English quotations from the *Confessions* are taken from Saint Augustine, *The Confessions*, trans. R. S. Pine-Coffin (New York: Penguin Books, 1961). My study owes a great deal to E. P. Meijering's scholarly commentary, *Augustin über Schöpfung, Ewigkeit und Zeit. Das elfte Buch des Bekenntnisse* (Leiden: E. J. Brill, 1979). I place greater emphasis than he does on the aporetical character of the discussion and especially on the dialectic between *distentio* and *intentio*, which, however, is heavily stressed by A. Solignac in his "Notes Complémentaires" (pp. 572–91) to the French translation by E. Tréhorel and G. Bouissou, based on the text of M. Skutella (Stuttgart: Teubner, 1934), with an introduction and notes by Solignac, in the "Bibliothèque Augustinienne," vol. 14 (Paris: Desclée de Brouwer, 1962). Jean Guitton's work, *Le Temps et l'Eternité chez Plotin et saint Augustin* (Paris: Vrin, 1933), has lost none of its acuteness. For the references to Plotinus, I have made use of the introduction and commentary of Werner Beierwaltes, *Plotin über Ewigkeit und Zeit: Enneade III 7* (Frankfurt: Klostermann, 1967). Other works that will also be referred to are E. Gilson, "Notes sur l'être et le temps chez saint Augustin," *Recherches Augustiniennes* 2 (1962): 204–23; and John C. Callahan, *Four Views of Time in Ancient Philosophy* (Cambridge: Harvard University Press, 1948), pp. 149–204. On the history of the problem of the instant, see P. Duhem, *Le Système du monde* (Paris: A. Hermann, 1913), vol. 1, chap. 5.

2. This meditation extends from 1:1 to 14:17 and is taken up again in 29:39 and carried to the end, 31:41.

3. J. Guitton, attentive to the tie between time and consciousness in Augustine, observes that the aporia of time is also the aporia of the self (Guitton, p. 224). He quotes *Confessions* 10, 16:25: "O Lord, I am working hard in this field, and the field of my labours is my own self. I have become a problem to myself, like land which a farmer only works with difficulty and at the cost of much sweat. For I am not now investigating the tracts of the heavens, or measuring the distance of the stars, or trying to discover how the earth hangs in space. I am investigating myself, my memory, my mind [ego sum, qui memini, ego animus]."

4. This audacious assertion, which is taken up again at the end of Part I, will be the object of a long discussion in volume 2.

5. I shall henceforth simply give the reference 14:17, 15:18, etc., whenever I am citing Book 11 of the *Confessions*.

6. Here the contrast with eternity is decisive: "As for the present, if it were always present and never moved on to become the past, it would not be time but eternity" (14:15). We can, however, note in this respect that, regardless of the understanding we may have of eternity, the argument can be limited to appealing to our use of language involving the word "always." The present is not always. In this way passing requires the contrast of remaining. (Meijering refers in this regard to *Sermo* 108 in which passing is opposed in a number of different ways to remaining.) As the argument continues we shall see the definition of the present become finer and finer.

7. This role of anticipation is well noted by Meijering in his commentary.

8. Regarding God's laughter, see Meijering, pp. 60–61.

9. No more than did classical antiquity, Augustine has no word for units smaller than the hour. This does not change until the eighteenth century. Meijering (p. 64) refers in this regard to H. Michel, "La Notion de l'heure dans l'antiquité," *Janus* 57 (1970): 115–24.

10. Concerning the argument of the indivisible instant that has no extension, there is in Meijering (pp. 63–64) a reference to the texts of Sextus Empiricus and a fortunate reminder of the Stoic discussion presented by Victor Goldschmidt in *Le Système stoïcien et le Temps*, pp. 37ff., and pp. 184ff. It will have been noted that Augustine is perfectly aware of the dependence of his analysis on a speculative argumentation: *si quid intelligitur temporis. . . .* Here there can be no pretence of a pure phenomenology. In addition, the appearance of the notion of temporal extension should be noted, but this is not yet at the stage where it will take root: "For if its duration [that of the present] were prolonged, it could be divided into past and future [nam si extenditur, dividitur . . .]" (15:20).

11. Meijering (p. 66) recognizes in the Augustinian *quaero* the Greek *Zetein* which makes the difference between the Augustinian aporia and the complete ignorance of the skeptics. Jean Guitton discerns a non-Greek source for the *Zetein* in the Hebrew wisdom tradition which finds an echo in Acts 17:26.

12. It is only after having resolved the first paradox of being and nonbeing that Augustine will be able to return to this assertion in more or less the same terms: "we measure time while it is passing" (21:27). It is thus always in relation to the notion of measurement that the idea of passing imposes itself. But as yet we do not have the means at our disposal to understand the latter.

13. The argument about prediction which concerns all human beings must be clearly distinguished from the argument about prophecy which concerns only the inspired prophets. This second argument presents a different problem, that of the way in which God (or the Word) "reveals" the future to the prophets (see 19:25). On this point, cf. Guitton, pp. 261–70. He stresses the liberating character of the Augustinian analysis of *expectatio* in relation to the entire pagan tradition of divination and manticism. To this extent, prophecy remains an exception and a gift.

14. The entire paragraph must be cited: "When we describe the past correctly, it is not past facts which are drawn out of our memories but only words based on our memory-pictures of those facts, because when they happened they left an impression on our minds, by means of our sense-perception" (18:23). The number of prepositions concerning place or location is striking: it is out of (*ex*) our memories that we draw words based on (*ex*) memories that leave an impression on (*in*) our minds. My "own childhood, which no longer exists, is in [in] past time, which also no longer exists. But when I remember those days . . . it is in [in] the present that I picture them to myself, because their picture is still present in [in] my memory" (ibid.). The question "where"

("if the future and the past do exist, I want to know where [ubicumque] they are") calls for the response, "in."

15. Perhaps it is even a little more so. Consider the premeditation of a future action. Like expectation, it is present, whereas the future action does not yet exist. But the "sign"-"cause" is here more complicated than mere prediction. For what I am anticipating is not only the beginning of an action but its completion. Carrying myself forward beyond its beginning, I see its beginning as the past of its future completion. We then use the future perfect: "Once we have set to work [aggressi fuerimus] and started to put our plans into action [agere coeperimus], that action exists, because it is not future but present" (18:23). The future present is anticipated here through the use of the future perfect. The systematic study of verbal tenses by Harald Weinrich in his *Tempus* will pursue further this sort of investigation. See volume 2, chapter 3.

16. The quasi-kinetic language of the transition from the future toward the past through the present (cf. below) will help to further consolidate this quasi-spatial language.

17. Meijering stresses in this regard the role of concentration which, at the end of the book, will be related to the hope of stability which gives the human present a certain resemblance to God's eternal present. We might also say that the narrative of Books 1–9 is the history of the quest for this concentration and this stability. On this point, see volume 2 of this study.

18. This substitution explains why Augustine no longer makes use of the distinction between *motus* and *mora*: "my question is whether a day is that movement [motus] itself, the time needed [mora] for its completion, or a combination of both" (23:30). Since all three hypotheses are discounted and the investigation into the very sense of the word "day" is abandoned, the distinction has no real consequences. With Guitton (p. 229), we can say that for Augustine "time is neither *motus* nor *mora* but more *mora* than *motus*." The *distentio animi* has no more tie to *mora* than it does to *motus*.

19. Augustine's hesitation can be related to two other assertions: first, that the movement of the lights of the sky "marks out" time, then, in order to distinguish the moment when an interval of time begins and the moment when it stops, we must "mark" (*notare*) the place where the moving body starts out and the place where it arrives; if not, we are unable to say "how much time is needed for the body to complete its movement between the two points" (24:31). This notion of "marking" seems to be the only point of contact remaining between time and movement in Augustine. The question, then, is to know whether these spatial marks, in order to fulfill their role as points of reference for the length of time, do not make the measurement of time necessarily dependent on the regular motion of some moving body other than the soul. I shall return to this difficulty below.

20. On this point, cf. Beierwaltes's commentary on *Enneads* III 7, 11, 41, *diastasis zoes*; A. Solignac, "Notes complémentaires," pp. 588–91; and Meijering, pp. 90–93. The free adaptation of the Plotinian terms *diastēma—diastasis* by Christian writers goes back to Gregory of Nyssa, as has been established by J. Callahan, the author of *Four Views of Time in Ancient Philosophy*. See his essay "Gregory of Nyssa and the Psychological View of Time," in *Acts of the Twelfth International Congress of Philosophy* (Florence: Sansoni, 1960), p. 59. Confirmation of this claim can be found in David L. Balas, "Eternity and Time in Gregory of Nyssa's *Contra Eunomium*," in H. Dorrie, M. Altenburger, and U. Sinryhe, eds., *Gregory von Nyssa und die Philosophie*, The Second International Colloquy on Gregory of Nyssa, 1972 (Leiden: E. J. Brill, 1976), pp. 128–53. In the same collection, T. Paul Verghese establishes that the notion of *diastēma* is used essentially as a criterion for distinguishing the divine trinity from the creature. In God there is no *diastēma* between the Father and the Son, no interval, no distance. Consequently *diastēma* characterizes creation as such, partic-

ularly the interval between the Creator and the creature. See T. Paul Verghese, "Diastema and Diastasis in Gregory of Nyssa: Introduction to a Concept and the Posing of a Concept," in ibid., pp. 243–58. Even assuming that this adaptation of the Plotinian terminology by the Greek fathers was known to Augustine, his originality remains. He is the only one to derive the *distentio* from just the extension of the soul.

21. Note the slight shift in the expression. A bit earlier Augustine rejected the possibility of measuring the pointlike present: *quia nullo spatio tenditur*, "because it has no extent" (26:33). In my opinion, *tenditur* announces the *intentio* of which the *distentio* is but the reverse side. In fact, the pointlike present has neither tension or distension; only the "time that passes" can admit these. This is why in the following paragraph it must be said of the present, inasmuch as it passes (*praeteriens*), that it "gains some extent" as a sort of lapse of time. This is no longer the present considered as a point but the living present, both under tension and distended.

22. Solignac stresses the aporetical character of this page by giving as the subtitle of his translation of 27:34 "Deeper Analysis. New Aporias" (p. 329).

23. If the *sensitur* confounds the skeptics, the *quantum*, notes Meijering (p. 95), indicates a certain reservation with respect to the Epicureans and their overconfidence in sensation. Here, Augustine is following the middle road of Platonism, that of a guarded confidence in the senses controlled by the intelligence.

24. My analysis differs here from that of Meijering, who pays almost exclusive attention to the contrast between eternity and time and does not stress the internal dialectic of time itself, involving intention and distension. It is true, as will be stated later, that this contrast is accentuated by the striving for eternity that animates the *intentio*. However, Guitton strongly emphasizes this tension of the mind with respect to which *distentio* stands as the reverse side: "Saint Augustine, as his reflection progressed, was obliged to attribute opposing qualities to time. Its duration is an *extensio*, a *distentio* which includes within it an *attentio*, an *intentio*. As a result of this, time is closely related to *actio*, of which it is the spiritual form" (p. 232). Thus the instant is "an act of the mind" (p. 234).

25. Kant will encounter the same enigma of a passivity that is actively produced with the idea of *Selbstaffektion* in the second edition of *The Critique of Pure Reason*. See B67–69. (Immanuel Kant, *Critique of Pure Reason*, trans. Norman Kemp Smith [New York: St. Martin's Press, 1965], pp. 87–89.) I shall return to this point in volume 2.

26. Two other objections might also arise. First of all, what is the relation of the Augustinian *distentio animi* to Plotinus's *diastasis zoes*? And what is the relation of the whole of Book 11 to the narration of the first nine books of the *Confessions*? To the first objection, I would reply that my purpose here does not allow me to treat the relation of Augustine to Plotinus in terms of the history of ideas. However I readily acknowledge that a good understanding of the mutation undergone by the Plotinian analysis of time can contribute to deepening the enigma that Augustine willed to posterity. A few footnotes obviously do not suffice in this regard. I would refer the reader to the commentaries of Solignac and Meijering on the *Confessions* to fill this gap, as well as to Beierwaltes's study on *Plotin über Ewigkeit und Zeit*. With regard to the speculation on time and the narration of the first nine books, this is of particular interest to me. I shall return to it in the second volume of the present work within the framework of a reflection on repetition. Something in this regard can already be intimated here if we refer to the *confessio* within which Augustine's entire work is cloaked.

27. In this respect, we cannot consider the great prayer of 2:3 to be a mere rhetorical ornament. (The French translator has very judiciously chosen to give a version in verse.) It contains the melodic line that speculation, along with the hymn, will develop: "Yours is the day, Yours the night. No moment of time passes except by your

will. Grant me some part of it for my meditations on the secrets of your law. Do not close your door to those who knock: do not close the book of your law to me." Speculation and hymn are joined together in the "confession." It is in a confessional tone that the *principium* of Genesis 1:1 is invoked in the prayer of 2:3: "Let me acknowledge [confitear tibi] as yours whatever I find in your books. Let me listen to the sound of your praises. Let me drink you in and contemplate the wonders of your law from the very beginning, when you made heaven and earth, to the coming of your kingdom, when we shall be forever with you in your holy city."

28. In this knowledge is summed up both the affinity and the radical difference between Plotinus and Augustine. The theme of the creation constitutes this difference. Guitton takes the measure of this gap in a few pages (pp. 136–45). Augustine, he says, "poured into the mold provided by the *Enneads* an inspiration that was foreign to Plotinus, even opposed to his thinking, and such that its entire dialectic tended to deny it, to prevent it from emerging, or to dissolve it" (ibid., p. 140). From the idea of creation resulted a temporary cosmos, a temporal conversion, and a historical religion. In this way time is justified as well as founded. As for the anthropomorphism which Plotinian emanationism seems to avoid, we might wonder whether the metaphorical resources of Augustine's material anthropomorphism are not more precious as regards the schema of creative causality than the Neoplatonic exemplarism which reposes in the identity of "the one" and which does not avoid a more subtle, because it is purely formal, anthropomorphism. The metaphor of creation keeps us attentive as well as on our guard, whereas exemplarism attracts us by its philosophical character. On this point, see Guitton, pp. 198–99. On the "eternal creator and temporal creation," cf. Meijering's exhaustive commentary, pp. 17–57. He gives all the pertinent references to the *Timaeus* and the *Enneads*.

29. If this ontological deficiency has a function in the argumentation other than that of the nonbeing of the skeptical argument about time, tied to the "not yet" of the future and the "no longer" of the past, nevertheless it stamps this nonbeing with the seal of the lack that is peculiar to created beings: "for we know, O Lord, that the extent to which something once was, but no longer is, is the measure of its death; and the extent to which something once was not, but now is, is the measure of its beginning" (7:9). Henceforth the two adjectives "eternal" (along with its synonym "immortal") and "temporal" are opposed to each other. Temporal means not eternal. Later, we shall wonder if the negation does not work both ways. Already here, in 7:9, to be eternal implies *not* "giving place to the next." With respect to the synonyms of eternity (*immortalitas, incorruptibilitas, incommutabilitas*), see Meijering, p. 32, who refers to *Timaeus* 29c. Let us therefore retain these first two moments of the limiting function of the idea of eternity contained in the two negatives: it is not like an artisan working with some earlier material that the Word creates; it is not with a voice that sounds in time that the Word speaks.

30. The translators and the interpreter of the *Confessions* in the "Bibliothèque Augustinienne" indicate a caesura between 10:11 and 10:12, and divide Book 11 in the following way: I. The creation and the creating Word (3:5–10:12). II. The problem of time: (a) before the creation, 10:12–14:17; (b) the being of time and its measurement, 14:17–29:39. My own analysis leads me to group together I and II(a) under the simple heading: the intensification of the *distentio animi* by its contrast with eternity. In addition, the apparently preposterous question that begins at 10:12 possesses the same aporetical style characterized by the questions "How?" (5:7) and "Why?" (6:8), which appeared to us to be provoked by the very confession of eternity. Finally, the aporia and the responses to it will give rise to the same sort of deepening reflection concerning the negative discussion of temporality begun at 3:5.

31. Already in *Timaeus* 37e, Plato had excluded the past and the future from eter-

nity without yet speaking of the eternal present. Meijering, p. 46, cites other texts of Augustine that interpret the *stare* and the *manere* of God as the eternal present. He strongly emphasizes (p. 43) that Augustine accepts the part of the argument of 10:12 that says that "the will of God is not a created thing. It is there before any creation takes place. . . . The will of God, then, is part of his substance." Meijering also likens this text to Plotinus's *Enneads* VI 8:13 and 9:14. He identifies the first expression of the eternal present in the middle Platonism of Numenius before its formulation in Plotinus (he refers in this regard to Beierwaltes, pp. 170–73), then in Gregory of Nyssa and Athanasius.

32. Today we have trouble imagining how animated—not to say violent—were the quarrels to which the idea of a temporal creation gave rise. Guitton shows how they were exacerbated by the conflict between literal exegesis and allegorical exegesis incited by the biblical narrative of creation "in six days" and, more especially, by the sense to be given to the "three days" preceding the creation of the great heavenly lights. Cf. Guitton, pp. 177–91.

33. The question here is not that of the faithfulness of the Latin translation to the Hebrew, but that of its influence within the philosophical tradition.

34. A. Solignac (pp. 583–84) refers here to Etienne Gilson, *Philosophie et Incarnation chez saint Augustin*, in which he studies the principal texts of Augustine's work concerning the famous verse from Exodus and other verses from the psalms, in particular *Sermo* 7. Solignac comments, "the transcendence of eternity in relation to time for Augustine is the transcendence of a personal God who created other persons and who converses with them. It is thus the transcendence of a *being* who possesses himself in an endless present in relation to the *existence* of beings whose contingency is manifestly within the vicissitudes of time" (ibid., p. 584).

35. I am not discussing here the question whether the idea of eternity is itself entirely positive, as we are led to believe by the terms *manere, stans, semper, totum esse praesens*. To the extent that "beginning," "ceasing," and "passing" are themselves positive terms, eternity is also the negative of time, "the other" of time. Even the expression "completely present" denies that God's present has a past and a future. Memory and expectation are positive experiences due to the presence of the vestige-images and sign-images. The eternal present does not appear to be a purely positive notion except by reason of its homonymy with the present that passes. To say that it is eternal, we must deny that it is the passive and active transit from the future toward the past. It is still insofar as it is not a present that is "passed through." Eternity is also conceived of negatively, as that which does not include time, as that which is not temporal. In this sense, there is a double negation: I must be able to deny the features of my experience of time in order to perceive this experience as a lack with respect to that which denies it. It is this double and mutual negation whereby eternity is the other of time that, more than anything else, intensifies the experience of time.

36. Pierre Courcelle, *Recherches sur les Confessions de saint Augustin* (Paris: de Boccard, 1950), chapter 1, emphasizes that the term "confession" in Augustine goes far beyond the confession of sins and includes the confession of faith and the confession of praise. The analysis of time and the *elegia* of the *distentio animi* are related to the second and third senses of the Augustinian *confessio*. Narrative, as I shall state below, is also included within it.

37. The expression *in regione dissimilitudinis* has inspired a number of works which are recalled in a lengthy note, no. 16, in A. Solignac (pp. 689–93). The fortune of this expression from Plato to the Christian Middle Ages is particularly stressed in Etienne Gilson, "*Regio dissimilitudinis* de Platon à saint Bernard de Clairvaux," *Medieval Studies* 9 (1947): 108–30, and Pierre Courcelle, "Traditions néo-platoniciennes et traditions chrétiennes de la région de dissemblance," *Archives d'Histoire Littéraire et*

Doctrinale du Moyen Age 24 (1927): 5–33, reprinted as an appendix to his *Recherches sur les Confessions de saint Augustin*.

38. But must we go so far as to distinguish, as does Guitton, "two internal movements which can be distinguished by consciousness, although they are mutually interrelated, *expectatio futurorum* which bears us toward the future and *extentio ad superiora* which orientates us, once and for all, toward the eternal"? (p. 137). Do these constitute "two forms of time" (ibid.), where the ecstasy of Ostia would illustrate the second form? I do not think so, if we consider the third way in which eternity affects the experience of time, which I shall discuss below. Guitton himself is prepared to agree. What basically distinguishes Augustine from Plotinus and from Spinoza is the impossibility of "separating ontologically" (ibid., p. 243) the *extensio ad superiora*, which in Spinoza will be called *amor intellectualis*, from the *expectatio futurorum*, which in Spinoza becomes *duratio*. The ecstasy of Ostia confirms this. Unlike Neoplatonic ecstasy, it is a weakness as well as an ascension. I shall return to this in volume 2. Narration is possible wherever eternity attracts and elevates time, not where it abolishes it.

39. Stanislas Boros, "Les Catégories de la temporalité chez saint Augustin," *Archives de Philosophie* 21 (1958): 323–85.

40. To which must be added admonition (*admonitio*), which is commented on by A. Solignac (p. 562).

Chapter Two

1. See below, n. 4.

2. We shall, nevertheless, be interested in, without overestimating, all the references in Aristotle's text that suggest a referential relation between the "poetic" text and the real "ethical" world.

3. G. F. Else, *Aristotle's Poetics: The Argument* (Cambridge: Harvard University Press, 1957). Aristotle, *Poetics*, introduction, commentary, and appendices by Frank L. Lucas (Oxford University Press, 1968). L. Golden and O. B. Hardison, *Aristotle's Poetics: A Translation and Commentary for Students of Literature* (Englewood Cliffs, N.J.: Prentice-Hall, 1968). Aristotle, *Poétique*, texte établi et traduit par J. Hardy (Paris: Les Belles Lettres, 1969). Aristotle, *La Poétique*, texte, traduction, notes par Roselyne Dupont-Roc et Jean Lallot (Paris: Seuil, 1980). I must also acknowledge my indebtedness to James M. Redfield, *Nature and Culture in the Iliad: The Tragedy of Hector* (Chicago: University of Chicago Press, 1975).

4. In the French text of this work I adopted the translation by Dupont-Roc and Lallot, only replacing *histoire* by *intrigue* for the word *muthos*. I did so because of the importance of "history" in later chapters of this work. Here I will cite the recent translation by James Hutton: *Aristotle's Poetics*, trans., with an introduction and notes by James Hutton (New York: W. W. Norton & Company, 1982).

5. Cf. G. Else ad 47a8–18. He even suggests translating the term *mimēsis* when it appears in the plural by "imitatings" to make clear that the mimetic process expresses the poetic activity itself. The *-sis* ending common to *poiēsis* and *sustasis* as well as *mimēsis* underlines the process-character of each of these terms.

6. The "representations in images" (47a19), referred to in Chapter 1—which is devoted to the "how" of representation, not to its "what" or its "mode" (see below)—continue to provide illuminating parallels borrowed from painting.

7. "Tragedy is an imitation of an action that is serious, complete, and possessing magnitude; in embellished language, each kind of which is used separately in the different parts; in the mode of action and not narrated [apangelia]; and effecting through pity and fear [what we call] the *catharsis* of such emotions" (49b24–28).

8. Aristotle here is replying to Plato who is replying to Gorgias. See Redfield, pp. 45f. Gorgias praises painters and artists for their skill in deceiving us (in his *Dissoi Logoi* and *In Praise of Helen*). Socrates draws from him an argument against art and the power it provides for manipulating opinions. The whole discussion of mimesis in Book 10 of the *Republic* is dominated by this distrust. The famous definition of art as the imitation of an imitation, twice removed from reality (596a–597b) and as moreover condemned to "imitating the *pathos* of others" (604e) is well known. The legislator therefore can only see in poetry the contradiction of philosophy. Aristotle's *Poetics* thus is a reply to Book 10 of the *Republic*. For Aristotle, imitation is an activity and one that teaches us something.

9. The "means" of representation, which we have already alluded to, and which are much more numerous than those tragedy, comedy, and epic make use of, are always arts of composition.

10. I prefer this Husserlian vocabulary to the more Saussurean one chosen by Dupont-Roc and Lallot, who take mimesis as the signifier and *praxis* as the signified, to the exclusion of any extralinguistic referent. See Dupont-Roc and Lallot, pp. 219–20. First of all, the pair signifier/signified seems inappropriate to me, for reasons I explain in my *Rule of Metaphor* and which I borrow from Benveniste, for the semantic order of the sentence of discourse and *a fortiori* for that of the text, which is a composition of sentences. Furthermore, the noetic-noematic relation does not exclude a referential development, represented in Husserl by the problematic of "fulfillment." I hope to show below that Aristotelian mimesis is not exhausted by the strict noematic correlation between representation and what is represented, but rather opens the way to an investigation of the referents of poetic activity intended by emplotment on the two sides [*en amont et en aval*] of mimesis/muthos.

11. Dupont-Roc and Lallot: *les aggissants*.

12. Better or worse than what? The text says "better than we are" (48a18). Below I shall discuss this reference in the *Poetics* to a feature of ethical action in the "real" world. I shall attach this reference to a usage of the term mimesis less strictly governed by the noematic correlation to muthos. It should be noted that this reference to ethics rightly applies to the whole field of mimetic activity, in particular to painting. The distinction between comedy and tragedy is in this sense only one application of the criterion of "how" to the arts of versified language. Cf. 48a1–18.

13. In his commentary on Chapter 3, devoted to the mode of mimesis, Else notes that the three modes—narrative, mixed, and dramatic—constitute a progression that makes the dramatic mode the imitation par excellence, thanks to the direct character of the expression of human truth, the characters themselves doing the represented or imitated action. See Else, p. 101.

14. Aristotle uses both *apangelia* (chap. 3) and *diēgēsis* (chaps. 23 and 26): "in epic the narrative form [en de tē epopoiia dia to diēgēsin]" (59b26). This vocabulary comes from Plato, *The Republic*, 392c–394c. But while for Plato narrative "by mimesis" was opposed to "simple narrative," as narrative delegated to a character versus direct narrative, with Aristotle mimesis becomes one large category encompassing both dramatic and diegetic composition.

15. Dupont-Roc and Lallot, in their commentary (p. 370), do not hesitate to speak of *récit diégétique* and *récit narratif* in order to designate narrative as narrated by the narrator (following the definition in Chapter 3 of the *Poetics*). We may therefore also speak of dramatic narrative and thereby give the term "narrative" a generic character in relation to its two species, the dramatic and the diegetic.

16. We may attenuate the contradiction between his two judgments about the spectacle, and also his slight bad faith which wants to gain acceptance for his preference for tragedy without compromising his formal model that excludes the need for an ac-

tual performance, in the following way. We may say, with Dupont-Roc and Lallot (pp. 407–8), that the script contains all the constitutive features of the mimetic activity, without the existence of the spectacle, and also that the way the dramatic text is stated contains the requirement that it be seen. I would put it this way: the script, without the spectacle, is a prescription for the spectacle. The actual spectacle is not necessary for the existence of this prescription. This status also applies to the orchestral score.

17. Henry James, "Preface to *The Portrait of a Lady*," in R. P. Blackmur, ed., *The Art of the Novel* (New York: Charles Scribner's Sons, 1934), pp. 42–48.

18. Frank Kermode, *The Genesis of Secrecy* (Cambridge: Harvard University Press, 1979), pp. 75–77. In the same way, Redfield observes that the *Iliad* is constructed around Achille's anger as well as Hector's tragic fate. But in an epic where the characters have no declared inwardness, only the interaction among them counts. Consequently a character only acquires significance by engendering a plot (Redfield, p. 22). There is no longer a quarrel over priority if we further understand by plot "that implicit conceptual unity which has given the work its actual form" (ibid., p. 23). This is the choice I have made throughout this work.

19. "I have posited that tragedy is an imitation of an action that is whole [teleios] and complete in itself [holēs] and of a certain magnitude [megethos]" (50b23–25).

20. Else is particularly firm about this disjunction between logic and chronology (see his commentary on 50b21–34). The only thing that counts is internal necessity that makes probability or necessity "the grand law of poetry" (ibid., p. 282). He goes so far as to see in this ideally dense temporal schema "a kind of Parmenidian '*on*' in the realm of art" (ibid., p. 294). He bases his argument on the fact that, in speaking of epic in Chapter 23, Aristotle cautions that "its structure should not resemble histories, which necessarily present not a single action but a single period of time [henos khronou]" (59a22–23). To this "report of a single time" Aristotle will oppose his universals that are "timeless" (Else, p. 574). I do not believe it necessary to push the opposition between logic and chronology so far, at the price of having to renounce the kinship between the *Poetics* and the *Ethics*. For my part, I shall attempt in the following chapter to elaborate an achronological notion of narrative temporality. Does not Else himself speak of the events contained within a drama as "events which are not in time at least in the usual sense"? (ibid.). So dramatic time cannot be completely ignored as soon as we accord epic the privilege of representing "various parts [of the story] as being enacted simultaneously [hama]" (59b27). The unique temporal perspective imposed by an action performed by the characters themselves merits reflection about the time of the dramatic narrative as distinct from diegetic narrative and about the time of the plot that governs both of them.

21. Regarding our "intellectual response" to an artist's imitations, see G. Else's commentary on 48b4–24. James Redfield, too, strongly emphasizes that for this pedagogical function of imitation (see Redfield, pp. 52–55), the probable is universal in its own way (ibid., pp. 55–60). The plot gives rise to knowledge (ibid., pp. 60–67). In this, the *Poetics* remains close to fifth-century rhetoric and its emphasis on argumentation. Whereas in the law court the argument is added to the narrative, which is itself contingent, the drama includes its argument in its plot and constructs the conditions of the event on the basis of the plot: "we can then define fiction as the outcome of a hypothetical inquiry into the intermediate causes of action, an inquiry which has led the poet to the discovery and communication in a story of some universal pattern of human probability and necessity" (Redfield, pp. 59–60). So "fiction is the outcome of a kind of inquiry" (ibid., p. 79): how did it happen that . . . ? Who acted in such a way? Similarly, Golden says, "Through imitation, events are reduced to form and thus, however impure in themselves, the events portrayed are purified—clarified—into intelligibility" (Golden, p. 236).

22. Dupont-Roc and Lallot say "chronicle" rather than "history," which is their term for translating *muthos*. This choice does have the advantage of leaving room for a less negative judgment about the writing of history.

23. Else exclaims, "The maker of what happened! Not the maker of the actuality of events but of their logical structure, of their meaning: their having happened is accidental to their being composed." Else, p. 321.

24. We gave the fuller quotation earlier: "an action that is serious, complete, and possessing magnitude" (50b24–25). In the immediate context of this passage Aristotle only comments on "complete" and "magnitude."

25. Redfield translates 52a1–4 as follows. "The imitation is not only of a complete action but of things pitiable and fearful; such things must happen when they happen contrary to expectation because of one another [di'allēla]." Else has: "Contrary to experience but because of one another." Leon Golden: "unexpectedly, yet because of one another."

26. Does the tragedy of Oedipus preserve its character of peripeteia for us who know the framework of the story and its outcome? Yes, if we do not define surprise in terms of some external knowledge but in terms of the relationship of expectation created by the internal course of the plot. The reversal occurs in our expectation, but is created by the plot. See the discussion below of the relationship between this internal structure and the audience's dispositions.

27. It is the role of recognition, as a change from ignorance to knowledge, within the limits I shall speak of in the following note, to compensate for the surprising effect contained in the peripeteia through the lucidity it brings about. In escaping self-deception the hero enters into his truth and the spectator enters into knowledge of this truth. In this sense, Else is probably correct to tie together the problem of the tragic fault and that of recognition. The fault, at least insofar as it consists of ignorance and error, is truly the reverse side of recognition. It will be an important problem in volume 2 of this work to find a bridge between recognition in Aristotle's sense and in Hegel's sense, and repetition in Heidegger's sense.

28. Hermann Lübbe, "Was aus Handlungen Geschichten macht," in Jürgen Mittelstrass and Manfred Riedel, eds., *Vernünftiges Denken* (Berlin/New York: Walter de Gruyter, 1978), pp. 237–50.

29. The model's limits are perhaps more apparent in the case of recognition, where the changes from ignorance to knowledge take place within relationships "leading either to friendship or to hostility on the part of those persons who are marked for good fortune or bad" (52a31). Friendship certainly goes beyond blood relations, but it constitutes a very narrow constraint. We might inquire whether the modern novel, at least in the form it took with Richardson's *Pamela*, making love the only outcome of action, does not reconstitute the equivalent of this constraint of friendship or hostility, as a labor of lucidity itself equivalent to Aristotelian recognition.

30. Redfield says, "*pathē* and learning together constitute the characteristic value to us of a well-made narrative. I suspect that Aristotle meant by *katharsis* exactly this combination of emotion and learning" (p. 67).

31. The *hamartia* is not just an extreme case of discordance. It contributes much to the tragic work's character of being an investigation. It makes the unmerited misfortune problematic. Interpreting the tragic error is the task of tragedy as "inquiry into the strengths and weaknesses of culture" (Redfield, p. 89). I shall return again to this role of the poetic work as revelatory of the "dysfunctions" (ibid., p. 111, n. 1) of a culture.

32. Else notes correctly that this discernment makes us judges. However it is "as a court of fellow human beings," not as ministers of the law, that we pass judgment. The

catharsis of pity and fear thus takes the place of condemnation and execration. And it is not we who bring about this purification, but rather the plot. See Else, p. 437. We rediscover here the connection suggested above between the tragic fault and recognition. Catharsis is the whole process governed by its structure as culminating in recognition.

33. Golden translates this as: "Since the poet should produce pleasure from [apo] pity and fear through [dia] imitation, it is apparent that this function must be worked into the incidents [en tois pragmasin empoiēteon]" (p. 23). Else comments, "the pleasure is derived *from* [apo] the pity and fear but *by means of* [dia] the imitation" (p. 411, his emphasis).

34. It will have been noted that I have not discussed the distinction between "complication" (*desis*) and "denouement" (*lusis*) in Chapter 13. The fact that Aristotle includes the complication among the events "outside" the plot makes me think we ought not to place this distinction on the same plane as the other features of the complex plot, all of whose criteria are "inside" it. This is why a critique of the concept of narrative closure whose argument draws on the aporias of this analysis, only touches a peripheral and heterogeneous category and perhaps one added later by Aristotle (see Else, p. 520), not the core of his concept of plot.

35. James Redfield forcefully emphasizes this tie between ethics and poetics. It is visibly warranted by the common terms *praxis*, action, and *ēthos*, character. More profoundly, both disciplines are concerned with the realization of happiness. Ethics, in effect, deals with happiness in its potential form. It considers its conditions, the virtues. But the connection between these virtues and the circumstances of happiness remains dependent upon contingencies. In constructing their plots, poets give intelligibility to this contingent connection. Whence the apparent paradox: "Fiction is about unreal happiness and unhappiness, but these in their actuality" (Redfield, p. 63). It is at this price that narration "teaches" about the happiness *and life* named in the definition of tragedy: "For tragedy is not an imitation of men but of actions and of life. It is in action that happiness and unhappiness are found" (50a17–18).

36. In volume 2, we shall see what use Claude Bremond makes of these notions of improvement and harm in his "logic of possible narratives." We might follow Dupont-Roc and Lallot when they state that the *Poetics* inverts the relationship of priority ethics establishes between the action and the characters. In ethics, they say, the characters are first, in poetics they move to the second rank: "this inversion in the relationship of priority between agent and action results directly from the definition of dramatic poetry as the representation of action" (p. 196; see also pp. 202–4). Or we might note, with Else (on 48a1–9), that for ethics too it is action that confers moral quality on the characters. In any case, how would this alleged reversal be perceived if the order of precedence that the *Poetics* inverts were not preserved by the reversal? Dupont-Roc and Lallot would no doubt agree. For them, the object of mimetic activity conserves, not just in this chapter but perhaps to the end, the ambiguous meaning of being a model of the object (the natural object imitated) and a copy (the artifact created). They note, regarding 48a9: "the mimetic activity (*of those who represent actions*) establishes a complex relation between the two objects, model and copy. It implies at the same time resemblance and difference, identification and transformation, in one and the same movement" (ibid., p. 157).

37. 51a16–20 is striking in this regard in that it speaks of actions one person performs "that do not go together to produce a single unified action."

38. Redfield (pp. 31–35) observes that the stories about heroes, received from the tradition, are, unlike the stories of the gods, stories about disasters and sufferings,

sometimes overcome, but more often endured. They do not talk of the founding of cities but of their destruction. The epic poet takes from them the "famous" person, the *kleos*, and writes his memorial. The tragic poet, too, draws on this source, with this reservation: "stories can be borrowed, plots cannot" (ibid., p. 58).

39. My position, which I shall argue for in the next chapter, is close to that of Hans Robert Jauss, in *Toward an Aesthetic of Reception*, trans. Timothy Bahti (Minneapolis: University of Minnesota Press, 1982), pp. 3–75 , and also to his notion of amusement. See also Jauss, *Aesthetic Experience and Literary Hermeneutics*, trans. Michael Shaw (Minneapolis: University of Minnesota Press, 1982), pp. 3–220.

40. The mixed status of pleasure, at the interface of the work and the public, no doubt explains why spectacle has such a fluctuating place in the course of the *Poetics*. On the one hand, it is said to be "least germane to the art of poetry" for tragedy "fulfills its function even without a public performance and actors" (50b16). On the other, it is one of the "parts" of tragedy. So although inessential, it cannot in fact be excluded since the text gives us something to see, and when it does not give us something to see it gives us something to read. Reading, the theory of which Aristotle does not present, is always only a substitute for spectacle. For who, if not the spectator or his substitute the reader, can appreciate the "right length" of a work, if we define this so that "it should be possible to embrace the beginning and the end in one view"? (59b19). The pleasure of learning takes place through seeing.

41. Dupont-Roc and Lallot rightly say, "the persuasive is only the probable considered in terms of its effect on the spectator, and, consequently, the ultimate criterion of mimesis" (p. 382).

42. See Wolfgang Iser, *The Implied Reader* (Baltimore: The Johns Hopkins University Press, 1974), pp. 274–94.

43. For Else, what brings about the purification is the very process of imitation. And since the plot *is* the imitation, purification is brought about by the plot. The allusion to catharsis in Chapter 6 does not therefore constitute an addition, but rather presupposes the entire theory of the plot. See also Leon Golden, "Catharsis," *Transactions of the American Philological Association* 43 (1962): 51–60. For his part, James Redfield writes, "Art . . . insofar as it achieves form, is a purification. . . . As the work reaches closure, we come to see that everything is as it should be, that nothing could be added or taken away. Thus the work takes us through impurity to purity; impurity has been met and overcome by the power of formal art" (p. 161). Purification is a purgation, to the extent that the artist gives form through a "reduction," to use an expression borrowed from Lévi-Strauss: "the mark of this reduction is artistic closure" (ibid., p. 165). It is because the work of fiction is "self-contained" (ibid.) that "art in imitating life can make intelligible (at the price of reduction) situations unintelligible in life" (ibid., p. 166). Dupont-Roc and Lallot are therefore fully justified in translating *catharsis* as *épuration*. Cf. their commentary, pp. 188–93.

44. Paul Ricoeur, "The Metaphorical Process as Cognition, Imagination, and Feeling," *Critical Inquiry* 5 (1978): 143–59.

45. Redfield's whole work is oriented in terms of this theme of the effect of poetic thinking on culture, where culture is defined in the following terms: "Those things which can be made otherwise by choice, effort, and the application of knowledge constitute the sphere of culture" (ibid., p. 70). The opposition between nature and culture consists essentially in the opposition between constraint and contingency: "values and norms are . . . not constraints on action but (teleologically) the sources of action" (ibid.). "Constraints constitute the sphere of nature; they are things which cannot be made otherwise" (ibid., p. 71). As a result, the meaning of a work of art is only fulfilled in its effect on culture. For Redfield, this effect is principally a critical one. The drama is born out of the ambiguities of cultural values and norms. With his eyes fixed on the norm, the poet presents his audience a story that is problematic with a character

that is deviant (ibid., p. 81). "The tragic poet thus tests the limits of culture. . . . In tragedy culture itself becomes problematic" (ibid., p. 84). Epic, before tragedy, already exercised this function by means of its "epic distance." "Epic describes the heroic world to an audience which itself inhabits another, ordinary world" (ibid., p. 36). The poet exercises his teaching authority at first by disorienting his audience, then in offering it an ordered representation of the themes of ruin and disorder from its heroic songs. But he does not resolve life's dilemmas. In the *Iliad*, for example, the funeral ceremony of reconciliation reveals no meaning, rather it makes manifest the absence of meaning in every warlike undertaking. "Dramatic art rises from the dilemmas and contradictions of life, but it makes no promise to resolve these dilemmas; on the contrary tragic art may well reach its highest formal perfection at the moment when it reveals to us these dilemmas as universal, pervasive, and necessary" (ibid., p. 219). "Poetry offers [humanity] not gratification but intelligibility" (ibid., p. 220). Such is the case, particularly, in the case of unmerited suffering, aggravated by the tragic fault. "Through the undeserved sufferings of the characters of tragedy the problem of culture is brought home to us" (ibid., p. 87). The *hamartia*, as the blind spot of discordance, is also the blind spot of "what tragedy teaches." It is in this sense we can risk calling art "the negation of culture" (ibid., pp. 218–23). I shall return in volume 2, with Jauss's help, to this function of the literary work where it makes problematic the lived experience of a culture.

CHAPTER THREE

1. See my contribution, "Le Discours de l'action," in Paul Ricoeur et le Centre de Phénoménologie, *La Sémantique de l'action* (Paris: Editions du Centre National de la Recherche Scientifique, 1977), pp. 3–137, especially pp. 21–63.

2. For the concept "basic action," see Arthur Danto, "Basic Actions," *American Philosophical Quarterly* 2 (1965): 141–48; reprinted in Alan R. White, ed., *The Philosophy of Action* (New York: Oxford University Press, 1968), pp. 43–58. Cf. E. Anscombe, *Intention* (Oxford: Basil Blackwell, 1957). Finally, regarding the concept of interference in relation to the notion of a closed physical system, see G. H. von Wright, *Explanation and Understanding* (Ithaca: Cornell University Press, 1971).

3. See "Le Discours de l'action," pp. 113–32.

4. See Clifford Geertz, *The Interpretation of Cultures: Selected Essays* (New York: Basic Books, 1973).

5. In one essay where I first set forth most of the notations devoted to the symbolic mediation of action, I distinguished between a constitutive and a representative symbolism. ("La Structure symbolique de l'action," in *Symbolism*, Acts of the 14th International Conference on Sociology of Religion, Strasbourg, 1977 [Paris: Editions du Centre National de la Recherche Scientifique, n.d.], pp. 31–50.) Today this vocabulary seems inadequate to me. I also took up this topic in "L'Imagination dans le discours et dans l'action," in *Savoir, faire, espérer: les limites de la raison* (Brussels: Publications des Facultés Universitaires Saint-Louis, 1976), vol. 1, pp. 207–28.

6. This is the point where the sense of the word "symbol" I am emphasizing comes closest to the other two senses I have distanced myself from. As an interpretant of behavior, any symbolism is also a notation system that abbreviates, as does mathematical symbolism, a great number of the details of action, and prescribes, as does musical symbolism, the course of executions or performances capable of actualizing it. However it is also as an interpretant governing what Geertz calls a "thick description" that the symbol introduces a twofold relation of meaning into the gesture or the behavior whose interpretation it governs. We may take the empirical configuration of a gesture as the literal meaning bearing a figurative one. At the limit, this meaning can appear, in certain conditions neighboring on secrecy, as a hidden meaning to be de-

coded. This is how any social ritual appears to strangers, without any need for turning their interpretation toward something esoteric or hermetic.

7. See my article "The Model of the Text: Meaningful Action Considered as a Text," *Social Research* 38 (1971): 529–62.

8. See Peter Winch, *The Idea of a Social Science and Its Relation to Philosophy* (London: Routledge and Kegan Paul, 1958), pp. 40–65.

9. I cited one example earlier: James Redfield's treatment of the relation between art and culture in his *Nature and Culture in the Iliad*. See above, pp. 50–51.

10. I shall return at length to the role of "repetition" in my general discussion of the phenomenology of time in volume 2.

11. See *Being and Time*, sections 78–83. Martin Heidegger, *Being and Time*, trans. John Macquarrie and Edward Robinson (New York: Harper and Row, 1962), pp. 456–88.

12. "Dasein historicizes *from day to day* by reason of its way of interpreting time by dating it. . . ." (ibid., p. 466). Recall Augustine's reflections on the "day," which he refuses to reduce purely and simply to one revolution of the sun. Heidegger does not follow him in this way. He puts the difference between the "most natural measure of time" (ibid., p. 465) and all artificial, instrumental ones. The time "within" which we are is world-time (*Weltzeit*) (ibid., p. 471)—"more objective" than any possible object and "more subjective" than any possible subject. Hence it is neither inside nor outside.

13. Wolfgang Iser, *The Act of Reading: A Theory of Aesthetic Response* (Baltimore: The Johns Hopkins University Press, 1978), chap. 3.

14. At the price of this generalization a historian such as Paul Veyne will be able to define plot as a combination in varying proportions of goals, causes, and chance, and make it the guideline for his historiography in *Comment on écrit l'histoire*. See below, pp. 169–74. In a complementary but not contradictory way, G. H. von Wright sees in historical reasoning a combination of practical syllogisms and chains of causality governed by systemic constraints. Again, see below, pp. 132–43. In numerous ways, therefore, plot composes heterogeneous series.

15. I am borrowing the notion of a "configurational act" from Louis O. Mink. He applies it to historical comprehension and I am extending it to the whole field of narrative understanding. See below, pp. 155–61.

16. Below in chapter 6, I shall consider some other implications of the reflective character of judgment in history.

17. I borrow this concept of "followability" from W. B. Gallie, *Philosophy and the Historical Understanding* (New York: Schocken Books, 1964). In Part II, I discuss the central thesis of Gallie's book, namely, that history is a species of the genre story.

18. This typology, however, does not abolish the eminently temporal character of the schematism. We ought not to forget the way Kant relates the constituting of the schematism to what he calls the *a priori* determinations of time: "The schemata are thus nothing but *a priori* determinations of time in accordance with rules. These rules relate in the order of categories to the *time-series*, the *time-order* and lastly to the *scope of time* in respect of all possible objects" (B184). (Immanuel Kant, *Critique of Pure Reason*, trans. Norman Kemp Smith [New York: St. Martin's Press, 1965], p. 185.) However Kant only recognized those determinations of time that contribute to the objective constitution of the physical world. The schematism of the narrative function implies determinations of a new genre which are precisely the ones we have just designated by the dialectic of the episodic characteristics and the configuring of emplotment.

19. Robert Scholes and Robert Kellogg, in *The Nature of Narrative* (New York: Oxford University Press, 1966), are correct in prefacing their analysis of the major cate-

gories of narrative activity with an ample review of the history of narration in the West. What I am calling the schematization of emplotment exists only through this historical development. This is why Eric Auerbach, in his magnificent work *Mimesis*, trans. Willard R. Trask (Princeton: Princeton University Press, 1953), chooses to graft his analysis and evaluation of the representation of reality in Western literature to a sample of numerous, yet strictly delimited, texts.

20. Aristotle notes that we only *know* universals—the individual is ineffable. But we *make* individual things. Cf. G. G. Granger, *Essai d'une Philosophie du Style* (Paris: Armand Colin, 1968), pp. 5–16.

21. See Roy Schafer, *A New Language for Psychoanalysis* (New Haven: Yale University Press, 1976); *Language and Insight* (New Haven: Yale University Press, 1978); and "Narration in the Psychoanalytic Dialogue," *Critical Inquiry* 7 (1980): 29–53. Cf. my own "The Question of Proof in Freud's Psychoanalytic Writings," in Charles E. Reagan and David Stewart, eds., *The Philosophy of Paul Ricoeur* (Boston: Beacon Press, 1978), pp. 184–210. This article was first published in a slightly different form as "The Question of Proof in Psychoanalysis," *Journal of the American Psychoanalytic Association* 25 (1977): 835–72.

22. Wilhelm Schapp, *In Geschichten Verstrickt* (Wiesbaden: B. Heymann, 1976).

23. Frank Kermode, *The Genesis of Secrecy: On the Interpretation of Narrative* (Cambridge: Harvard University Press, 1979).

24. Roman Ingarden, *The Literary Work of Art: An Investigation on the Borderlines of Ontology, Logic, and Theory of Literature*, trans. George G. Grabowica (Evanston: Northwestern University Press, 1973).

25. Greimas's concept of *verediction* provides a noteworthy example of the return of this dialectic, even within a theory that excludes without any concession any recourse to an external referent. See the article "Verediction" in A.-J. Greimas and J. Courtés, *Semiotics and Language: An Analytical Dictionary*, trans. Larry Christ, Daniel Patte, et al. (Bloomington: Indiana University Press, 1982), pp. 367–68.

26. See *The Rule of Metaphor*, Study VII, pp. 216–56.

27. Besides the previous reference to my *Rule of Metaphor*, see Paul Ricoeur, *Interpretation Theory: Discourse and the Surplus of Meaning* (Fort Worth: Texas Christian University Press, 1976), pp. 36–37, 40–44, 80, 88.

28. François Dagognet, *Ecriture et Iconographie* (Paris: Vrin, 1973).

29. Eugen Fink, *De la Phénoménologie*, trans. Didier Frank (Paris: Minuit, 1975); Hans-Georg Gadamer, *Truth and Method* (New York: Seabury Press, 1975), pp. 119–26.

30. Paul Ricoeur, "The Task of Hermeneutics," *Philosophy Today* 17 (1973): 112–28.

31. Nelson Goodman's saying, in *Languages of Art* (Indianapolis: Hackett, 1976), that literary works ceaselessly make and remake the world holds particularly for narrative works, to the extent that the *poiēsis* of emplotment is a making that, also, bears on what is made. Nowhere is the formula of the title of Goodman's opening chapter, "Reality Remade," more appropriate, as is his maxim about "reorganizing the world in terms of works and works in terms of the world" (ibid., p. 241).

32. Martin Heidegger, *The Basic Problems of Phenomenology*, trans. Albert Hofstadter (Bloomington: Indiana University Press, 1982), par. 19, "Time and Temporality," pp. 229–74.

33. In earlier establishing a homology between the praxic time of mimesis₁ and the last of the forms derived from temporality in *Being and Time*, "within-time-ness" or "being-'within'-time," I have in fact chosen the reverse order of *Being and Time*, that of the *Basic Problems*.

PART TWO

1. This does not exclude that historical explanation can be described as "mixed." In this regard I accept the thesis of Henrik von Wright to whom a part of chapter 5 is devoted. "Mixed," however, means neither confused nor ambiguous. A "mixed" form of discourse is something wholly other than a compromise, if it is carefully constructed as "mixed" on the appropriate epistemological plane.

2. "Explanation and Understanding," trans. Charles E. Reagan and David Stewart, in *The Philosophy of Paul Ricoeur: An Anthology of His Work*, ed. Charles E. Reagan and David Stewart (Boston: Beacon Press, 1978), pp. 149–66.

CHAPTER FOUR

1. Pierre Chaunu wrote in 1960, "epistemology is a temptation that we must resolutely resist. Does not the experience of these past years demonstrate that it can be a lazy solution for those who lose themselves in it with delight—one or two brilliant exceptions only serving to confirm the rule—the sign of an inquiry that marches in place and becomes increasingly sterile. At most it is opportune that some leading lights—which we do not in any way claim to be—devote themselves to it in order better to preserve the robust artisans of knowledge under construction—the only title we do claim—from the dangerous temptations of this morbid *Capoue*" (*Histoire quantitative—Histoire sérielle* [Paris: A. Colin, 1978], p. 10).

2. Certain analyses in this section are an abridgment of developments treated in greater detail in my essay *The Contribution of French Historiography to the Theory of History*, the Zaharoff Lecture for 1978–79 (Oxford: Clarendon Press, 1980). In chapter 6 below I present some further analyses of works by French historians not treated in that lecture.

3. Raymond Aron, *Introduction to the Philosophy of History: An Essay on the Limits of Historical Objectivity*, trans. George J. Irwin (Boston: Beacon Press, 1961).

4. Charles Victor Langlois and Charles Seignobos, *Introduction to the Study of History*, trans. G. G. Berry (New York: Henry Holt, 1898).

5. Henri I. Marrou, *The Meaning of History*, trans. Robert J. Olson (Baltimore: Helicon, 1966).

6. Logically speaking, "there is nothing unique in our understanding with regard to the past. It is definitely the same process that takes place in our understanding of other men in the present, and particularly in the understanding of articulated language. (Most frequently, and in the best examples, the document under consideration is a 'text' of some kind or another)" (ibid., pp. 91–92). For Marrou, the passage from individual memory to the historical past is not a problem, inasmuch as the real break is between an attachment to oneself and openness to others.

7. Here, Marrou takes his distance from one of the thinkers he most admires, Collingwood. But perhaps a rereading of Collingwood would put him closer to the thesis being defended here.

8. Quoting the passage by Aron I have already cited, Marrou writes, "In any case, 'there is no *historical reality*, ready-made, prior to knowledge, which need only be reproduced with fidelity.' History is the result of the creative effort, by which the historian, as the conscious subject, establishes a relationship between the past which he evokes and the present which is his own" (ibid., pp. 56–57).

9. For a brief history of the founding, the antecedents, and the development of the Annales school, see Jacques Le Goff, "L'Histoire nouvelle," in Jacques Le Goff, Roger Chartier, and Jacques Revel, eds., *La Nouvelle Histoire* (Paris: Retz-C.E.P.L., 1978), pp. 210–41.

10. Marc Bloch, *The Historian's Craft*, trans. Peter Putnam (New York: Knopf, 1953).

11. I shall return, in volume 2, to the question that occupies Bloch in his first chapter, the relationships among "history, men, and time." That history knows the past only insofar as it is human and can be defined as the science of "men in time" (ibid., p. 27); that historical time is both continuous and dissimilar; that history must abstract itself from the obsession with origins; that our knowledge of the present would be impossible without our knowledge of the past and vice versa; all these themes will return when we raise the question of the referents of history. Here we shall limit ourselves to the few epistemological insights Bloch attaches to his rapid reflections about the object of history, and especially to the status of the notions of "track" [*trace*] and "testimony." His audacity surely is to have linked his principal methodological notations to his definition of history as "knowledge of their tracks," to use François Simiand's apt expression. These tracks upon which we establish a science about human beings in time are essentially "the accounts of eye-witnesses" (p. 48). As a result, "historical observation"—the title of chapter 2—and "historical criticism"—the title of chapter 3—are essentially devoted to a typology and a criteriology of evidence. It is noteworthy that in *The Historian's Craft* narrative only appears as one species of testimony which the historian uses critically—namely, those intentional accounts destined to inform the reader—and never as the literary form the historian writes (see pp. 44, 61, 111, 177).

12. The considerable role of falsehoods in medieval history also contingently explains the emphasis given to the criticism of testimony.

13. "To evaluate the probability of an event is to weigh its chances of taking place" (ibid., p. 124). Bloch is not far from Weber and Aron when he observes the singularity of this mode of reasoning, which appears to apply foresight to the past: "since the line of the present has somehow been moved back in the imagination, it is a future of bygone times built upon a fragment which, for us, is actually the past" (ibid., p. 125).

14. "And so, to add it all up, the criticism of evidence relies upon an instinctive metaphysics of the similar and the dissimilar, of the one and the many" (ibid., p. 116). It is summed up therefore in the handling of the principle of "limited similarity" (ibid., p. 118).

15. Henri Focillon, *The Life of Forms in Art*, trans. Charles Beecher Hogan and George Keebler (New Haven: Yale University Press, 1942).

16. Narrative is associated with this reconstructive phase just once, this time under the cover of a quotation from Michelet: "But a great vital movement was needed, because all these diverse elements gravitated together in the unity of the story [*récit*]" (ibid, p. 154). Perhaps the greatest lack in *The Historian's Craft*, in its published part, is some reflection on the way the question of "historical analysis" (which implies the question of historical causation) is articulated in terms of "historical observation" (which includes the questions about historical facts and events). This is the point of articulation where a reflection on narrative and the connection between event and narrative could have been enlightening.

17. Trans. Siân Reynolds, 2 vols. (New York: Harper and Row, 1972–74). First published in 1949, it underwent two important revisions leading up to the fourth edition published in 1979 (Paris: A. Colin). See also the pieces collected in Fernand Braudel, *On History*, trans. Sarah Matthews (Chicago: University of Chicago Press, 1980), including an extract from the Preface to *The Mediterranean . . .* , Braudel's inaugural lecture at the Collège de France, "The Situation of History in 1950," his famous *Annales* article, from 1958, on the *longue durée*, and other essays dealing with the relationships between history and other human sciences.

18. See his "Leçon Inaugurale" at the Collège de France (1933), in Lucien Febvre,

Combats pour l'Histoire (Paris: A. Colin, 1953), p. 7. There is no article titled *récit* or *narratif* in *La Nouvelle Histoire*.

19. Paul Lacombe, *De l'histoire considérée comme une science* (Paris: Hachette, 1894); François Simiand, "Méthode historique et science sociale," *Revue de synthèse historique* 6 (1903):1–22, 129–57; Henri Berr, *L'Histoire traditionelle et la Synthèse historique* (Paris: Alcan, 1921).

20. Huguette and Pierre Chaunu, *Séville et l'Atlantique: 1504–1650*, 12 vols. (Paris: SEVPEN, 1955–60).

21. Below, I shall compare Braudel's practice in *The Mediterranean* to his theoretical declarations in *On History*, to which I have limited myself here.

22. Pierre Chaunu, *Histoire quantitative—Histoire sérielle*.

23. The concept of "conjuncture," forged by economists, "expresses the desire to surpass the discontinuity between the various curves established by *statisticians* to grasp the interdependence of all the variables and factors isolated at a given moment, and to follow—hence predict—their evolution over time" (from the article "Structure/Conjuncture," in *La Nouvelle Histoire*, p. 525, emphasis in original).

24. His "General Introduction" to *La Crise de l'économie française à la fin de l'Ancien Régime et au début de la Révolution française* (Paris: Presses Universitaires de France, 1944), was economic history's Discourse on Method. According to Pierre Chaunu, "Labrousse marked out the boundaries of meaning for a conjuncture that could speak only within a structure" (*Histoire quantitative—Histoire sérielle*, p. 125).

25. "In the beginning was economics, but at the center of everything was man, man confronted with himself, hence with death, in the succession of generations, whence demography" (Pierre Chaunu, "La Voie démographique et ses dépassements," in *Histoire quantitative—Histoire sérielle*, p. 169).

26. P. Goubert's work, *Beauvais et le Beauvaisis du 1600 à 1730* (Paris: SEVPEN, 1960), reprinted under the title *Cent Mille Provinciaux au XVII* siècle (Paris: Flammarion, 1968), in this regard marks the full integration of demographic history and economic history into the framework of the regional monograph. In this sense, it has been perhaps demographic history more than anything else that has allowed the idea of a system of civilization to be joined to that of a structure, and the delimiting of such a system from the turn of the thirteenth century to the beginning of the twentieth century, that is, to the end of rural Europe. The outline of this system of civilization only appears if demography does not confine itself to counting people, if it aims at extricating the cultural and nonnatural characteristics that govern the uneasy equilibrium of this system.

27. F. Braudel, *Civilization matérielle. Economie et Capitalisme XV*—*XVIII* siècle: vol. 1, *Les Sructures du quotidien*; vol. 2, *Les Jeux de l'échange*; vol. 3, *Le Temps du monde* (Paris: A. Colin, 1967–79). To date the first two volumes have been translated into English: *The Structures of Everyday Life*, trans. Miriam Kochan, revised Siân Reynolds (New York: Harper and Row, 1981); *The Wheels of Commerce*, trans. Siân Reynolds (New York: Harper and Row, 1983).

28. See below, chapter 6, pp. 208–14.

29. Jacques Le Goff, *Time, Work, and Culture in the Middle Ages*, trans. Arthur Goldhammer (Chicago: University of Chicago Press, 1980). This work stems from a long time-span history: "the long period of the Middle Ages," "the long period relevant to our history" (p. x). I shall return to some statements by Le Goff concerning the relationships between this "total," "long," "deep" Middle Ages and our present in volume 2 of my study.

30. Refusing to "give himself over to an ethnology that stands outside time" (ibid., p. 246), Le Goff sees diachrony as working according to "abstract systems of transformation very different from the evolutionary schemes used by the historian in attempt-

ing to apprehend the process of becoming in the concrete societies he studies" (ibid., p. 235). The problem, he says, is to transcend the "false dilemma of structure versus conjuncture, and, even more important, structure versus event" (ibid.).

31. See below, pp. 206–25.

32. See Michel Vovelle, *Piété baroque et Déchristianisation en Provence au XVIIIe siècle: les attitudes devant la mort d'après les clauses des testaments* (Paris: Plon, 1973); Pierre Chaunu, *La mort à Paris, XVIe, XVIIe, XVIIIe siècles* (Paris: Fayard, 1978).

33. Pierre Chaunu, "Un Champ pour l'histoire sérielle, l'histoire au troisième niveau," in *La mort à Paris*, p. 227.

34. Georges Duby, "Histoire sociale et idéologies des sociétés," in Jacques Le Goff and Pierre Nora, eds., *Faire de l'histoire* (Paris: Gallimard, 1974), vol.1, p. 149.

35. Philippe Aries, *The Hour of Our Death*, trans. Helen Weaver (New York: Knopf, 1981).

36. Michel Vovelle presents a critical summary of the results and the dead ends of twenty years of long time-span history, starting with Braudel's celebrated article of 1958 ("History and the Social Sciences: the *Longue Durée*"), in *La Nouvelle Histoire*, pp. 316–43. Accepting that "the death of a certain historicizing history is today an accomplished fact" (p. 318), he asks whether the event struck down by Braudel has really disappeared from the historical field. He doubts that the model of embedded times, practiced by Braudel, can be transposed to other historical regions, especially social history. On the one hand, the heterogeneity of rhythms and correspondences between different time-spans tends to nullify the idea of a total history. On the other hand, the polarization between the quasi-immobility of the great mental structures and the return of the event, brought about by the recent interest in ideas about cut-off points, traumas, breaks, and revolutions, calls into question the very idea of a graduated scale of time-spans. For example, the most recent history seems to be seeking a new dialectic of short spans of time and long ones, a "concordance of times" (p. 341). I shall return in chapter 6 to this problem, which perhaps does not have a solution at the level of the historian's profession but rather on the level of a more subtle reflection about historical intentionality. Aside from this reflection, the historians' intellectual honesty undoubtedly lies in rejecting both immobile history and that of the event as an outburst and, within this wide interval, giving free reign to the multiplying of historical times, depending on the requirements of the object under consideration and the method chosen. Thus, for example, we can see the same author, Emmanuel Le Roy Ladurie, illustrating in turn the short time-span and even the use of a narrative form in his famous *Montaillou: The Promised Land of Error* (trans. Barbara Bray [New York: G. Braziller, 1978]); the long time-span in *The Peasants of Languedoc* (trans. John Day [Urbana: University of Illinois Press, 1974]); and the extreme long time-span in *Times of Feast, Times of Famine: A History of Climate Since the Year 1000* (trans. Barbara Bray [Garden City, N.Y.: Doubleday, 1971]), and in Part IV of *The Territory of the Historian*, trans. Ben Reynolds and Siân Reynolds (Chicago: University of Chicago Press, 1979): "History without People: The Climate as a New Province of Research," pp. 285–319.

37. Wilhelm Windelband, "Geschichte und Naturwissenschaft (Strassburger Rektorede, 1894)," in *Präludien: Aufsätze und Reden zur Philosophie und ihrer Geschichte*, vol. 2 (Tubingen: J. C. B. Mohr, 1921), pp. 136–60.

38. See Raymond Aron, *La Philosophie Critique de l'histoire: essai sur une theorie allemande de l'histoire* (Paris: Vrin, 1938, 4th. ed. 1969). See especially the footnote on the relationships between Windelband and Rickert, pp. 306–7.

39. *The Journal of Philosophy* 39 (1942): 35–48; reprinted in Patrick Gardiner, ed., *Theories of History* (New York: The Free Press, 1959), pp. 344–56. I shall cite the latter.

40. "By a general law, we should here understand a statement of universal conditional form which is capable of being confirmed by suitable empirical findings" (ibid. p. 345).

41. Bertrand Russell, "On the Notion of Cause," *Proceedings of the Aristotelian Society* 13 (1912–13): 1–26.

42. Hempel's refusal to give a distinct status to the causal relation is directed against Maurice Mandelbaum, who, in chapters 7 and 8 of his *The Problem of Historical Knowledge* (New York: Liveright, 1938), had attempted to distinguish the "causal explanation" practiced by historians from "causal analysis," identical to explanation by causal laws. See Hempel, p. 347 n.1. I shall return to Mandelbaum's thesis, in its more recent form, in chapter 6.

43. Charles Frankel, "Explanation and Interpretation in History," *Philosophy of Science* 24 (1957): 137–55; reprinted in *Theories of History*, pp. 408–27. I shall cite the latter.

44. The way had been opened, in fact, by Hempel himself, with his notion of an "explanation sketch." We need to understand this strategy if we are to fully comprehend the breakthrough created by Dray's work, which we shall come to below.

45. Having to take a "weak" model of explanation into account will be a sufficient reason for us not to give in to a directly narrativist thesis and to appeal to a more indirect method of relating explanation to understanding.

46. The adversaries of the covering law model will see in this a sign that explanation in history is grafted to the prior intelligibility of narrative, which it reinforces, as it were, by interpolation.

47. Patrick Gardiner, *The Nature of Historical Explanation* (Oxford: Clarendon Press, 1952).

48. Ernst Nagel, "Some Issues in the Logic of Historical Analysis," *Scientific Monthly* 74 (1952): 162–69; reprinted in Gardiner, *Theories of History*, pp. 373–86. I cite the latter.

49. It is remarkable that the question of selectivity should never be related to one specific feature of history, namely, that historians belong to the field of their objects in a different way than physicists belong to the physical world. I shall return to this point in volume 2.

50. Here again it is remarkable that the question of knowing why there is a question of importance in history is avoided. That the weighing of degrees of importance arises from a logic of relative guarantees is beyond question. On this point Nagel has added to the model in defending it. And a dialectic of explanation and understanding will have to take account of this. But, however indisputable it may be that such weighing concerns history as "inquiry," the question remains of situating this inquiry within the total process of historical understanding.

51. We shall see later what other use may be made of this important concession. Frankel makes several others as well that weaken the model to the point of abandoning it. For example, he concedes to Isaiah Berlin (referring to Berlin's "Historical Inevitability," the Auguste Compte Memorial Lecture, 12 May 1953, in idem, *Four Essays on Liberty* [London: Oxford University Press, 1969], reprinted in Patrick Gardiner, ed., *The Philosophy of History* [London: Oxford University Press, 1974], pp. 161–86), that if history is written in ordinary language, and if the reader does not expect specialized scientific language, it is because the success of an explanation is not measured in terms of a theory but "by the account he gives of concrete affairs." Causal explanations, and even commonsensical ones, skirt the rules of wisdom—such as the adage that power corrupts and absolute power corrupts absolutely. We are not far here from a narrativist theory: we want a historian "to tell a story and to make it come to life" (in *Theories of History*, p. 414).

52. I shall return in chapter 6 below to the variety of meanings that adorn the notion of a cause in history.

53. Here again Frankel's argument skirts the narrativist conception. The choice of terminal consequences by the historian is called "the frame of his story" (ibid., p. 421). In discussing the question of the "true" cause, Frankel, following Gardiner on this point, shows that when the disagreements have to do not with perspective but with connections, they are "about what . . . should or should not be included in the historian's story to make that story an adequate answer to the question that has been raised" (ibid., p. 427). When a historian proposes his interpretation of a period or an institution, "he is telling a story of a sequence of causally related events that have consequences of value or dis-value" (ibid., p. 421).

54. In volume 2 I shall return to this problem of the relationships between explaining the past and action in the present, which the theory of progress pushed to the front rank in the philosophy of history. At the present stage of our discussion, the only thing at stake is whether this choice of terminal consequences need not first satisfy a good causal connection on the factual level.

55. A fine passage of Frankel's bears witness to this delicate equilibrium between a methodological pluralism and a noncomplacent attitude as regards skepticism. Having spoken favorably of interpretations in terms of terminal consequences, Frankel notes that if the scheme proposed for history does depend on the facts, the limited opportunities, and the possibilities raised by circumstances, and if also the historian is not sectarian and provincial, but open and generous, then "history which is lit by some clear and circumspect idea of what human life can be is generally preferred to the history that is impassive, that never commits itself, and that lacks a guiding ideal or the irony or tears that go with applying such an ideal to the record of human affairs" (ibid., p. 424). The whole of Charles Frankel's liberalism and humanism is contained in these phrases.

CHAPTER FIVE

1. W. H. Dray, *Laws and Explanations in History* (London: Oxford University Press, 1957).

2. I shall return to the notion of causal explanation in the next chapter.

3. To be entirely convincing, the argument must be stated as follows. The physical and mechanical laws set in play by the accident, which as such do not involve a temporal order, require reconstituting the accident phase by phase in order to apply the laws seriatim. It is this application ad seriatim that makes knowing the laws a necessary condition of the explanation. If Dray did not give his argument this form, it is because he takes as his model the mechanic who perfectly understands each phase of the accident without himself being a physicist. Does Dray thereby mean to situate the historian's knowledge on the same plane as the mechanic's? If so, we risk falling into a summarily pragmatic conception of explanation in history, substituted for a theoretical one. Dray's work presents numerous traces of such a conception. See ibid., pp. 70–76.

4. "No matter how complicated the expression with which we complete a statement of the form 'E because . . .', it is a fact of the 'logic' of such 'because' statements that additions to the explanatory clause are never ruled out by our acceptance of the original statement" (ibid., p. 35).

5. This argument, we shall see, can easily be incorporated into the thesis that an event, as what contributes to the progression of a plot, shares with this plot the property of being both singular and typical at the same time.

6. Dray (ibid., p. 2) refers to Karl Popper, *The Open Society and Its Enemies*

(London: Routledge and Kegan Paul, 1952,) vol. 2, p. 262. For many authors, asking about causality in history is simply to repeat the discussion about the place of laws in history, given either that we take cause to mean exactly the same thing as does law—when it is better to avoid speaking of a cause since the term is so equivocal—or that we take causes as specific kinds of laws, "causal laws"—then we have just a causal version of the covering law model. Saying X causes Y is equivalent to saying whenever X, Y.

7. Collingwood tried to do this in his *An Essay on Metaphysics* (Oxford: Clarendon Press, 1948), where he distinguished three senses of the term. According to the first sense, the only one he takes as proper to history, and also as the primitive one, a person *makes* another person act in a certain way by providing him with a motive for so acting. According to the second sense, the cause of something is "the handle" by means of which we control it. Therefore it is what is in our power to produce or prevent. (For example, the cause of malaria is the bite of a mosquito.) He derives this second sense from the first one by broadening the notion of an effect resulting from human actions on the behavior of anyone to anything in general. Collingwood excludes this second sense from history, reserving it for the practical natural sciences and the discovery of causal laws by experimentation. Dray retains something from it, however, in his pragmatic criterion for causal attribution, although he sets it within the framework of a specific activity of judging. The third sense establishes a one-to-one relation, thanks to logical necessity, between two events or states of affairs. It is equivalent to the notion of a sufficient condition.

8. Max Weber and Raymond Aron will help us in the next chapter to push this analysis even further.

9. Cf. here H. L. A. Hart, "The Ascription of Responsibility and Rights," *Proceedings of the Aristotelian Society* 49 (1948): 171–94, and Stephen Toulmin, *The Uses of Argument* (Cambridge: Cambridge University Press, 1958). Both authors invite us to bring together explanation and the justification of one "claim" against another "claim" by providing "warrants."

10. I am saving this apology for singular causal imputation for my own attempt to articulate historical explanation in terms of our narrative understanding. Particular causal imputation can constitute the intermediary link between levels, to the extent that, for one thing, it is already an explanation and, for another, that it is established upon a narrative base. However as regards this aspect of the problem, there is only one brief allusion in Dray's book: "to give and defend a causal explanation in history is scarcely ever to bring what is explained under a law, and almost always involves a descriptive account, a narrative of the actual course of events, in order to justify the judgement that the condition indicated was indeed the cause" (ibid., pp. 113–14). Note also the allusion to diagnosis as the medical equivalent of individual causal imputation in history.

11. In this sense, it is an attempt to "make sense," but through arguments independent "of what Collingwood in particular has to say about historical understanding" (ibid., p. 122).

12. "Taken in isolation, it is very seldom beyond all doubt whether a given explanatory statement of the form 'He did *x* because of *y*' is to be taken in the rational sense or not. . . . The particular 'because' does not carry its language level on its face; this has to be determined by other means" (ibid., p. 133). The ambiguity of the term "because" increases if we take into account its use in explanations in terms of dispositions, which Gilbert Ryle distinguishes from explanations in terms of empirical laws and which Gardiner takes up again in *The Nature of Historical Explanation*, pp. 89–90 and 96–97.

13. Regarding this point, cf. Hermann Lübbe," "Was aus Handlungen Geschichten macht: Handlungsinterferenz; Meterogonic der Zwecke; Widerfahrnis; Handlungsge-

mengelagen; Zufall," in J. Mittelstrass and M. Reidel, eds., *Vernünftiges Denken. Studien zur praktischen Philosophie und Wissenschaftstheorie* (Berlin/New York: Walter de Gruyter, 1978), pp. 237–68.

14. G. H. von Wright, *Explanation and Understanding* (Ithaca: Cornell University Press, 1971).

15. See G. H. von Wright, *Norm and Action* (London: Routledge and Kegan Paul, 1963); idem, *An Essay in Deontic Logic and the General Theory of Action* (Amsterdam: North Holland, 1968).

16. He pays particular attention to the threefold criticism directed against this dichotomy that he finds in Dray's *Laws and Explanations in History*, and in G. E. M. Anscombe, *Intention* (Oxford: B. Blackwell, 1957), Peter Winch, *The Idea of A Social Science* (London: Routledge and Kegan Paul, 1958), and Charles Taylor, *The Explanation of Behavior* (London: Routledge and Kegan Paul, 1964). Also, he shows much interest in the convergence between developments he sees, on the European continent, in the hermeneutical or dialectical-hermeneutical current of philosophy. Given the perspective of these intersecting influences, von Wright expects Wittgenstein's philosophy to have an impact on hermeneutical philosophy equal to the one it has had on analytic philosophy, thereby contributing to the drawing together of these two traditions. He interprets hermeneutics' orientation toward questions of language as one favorable sign. In dissociating "understanding" and "empathy," recent hermeneutical philosophy, that of Gadamer in particular, makes understanding "a semantic rather than a psychological category" (*Explanation and Understanding*, p. 30).

17. Cf. J. L. Petit, "La Narrativité et le concept de l'explication en histoire," in Dorian Tiffeneau, ed., *La Narrativité* (Paris: Centre National de la Recherche Scientifique, 1980), pp. 187–201.

18. See *Explanation and Understanding*, pp. 43–50.

19. Von Wright includes the concept of event within that of a state of affairs: "an event, one could say, is a pair of successive states" (ibid., p. 12). This definition is justified in his earlier work, *Norm and Action* (London: Routledge and Kegan Paul, 1963), chapter 2, section 6.

20. Furthermore, causality, even when divested of any anthropomorphic interpretation, preserves an implicit tie to human action in that we call a cause either what it is sufficient to produce to obtain an effect, or what it is necessary to suppress to make the effect disappear. In this sense, to conceive of a relation between events in terms of causality is to conceive it under the aspect of possible action. Von Wright thereby rejoins Collingwood's description of a cause as a "handle." I have already referred to this problem of non-Humean uses of the idea of a cause in speaking of Dray's work. I shall return to it again in the next chapter with Max Weber, Raymond Aron, and Maurice Mandelbaum.

21. Arthur C. Danto, "What Can We Do?" *The Journal of Philosophy* 60 (1963): 435–45; idem, "Basic Actions," *American Philosophical Quarterly* 2 (1965): 141–48.

22. I am leaving aside the long analysis by means of which he undertakes to ameliorate the theory of practical inference stemming from Aristotle and taken up again in the modern period by Anscombe, Taylor, and Malcolm. What von Wright calls the "Logical Connection Argument"—in opposition to the argument for a nonlogical, that is, extrinsic, causal connection—was not presented, he says, in a convincing way by his predecessors. He wants to pose the problem instead in terms of *verification*. The question is a twofold one. How, we will ask, do we assure ourself that an agent has a certain intention? And how do we discover that his behavior is of the kind for which the intention is taken to be the cause? The argument then runs as follows. If it seems as though we cannot answer the first question without answering the second one, then the intention and the action are not logically independent. "In this mutual dependence of the verification of premises and the verification of conclusions in practical syllogisms

consists, as I see it, the truth of the Logical Connection Argument" (ibid., p. 116). I shall not pursue further the demonstration of this circular relationship, which is not necessary for my own proposal.

23. I am also ignoring von Wright's discussion of the compatibility between teleological and causal explanation. I will only speak of it insofar as his argument confirms the irreducibility of the first to the second. The argument essentially consists in saying that the two forms of explanation do not have the same *explanandum*. It is a question of different phenomena put into different descriptions: bodily movements on the side of causal explanation, intentional behavior on the other side. Not having the same *explanandum*, the two types of explanation are compatible. What is excluded is the possibility of adopting both explanations at the same time. Thus I cannot at the same time raise my arm and observe, on some screen, the changes taking place in my brain. When I am observing, I let things happen. When I am acting, I make them happen. It is a contradiction in terms therefore to let something happen and at the same time to make the same thing happen on the same occasion. No one, consequently, can observe the causes of the results of his own basic actions, in the sense of the word "result" adopted earlier. Causal and teleological explanation—irreducible to each other, and compatible—fuse in the meaning we attach to an action. "The conceptual basis of action, one could therefore say, is partly our ignorance (unawareness) of the operation of causes and partly our confidence that certain changes will happen only when we happen to be acting" (ibid., p. 130).

24. In an important note (ibid., pp. 200–201), remaining faithful to Wittgenstein, von Wright resists any linguistic reform that would exclude causal terminology from history, owing to the confusion possible between causal categories too exclusively dependent upon the Hempelian model. It is one thing to ask if causal terminology is appropriate to history, another to ask whether this or that causal category applies in this discipline.

25. This first type can be schematized as follows (see ibid., p. 137).

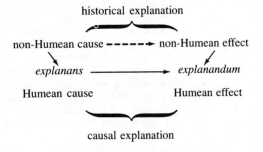

26. This second form of explanation can be schematized as follows (see ibid., p. 138).

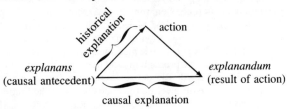

27. The independence of two events is debatable, von Wright notes, if the described event is that the First World War "broke out." Is this not a "colligation," whose complete description includes the incident at Sarajevo? The discussion never ends if we lose sight of the fact that it is always in terms of some description or another that an event is dependent or independent. In this sense, quasi-causal explanation is tributary to a particularly analytic description of events. Mandelbaum would certainly recall here that this atomistic use of causality derives from an overall grasp of an uninterrupted process, affecting continuous entities such as nations. See below, pp. 194–206.

28. Quasi-causal explanation is thus schematized as follows (see ibid., p. 143).

Practical premises

explanans   *explanandum*

29. See Part I, chap. 3, on the temporal implications of mimesis$_2$.

30. Arthur C. Danto, *Analytic Philosophy of History* (New York: Cambridge University Press, 1965).

31. This definition of the task of analytic philosophy is akin to the plea Peter Strawson makes, at the beginning of his *Individuals: An Essay in Descriptive Metaphysics* (London: Methuen, 1959), in favor of a descriptive metaphysics, which he opposes to a revisionist metaphysics. In return, this implication of a descriptive metaphysics in an analysis of our conceptual and linguistic network is strongly opposed to French structuralism's tendency to conceive of this network as closed in on itself, excluding any extralinguistic reference. Applied to history, this latter conception tends to make an event a simple "effect of discourse." This linguistic idealism is completely foreign to analytic philosophy, for which the analysis of our ways of thinking and talking about the world and its descriptive metaphysics are mutually convertible. On this point analytic philosophy comes much closer to hermeneutic philosophy, although this latter form of philosophy proceeds more deliberately from an explication of historical existence in the direction of a language appropriate to it.

32. I shall return in volume 2 to the question of testimony as an irreducible category of our relation to the past.

33. I shall return to this distinction, which has no place here. It does not concern a difference in epistemological degree but a different relation to the past. For Croce, a chronicle is history cut off from the living present and, in this sense, applied to a dead past. History properly speaking is viscerally linked to the present and to action. This is the sense in which all history is contemporary history. The framework of this affirmation is not a conflict over method nor a conflict between method and truth, but the larger problem of the relationships between historical retrospection and the anticipation of the future tied to action.

34. This seems so in the case of *consequential significance*: "If an earlier event is not significant with regard to a later event in a story, it does not belong to that story" (ibid., p. 134). But there are other modes of meaning or importance for which textual structure and the structure of the sentence are superimposed less easily: pragmatic, theoretical, or revelatory meaning or importance, and so on.

35. See Danto, chapter 10, "Historical Explanation: The Problem of General Laws," pp. 201–32.

36. W. B. Gallie, *Philosophy and the Historical Understanding* (New York: Schocken Books, 1968).

37. See above, Part I, chapter 3, on mimesis$_2$.

38. The place given to sympathy in what I am calling subjective teleology confirms this diagnosis. What governs our expectation, Gallie says, is not some truth of an inductive kind but our sympathy or antipathy. Once embarked on a good story, "we are pulled along by it, and pulled by a far more compelling part of our human make-up than our intellectual presumptions and expectations" (ibid., p. 45). His concern to distinguish his analysis from the logic of the covering law model risks, then, swinging over to the side of a psychology based on our emotional response. Unfortunately this tipping toward psychology facilitated criticism of Gallie's work by Hempel's successors. For my part, I see nothing to condemn in such an interest in the psychological conditions of the reception of a work (whether narrative or not). It has its place for a hermeneutics in which the meaning of a work is fulfilled in reading. But, according to the analysis I proposed in Part I of the relationships between mimesis$_2$ and mimesis$_3$, the rules for acceptability must be constructed at the same time *inside* and *outside* the work. Similarly, the notion of interest, which I shall return to in volume 2, cannot be eliminated from a theory of narrative. To accept or receive is to be interested.

39. In his criticism of nominalism, Gallie is not far from the major assumption of the historians of the Annales school: "Historical understanding therefore is not founded on individual Kings—or chaps—but on those changes in a given society which can be seen to make sense in the light of our general knowledge of how institutions work, or what can be and what cannot be done by means of them" (ibid., p. 83).

40. Gallie likes General de Gaulle's statement in *Le Fil de l'Epée*, "c'est sur les contingencies qu'il faut construire l'action" (ibid., p. 98).

41. Louis O. Mink, "The Autonomy of Historical Understanding," *History and Theory* 5 (1965): 24–47; reprinted, with minor changes, in William H. Dray, ed., *Philosophical Analysis and History* (New York: Harper and Row, 1966), pp. 160–92. I shall cite this latter version.

42. Louis O. Mink, "Philosophical Analysis and Historical Understanding," *Review of Metaphysics* 20 (1968): 667–98. He also considers Morton White's *Foundations of Historical Knowledge* (New York: Harper and Row, 1965), and Danto's *Analytic Philosophy of History*.

43. This argument fits perfectly with Danto's analysis of "narrative sentences" in terms of an original theory of descriptions. History, it will be recalled, is one description of human actions (or passions), namely, the description of earlier events in terms of later events unknown to the agents (or recipients) of the first occurrence. According to Mink, there is more to be said concerning historical understanding, not less. There is more to be said inasmuch as the redescription of the past implies recently acquired techniques of knowing (economic, psychoanalytic, etc.) and especially new tools of conceptual analysis (as, for example, when we talk about the "Roman proletariat"). Consequently, we need to add to the temporal asymmetry presented by Danto between the earlier event that is described and the later event whose descriptive terms are used for the first description, the conceptual asymmetry between the systems of thought available to the original agents and those introduced by later historians. This type of redescription, like Danto's, is a description *post eventum*. However, it stresses the process of reconstruction at work here rather than the duality of events implied by narrative sentences. In this way, "historical judgment" says more than does "narrative sentence."

44. In another article, Louis O. Mink, "History and Fiction as Modes of Comprehension," *New Literary History* (1970): 541–58, we read: "the difference between following a story and *having followed a story* is more than an incidental difference between present experience and past experience" (p. 546, his emphasis). What the logic of narration neglects is "not what the structure of generic features of narratives

are, not what it means to 'follow,' but what it means *to have followed a story*" (ibid., his emphasis).

45. "Philosophical Analysis and Historical Understanding," p. 686.

46. "History and Fiction as Modes of Comprehension."

47. It is true that Mink does nuance in two ways his thesis that it is as a function of the ideal goal that all partial comprehension can be judged. First, there are different descriptions of this ideal goal of comprehension. Laplace's model of a world predictable in its smallest detail does not coincide with Plato's synopsis in Book VI of *The Republic*. Second, these descriptions are extrapolations of the three different and mutually exclusive modes of comprehension. However, these two corrections do not really affect the principal argument, namely, that the goal of comprehension is to abolish the *seriatim* character of experience in the *totum simul* of comprehension.

48. Hayden White, *Metahistory: The Historical Imagination in Nineteenth-Century Europe* (Baltimore and London: The Johns Hopkins University Press, 1973). The Introduction (pp. 1–42) is entitled "The Poetics of History."

49. Michel de Certeau, *L'Ecriture de l'histoire* (Paris: Gallimard, 1975).

50. In an article entitled "The Historical Text as Literary Artifact," *Clio* 3 (1974): 277–303, reprinted in idem, *The Tropics of Discourse* (Baltimore and London: The Johns Hopkins University Press, 1978), pp. 81–100 (I shall cite this version), White defines a verbal artifact as "a model of structures and processes that are long past and cannot therefore be subjected to either experimental or objectal controls" (ibid., p. 82). In this sense, historical narratives are "verbal fictions the contents of which are as much *invented as found and the forms of which have more in common with their counterparts in literature than they have with those in the sciences*" (ibid., his emphasis).

51. See Northrop Frye, "New Directions from Old," in his *Fables of Identity: Studies in Poetic Mythology* (New York: Harcourt Brace and World, 1963), p. 55.

52. "My method, in short, is formalist" (*Metahistory*, p. 3). We shall see in what sense his theory of emplotment distinguishes this formalism from French structuralism and puts it closer to that of Northrop Frye.

53. Hayden White, "The Structure of Historical Narrative," *Clio* 1 (1972): 5–19.

54. "Motific organization, then, is an aspect of story elaboration; it provides a kind of explanation, the kind which Mink may have in mind when he speaks of historians providing 'comprehension' of events in their stories by 'configuring' them" ("The Structure of Historical Narrative," p. 15). *Metahistory* confirms this when it speaks of the transformation of chronicle into story as effected "by the characterization of some events in the chronicle in terms of inaugural motifs, of others in terms of terminating motifs, and of yet others in terms of transitional motifs" (ibid., p. 5). A story, in opposition to a chronicle, is "motifically encoded" (ibid., p. 6). I am not in agreement with this reduction of the field of what Mink calls the configurational act to just "story." However, White believes there is a confirmation of his correlation between configurational act and explanation by story in the distribution Mink makes between configurational, categoreal, and theoretical comprehension. White thinks we can assign the categoreal mode to explanation by emplotment and the theoretical mode to explanation by argument. Aside from the fact that neither of these two divisions—Mink's and White's—can be superimposed on the other, one hardly does justice to Mink's analysis of the configurational act by reducing its field of applicabililty to the organization of a story, to the exclusion of both emplotment and argument. Like my concept of plot, Mink's configurational act seems to me to cover all three fields that White distinguishes from one another. The key to this divergence between us lies, in my opinion, in the opposite reduction White imposes on explanation by emplotment, namely, identifying plot with a type, that is, the category of plot which a story belongs to. This reduction seems arbitrary to me.

55. This regression from story to chronicle, then from chronicle to the historical field, in *Metahistory*, resembles the regression undertaken by Husserl in his genetic phenomenology from active syntheses to always prior passive syntheses. In both cases, the question arises about what precedes every active or passive synthesis. This heady question led Husserl to the problematic of the *Lebenswelt*. It leads White to a wholly different one, which we shall encounter again in volume 2, namely, the tropological articulation that "prefigures" (ibid., p. 5) the historical field and opens it to narrative structures. The concept of the historical field does not, therefore, serve just as a limit underlying the classifying of the narrative structures, it more fundamentally marks the transition from studying "explanatory effects" of narrative to its "representative" function.

56. See White, "The Structure of Historical Narrative," p. 17.

57. For the details of this construction and its illustration through the great historians of the nineteenth century, see *Metahistory*, pp. 13–21, and passim.

58. "By the term 'ideology' I mean a set of prescriptions for taking a position in the present world of social praxis and acting upon it . . . such prescriptions are attended by arguments that claim the authority of 'science' or 'realism' " (ibid., p. 22). Here White links up with the attempts of the Frankfurt School philosophers, followed by Karl-Otto Apel and Jürgen Habermas, as well as by some anthropologists such as Clifford Geertz—and even some Marxists such as Gramsci and Althusser—to free the concept of ideology from the purely pejorative connotations which Marx saddled it with in *The German Ideology*.

59. We might ask what accounts for the unity of a narrative, its domain being apparently so dismembered. As usual, recourse to etymology (see White's "The Structure of Historical Narrative," pp. 12–13) is not very illuminating. The Roman *narratio* is too polysemic and too dependent upon its own contexts, and the root *gna*—said to be common to every mode of knowing and knowability—does not provide any further determining criterion. The following suggestion is more interesting. Behind every narration is a narrator. Is it not then on the side of the narrative voice that we should seek the unity and diversity of its explanatory effects? "We might say then that a narrative is any literary form in which the voice of the narrator rises against a background of ignorance, incomprehension, or forgetfulness to direct our attention, purposefully, to a segment of experience organized in a particular way" (ibid., p. 13). But then the unity of the narrative genre is not to be sought on the side of the narrative structures, or their utterance, but on the side of narration as utterance.

60. *Metahistory*, p. 29. On the same page White presents a table of the affinities that govern his reading of the four major historians and four philosophers of history to whom his work is principally devoted.

61. Slipping from one configuration to another is always possible. The same set of events may lead to a tragic or a comic history, according to the choice of plot structure made by the historian, just as for one class, as Marx said, the eighteenth Brumaire of Louis-Napoleon Bonaparte could be a tragedy, while for another class it was a farce. See White, "The Historical Text as Literary Artifact," p. 84.

62. White, too, acknowledges his debt in this regard to Kermode's *The Sense of an Ending* (see his "The Structure of Historical Narrative," p. 20).

63. White's theory of tropes, which I shall not discuss here, adds a supplementary dimension to historical style. But it does not add anything to explanation properly speaking. See *Metahistory*, pp. 31–52, and "The Historical Text as Literary Artifact," pp. 88–100, on the mimetic aspect of narrative. I shall return to it in volume 2, in terms of my discussion of the relationships between the imaginary and the real in the notion of the past.

64. This rule of tradition in narrative encoding provides a response to the objection

that the three typologies used by this theory of historiographical style are borrowed. We must say of the inherited forms of encoding what we have said about laws: historians do not establish them, they employ them. This is why recognition of a traditional form can take on in history the value of an explanation. In this regard, White compares the process of becoming familiar again with elements with which the subject has become unfamiliar with what happens in psychotherapy. ("The Historical Text as Literary Artifact," pp. 86–87.) The comparison works in both directions, inasmuch as the events that the historian seeks to make us familiar with have often been forgotten due to their traumatic character.

65. Paul Veyne, *Comment on écrit l'histoire*, augmented with "Foucault révolutionne l'histoire" (Paris: Seuil, 1971). A more complete examination of this work can be found in my essay *The Contribution of French Historiography to the Theory of History*. See also Raymond Aron, "Comment l'historien écrit l'épistémologie: à propos du livre de Paul Veyne," *Annales* no. 6 (November-December, 1971): 1319–54.

66. Neither Aron, nor above all Marrou, would have so cleanly cut the vital thread that still ties history to the understanding of others, hence to a certain aspect of lived experience.

67. See the next chapter.

CHAPTER SIX

1. For example, Paul Veyne, in his essay "L'histoire conceptualisante," in *Faire de l'histoire*, vol. 1, pp. 62–92. Recall also my reference to the lengthy analyses that Marc Bloch devotes to the problem of "nomenclature" in history. See above, p. 101.

2. Maurice Mandelbaum, *The Anatomy of Historical Knowledge* (Baltimore and London: The Johns Hopkins University Press, 1977), p. 150.

3. Edmund Husserl, *The Crisis of European Sciences and Transcendental Philosophy*, trans. David Carr (Evanston: Northwestern University Press, 1970).

4. I am keeping the other side of the paradox for volume 2: the return from poetic composition to the order of action, which contains the seed of the classical problem of the relation between history, the science of the past, and present action (principally political action) which is open to the future.

5. Max Weber, "Critical Studies in the Logic of the Cultural Sciences," in idem, *The Methodology of the Social Sciences*, trans. Edward Shils and Henry A. Finch (Glencoe, Ill.: The Free Press, 1949), pp. 113–88.

6. The place Aron ascribes to historical causality is important. Gaston Fessard, in *La Philosophie historique de Raymond Aron* (Paris: Julliard, 1980), makes us aware of the rational order of Aron's book by means of a daring comparison with Ignatius Loyola's *Spiritual Exercises* (see especially pp. 55–86, dealing with the reconstruction of the stages and the order of development of Aron's work). Aron's analysis of historical causality comes directly after the theory of understanding presented in section 2, in the conclusion of this section dealing with "The Limits of Understanding" (see Aron, *Introduction to the Philosophy of History*, pp. 151–55). Placed at the start of section 3, entitled "Historical Determinism and Causal Thought," this analysis begins a three-stage inquiry, placed in succession under the auspices of the judge, the scientist, and the philosopher. The first is devoted to "the causes of a single fact," the second to "relations comparable to those of the physical sciences," and the third to "the nature of historical determinism" (ibid., p. 158). This final stage leads in turn to part 4, which is the philosophical section properly speaking: "History and Truth." The inquiry of causality is thus delineated in two ways: first by the place occupied by the third section, within the framework of the book as a whole, and then by the place within the third section, occupied by historical causality in relation to sociological

causality and to the alleged laws of history. There is no better way of emphasizing the transitional role ascribed to historical causality, set in this way between understanding, which possesses all the features of narrative understanding, and sociological causality, which has all the features of nomological explanation.

7. This is found in the second part of his essay, under the heading "Objective Possibility and Adequate Causation in Historical Explanation" (pp. 164–88). I shall return below to Part I of the essay. Raymond Aron begins his own study with a presentation of the "logical schema" of the argument he calls "retrospective probability" (pp. 158–66). We shall see what Aron adds to the strictly logical analysis.

8. See the lengthy notes on pp. 167–68 concerning the use von Kries makes of the probabilist argument and its transposition into the sphere of criminology and jurisprudence.

9. See above, p. 163.

10. The discussion that follows takes us back to the first part of Weber's essay, entitled "A Critique of Edward Meyer's Methodological Views" ("Critical Studies," pp. 113–63).

11. Aron distinguishes in the same way between moral responsibility, legal responsibility, and historical responsibility: "The moralist views the *intentions*, the historian the *acts*, the jurist compares *intentions and acts* and measures them with *judicial concepts*" (*Introduction to the Philosophy of History*, p. 166, his emphasis). "*Historically* responsible is the man who by his acts sets in motion the event the origins of which are being sought" (ibid., his emphasis). In so doing the historian contributes, I would say, to dissociating the notion of imputation from that of incrimination: "War . . . , as seen by the historian, is not a crime" (ibid., p. 173). If we add that causal imputation must also be distinguished from the psychological interpretation of intentions, then it must be admitted that these distinctions are subtle and even fragile. This explains Aron's tone, which is quite different from Weber's. The latter conducts his analysis with a great deal of self-assurance. Aron is more sensitive to all that complicates and, up to a certain point, blurs "the logical schema." We have already observed this in connection with his analysis of chance.

12. Weber is alluding here to the distinction made by Windelband in his Strasbourg lecture, which I referred to earlier, between the nomothetic procedure (peculiar to the sciences of nature) and idiographic procedure (peculiar to the sciences of culture).

13. Weber makes this distinction by opposing *Real-Grund*, ontological ground, and *Erkenntnis-Grund*, epistemological ground: "For the meaning of history as a *science of reality* can only be that it treats particular elements of reality not merely as heuristic *instruments* but as the *objects* of knowledge, and particular causal connections not as premises of knowledge but as *real* causal factors" (ibid., p. 135, his emphasis).

14. Max Weber, *The Protestant Ethic and the Spirit of Capitalism*, trans. Talcott Parsons (New York: Charles Scribner's Sons, 1958).

15. There is no doubt that Maurice Mandelbaum introduced this distinction in order to minimize his concessions in the debate on objectivity in history that he himself provoked with his 1938 work *The Problem of Historical Knowledge*. Greater objectivity can, in fact, be attained in "general" history than in "special" history because the continuous existence of its object is given prior to historians' efforts to delimit their subject and to make correlations. An "interlocking" is therefore possible here, in principle, between different viewpoints on the same events, or between various facets (political, economic, social, and cultural) of the same events. Specialized histories are much more clearly relative to the controversial conceptions of historians, so widely do their criteria for classification vary. This is why it is much more difficult to apply to them the procedures for corroboration, rectification, and refutation which the objectivity of general history is based upon. For my part, it is not the debate on objectivity

that interests me here, but rather the resources offered by the distinction between the singular character of societies and the general nature of the phenomenon of culture for a genetic phenomenology applied to the entities of historical discourse.

16. I shall return in volume 2 to this threefold temporal structure of the we-relation, as it is so masterfully analyzed by Alfred Schutz. In Mandelbaum, too, there is an argument in favor of this oblique reference. He grants that explanation, with its analytical and discontinuous style, could not propose to reconstruct the totalizing and continuous process of a particular society, if historians were not already familiar with global changes such as these in their own experience of life in society: "the original basis for our understanding of societal structures is, then, the experience of an individual in growing up in his society, and the enlargement of horizons that comes through a knowledge of other societies" (ibid., p. 116). History, he recalls, is not born out of nothing. It does not start from a dust cloud of facts that await history's work of synthesis in order to receive a structure. History is always born out of an earlier history that it comes to correct. And behind this primordial history lies social practice, with its internal contradictions and its external challenges.

17. I shall return in volume 2 to the ontology of the we-relation that is presupposed in the present argument. I shall ask whether Husserl, at the end of the Fifth Meditation, was successful in his attempt at deriving higher-order communities from intersubjectivity. I shall also ask if Max Weber's definition of "social action," at the beginning of *Economics and Society*, enables him to avoid the difficulties of methodological individualism. I wish to express here my debt to the thought and work of Alfred Schutz in his *The Phenomenology of the Social World*, trans. George Walsh and Frederick Lehnhart (Evanston: Northwestern University Press, 1967). Schutz did not, in fact, limit himself to reconciling Husserl and Weber. He integrated their concepts of intersubjectivity and social action with a concept of the we-relation borrowed from Heidegger, without losing the force of the first two thinkers' analyses, and without limiting himself to a convenient eclecticism combining all these masters. Schutz's phenomenology of social existence receives, in addition, a decisive assist from the anthropology of a George Herbert Mead, a Victor Turner, and a Clifford Geertz. My debt to them is no less than what I owe to Schutz.

18. His thesis owes a great deal to the work by H. L. A. Hart and A. M. Honoré, *Causation in the Law* (Oxford: Clarendon Press, 1959). "It is no exaggeration to say that since its appearance in 1959 the whole tenor of discussions of causation in Anglo-American philosophy has changed" (Mandelbaum, p. 50). He does not, however, follow these authors in their claim that causal explanation and the formulation of general laws apply to two separate domains of knowledge—history and law, on the one hand, and the sciences, on the other. Adhering instead to J. L. Mackie's analyses in *The Cement of the Universe: A Study of Causation* (Oxford: Clarendon Press, 1974), Mandelbaum perceives, rather than a dichotomy between two vast areas of explanation, a series of explanatory levels indifferent to their areas of application, starting with the perception of causality, moving through causal attribution at the level of judgment, and reaching the establishment of laws, as the "cement" of the causal connection. This thesis moves away from that of W. Dray, having first moved toward it. With Dray and against the proponents of the covering law model, Mandelbaum affirms the primacy and the irreducibility of singular causal attribution; against Dray, he refuses to oppose once and for all singular causality and regularity, and admits that explanation in terms of laws does "cement" causal attribution.

19. In this regard, we can note that the occurrence "not being different" authorizes a comparison between this analysis and the constitution of unreal series in the reasoning of retrospective probability, as this is understood by Weber and Aron.

20. This argument holds for Hempel's example of the explosion of a radiator filled

with cold water. The physical laws set into play do not apply *all at once* to the initial conditions. They apply to a series of occurrences. They are instruments for the causal explanation, not substitutes for that explanation (Mandelbaum, p. 104).

21. This argument recalls that of von Wright concerning the explanation of closed systems. See above, p. 136.

22. This concept of unlimited variable density will enable us in the following section to reconsider in a new light the question of nonevent history [*histoire non-événementielle*]. It already allows us to assert that the short term and the long term are always permutable in history. In this respect, Braudel's *The Mediterranean* and Le Roy Ladurie's *Carnival in Romans* (trans. Mary Feeney [New York: George Braziller, 1979]) provide a marvelous illustration of this permutation allowed by the degrees of density of the temporal fabric of history.

23. Paul Veyne, *L'Inventaire des Différences*, "Leçon inaugurale" au Collège de France (Paris: Seuil, 1976). I discuss this work at greater length in *The Contribution of French Historiography to the Theory of History*.

24. "In accordance with its formulation, historical knowledge reveals its radical nominalism, much more radical than Max Weber ever imagined it, in spite of his profession of faith" (ibid., p. 173). Speaking more specifically of the singular terms that occupy his fifth class of concepts, Marrou goes on to say, "The use of such ideas is perfectly legitimate if we are always careful to retain their strictly nominal character" (ibid., p. 174).

25. The reader may find it unfortunate that causal analysis in history has been discussed in three different contexts: first with William Dray, within the framework of the discussion of the covering law model; a second time with Max Weber and Raymond Aron, under the heading of the transitional procedures between narrative and explanation; and a third time with Maurice Mandelbaum, in connection with the status of the first-order entities. It did not seem to me that I could avoid this triple approach. For these are indeed three different problematics: the first is determined by the appearance in analytic philosophy of a subsumption model, with which neither Max Weber nor Raymond Aron had to come to terms; the second is determined by the question posed within the German tradition of *Verstehen* of the exact scientific status that can be claimed by the idiographic sciences, whose autonomy is in no way contested; the third is related to the new series of questions posed by the correspondence between the continuity of the final entities posited by history on the plane of existence and that of the causal process on the epistemological level.

26. In order to link up with the problems discussed in the two preceding sections, I will simply recall the close kinship between this major presupposition and the other innovations claimed by the Annales school: the documentary revolution, the extending of the questionnaire, the primacy of the problematic over the given historical "fact," the deliberately conceptualizing cast of the investigation. In this sense the long timespan is only one component of the overall shift in direction in the field of historical research. Still it has its own peculiar criteria which do call for discussion.

27. The English translation is of the the second edition of 1966. Fernand Braudel, *The Mediterranean and the Mediterranean World in the Age of Philip II*, trans. Siân Reynolds (New York: Harper and Row, 1972), 2 vols. I will cite from this edition, which contains all of the passages from the third edition that I refer to.

28. Placed under the heading of a certain type of geography that is especially attentive to human destinies, the first-level inquiry is "the attempt to convey a particular kind of history" (*The Mediterranean*, p. 23). A "history in slow motion from which permanent values can be detected" (ibid.), which therefore makes use of geography as one of its media. In this respect it is striking that the author waits until past page

200 before making any reflections on the "physical unity" of the Mediterranean. We may readily admit that the "Mediterranean itself is not responsible for the sky that looks down on it" (ibid., p. 232), but the physical unity that is in question here is above all the permanence of certain constraints—the hostile sea, the harsh winters, the burning sun—and all that contributes to the identity of the Mediterranean people, as they make up for all that is lacking, and adjust their wars, their treaties, and their conspiracies to the rhythm of the seasons, under the sign of the eternal trinity: wheat, olive tree, and vine—"in other words an identical agrarian civilization, identical ways of dominating the environment" (ibid., p. 236).

29. "Man has been the laborer of this long history" (ibid., p. 64). "Spain sent all her sons down to this southern region opening to the sea" (ibid., p. 84). "All of these movements require hundreds of years to complete" (ibid., p. 101). In short, "geographical observation of long term movements guides us towards history's slowest processes" (ibid., p. 102).

30. "The new element was the massive invasion by Northern Nordic ships, after the 1590's" (ibid., p. 119). Nor is it possible not to mention the war of Grenada.

31. "These two different Mediterraneans were vehicles, one might almost say they were responsible for the twin empires" (ibid., p. 136).

32. "Politics merely followed the outline of an underlying reality. These two Mediterraneans, commanded by warring rulers, were physically, economically, and culturally different from each other. Each was a separate historical zone" (ibid., p. 137).

33. "These liaisons and partnerships, successively created and destroyed, summarize the history of the sea" (ibid., pp. 165–66).

34. "The Mediterranean (and the accompanying Greater Mediterranean) is as man has made it. The wheel of human fortune has determined the destiny of the sea, expanding or contracting its area" (ibid., pp. 169–70).

35. The city brings about, in the geographer-historian's discourse, a flood of dates (see, for example, ibid., pp. 332–34), so pregnant is the history of cities, as they confront the designs of territorial states, expanding or dying out in the wake of economic conditions. Yes, cities speak "of evolution and changing conditions" (ibid., p. 352) against the backdrop of constancies, permanence, and repetitions that are established on the first level of analysis.

36. In the chapter on precious metals, money, and prices (ibid., pp. 462–542), the changes in commercial practices, the influx and outflow of metals cannot help but be dated: "The advance of the Portuguese along the Atlantic coast of Africa was an event of major importance" (ibid., p. 469). And further on: "During the difficult war years, 1557–58, the arrival of the ships carrying bullion were the great events of the port of Antwerp" (ibid., p. 480). A profusion of dates accompanies the cycle of metals on the western routes. Royal bankruptcies are dated (1596, 1607). It is a question, of course, of grasping the stable factors in order to verify the explanatory schema. But this requires passing through the history of events with its dates, its proper names, naming Philip II and considering his decisions. In this way, level three casts a shadow on level two, due to the interferences between politics and war, on the one hand, and different economies, on the other.

37. "All these explanations which are in fact so many *events* in the pepper and spice world, tend to obscure the problem in its entirety, a problem that is best appreciated when viewed in a world context—from the American silver mines to the Moluccas or the Western tip of Sumatra" (ibid., pp. 568–69, his emphasis).

38. "The life-span of empires cannot be plotted by events, only by careful diagnosis and auscultation—and as in medicine there is always room for error" (ibid., p. 661).

39. The state, "quite as much as capitalism, was the product of a complex evolu-

tionary process. The historical conjuncture, in the very widest sense of the term, carries within it the foundations of all political power; it breathes life or death into them" (ibid., p. 681).

40. "Of all the possible solutions, Spain chose the most radical: deportation, the uprooting of a civilization from its native soil" (ibid., p. 796).

41. "Has there been any civilization at any time in the past which has sacrificed its own existence to that of another? . . . the economic situation . . . must take its share of the blame" (ibid., p. 823).

42. It is in this way that Lepanto, which Voltaire ridiculed as being so unimportant, was, indeed, "the most spectacular military event in the Mediterranean during the sixteenth century. Daring triumph of courage and naval technique though it was, it is hard to place convincingly in a conventional historical perspective" (ibid., p. 1088). Lepanto would probably have had important consequences if Spain had been determined to pursue them. But on the whole, "Lepanto had not accomplished anything." In this regard, we may note the fine pages devoted to Don John's calculations, that "instrument of destiny" (ibid., p. 1101)—the explanatory reflection corresponds exactly to William Dray's model of rational explanation, as well as to the Weberian model of explanation by means of contrary assumptions.

43. From time to time we see Braudel waging war against the history of events and allowing himself to be tempted by the history of conjunctures, not only with regard to Lepanto, as has been stated, but also when he is confronted with the sheer phenomenon of renunciation observed in the two political leviathans in conflict, and by the general decline of warfare. Did Spain, then, miss its geographical mission by deciding not to go into Africa? "But for what they are worth, these questions have yet to receive a proper hearing. Tomorrow's historians of political change will have to reconsider them and perhaps make some sense of them" (ibid., p. 1142).

44. Here is Braudel speaking of the chance missed in 1601: "In its own way, the degeneration of official war was a warning sign of the general decline of the Mediterranean, which, there can be no doubt, was becoming clearer and more apparent with the last years of the sixteenth century" (ibid., p. 1234).

45. "I do not believe that the word Mediterranean itself ever floated in his consciousness with the meaning we now give it, or that it conjured up for him the images of light and blue water it has for us; or even that it signified a precise area of major problems or the setting for a clearly conceived policy. Geography in the true sense of the word was not a part of a prince's education. These are all sufficient reasons why the long agony which ended in September 1598 was not a great event in Mediterranean history; good reasons for us to reflect once more on the distance separating biographical history from the history of structures, and even more so from the history of geographical areas" (ibid., pp. 1236–37).

46. This man "can only be understood in relation to a life of the purest religion, perhaps only in the atmosphere of the Carmelite revolution" (ibid. 1236).

47. In Braudel's article "History and the Social Sciences," we read: "A new kind of historical narrative has appeared, that of the conjuncture [le récitatif de la conjuncture], of the cycle, and even of the 'intercycle,' covering a decade, a quarter of a century, and, at the outside, the half-century of Kondratiev's classic cycle" (On History, p. 29). In the Cambridge Economic History of Europe, vol. 4, Braudel defines the cycle in the following way: "Because the word cycle might be applied to a seasonal movement we should not be misled. The term designates a double movement, a rise and fall with a peak in between which, in the strictest sense of the term, is called a crisis" (ibid., p. 430). I am indebted to M. Reep, in an unpublished essay, for the reference to this text, as well as for the suggestion that the notion of cycle shares with the Aristotelian muthos the twofold feature of constituting a mimesis of economic life

(in the sense of mimesis$_2$, of course) and of presenting a median structure, a reversal— that, precisely, which the notion of crisis introduces—between two intercycles.

48. The title itself, *Le Temps du Monde*, promises more than it can deliver, as the author admits (Avant-Propos, p. 8). If it is his ambition to grasp the history of the world "in its chronological developments and its diverse temporalities" (ibid.), he has the modesty not to hide the fact that this world time does not cover the totality of human history. "This exceptional time governs, depending on the place and the age, certain spaces and certain realities. But other realities, other spaces escape it and remain foreign to it. . . . even in advanced countries, economically and socially speaking, world time does not include everything" (ibid). The reason is that the book follows a particular line that privileges a certain sector of material and economic history. Within these avowed limits, the historian strives "to study by means of comparisons on a world-wide scale, the sole variable" (ibid., p. 9). From such a height, the historian can attempt "to dominate time, henceforth our principal, or even our only, adversary" (ibid., p. 10). It is again the long time-span that permits us to link together the successive experiences in Europe which deserve to be considered as world-economies (1) in a space that varies only slowly, (2) around a few dominant capital cities (Venice, Amsterdam, etc.) which one after the other come to predominate, and (3) finally according to a principle of hierarchization concerning the zones of contact. The subject matter is therefore the division of time (and space) as a function of conjunctural rhythms, among which the secular trend—"the most neglected of all the cycles" (ibid., p. 61)—proves to be the most fruitful. For my own reflection on time, I take note that "the trend is a *cumulative* process. It adds on to itself; everything happens as if it raised the mass of prices and economic activities little by little until the moment when, in the opposite direction, with the same stubbornness, it began to work to lower them through a general, imperceptible, slow, and prolonged reduction. Year by year, it is barely noticeable; century by century, it proves to be an important actor" (ibid.). The image of a tide, with wave upon wave, intrigues us more than it explains anything to us: "the final word escapes us and, along with it, the exact meaning of these long cycles that seem to obey certain laws or rules governing tendencies unknown to us" (ibid., p. 65). Must we then say that what seems to explain the most is at the same time what helps us understand the least? In volume 2, I shall take up the problem of giving a real meaning to what is here no more than an admission, even a truism, that "short time and long time exist together and are inseparable . . . for we live all at once in short time and in long time" (ibid., p. 68).

49. "For it was the interaction of such pressing need, such disturbances and restorations of economic balance, such necessary exchanges, which guided and indirectly determined the course of Mediterranean History" (ibid., p. 138). Further on, Braudel speaks of the "general outline" (ibid., p. 230), the retreat of the Mediterranean from general history, a retreat delayed until the middle of the seventeenth century. Referring once more to the gradual replacement of city-states by capital cities, he writes: "Their message is one of evolution and changing conditions [*conjuncture*] which hints at their approaching destiny: that decline proclaimed by so many signs at the end of the sixteenth century and accentuated in the seventeenth century" (ibid., p. 352).

50. Discussing forms of war, especially of foreign wars (the Crusades, jihads), Braudel mentions once again the role of civilizations, those "major participants [*personnages*]" (ibid., p. 842). These "characters," like the events in question, are defined in classical terms by their contribution to the main plot.

51. I wonder if Braudel did not think he had avoided the problem of the overall unity of his work by letting the problem of reuniting the pieces of fragmented duration be taken care of by physical time. In *On History* we read: "These fragments are reunited at the end of all our labors. The *longue durée*, the conjuncture, the event all fit into

each other neatly and without difficulty, for they are all measured on the same scale" (*On History*, p. 77). What scale, if not that of physical time? "For the historian everything begins and ends with time, a mathematical, godlike time, a notion easily mocked, time external to men, 'exogenous,' as economists would say, pushing men, forcing them, and painting their own individual times the same color: it is, indeed, the imperious time of the world" (ibid., p. 78). But then the long time-span becomes one of the paths by which historical time is led back to cosmic time, rather than one way of increasing the number of time spans and speeds. Of course, historical time builds its constructions against the backdrop of cosmic time. But it is within physical time that the unifying principle of "the diverse colors of individual times" is to be sought.

52. The polyphony comes from dozens of measures of time, each of them attached to a particular history. "Only the sum of these measures, brought together by the human sciences (turned retrospectively to account on the historian's behalf) can give us that total history whose image is so difficult to reconstitute in its rich entirety" (*The Mediterranean*, p. 1238). This total image would require the historian to have at once the geographer's, the traveler's, and the novelist's eye. The following are mentioned at this point by Braudel: Gabriel Audisio, Jean Giono, Carlo Levi, Lawrence Durrell, and André Chamson (ibid., p. 1234).

53. His frank statement on structure and structuralism should be taken into consideration: "I am by temperament a 'structuralist,' little tempted by the event, or even by the short-term conjuncture which is after all merely a grouping of events in the same area. But the historian's 'structuralism' has nothing to do with the approach which under the same name is at present causing some confusion in the other human sciences. It does not tend towards the mathematical abstraction of relations expressed as functions, but instead towards the very sources of life in its most concrete, everyday, indestructible and anonymously human expression" (ibid. p. 1244).

54. One last time, in the conclusion to his great work, the historian reasserts his suspicion concerning those "essentially *ephemeral* yet moving occurrences, the 'headlines' of the past" (ibid., p. 1243, his emphasis).

55. "A specialist in change (by saying *transformation*, the historian places himself sooner or later on potentially common ground with the ethnologist, providing he does not revert to the notion of the *diachronic*), the historian should be aware of becoming insensitive to change" (ibid., p. 236, his emphasis).

56. Georges Duby, "Histoire sociale et idéologies des sociétés," in *Faire de l'histoire*, vol. 1, p. 157. As early as my first chapter I stated how this attention to the temporal models of change leads to a conceptual reconstruction of a chain of events such as the Crusades.

57. Georges Duby, *The Three Orders: Feudal Society Imagined*, trans. Arthur Goldhammer (Chicago: University of Chicago Press, 1980).

58. Georges Dumézil, *Les Dieux souverains des Indo-Européens* (Paris: Gallimard, 1977), p. 210, quoted by Duby, p. 6.

59. "The principle or necessary inequality accounts for the addition of a third function. This explains why the trifunctional schema came either before or after a treatise on submission and on the structure of a society in which the high reigned in perfection and the low grovelled in sin. Triplicity arose out of the conjunction of two kinds of dissimilarity, that instituted by the *ordo*—there were the priests and the others—conjoined with that instituted by *natura*—there were nobles and serfs" (Duby, p. 59).

60. "Establishing the system's genealogy will aid in understanding its structure, and the place within it assigned to the trifunctional figure" (ibid., p. 65).

61. "A crisis. Ideological formations reveal themselves to the historian in periods of tumultuous situation. In such grave times, the custodians of the word speak incessantly. The time has now come for us to step outside the cathedral workshop. Then

perhaps we may be able to gain a understanding of why tools and material were put to the uses we have seen as we followed the meanderings of memory and the hazards of action" (ibid., pp. 118–19).

62. "Thus the postulate of social trifunctionality was also leveled at the monks, and specifically at monks fallen under Cluny's spell. It was dredged up at the very moment of reformed monasticism's triumphing" (ibid., p. 142).

63. "A bright future lay in store for it. Nevertheless, at the time it was set forth by the bishop of Adalbero and the bishop of Laon, it was rightly looked on as backwards. Thus for a considerable period it was not accepted" (ibid., p. 166).

64. In fact, what remains until 1789 is the binary principle of inequality. The functional tripartition now occurred in "the breach between the monarch and 'plebs' and helped hold the latter in check" (ibid., p. 355).

65. "I have chosen to conclude this study with Bouvines: this was not a choice made out of force of habit, nor was it made because I overestimate the importance of the event. I am convinced that 1214 was the year in which the primitive history of the trifunctional figure came to an end. By that date—its form crystallized and superimposed upon the French kingdom as a whole—that figure was to emerge from the realm of the imaginary, ripe for embodiment in an institution" (ibid., p. 346). And further on: "I end here, because at this point the trifunctional postulate has come full circle back to its origins" (ibid., p. 354).

66. François Furet, *Interpreting the French Revolution*, trans. Elborg Forster (Cambridge: Cambridge University Press/Paris: Editions de la Maison des Sciences de l'Homme, 1981), p. ix.

67. Thus the final word of the beautiful chapter that synthesizes the various aspects of Furet's work implicitly concedes: "What sets the French Revolution apart is that it was not a transition but a beginning and a haunting vision of that beginning. Its historical importance lies in one trait that was unique to it, especially since this 'unique' trait was to become universal: it was the first experiment with democracy" (ibid., p. 79). Does not this admission concerning the event contain within it another one concerning the relation between the explanation and the narrative, and, finally, concerning the very attitude of distanciation? If this unique trait has become universal—at least the universal of our present political reality—must it not be said that a little disinvolvement leads us away from commemoration but that a lot takes us back again?

CONCLUSIONS

1. In this regard, I would like to recall the terminological convention I am trying to respect. I do not take the term "fiction" as a general synonym for "imaginary configuration." The latter is an operation common to history and to the fictional narrative, and as such it falls within the sphere of mimesis₂. On the other hand, in my vocabulary the term "fiction" is defined entirely by the antithesis it forms with respect to true narrative. It is thus inscribed on one of the two trajectories of the reference of narrative and falls under the heading of mimesis₃, which will be dealt with explicitly only in volume 2. As I stated above, this choice is not without certain drawbacks. Many authors make no distinction between fiction and configuration, inasmuch as every configuration is feigned, that is to say, not given in the materials arranged by the narrative. These authors can legitimately take every narrative to be a fiction, insofar as they do not take into consideration the whole of the genre of narrative. Since they are not obliged to account for history's claim to constitute a true narrative, they do not need a special term to distinguish between the two referential modalities into which narrative configurations are, on the whole, divided.

Index

Action, ix, x, xi, 8, 9, 22, 32, 33, 34, 40,
46, 47, 54, 55, 57, 58, 59, 64, 71, 76, 81,
83, 92, 101, 119, 128, 132, 134, 135, 136,
137, 140, 141, 145, 146, 149, 151, 158,
172, 177, 179, 180, 181, 182, 189, 198,
200, 206, 215, 222, 229, 230; basic actions, 55, 136, 137, 254; intentional
character of, 137, 138, 139, 147, 183; semantics of, 54, 56, 61, 81, 205; theory of,
55, 130, 131, 135, 137, 147, 229
Adalbero of Laon, 219, 221
Althusser, Louis, 110, 258
Ambrose, Saint, 17
Analogy, 189, 190, 192, 197, 198, 199, 205,
224, 230
Anscombe, G. E. M., 243, 253
Anthropology, historical, 109, 110, 217–18
Apel, Karl-Otto, 258
Arendt, Hannah, 199
Aries, Philippe, 111, 249
Aristotle, x, xi, 3, 4, 6, 15, 22, 31–51, 52,
53, 54, 56, 59, 64, 65, 66, 68, 69, 70, 71,
76, 84, 112, 129, 130, 132, 141, 145, 151,
152, 154, 156, 158, 162, 164, 170, 171,
172, 173, 178, 185, 207, 215, 216, 224,
227, 229, 230, 238, 239, 240, 253
Aron, Raymond, 95, 97–98, 116, 165, 169,
170, 171, 183, 186–88, 192, 200, 203,
213, 246, 247, 249, 252, 253, 259, 260,
261, 262
Athanasius, 236
Audisio, Gabriel, 266
Auerbach, Eric, 163, 245
Augustine, Saint, xi, 3, 4, 5–30, 31, 32, 52,
54, 60, 61, 68, 71, 72, 82, 83, 84, 85, 86,
160, 220, 232, 233, 234, 235, 236, 237,
244
Austin, J. L., 62

Balas, David, 233
Barthes, Roland, 77
Beierwaltes, Werner, 231, 233, 234, 236
Benjamin, Walter, 79
Benveniste, Emile, 77–78, 238
Bergson, Henri, 227
Berlin, Isaiah, 178, 250
Berr, Henri, 102, 248
Bien, Joseph, xii
Bismarck, Otto von, 183, 184, 185, 189
Bloch, Marc, 97, 99–101, 102, 107, 169,
173, 247, 259
Boethius, 159–160
Bonaparte, Louis-Napoleon, 258
Booth, Wayne, 163
Boros, Stanislas, 28, 237
Brande, Karl, 224
Braudel, Fernand, 101–6, 108, 109, 169,
177, 194, 208–17, 219, 224, 225, 230,
247, 248, 262, 265
Bremond, Claude, 241
Burckhardt, Jacob, 162, 167

Caesar, Julius, 184
Callahan, John C., 231, 233
Cassirer, Ernst, 54, 57
Catharsis, 42, 43, 50
Causal analysis, 122, 125–27, 134, 178,
183
Chamson, André, 266
Character, in narrative, xi, 36, 37, 46–47,
59, 177, 178, 181, 193, 194, 197, 198,
199, 200, 224, 229, 239, 241, 265. See
also Quasi-characters
Charles V, 211
Chaunu, Huguette, 102, 248
Chaunu, Pierre, 102, 106, 110, 111, 246,
248, 249

269

Index

Index

Fiction, 45, 59, 64, 72, 79, 81, 82, 84, 85, 151, 152, 158, 161, 163, 227, 239, 267
Fink, Eugen, 81, 245
Focillon, Henri, 100, 247
Followability, 66, 67, 76, 91, 149–52, 207, 244
Frankel, Charles, 115, 117–19, 250, 251
Freud, Sigmund, 74
Frye, Northrop, xii, 67, 68, 163, 166, 186, 257
Furet, François, 199, 221–24, 267

Gadamer, Hans-Georg, 70, 77, 81, 245, 253
Galileo, 132
Gallie, W. B., 149–55, 157, 158, 177, 179, 207, 244, 255, 256
Gardiner, Patrick, 115, 178, 185, 250, 251, 252
Geertz, Clifford, 57, 58, 243, 258, 261
Generation, 199
Genre, 35, 69, 70, 76, 229
Gerard of Cambrai, 219, 221
Gilson, Etienne, 231, 236
Goethe, Johann Wolfgang von, 190
Golden, L., 50, 237, 239, 240, 241, 242
Goldschmidt, Victor, 232
Gombrich, E. H., 164
Goodman, Nelson, 245
Gorgias, 238
Goubert, P., 248
Gramsci, Antonio, 258
Granger, G. G., 245
Gregory of Nyssa, 233–34, 236
Gregory the Great, 220
Greimas, A.-J., 56, 245
Guitton, Jean, 231, 232, 233, 234, 235, 236, 237

Habermas, Jürgen, 96, 258
Hardison, O. B., 32, 237
Hardy, J., 237
Hart, H. L. A., 252, 261
Hegel, G. W. F., 58, 59, 95, 102, 104, 131, 144, 162, 177
Heidegger, Martin, 16, 54, 60–64, 83, 84, 85, 86, 87, 160, 177, 227, 244, 245, 261
Hempel, Karl, 112–15, 118, 129, 149, 164, 250, 256, 261
Hermeneutical circle, 72, 76, 84, 86
Hermeneutics, 53, 71, 81, 256
Herodotus, 40
Hierarchical structure, 22, 37, 86, 179, 213, 265; of discourse, 194; of entities in history, 181; of temporal experience, 85; of temporality, 28, 30, 84; of time, 61; of tragedy, 34

Historicality, 62, 63, 85
Historiography, 30, 84, 85, 91, 92, 93, 100
History, 32, 33, 40, 82, 85, 86, 91, 102, 106, 108, 109, 114, 133, 136, 139, 144, 151, 157, 161, 162, 163, 173, 177, 178, 187, 194, 195, 197, 206, 227, 228, 255, 267; of conjunctures, 264; demographic, 108, 248; economic, 106, 107, 110, 154, 214, 248; of events, 96, 101, 108, 174, 189, 208, 210, 213, 216, 264; first-order entities, 193–206, 229, 230; general, 195, 203, 204; of long time-span, 208, 216, 217, 224, 248, 249; of *mentalités*, 108, 109, 218; narrative, 91, 93, 101, 102, 151; philosophy of, 3, 30, 84, 91, 95, 111, 118, 144, 162, 224, 251; political, 101, 102; quantitative, 108, 170; second- and third-order entities, 203–4; serial, 106, 107, 108, 110; social, 102, 103, 106, 107, 131, 154; special, 195, 203, 204, 206; structural, 174; theory of, 44, 98, 113, 128, 130, 135, 137, 147, 201, 229, 230
Hölderin, F., 79
Homer, 37, 216, 219
Honoré, A. M., 261
Hope, 30, 85, 144
Hume, David, 113, 136, 137, 140, 201, 202, 253
Husserl, Edmund, 16, 83, 84, 85–86, 179, 180, 181, 198, 227, 228, 238, 258, 259, 261
Hutton, James, 237

Iconic augmentation, 80–81, 82
Ideal-types, 153, 173, 205
Ideology, 79, 110, 141–42, 165, 176–77, 180, 197, 198, 202, 212, 218–21, 222, 223, 258
Imagination, ix, 46, 50, 69, 82, 183, 184, 186, 188, 192; productive, ix, x, 68, 69, 70, 73, 76; social, 49
Ingarden, Roman, 77, 245
Innovation and sedimentation, 68, 69, 77, 79, 166, 208
Intentionality, historical, 82, 85, 92, 180, 193, 194, 229, 249
Interpretation, 72, 73, 114, 115, 118, 119
Iser, Wolfgang, 50, 64, 77, 242, 244

James, Henry, 37, 239
Jauss, Hans Robert, 77, 242, 243
Jesus, 75
Joyce, James, 77
Judgment, 66, 68, 76, 125, 126, 127, 155, 156, 157, 176, 178, 185, 186, 216, 244, 256

271

Index

Kafka, Franz, 75
Kant, Immanuel, 66, 68, 99, 156, 159, 160, 173, 176, 234, 244
Kellogg, Robert, 163, 178, 244
Kermode, Frank, 37, 67, 73, 75, 231, 239, 245, 258
Kuznets, Simon, 107

Labrousse, Ernest, 107, 248
Lacombe, Paul, 102, 248
Ladurie, Emmanuel Le Roy, 249, 262
Lallot, Jean. *See* Dupont-Roc, Roselyne
Langlois, Charles Victor, 97, 246
Language, ix, x, 7, 8, 9, 11, 12, 27, 29, 34, 48, 54, 62, 69, 78, 79, 101, 139, 147, 178, 232, 255
Laplace, P., 159, 257
Le Goff, Jacques, 109, 217–18, 246, 248
Leibniz, Gottfried Wilhelm, 57, 176
Levi, Carlo, 266
Lévi-Strauss, Claude, 105, 109, 242
Linguistics, 78
Literary criticism, 64, 75, 83, 84, 85, 155, 161, 162, 163, 164
Logic, 38, 47, 49, 52, 107, 122, 129, 132, 171, 185; of narrative, 56; of probability, 184
Long time-span, 102, 104, 105, 106, 109, 177, 207, 208, 209, 210, 211, 224, 225, 227, 265, 266
Louis XIV, 123, 128, 172
Loyseau, Charles, 219
Lübbe, Hermann, 44, 172, 240, 252
Lucas, Frank L., 32, 237

Mackie, J. L., 261
McLaughlin, Kathleen, xii
Malcolm, Norman, 253
Mandelbaum, Maurice, 171, 172, 178, 194–203, 250, 253, 255, 259, 260, 261, 262
Mannheim, Karl, 165
Marczewski, Jean, 107
Mark, gospel of, 75
Marrou, Henri-Irénée, 95, 98–99, 165, 169, 205–6, 246, 259, 262
Marx, Karl, 107, 119, 162, 202, 258
Mauss, Marcel, 102
Mead, George Herbert, 261
Meaning, ix, x, 8, 28, 57, 63, 67, 70, 72, 77, 80, 92, 118, 119, 132, 137, 144, 146, 147, 148, 149, 158, 168, 179, 180, 182, 190, 223, 226, 240, 243, 254, 255, 256, 265
Meijering, E. P., 10, 14, 231, 232, 233, 234, 235, 236
Merleau-Ponty, Maurice, 16

Metabolé, 43, 224
Metaphor, ix, 21, 28, 104, 105, 205, 235
Metaphorical process, 50
Meyer, Edward, 183, 189, 190, 192
Michel, H., 232
Michelet, Jules, 162, 167, 247
Mimēsis, xi, 31, 33, 34, 35, 37, 41, 42, 45, 48, 158, 180, 215, 237, 238, 264; mimesis$_1$, 46, 47, 53, 54–64, 66, 71, 73, 81, 92, 131, 180, 182, 200, 205, 256; mimesis$_2$, 46, 47, 53, 64–70, 71, 73, 76, 77, 92, 93, 131, 152, 163, 180, 182, 200, 207, 227, 230, 254, 255, 264, 267; mimesis$_3$, 46, 48, 50, 53, 68, 70–87, 92, 163, 267
Mink, Lewis O., 41, 155–61, 170, 179, 207, 244, 256, 257
Minkowski, Eugène, 26
Muthos, 31, 33, 34, 35, 36, 43, 45, 64, 69, 81, 151, 162, 180, 229, 264. *See also* Emplotment; Plot
Myth, 106, 151

Nagel, Ernst, 116–17, 250
Narrative, ix, x, xi, 3, 22, 36, 56, 60, 63, 66, 70, 72, 81, 86, 94, 111, 121, 142, 143, 148, 150, 152, 158, 171, 178, 181, 182, 192, 194, 195, 200, 206, 208, 227, 236, 238, 247; competence, 93; configurational dimension, 66, 67, 225; diegetic, 238, 239; discourse, 56; episodic dimension, 66, 67; fiction, fictional, xi, 3, 33, 52, 53, 64, 81, 91, 94, 102, 155, 162, 226, 267; field, 227, 228, 258; function, 3, 68, 179, 244; historical, 3, 52, 64, 82, 94, 155, 226; sentence, 56, 143–49, 179, 256; temporality of, 158, 182, 206, 207, 239; text, 149; theory of, 30, 55, 130, 147, 160, 256; time, 59, 67, 92, 208, 225; voice, 215, 258. *See also* Understanding
Narratology, 30, 85
Narrator, 36, 172, 178, 188, 258
Nietzsche, Friedrich, 72, 162
Nominalism, 152–54, 173, 178, 205, 206, 256, 262
Novel, the, 32
Numenius, 236

Objectivity, 120, 161, 178, 204, 260
Ontology, xi, 5, 24, 26, 27, 48, 60, 78, 80, 84, 85, 93, 94, 96, 97, 155, 158, 160, 198, 199, 207, 226, 235, 237, 260, 261

Paradigm, 68, 69, 73, 76, 77, 79, 83, 166, 184, 207
Paradigmatic, syntagmatic, 56, 66
Participatory belonging, 181, 182, 193, 194, 198, 199, 200, 203, 229

272

Index

273